Trekking in
RUSSIA
& CENTRAL ASIA
A Traveler's Guide

Frith Maier

THE
MOUNTAINEERS

Published by
The Mountaineers
1011 SW Klickitat Way
Seattle, Washington 98134

Published simultaneously in Canada by Douglas & McIntyre, Ltd.,
1615 Venables Street, Vancouver, B.C. V5L 2H1

Published simultaneously in Great Britain by Cordee,
3a DeMontfort Street, Leicester, England, LE1 7HD

Edited by Kris Fulsaas
Maps by Sergei Beskov
Photographs by the author except those credited otherwise
Cover design by Watson Graphics
Book layout by Nick Gregoric
Book design and typesetting by The Mountaineers Books

Cover photograph: Trekking on Kamchatka (Photo: Patrick Morrow)

Library of Congress Cataloging in Publication Data
Maier, Frith.
        Trekking in Russia & Central Asia : a traveler's guide / Frith Maier.
            p.   cm.
        Includes bibliographical references and index.
        ISBN 0-89886-355-4
        1. Former Soviet republics--Guidebook. I. Title. II. Title: Trekking in Russia
and Central Asia.
        DK16.M32   1993
        914.704'86--dc20
                                                                94-4780
                                                                CIP

Contents

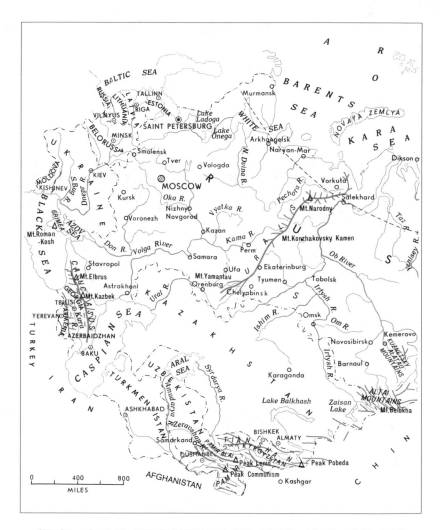

SECTION II. THE TREKS, TRAILS, AND CLIMBS

Part 1. Western Russia 98

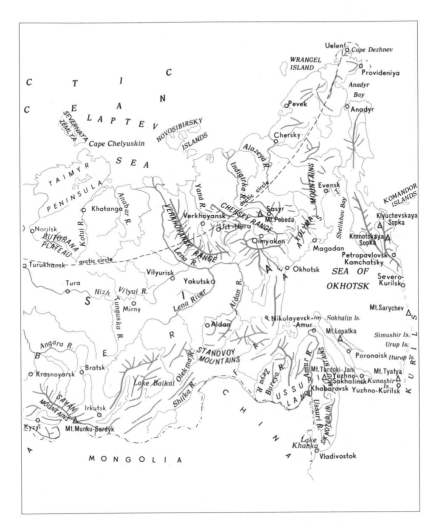

Part 2. Central Asia (Turkestan) 156

Part 3. Siberia and the Russian Far East 233

APPENDICES

LEGEND

⌇	STREAM, RIVER	⋏	MOUNTAINS, RANGE
⌢⌢	BORDER OF NATIONAL PARK	⌒	CAVE
——	COAST LINE	Δ	MOUNTAIN
—•—	RAILROAD	X	PASS
- - - -	TRACK	.•	KOSH, CABIN
——	ROAD	⬠ ⊘	VILLAGE, CITY
═══	HIGHWAY	⚲	SPRING
⬭	GLACIER		

Preface

A "guidebook" to what was the largest country in the world can only be an overview; in writing it, I was constantly frustrated by the lack of space for thoroughness. My goal is to provide information not available elsewhere. For instance, I've included more about the cities of the Far East because you won't find it in other books.

This book is not a guidebook in the traditional sense; you won't find much here about specific hotels, restaurants, or bus numbers. Nor does this book pretend to be a definitive hiking guide; to describe all the trekking opportunities in Russia and Central Asia would fill a large bookshelf. I've attempted to present a mix of hikes, some easily accessible from major population centers, others in very remote areas. Some of the trips are on well-marked trails that are easily followed, others are the dreams of intrepid explorers well versed in the arts of backcountry travel, with loose feet and loose schedules. Hopefully this book will help inspire you for outdoor adventures in diverse areas, from the Crimea to the Kurils.

Use this book as an appetizer, not the last word. Just because you don't find a region described here does not mean it's not interesting. There's excellent ski touring on the Kola Peninsula and fascinating desert walking in Turkmenistan, but the book doesn't describe either of these areas. Likewise, one of the more exotic parts of Russia and Central Asia is the Trans-Caucasus—Armenia, Azerbaidzhan, and Georgia—which this book does not cover, due to local wars. In some cases, the decision was made to exclude an area because of space considerations, and elsewhere simply because adequate, accurate information was not available.

This book includes some very basic descriptions of standard climbing routes on some of the former Soviet Union's most popular peaks. This information is provided because it is not easily available elsewhere, and because some travelers venturing into the mountains of Russia and Central Asia will want to combine trekking and climbing. The climbing routes are described solely for the benefit of experienced mountaineers and should not be misconstrued as options for backpackers.

In addition to trekking and a few climbs, I touch just in passing on some of the vast opportunities for other kinds of outdoor adventures in Russia and Central Asia—like white-water rafting, kayaking, bicycling, and skiing.

Now that the tightly sealed borders of the former Soviet Union have been pried open, many interesting cross-border journeys can be done. You can go from Kyrgyzstan to Xinjiang Province in western China, from Siberia to Mongolia or China, or from the Caucasus to Turkey. I mention some of these opportunities in this book.

Russia and Central Asia have changed tremendously since the late 1980s, and this includes travel conditions. These countries continue to evolve at a rapid pace and almost certainly these ongoing changes will make parts of this book out of date or inaccurate. I encourage you to supplement the information

Sashliki, *or shishkabob, kiosks are the Russian equivalent of hot dog stands.*

in these pages with your own research. It is essential that the independent traveler stay informed. This book especially, about a part of the world undergoing revolutionary changes in its social fabric, should not be considered an absolute authority. Please let me know about suggestions or changes in information that you come across in your travels.

There is no good name for the conglomeration of countries that used to make up the fifteen republics of the Soviet Union. Officially, Russia, Kyrgyzstan, Tajikistan, Uzbekistan, Turkmenistan, and Kazakhstan declared themselves the *Soobshcestvo Nezavisimykh Gosudarstv*, abbreviated SNG in Russian (Georgia joined in 1993). This translates as Commonwealth of Independent States, or CIS, but it doesn't roll easily off the tongue. Citizens of the former USSR continue to refer to their sectioned country as the *Soyuz* (the Union), using SNG only sarcastically. Ukraine, Lithuania, Latvia, and Estonia refused to join the CIS. The U.S. State Department refers to the whole lot as the Newly Independent States (NIS), and I use this abbreviation occasionally in this book.

No suitable broad term has emerged yet to replace the term *Soviet Central Asia*, which distinguished Uzbekistan, Tajikistan, Kyrgyzstan, Turkmenistan, and southern Kazakhstan from the rest of Central Asia. In ancient times, it was Bactria. Later, Europeans called it Tartary, but this too refers to a larger area, much of which lies in present-day China's Xinjiang Province. Turkestan is a traditional name that more narrowly denotes the region formerly known as Soviet Central Asia. This book uses Turkestan and Central Asia interchangeably. In conversations with Soviets you hear the region called "Central Asia."

"Soviet" is by far the simplest way to refer generically to the people who live in the former Soviet Union, many of whom are not Russians. I sincerely hope the occasional use of this word here will not offend any-one. It is not intended as a political insult.

I've lived about four years in Russia and Turkestan, and taken twenty-some extended trips all over the former Soviet empire—and still plenty of places there entice me. When I first lived in Leningrad (now called St. Peters-burg) as a student in 1984–85, independent travel was impossible for an American; my journeys were social and spiritual ones. The friends I made then drew me back again and again. In my travels to every corner of Russia and Central Asia I have found countless warm, genuine, colorful, and remark-able people. My adventures there have thrust me into many delightful and un-believable situations. I have watched hundreds of enduring friendships be-tween Americans and Soviets come out of the wilderness programs I've been involved with there. These experiences, not the hardships and frustrations of travel there, are what stay with me.

Countless books and poems have been written in attempts to capture the essence of Russia, that enigmatic country that spans two continents. None ever quite succeeds in explaining the elusive qualities that make Russians fondly call their land *rodina* ("the motherland"), that makes travelers return over and over again. I have written this book to help inspire those who love outdoor travel adventures and who thrive on challenge, uncertainty, and breaking new ground to explore this maddening and amazing country.

Frith Maier

A Note About Safety

Safety is an important concern in all outdoor activities. No guidebook can alert you to every hazard or anticipate the limitations of every reader. There-fore, the descriptions of roads, trails, routes, and natural features in this book are not representations that a particular place or excursion will be safe for your party. When you follow any of the routes described in this book, you as-sume responsibility for your own safety. Under normal conditions, such ex-cursions require the usual attention to traffic, road and trail conditions, weather, terrain, the capabilities of your party, and other factors. Keeping in-formed on current conditions and exercising common sense are the keys to a safe, enjoyable outing.

Political conditions may add to the risks of travel in Russia and Central Asia in ways that this book cannot predict. When you travel, you assume this risk, and should keep informed of political developments that may make safe travel difficult or impossible.

The Mountaineers

Acknowledgments

Thanks to Judith and Frank Maier for raising me on wet and wild mountain adventures with uncertain outcomes. Thanks also to Brian Povolny, Tom Hargis, Bill Sumner, and Kathy Phibbs, who taught me to climb. And thanks to the numerous other mentors who have encouraged and supported me in the explorations that led to this book.

In 1986, with the help of dozens of Seattle people, I created the Seattle–Tashkent Mountaineering Exchange. That was the beginning of the extensive travel around the former USSR that inspired this book. I'm grateful to Hal Green, Fred Noland, Rosanne Royer, Virginia Westberg, and other members of the Seattle–Tashkent Sister City Committee who were committed to citizen exchange with the Soviet Union, and also believed in a young person who had a dream. Most of my subsequent travel in the wild places of Russia and Soviet Central Asia was through my work designing and leading REI Adventures trips; thanks to Dennis Madsen, Bob Korbol, and Wally Smith for the opportunity to develop a very unusual program at REI. Tanya Pogossova, Mark Dudley, and Carol Woodhull are among the talented and adventurous people who helped that program flourish and grow.

Steve Bezruchka, M.D.; Rob Perkins; Alana Bradley; and Brian "Dr. Dr." Povolny provided professional advice and encouragement throughout the writing of the book. Dr. Anya Maier's practical support was indispensable. Matt Wood, Sarah Peyton, and Peter Christiansen generously proofread the manuscript. Thanks also to Bill Dawson and my colleagues at REI Adventures: Paul Schicke, Linda Pearson, Rusty Brennan, Cynthia Dunbar, Charlie Lippthratt, Joe Staiano, Michelle Baker, and Rhonda Caldwell. Without their flexibility, I would not have been able to complete this project.

The individuals who assisted with this book share a wealth of first-hand experience living and traveling in Russia and Turkestan; their contributions make this a much more useful book. I am also grateful to the photographers who shared their work.

Thanks to Stephen Cunha, Tyler Norris, and Dan Waugh for their input on chapter 9, the Pamir Mountains. Tyler Norris, Andy Turnage, Jonathan Bobaljik, and Peter Bogardus contributed to chapter 10, the Tian Shan. Jonathan also provided invaluable information about the Caucasus based on several summers guiding there. In the Northern Tian Shan section of the Tian Shan chapter, the Kul Sai hike description is courtesy of American journalist Vlad Klimenko.

Thanks to Peter Christiansen for the Kuznetsky Alatau section of chapter 11, Siberia. Thanks to Michael Tripp, Gary Cook, Ben Hanson, Paul Schicke, the Russian Geographic Society, and the Baikal Ecological Museum for their contributions to the Lake Baikal section of chapter 11, Siberia. I am particularly indebted to Michael Jones, who wrote much of this section.

Thanks to the National Audubon Society, Judy Brakel, and Don Croner of *Russian Far East* Magazine for assistance preparing the Chukotka section of chapter 12, The Russian Far East. Thanks to T. Scott Bryan for his contribution on Kronotsky Nature Preserve in the Kamchatka section of chapter 12, The Russian Far East. Thanks to Mark Dudley, Bill Pfeiffer, and Anatoly Lebedev for consultation about the Ussuriland section in chapter 12, The Russian Far East. Mark Dudley, the first American to reside in Magadan in the second half of the twentieth century, wrote about that city, and Carrie Mackay helped write the information on Khabarovsk in the Ussuriland section of chapter 12, The Russian Far East. Thanks to Bob Moore, who reported on Kunashir Island in chapter 12, The Russian Far East, with the thoroughness he uses preparing legal briefs in his Washington, D.C. practice; Bob participated in a 1991 Earthwatch trip to the island.

Thanks to Russell McMullen, M.D. and Elaine Jong, M.D. of the University of Washington Travel Medicine Clinic, and to Oleg Ashirov for their assistance with the Health Considerations section of chapter 3, Staying Safe and Healthy.

Sergei Beskov drew the beautiful maps as well as consulting about Chukotka, an area he knows well. He was patient with my always-expanding schedule and was a pleasure to work with, even though I was in Seattle and he in Moscow. Mark Blitshtein, Kolya Kosterov, Boris Kosmakov, and Sergei Vyukov of Pilgrim Tours in Moscow very graciously loaned me their personal libraries of Russian guidebooks. They also helped me collect volumes of reference materials and generously advised me on numerous questions about routes.

Working with all the nice people at The Mountaineers Books mitigated the drudgery of writing a book. I'm especially grateful to my editor, Margaret Foster, and copy editor Kris Fulsaas, both of whom kindly coached me along my hesitant digression into guidebook writing.

How to Use This Book

Section I, About Trekking, consists of five chapters that give you background information to use before you begin your trek. These chapters include discussions on preparations, safety and health, travel in Russia and Central Asia, and environmental issues.

Section II, The Treks, Trails, and Climbs, is broken down into three geographical regions: Part 1, Western Russia; Part 2, Central Asia (formerly Turkestan); and Part 3, Siberia and the Russian Far East. Each part has a general description of its geographical area and the chapters it contains. The chapters are broken down into sections that consist of major mountain ranges or systems, or other major landforms. In general, the parts and their chapters progress from west to east.

Each of the seven chapters in Section II has a general description of its geographical area and the sections it contains. Each of these chapter sections also has a general description of its geographical area.

For each of these general descriptions—introducing the three parts of Section II, the seven chapters, and their sections—the reader will find discussions of geology, environment, flora/fauna, and climate; history; the people and their culture, language(s), religion(s), customs, and cities; current political conditions and how they affect the trekker; and general trekking information for that area.

In the sections within each chapter, this general description is then followed by an information block containing practical information under the headings of Getting There, Where to Stay, When to Go, and Equipment and Supplies. Where the information is pertinent to a particular hike, the hike name is highlighted in bold so that the reader can easily refer to it as necesssary.

After the practical information are the hikes, treks, and climbs for that section. For each hike description, the first paragraph is an overview of the hike, including where it goes, what you'll see, the duration (in hours or days), the distance (in kilometers), and the rating (easy, moderate, strenuous, et cetera). Within this first paragraph, the pertinent information is boldfaced; within the description of each hike, milestone place names and the distance/duration between them, as well as campsites, are boldfaced. As often as possible, these milestones indicate day-long segments.

Remember, remote areas of Russia and Central Asia are wild places. Even frequently traveled trails and roads are generally not marked. Trails are not graded or groomed according to standards you may be accustomed to in your own country. The traveler must be much more resourceful in gathering information than in many other countries.

This book describes some treks in extensive detail; others are broadly outlined and would be hard to follow without map, compass, and orienteering experience or a knowledgeable local guide. There's much less hard data on hiking routes in Siberia and the Far East than on those in Western Russia and

Central Asia, so the descriptions of backcountry recreation opportunities in the wild east are more abstract.

The descriptions of roads, trails, routes, and natural features that are given in this book are not representations that a particular place or excursion will be safe for your party. If you are planning on traveling independently, please read carefully about the area you're interested in, so that you know before you get there what additional information you need.

At the back of the book are some appendices for reference. Appendix A, General Resources, contains the names and addresses of the many travel resources found throughout the book. This appendix is broken down into categories such as travel agencies, medical resources, environmental organizations, et cetera, for greater ease of use. Appendix B, Contacts, contains a region-by-region listing of useful contacts that corresponds with the chapters of Section II, The Treks, Trails, and Climbs.

You'll also find Appendix C, Bibliography, which I've broken down into sections for easier use; I strongly encourage the reader to supplement this book with the resources listed in the Bibliography. Appendix D, Trekkers' Phrasebook, contains a glossary from English to Russian, as well as a glossary of other foreign-language words found throughout this book.

About the Russian Language

Russian and the languages of Turkestan are written in the Cyrillic alphabet. There are several accepted systems for writing Cyrillic in roman letters. Since this book is not an academic text, I've chosen to use spellings that I think will be easiest for the reader to decipher and pronounce. This book does not strictly follow the Library of Congress transliteration system. Technically, soft signs are indicated by an apostrophe, but I've dropped these, as we don't have the soft sign or hard sign in English.

You may find yourself using German-prepared maps; the German transliteration system can be quite different. Also, Russian spellings may differ from local spellings of Turkestan place names, and even among the Turkic languages of Turkestan there are variations. I refer to Lake Issyk Kul, which is funny grammatically because it's the same as saying Lake Issyk Lake. According to Russian grammar rules, the letter *e* is sometimes pronounced "yo." In most cases, I have transliterated this the way it sounds, unless it is already familiar to English readers spelled with an *e*. An *e* at the beginning of a word is pronounced "ye," as in Yeltsin. Again, as much as possible I've spelled these as they sound.

Russian is an inflected language: any word can have multiple endings depending on how it is used in the sentence. On top of this, Russian nouns are gender-specific, so in the idiosyncrasies of Russian grammar, lakes are neutral gender, a single mountain is feminine, but a mountain range is masculine. The adjectives or names modifying these nouns have different endings, *aya* for feminine nouns, *ii* for masculine nouns, and *oye* for neutral nouns. I have simplified many of these endings to *y*. Please do not be confused by this: virtually always, if the rest of the name matches, you can ignore the spelling of the last two or three letters. If you are referring to other guides, books, or

The Cyrillic alphabet, in which Russian is written, has also been adopted by other ethnic groups. These women are standing outside the city hall in a small Dagestani town. The Avarsky-language signs are written with Cyrillic letters.

maps, you may well find discrepancies in the way place names are spelled.

Russian is a difficult language; no crash course can teach you the intricacies of Russian grammar and pronunciation. I suggest you not worry too much if you see a place name spelled several different ways. In a few cases, though, you will encounter very similar names that actually *are* different places, such as the Adyl-Su and Adyr-Su valleys in Prielbrusye.

At the back of this book, in Appendix D, Trekkers' Phrasebook, you will find a glossary of terms useful to a trekker that you might not find in the typical Russian–English dictionary or phrasebook. Also included is a glossary of foreign words found throughout this book (which appear italicized in the text). The appendix, as well as the information given here, is intended to supplement your Russian–English phrasebook, dictionary, and other language guides you might use. The Russian language information given in this book is not intended to be a complete language reference for the traveler to Russia and Central Asia.

Overleaf: *Vitaly Nikolaenko, caretaker at the Valley of Geysers in Kamchatka, welcomes visitors with a banner: "Guests are my wealth."*

SECTION I
ABOUT TREKKING

Enjoy dramatic mountainscapes when trekking the Fanskie Gori's moderate passes (Photo: Dennis Madsen)

1   Introduction

For the adventurer, the former Soviet empire encompasses a greater variety of fantastic mountain and wilderness areas than any other country on earth. Cold War stereotypes left many Westerners with an impression of Russia as a frozen wasteland. In reality, Russia and Turkestan encompass a wealth of natural beauty, from pristine high mountains to blooming deserts, rolling steppe to Arctic tundra, great wild rivers to volcanic wonderlands, forests still thick with bears and wetlands that harbor birds migrating from several continents. And then some frozen wastelands, too!

In these varied natural landscapes live a vast array of rare species of wildlife and plants. The Soviet Union was the largest country in the world; the now independent countries it has been partitioned into span a larger range of climatic and physiographic zones than any other part of the planet. The traveler can pick anything from a subtropical rain forest to an arid mountainscape. This book is a smorgasbord: the sampling of areas mentioned here ranges from the coldest place on earth (Yakutsk) to some of the hottest places (the Turkestan lowlands in midsummer). It takes you from the Crimea, across the Black Sea from Istanbul, to Chukotka, whose nearest neighbor is Nome, Alaska.

Eleven time zones separate the western and eastern edges of the country. In between live Russians, Ukrainians, Jews, Germans, Tatars, Georgians, Bashkirs, Poles, Udmurts, Koreans, Buryats, Yakuts, Komi, Dargintsy, and dozens of other peoples—all told, more than ninety distinct ethnic groups are recognized among the Soviet population. Many of them speak their own language. Unlike in the American melting pot, many of these ethnic minorities have maintained their own culture and traditions and some live in communities and even provinces made up primarily of their ethnic group. Russian is the language spoken throughout the country, but many people speak it as a second language and some have only a rudimentary understanding of Russian.

The history of the Russian Empire's colonization campaigns, and the seven decades of Soviet rule (the communists came to power in November 1917 and the USSR was disbanded in December 1991) is full of black and brutal chapters. The people of the former Soviet Union have a collective memory of suffering and hardship, and the Soviet system destroyed much that was good in Russian society. Still, this is a resilient, intriguing, and dramatic country—or, more correctly, former country. The superpower is now a confusing mosaic of frail new countries that continues in a major way to affect the course of history throughout the world.

This is a fascinating time to visit Russia and Turkestan. Perhaps you have imagined being present at the writing of the American constitution, or the creation of a new system of government. It is these historical processes that are taking place now in Kyrgyzstan and elsewhere. At the same time that people are eagerly trying to learn Western ways and to survive in a capitalist economy, the fall of communism has opened up the whole huge country to travelers. For the explorer at heart, it presents the opportunity of a lifetime.

In remote places, you can meet people with amazing stories to tell. They may invite you into their homes, take you to their *dachas* (country houses), and share homegrown, homemade food and drink toasts to a peaceful world with you, if you're open to it. Especially in small towns that have seen few or no foreigners—and there are thousands of these—you'll be a celebrity. The travel approach you take will largely determine what kind of experiences you have. If you take time to get involved with people, and share something of yourself, you are more likely to see a community from the inside. There are many ways to do this. Perhaps it's volunteering to teach English for a while in a small community. Or exchanging visits with a Russian.

It's a truism of travel anywhere that you have memorable encounters with people when you spend some time in a place instead of hurrying through. Russia and Central Asia lend themselves to fascinating cross-cultural experiences, often quite bizarre unpredictable ones compared to the civilness of travel in, say, Western Europe. In provincial Russia and Central Asia, people starved by decades of isolation are very eager to learn about the rest of the world and interact with foreign travelers. To me, Moscow is just another city—a dirty, mean one at that—but in remote places in Russia and Central Asia you can have the sort of unique, life-touching travel encounters that are increasingly difficult to find in this well-traveled, late-twentieth-century world. A Russian acquaintance compared travel in America to his home country: "Traveling in the United States I had a feeling that, geographically speaking, the last frontier has been reached there. Russia, however wild and disorganized it can be, still gives an impression to a traveler that it has no limits. There are no private property signs. Civilization is in another world."

What to Expect

Travel in Russia and Central Asia is not for everyone. The place has a well-deserved reputation for tough traveling—for many of the wrong reasons. Food shortages, ethnic violence, political instability.... In reality, these affect the foreign traveler little. There's plenty of food around, at prices many Russians can't afford but which will seem cheap to the traveler accustomed to Western prices. Except for isolated trouble spots that should be avoided, Russia and Central Asia are still among the safer places in the world to travel. (See Political Conditions, chapter 3, Staying Safe and Healthy.)

You can now go to Moscow or St. Petersburg, check into a luxury hotel, and take in the sights with a minimum of discomfort and inconvenience. More adventurous travel in Russia and Central Asia, however, can be very wearing.

An independent, budget traveler is an oddity: for so many years, the only foreigners who traveled in Russia were packaged into Intourist tours, allowed very limited movement, and closely shepherded by tour guides. Even domestic Soviet travel was traditionally largely packaged: factories and institutes sent their employees on vacation at Black Sea resorts, or on organized tours to Baikal or Central Asia. Group travel fit communist "togetherness" principles, and it was usually subsidized by trade unions, so even if people preferred to travel independently, this wasn't an option. Soviets have little experience with independent travelers, let alone the independent foreign traveler.

This book, the first to give you the "inside scoop" on independent adventure travel in Russia and Central Asia, cannot make travel there easy or comfortable. There's no tradition of budget travel in Russia and Central Asia, nor any infrastructure to smooth the way for the independent traveler. In remote corners of the former Soviet Union, services for travelers are more Third World than in much of the Third World. Public toilets are usually filthy, if you're lucky enough to find one. You may end up setting a "personal best" for extended periods without a shower. Tourist information centers with free city maps and pleasant, helpful bilingual staff don't exist. Outside of Moscow and St. Petersburg, you'll have trouble finding a city map or information at all.

This is no Sweden, where train ticket agents in small rural towns speak English. Even in the cities, English will likely be understood only in offices or businesses that cater to foreigners. These same people often have a vested interest in giving you information that sells the services they provide. If you really want to take the road less traveled, you have to learn enough Russian to get by or be prepared for communication with gestures and guesswork. Train, plane, and bus schedules, movies, museums, road signs, and weather forecasts are all in—you guessed it—Russian (or Kyrgyz, Uzbek, Kazakh, et cetera). Sure, in deepest Pamir you can pick up the BBC on your shortwave radio and find out what's going on in the world, but you won't be able to understand the local weather forecast without a grasp of the local language.

Delays are the rule. You will spend many hours waiting for the delayed flight, waiting for a promised vehicle, waiting for gas, waiting hours for a call to the next town, waiting days to place a call overseas, waiting for your guide to show up with food ... travel in provincial Russia and Central Asia is an exercise in the zen of waiting. Sometimes you may not even know exactly why you're waiting. Uncertainty is the name of the game in travel in Russia and Central Asia. The best-laid plans will change, probably more than once.

You'll have to carry large sums of cash because, outside of Moscow, travelers checks may as well be Monopoly money, and credit cards are accepted only for a limited range of services. As a foreigner, you will be seen as an opportunity for making money, particularly if you are associating with people who are in the business of foreign tourism.

All of these cautions are intended not to discourage you from going, but to help you determine if you can enjoy Russia in spite of all the frustrations. If you travel for rest, fine food, and nice hotels, Russia is not for you. If you can't enjoy travel without convenience and being able to plan ahead, chances are you won't have a good time traveling independently in Russia and Central Asia.

However, if you travel to see remote, beautiful places with interesting, unforgettable people, if you're flexible and resourceful, chances are you will enjoy independent travel in Russia and Central Asia. Travelers to Russia have commented that it is not a place to go for a vacation; it is a place you go for adventure.

Even before the disintegration of the USSR, this was not one country but a conglomeration of vastly different cultures and natural environments. The Crimea, Caucasus, Central Asia, and Altai have long been popular with Soviet hikers. In these areas, you'll find established trail systems and a developed tourist infrastructure: *turbaza*, bus routes, locals used to seeing backpacks. In some places, there are actually established "routes": numbered trails at least partially marked. Most trails in Russia and Central Asia are not built or maintained by any agency. The trails go where the people (and animals) go: usually straight up to a pass, and straight down from a pass. As you can imagine, this means they often end up being *steep*. In Siberia and the Far East, trails tend to be game paths and hunters paths.

Because there is no tradition of porter- or pack-animal–assisted trekking in Russia, this book uses the term "trekking" interchangeably with "backpacking." Usually I refer to an extended backpacking trip in a remote area as a trek, and a shorter backpacking trip in a more well-traveled area as a hike.

Many of the treks described in this book require extensive experience with mountain travel. A two-week trek in a remote area with glaciated passes requires competence in a range of skills including route finding, crevasse rescue, and wilderness first aid. This book does not provide mountaineering instruction. You must carefully read all the information given and honestly evaluate your skill level before independently attempting any of the routes described here. You can increase your safety margin by hiring guides or joining an organized trip, but it is still up to you to be prepared. (For more information, see the Climbing section later in this chapter.)

A History of Backpacking and Mountaineering in Russia

The Russian word for hiker is *gorny turist*, literally "mountain tourist." They're often referred to simply as *turisti*, which results in some confusion because the same word is used for tourists sightseeing in tour buses, lining up at Lenin's mausoleum, or beached at the Black Sea. In the strictly regimented world of Soviet sports, *gorny turism* was a game in its own right.

The giant national sports clubs *Burevestnik, Trud, Spartak, TsSK, Dinamo, VTsSPS*, and others fielded the range of traditional sports teams (hockey, basketball, gymnastics, soccer, track and field, et cetera)—and *gorny turism* teams. Alpinism teams were parallel, separate entities.

In each sport, participants achieved ranks (*razryadi*), starting with Novice, followed by Third, Second, First, Candidate Master of Sport (*KMS* in Russian), and Master of Sport. The highest honor for an alpinist, in the days when ordinary Russians were not allowed to travel and only elite climbers made the rare expedition to the Alps, was International Master of Sport.

A *gorny turist* moved up in rank by completing mountain traverses of increasing duration and technical difficulty. To garner the coveted badges of KMS and Master of Sport, *alpinisti* climbed to progressively higher elevations and conquered extreme mountain faces on multiday aid-climbing epics. The progression from Novice up through the ranks takes years, with few mountaineers jumping ahead more than one rank a season, and even fewer ever making Master of Sport.

Climbers (*alpinisti*) look down their noses at *turisti*. They like to make jokes about the huge loads *turisti* carry and disparagingly refer to them as *chainiki* (literally "teapot," which corresponds to "bozo"). Curiously enough, the activities of *turisti* don't differ significantly from *alpinisti*. In fact, *turisti* do adventures that are often more committing than those done by *alpinisti*: while the *alpinisti* are waiting out bad weather in a base camp to go up and do a summit, *turisti* will be camped in the storm on some high pass days into a several-week-long expedition. But *alpinisti* are *alpinisti*, and *turisti*—even when they summit on Elbrus or Pik Communism—are only *turisti*.

Some hikers chose to do mountain trips independently of the clubs. Called *diki turisti* ("wild tourists"), they went where they chose, didn't document their conquests, sought no ranks or badges, and generally disdained the martial organization of Soviet sports. The rescue squad leaders and *alplager* bosses hassled these *diki turisti* at every turn: in a system where rules controlled every aspect of society, these renegades were challenging authority.

Martial and regimented as it was, the Soviet Mountaineering Federation under the USSR Sports Committee introduced thousands of city kids to the mountains. Climbing and hiking clubs flourished at the universities and technical colleges.

Hiking clubs went off every summer on extended mountain trips, sometimes several weeks long and completely self-supported. These youthful expeditions were particularly sporting considering they had no light-weight gear—neither food nor equipment. As rigorous as an intensive Outward Bound or National Outdoor Leadership School course, they exposed average kids from Moscow, Leningrad, and other big cities to wilderness summer after summer.

These kids, raised on communist propaganda in crowded Soviet cities, found in the mountains a spirit of freedom and camaraderie. Every group had at least one guitar player, and Russians know dozens of *turistky* songs (*alpinistky* songs, to the climbers) by the "bards" Vysotsky, Vizbor, Galich, Okudzhava, Dolina, and others. Some of these musical folk heroes' songs used the interdependent relationships between people in the mountains as a metaphor to criticize communist society between the lines:

> *If you have a new friend / and you're not sure if he's a good guy or bad / take him to the mountains, take a chance / don't leave him by himself / rope up with him and you'll find out just who he is*
> —Vysotsky

The bards represented social rebelliousness: none of them was allowed to record or perform in concert officially. Vysotsky, in particular, was a political outcast.

Russians hike and climb in groups: it's the communist way. While this may seem somewhat alien to us individualistic Westerners, it creates some very fine fellowships. The warm camaraderie I've found being in the mountains with Russians, especially the strong campfire singing tradition, is very moving.

Alpinist club members spent a month or more at a time at climbing camps (*alpbaza* or *alplager*) in the major ranges. The *alpbazas* hired instructors and provided campers with equipment. This gear—leather boots a size too large or

Campfire songs are a strong mountain tradition in Russia.

too small, canvas rucksacks, leaky army surplus–type tents—was hardly top of the line, but it gave young people who couldn't afford their own equipment a chance to mountaineer.

The *putevki* (vouchers) for stays at these climbing camps were already dirt cheap, and the trade unions subsidized them even further by paying half the cost for students. So a month in the mountains ended up costing a participant little more than the railroad ticket or airfare.

After World War II, the Soviet sports empire trained climbers and supported them, elevating top alpinists to the status of national heroes. A select group of high-altitude mountaineers drew salaries as coaches, spending all their time climbing on expense-paid expeditions. These professionals competed for alpinist glory on treacherous routes, often at high altitude, or in extreme winter conditions.

Moving in groups of four to six members, they aided their way up big mountain faces, with one person leading and the others jumaring fixed lines, spending multiple nights on ledges or hanging platforms. Judges awarded honors for these competitions based on time and difficulty. Most of the top teams came from Russian and Ukrainian cities, with Donetsk, Kharkov, and Leningrad especially noted for strong alpinists. Moscow teams frequently also took top honors—according to some, because Muscovites ran the Soviet Mountaineering Federation and judged the competitions. Mountainous areas produced few mountaineers, with the notable exception of Alma Ata, where many top alpinists climbed for the Club Army team.

In the 1970s, Mikhail Monastyrsky promoted the idea of inviting climbers from the West to the USSR's big mountains. On his initiative, international mountaineering camps (IMCs) were created at Mount Elbrus in the Caucasus, at Achik Tash (Peak Lenin), and at Fortambek and Moskvina (Peaks Communism and Korzhenevskaya). For a couple of years, a camp also operated at Mount Belukha in the Altai. The IMC—in Russian, *Mezhdunarodniye Alpinistskiye Lagerya (MAL)*—network was run by Sports Committee people in Moscow.

The camps handled hundreds of foreign climbers in the course of a season, all channeled through the official system, which provided guides and took responsibility for safety precautions and rescues. Every popular climbing area had a rescue service, *kontrolno-spasatelnaya sluzhba (KSS)*, based out of a rescue post, *kontrolno-spasatelny punkt (KSP)*. Most of these were outposts from the KSP headquarters located in the cities (Dushanbe, Osh, Tashkent, et cetera) with radio connections, so that in emergencies helicopters and other assistance could be requested.

In the late 1980s, the IMC was swallowed up by a new international marketing arm of the Sports Committee, Sovintersport. Sovintersport jacked up prices for stays at the camps, which had traditionally been reasonable. As soon as the political thaw loosened official organizations' stranglehold on tourism, non-governmental climbing clubs and private tour organizers easily undersold Sovintersport, spelling the beginning of the end for the international climbing camps. Now, a myriad of independent companies "host" foreign climbers in the Caucasus, Pamirs, and Tian Shan. The replacement of the IMC/Sovintersport network by competing agencies created more options in terms of access to new areas, custom trips, et cetera. From a safety standpoint, however, it was not an improvement.

Now, the government rescue services, underfunded and poorly equipped, only respond in major disaster situations—such as the avalanche that swept away forty-three climbers on Peak Lenin in 1990. Several accidents in the Baksan Valley tragically illustrate the result of this neglect of services. In 1992, one of the cablecars on Mount Elbrus fell to the ground, killing one passenger and critically injuring several others. In early 1993, a giant avalanche wiped out a Moscow State University lodge at the base of the mountain, burying a number of skiers. The slope that slid would have been dynamited by avalanche patrols in past years. In 1993, avalanche monitoring was cut back, and fatal volumes of snow loaded the slope above the lodge.

Ethnic politics also colors the climbing scene in Russia and Central Asia. Most of the IMC guides and staff came out of the Moscow and Leningrad old boys' climbing network. Few local mountaineers were trained to be climbing guides or included in the operation of the camps. Now locals, fueled by resentment of Moscow's long domination, assert their authority over the popular routes. In most cases, it is not even local climbers who claim ownership of camps, facilities, or even the mountain itself, but avaricious bureaucrats who see extortion of climbers as easy income. These people often have little understanding of climbing and less concern for safety. Fees collected for permits, waste disposal, et cetera, generally line the pockets of corrupt local chieftains rather than paying for equipment maintenance.

Today, many of the former professional Soviet climbers now guide foreign clients or are otherwise involved in commercial tourism. Climbing in the former Soviet Union has been reduced to what it is elsewhere: a sport for adults who can afford expensive equipment and travel. Russians managed to do mountain adventures in the old days on very little money: they sewed their own packs, down bags, tents, and clothing. Everyone knew someone in a machine factory who could turn out ice screws. Above all, travel was affordable even on a student stipend. Post–Communist party economics crushed this system.

Now, the harsh reality of survival keeps many people from the mountains. Instead of going on trips to the mountains, they spend their holidays and weekends at the *dacha* (country house), growing vegetables for the winter. The *alpbazas* charge too much for any student's budget. Some of them stand empty; others are successfully attracting a newly moneyed clientele. The well-organized mountain rescue structure formerly overseen by the Soviet Mountaineering Federation has fallen into disarray. The decline of the national outdoor education system, the most extensive in the world, is tragic.

Trekking with a Commercial Company

A number of Western adventure travel companies and some environmental groups offer organized trips. If you're short on time and want your vacation to go smoothly, an organized trip is by far the easiest way to go. This saves you the advance hassles of arranging visa authorization, negotiating by fax or telex with a Russian or Central Asian organization for services, and figuring out payment. Once you get there, it means things are more likely to go according to plan, without major changes and delays. The hassles are the responsibility of the adventure travel company.

Reputable adventure travel companies take pains to make you aware of what your trip includes, and guarantee that you get what you paid for. Check out the track record of the company whose trip you're looking at. Here are some things to consider:

How much experience do they have in Russia and Central Asia? How knowledgeable is the person selling the trip about the itinerary and the area? How thorough are the materials they send you about the trip? Are they involved in the operation of the program, or are they simply marketing it? Who leads the trip? What emergency medical precautions do they take? Ask to talk with a client who's participated in a similar trip in the area.

Depending on what you want to do, organized group travel can actually be more economical than independent travel, especially if it involves chartering small planes or helicopters, which is prohibitively expensive for one or two people. Even if you're planning extended independent travel in Russia or Central Asia, starting out on an organized group trip can be a good way to get into the country and get your "land legs."

Trekking as an Individual

If you're planning your own trip, it's very important to have current information about visas, costs, and what travel restrictions are being enforced. In an area changing as quickly as the former Soviet Union, no information source more than a year old, including this book, can be considered current for these details. Several books complement this one well, especially Lonely Planet's *USSR—A travel survival kit, Central Asia: The Practical Handbook,* and the *Russia Survival Guide;* check the Bibliography in the back of this book.

Because the requisite visa for Russia must be "supported" by a Russian individual, company, or organization, you're going to need sponsorship. Unless you have Russian friends who can invite you, you will need sponsorship from an organization. Appendix B, Contacts, lists local contact people and organizations for that area. You can arrange a trip through these contacts from abroad, and have them support your visa. You may find it difficult to reach contacts in more remote areas; telephone numbers change frequently (see the Communications section of chapter 4, Traveling in Russia and Central Asia).

I have tried to include as large as possible a selection of contact organizations in this book. I can't personally vouch for all of the firms and organizations listed, although I have excluded those that have a poor reputation. I make special note of those that I have experience dealing with, or have been able to check references for. The reality is that most of these companies are still learning the ropes. It's important to be a careful consumer, so that you can be *pleasantly* surprised.

SOVIET TRAVEL AGENCIES

Most of the fledgling *turagenstvo* (travel agencies) have a dozen employees, maybe a tour bus, and some interpreters and guides on contract. Others are larger and have already established themselves. Some of the travel agencies offer "outdoor programs." You can find out about these, or you can propose a customized itinerary you want to do. Some may not be interested in handling a special itinerary for one person, and they may demand more than you want to pay if you're not part of a group. This is understandable, considering the time, hassle, and communications expense for them to arrange visa permissions.

Many require payment in advance. While this is simpler than traveling with large wads of cash, it is not without risk. You should be very clear about what you're getting. If the services you pay a Soviet travel agency for are not provided, you have no legal recourse. Few will actually try to defraud you, but it's quite common for them to make promises that they cannot realistically fulfill.

Most have agreements with agencies in other cities to provide services, so that you can deal with one agency and have them make arrangements for an entire itinerary. The rule of thumb, however, is that you'll get better, less expensive service from a local agency. This is because, too often, if you pay one Russian company for services in another town, the money doesn't trickle down to those providing the services.

Travel agencies are more apt to help an individual at reasonable prices if you approach them locally for fairly limited services—for example, a vehicle and driver/guide, food, and possibly some equipment. You can find lists of Moscow and St. Petersburg travel agencies in the Yellow Pages for these cities; see the Bibliography at the back of this book.

HIRING LOCAL ASSISTANCE

Guides. Outdoorspeople with a background in *gorny turism* (mountain hiking) are more reliable and helpful for a hiking or overland trip than those who come out of the Soviet alpinism clubs. Some, not all, of the climbers have a chip on their shoulder and a condescending attitude to foreign trekkers.

Climbing guides. There are many excellent Russian mountain guides. Many have extensive experience with foreign clients in the Pamir and Tian Shan. The tendency of some to "show off" their manliness to clients with bravado and one-upmanship—"I jumped that crevasse, why can't you?"—gives a bad name to all of them, even the more professional ones. Some of the international mountaineering camps provide guides only as emergency rescuers, unless you specifically request a guide.

Some Russian mountaineers are confused by the standard of "climb safe, climb cautiously"; the Soviet school of alpinism trained climbers to be strong and bold and highly competitive. The pressure on teams to place in competitions didn't encourage caution—too often the only way to prove yourself was to do very high-risk routes. It's important that you, as the client, make it very clear what your expectations are: Do you want someone to climb with you as an equal, or do you want the guide to lead and make all climbing decisions?

Porters. It's possible to hire students as porters, but this is not Nepal, where porterage is an accepted practice, easily arranged, with going rates. Be aware of the porter's agenda: it's more likely he will be along for the opportunity to get to know foreigners than for the money. This is not necessarily a disadvantage, because it may lead to a more interesting cross-cultural experience.

Pack animals. In Siberia and the Far East, pack animals are not even an option because of the density of the taiga and generally unsuitable terrain. However, there are lots of horses in the Altai of Siberia, and some horseback riding outfits. In Turkestan, of course, animals carried loads over high passes for centuries on what we call the Silk Road. There are plenty of burros and horses in the Caucasus and Turkestan. If you're doing a trip through a travel agency, they may be willing to arrange for animals. It also may turn out to be more hassle than it's worth. Burros and horses only make life easier on the trail when they're accompanied by someone who knows how to load and handle them. As for hiring animals when you reach the mountains—good luck. Herders don't usually like to let their burros get too far away and who needs a burro for only three days? It's best not to count on having pack animals because then your plans won't be wrecked if they don't materialize. (For more information, see Part 2, Turkestan, in Section II.)

VAGABONDING

What passes for the norm of travel in Europe or most of the rest of the world—hitting the road and making plans as you go along—becomes extreme travel in Russia and Central Asia. But you *can* do it.

It's helpful to have friends there. If you don't know any Soviets, try to meet immigrants and visitors from the former USSR in your community. You can find them in English as a Second Language classes in churches and community colleges. Volunteer to teach English or tutor English. Immigrants probably have friends and relatives back home they can put you in touch with. Some other ideas of how to make Soviet friends: get involved in your community's sister city program (many cities have sister cities in Russia and Central Asia); get a Soviet pen pal; host an exchange student from Russia or Central Asia.

If you find someone you hit it off with, you can exchange visits: you invite him or her to your country and assist with his or her travel there, and he or she returns the favor and invites you to Russia or Central Asia. Or vice versa. Be careful about such arrangements, though, and who pays for what. The imbalance between Western and Soviet standards of living may mean you get stuck paying for more than you bargained if you don't work it all out in advance.

Once you've been invited by a friend and have a visa into the country, you'll find traveling easier with a Soviet traveling companion who speaks your language. Your "native escort" may want to be paid, or may be happy to have you pay his or her expenses.

In addition to helping you surmount the language barrier, having a native escort also keeps costs down by allowing you to pay rubles rather than dollars for many services (see the Money section of chapter 4, Traveling in Russia and Central Asia). Depending on this person's personality, he or she may not necessarily make it easier for you to get to know villagers. City people (Muscovites in particular) sometimes treat provincial folk (everyone outside of Moscow) with a certain snobbery, and Muscovites are particularly unpopular in the provinces these days. Try to find a traveling companion who is genuinely interested in people and will translate their conversations.

If you choose to go it alone, you'll have many interesting challenges. You *will* find people along the way who will help you, and circumstances will no doubt force you into many interesting encounters with people. If your native language is English, you'll find that even small towns usually have an English teacher. This person may have difficulty understanding even the simplest English phrases, but will probably be very eager to meet you and glad to help you. It's possible to run into Soviets who speak some German, French, Italian, or Spanish. In the Russian Far East, more and more local schools offer courses in Japanese and Chinese. And Russians, unlike the French, are delighted when foreigners try to learn their language.

Climbing

This is not a climbing guidebook, but it includes basic information about climbing the Soviet Union's four peaks higher than 23,000 feet (7000 m): Peaks Communism, Pobeda, Lenin, and Korzhenevskaya (a recent resurvey includes Khan Tengri as the fifth). It also covers the ascent of a number of other mountains, such as Mount Elbrus in the Caucasus and Mount Belukha in the Altai. These routes are mentioned because this is the first English-language guidebook to adventure travel in Russia and Central Asia, and up-to-date information about mountain-climbing opportunities in these areas is not available elsewhere.

Thanks to inflation and airfare increases, the mountains of Turkestan are no longer a high-altitude "steal." But the availability of helicopters and the organized base camps at the "7000-meterers" of the High Pamir and Tian Shan mean that high altitude there is still more easily accessible than just about anywhere else in the world.

The highest peaks are not necessarily the most aesthetically appealing or the best for climbing. There are hundreds of summits in the Caucasus more interesting than Mount Elbrus, yet thousands of people climb this Goliath every year, without venturing near anything else around. By the same token, there are countless fantastic peaks in the Pamir, Tian Shan, and Altai that no foreigner has ever climbed because they're shy of 23,000 feet. Siberia and the Far East are practically undiscovered as yet by foreign climbers. Hopefully, this book will inspire some exploratory climbing in the Altai Mountains, the Sayan Mountains, and the mountain ranges of Yakutia.

It is not advisable to attempt a 23,000-foot (7000-m) peak unless you have previously climbed to at least 18,000 to 20,000 feet (5500 to 6000 m). Strategies for climbing a 23,000-foot (7000-m) peak vary. If you arrive at a high base camp from sea level, it likely will take you between 15 and 30 days to summit one of the standard routes. If you arrive at base camp already acclimatized to 13,000 or 16,600 feet (4000 or 5000 m) from climbing in other areas, you may be able to climb a big peak from base camp to summit and back in 3 to 5 days. (The speed records for Khan Tengri, Korzhenevskaya, and Lenin, established by superalpinists, are under 20 hours round-trip.) Teams arriving unacclimatized generally take a "yo-yo" approach that might look something like this:

Day 1: Rest and acclimatize. Day 2: Easy hike. Day 3: Hike to Camp I. Overnight. Day 4: Climb to Camp II. Day 5: Descend to base. Days 6 and 7: Rest. Day 8: Back to Camp II. Overnight. Day 9: Ascend to Camp III. Overnight. Day 10: Descend to base. Days 11 and 12: Rest. Day 13: Overnight. Day 14: Overnight Camp III. Day 15: Overnight Camp IV. Day 16: Summit attempt. Day 17: Descend to base.

On the big Pamir and Tian Shan peaks, there are areas suitable for pitching a tent in a relatively safe location that are commonly used for intermediate Camps I, II, III, and IV. These are usually separated by about 1,500 to 2,500 feet (500 to 800 m). As you acclimatize, you will be able to move more quickly between the camps.

The above gameplan assumes perpetually good climbing weather, which rarely happens. A storm can blow in that keeps you grounded for days. If you're lucky, this will happen when you're in base camp, or close enough to retreat to base. The other factor, along with the weather, that usually dictates the climbing schedule is your health. Altitude, combined with travel in a foreign country, stresses the body and most climbers get sick at some point. Taking adequate rest days and staying healthy are important parts of the strategy for success on a 23,000-foot (7000-m) peak.

There is no one right way to climb a 23,000-foot (7000-m) peak. The best climbing strategy can be foiled by big storms blowing in at inopportune times and, unless you're prepared to spend an entire season waiting for the weather, you simply may not get a shot at your peak. Peak Lenin averages a summit success rate of 50 percent or less; the percentage of climbers attempting Peak

Communism who actually summit is significantly lower. In fact, during one recent season, so much snow fell repeatedly on Peak Communism that no one summited the peak all summer.

The risks associated with mountain climbing, especially at high altitudes, should never be underestimated. The standard route on Peak Lenin may have no more crevasses than Mount Rainier or Mont Blanc, but the objective hazards of mountaineering increase exponentially as you climb at higher altitudes. Altitude sickness and weather can quickly turn an apparently manageable mountaineering expedition into a tragedy. It doesn't work to rationalize: "I'll go to a 7000-meter peak and see how far I get." An expedition to the High Pamir is a big commitment of time and money. Once on the mountain, the drive to accomplish one's goal of summitting a big peak tends to subsume all else.

How high is too high? This depends very much on the individual. Most people experience some symptoms of altitude sickness if they go from sea level to above about 10,000 feet (3000 m) in the space of a few hours. By spending several days at altitude and then gradually moving higher, many people are able to climb a 23,000-foot (7000-m) peak without suffering acute mountain sickness. For others, this is not physiologically possible, no matter how long they spend acclimatizing.

As you climb incrementally higher peaks, you will become familiar with your individual tolerance for altitude and the rate at which you comfortably acclimatize. The gained awareness of your limits will help you climb higher safely. There is no magic formula, but I suggest pushing your personal altitude limits in increments of not more than 3,000 feet (1000 m) at a time. That is, if you've only climbed to 12,000 feet (3500 m), climb a 15,000-foot (4500-m) peak before you try something bigger; when you've been to 15,000 feet (4500 m), try an 18,000-foot (5500-m) summit.

Extensive research has been done on climbers' physiological responses to high altitude, including studies of various drug treatments. If you are not familiar with the literature, read up on the subject before attempting to do anything over about 14,000 feet (4000 m); see the Bibliography at the back of the book. Altitude drugs may be necessary when flying in to one of the High Pamir base camps above 14,000 feet (4000 m). The acclimatization process is less brutal if you arrange to spend several days at an intermediate elevation above 8,000 or 10,000 feet (2500 or 3000 m); see also the Altitude Sickness section of chapter 3, Staying Safe and Healthy.

If you have sufficient mountaineering experience, the high peaks of Russia and Central Asia are an excellent place to push your personal altitude record. A trip up Mount Elbrus can be quicker and less expensive than many other peaks of similar elevation. The 7000-meter peaks in the Pamir, also cost-competitive, offer much easier access than equivalent peaks elsewhere, due to the availability of helicopters.

This book provides only bare bones information about the standard routes on the most popular peaks in Russia and Central Asia. The reader is expected to evaluate whether he or she is physically and mentally prepared for a particular climb. It is also assumed that the basic route information supplied here will be supplemented by consultations with climbers in the base camps who know these routes well.

When you follow any of the routes described in this book, you assume responsibility for your own safety. The climbs should not be confused with treks. No high-altitude peak is a trek. Even Mount Elbrus, which is climbed by thousands of people every year, is only safe if you are properly prepared.

Some High Pamir base camps offer more comforts and services than others, but as a rule they have individual "suites" in spacious stand-up room tents, a mess tent where cooks dish up generous meals, and a *banya* (steam bath)—see *The Banya* section of chapter 4, Traveling in Russia and Central Asia. Russian climbing expeditions typically fly in huge loads of food and equipment to these base camps.

On steep, hazardous sections of popular routes, Russian climbers usually fix lines that are left in place throughout a season and are used by many groups attempting the mountain. While generally secure, these ropes deserve to be treated warily: since you didn't put them there, you can never be sure what they're attached to or what condition they're in.

SOVIET CLIMBING ROUTE RATING SYSTEM

The Soviets have their own system of grading alpine climbing routes that is different from the American or European system. If you are planning to climb in Russia or Central Asia, it will be helpful to be familiar with this system, so that in consulting with Soviet mountaineers you will understand the difficulty ratings of their routes. The following description of the Soviet climbing route rating system is reprinted with permission from *Classic Climbs in the Caucasus*, by Frederick Bender (see Bibliography).

The basic factors determining route grading are the technical difficulties of the crucial sections of the route, and their frequency; the height of the peak and height of the critical areas of the route independent of their grade of difficulty; the length of the route from the starting bivouac; the average steepness of the route; and the time required to climb the route by a suitably matched party. In addition, a shifting scale of rating makes allowance for height, so that at above 16,500 feet (5000 m), grades are usually moved up one level of difficulty.

Apart from these basic factors, there are further elements that play a part in determining a route's grade of difficulty: exposure; the nature of the terrain; the size, quantity, and shape of holds, cracks, and stances; the clarity of the route line; climbing techniques required; application of specific aids; objective danger; support possibilities; and the most rational, least dangerous, and most practicable method of descent. The main technical levels are:

I. Easy—Broad scree or snow ridges, broken rock ridges or snow/ice slopes at angles of up to 30 degrees. Basic alpine equipment only.

II. Simple—Snow and ice sections at an angle of up to 30 degrees and rocks requiring moderate climbing skills. Basic alpine equipment only.

III. Moderately difficult—Snow and ice sections at an angle of 35 to 45 degrees. Steep rock features with good and numerous holds, not requiring artificial aids—descent of such passages being done by free climbing or rappeling. Basic alpine equipment, plus normal rock climbing gear.

IV. More than moderately difficult—With steep rock sections suitable for free climbing. Snow and ice slopes at an angle of up to 55 degrees. Climbing with a rucksack is still possible but arduous. Descent of difficult areas is usually by rappel. Full alpine and rock climbing equipment required.

V. Difficult—Steep rock with a limited number of holds often needing artificial aids. Snow and ice slopes of more than 50 degrees and difficult corniced ridges. Full alpine and rock climbing equipment, plus etriers.

VI. Very difficult—Vertical and overhanging rocks or rock with very few holds, cracks, stances, et cetera, requiring mainly aid climbing. Hard mixed climbing or steep ice pitches. Maximum alpine ability and gear required.

The overall grade of a route is defined within a scale of 1 to 6, with subdivisions A and B, as follows:

Grade 1A. An easy ascent on a peak of up to 15,000 feet (4500 m).

Grade 1B. An ascent of a peak of between 6,000 and 16,500 feet (2000 and 5000 m) over rock, with sections of snow and ice or mixed ground.

Grade 2A. An ascent of more than 1,500 feet (500 m) on a peak of between 6,000 and 19,500 feet (2000 and 6000 m), or traverses at this height, on rock, snow, or ice with rock pitches of up to II-level difficulty, and/or II-level snow and ice sections of up to 300 feet (100 m).

Grade 2B. An ascent of a peak of between 6,000 and 19,500 feet (2000 and 6000 m), or traverses at this height, on rock, snow, and ice with short sections of III-level rock or ice. Requires use of some pitons for belaying.

Grade 3A. An ascent of a peak of between 8,000 and 21,000 feet (2500 and 6500 m), or traverses at this height, on rock, snow, and ice. Route length of up to 2,000 feet (600 m) with long passages of II-level rock and ice.

Grade 3B. An ascent of 2,000 feet (600 m) or longer on a peak of between 8,000 and 21,000 feet (2500 and 6500 m), or traverses at this height, on rock, snow, and ice. Might include rock pitches of 65 to 100 feet (20 to 30 m) or more and III-level snow and ice sections of 650 to 1,000 feet (200 to 300 m), or shorter passages of IV-level difficulty.

Grade 4A. An ascent of at least 2,000 feet (600 m) on a peak of between 8,000 and 23,000 feet (2500 and 7000 m), or traverses at this height. Would include 65- to 165-foot (20- to 50-m) rock pitches of IV-level difficulty, or IV-level snow and ice sections of 650 to 1,000 feet (200 to 300 m) or more. Might take 6 to 8 hours or more and require use of pitons for belaying. Traverses combine at least five routes of Grade 3B or combinations equivalent to this.

Grade 4B. An ascent of at least 2,000 feet (600 m) on a peak of between

8,000 and 23,000 feet (2500 and 7000 m), or traverses at this height, with IV-level rock sections of 130 to 260 feet (40 to 80 m) or short passages of V-level difficulty, and IV-level snow and ice sections of 1,000 to 1,300 feet (300 to 400 m) or more. Would normally take 8 to 10 hours or more and require use of 8 to 10 pitons or more for belaying. Traverses include at least two routes of Grade 4A.

Grade 5A. An ascent of at least 2,000 feet (600 m) on a peak of between 10,000 and 24,600 feet (3000 and 7500 m), or traverses at this height. Long rock sections of III- to IV-level difficulty, with some pitches of V level, or V-level snow and ice sections of 1,000 to 1,300 feet (300 to 400 m). Could take 10 to 15 hours or more and would require use of 20 to 40 pitons or more for belaying. Traverses combine at least two routes of Grade 4B and one route of Grade 4A.

Grade 5B. An ascent of at least 2,300 feet (700 m) on a peak of between 10,000 and 24,600 feet (3000 and 7500 m), or traverses at this height. Long sections of III- and IV-level difficulty, with pitches of up to 165 feet (50 m) of V level and short sections of IV level, or V-level snow and ice sections of 2,000 to 2,600 feet (600 to 800 m). Would take 15 to 20 hours and require the use of 30 to 50 pitons or more for belaying. Traverses combine at least two routes of Grade 5A.

Grade 6. An ascent of at least 2,600 feet (800 m) on a peak of more than 12,000 feet (3600 m), or traverses at this height, on rock or mixed ground. Sustained difficulty, with an average level of IV- or V- and VI-level pitches of 65 feet (20 m) or more. Would take 40 to 50 hours and require use of 100 to 150 pitons or more for belaying. Traverses combine at least three routes of Grade 5B.

SOVIET MOUNTAIN PASS RATING SYSTEM

In addition to the climbing route rating system, the Soviets have a system for gauging the difficulty of mountain passes. Most of the treks in this book are easy, over nonclassified (H/K) passes. Any trek that crosses a more difficult pass is mentioned, with the mountain pass rating system used to indicate the difficulty level. These classifications are indicated on some backpacker maps as well, and you may encounter these classifications when discussing various hiking routes with Soviet hikers.

H/K (Russian for "nonclassified"). These are the simplest passes, with no technical aspect.

1A. Simple scree, snow and rock slopes to 30 degrees, flat glaciers without open crevasses, steep grassy slopes, perhaps with rocky sections. Passes of this degree of difficulty usually are approached via trails. No special equipment is required.

1B. Easy rock, snow and scree slopes averaging 20 to 45 degrees with patches of ice (usually snow-covered) some years, closed glaciers with some hidden crevasses. Passes of this degree may require roping up.

2A. 20- to 45-degree rock, snow, and ice slopes with closed glaciers, and icefalls of moderate difficulty. Crampons or step-kicking are probably required. Ice screws may be necessary for belaying up steep sections.

2B. Steep snow, ice, and rock slopes (over 45 degrees), more difficult ice-falls, and some technical climbing. Probably necessary to overnight on snow on the pass or not far from it.

3A. Steep slopes (45 to 65 degrees), sections of technical climbing of 165 to 300 feet (50 to 100 m) in length, and difficult icefalls. Belay anchors and aid climbing may be necessary, as well as rappel descents. These pass routes require one or more overnights on snow.

3B. This most difficult rating for "tourist passes" includes extended sections of technical rock and ice slopes as steep as 60 degrees, requiring being roped during the entire ascent, possibly for several days.

Deciding Where to Go

If you're considering an extended trip to Russia and/or Central Asia, and you don't have a specific area you're already interested in, these criteria might help you narrow your choices:

Are you looking for lots of opportunities for cultural interaction? In Dagestan (in the eastern Caucasus), the Crimea, the vicinity of Lake Baikal (in Siberia), and much of Central Asia at lower elevations, you can trek beautiful country, passing through villages every few days.

What's your skill level? Some of the treks described here require mountaineering experience. Most of the treks in this book are easy, over nonclassified (H/K) passes. Any more difficult passes are mentioned.

Are you a mountain junkie? All of the regions covered in this book are mountainous. For high-altitude trekking, go to the High Pamir and Tian Shan in Turkestan. If you want to explore mountains where no foreigner has been before, consider most of the Sayan Mountains and the ranges north of Lake Baikal (in Siberia), and the Verkhoyansk, Chersky, and Kolyma mountains and Kamchatka's volcanoes (in the Far East). There are so many mountains in Russia and Central Asia that any of the ranges can be called remote. There is not a mountain range in all the former Soviet Union where you could not find a place to go and not see another person for a whole month. The mountains of Siberia and the north are just *more* remote.

Do you feel more at home in less extreme mountain settings? For easy, accessible trekking, the Crimea can't be beat. The Altai (in Siberia) also has great moderate trekking, farther from civilization.

Seeking close encounters with wilderness? If you want to see bears and birdlife, and few or no people, head for the wild east.

Trying to stretch your travel budget as far as possible? Among the places you can travel overland, which keeps costs down, are the Caucasus, Crimea, Turkestan, and Siberia's Lake Baikal and the Altai Mountains. On Kamchatka, and in much of Chukotka, Yakutia, and Khabarovskii Krai (all in the Far East), helicopter or small plane transportation is required to cover the huge distances. This can get expensive. If you're not already in the country for some other reason, you should also compare costs to get to eastern Russia or to the west.

How much time can you spend? Some wonderful areas, like the Altai, are so far from anywhere that you can spend days just getting into the mountains. If you can only go for a week, go somewhere more easily accessible, like the Caucasus, Turkestan, or Siberia's Lake Baikal.

If you're going to Russia or Central Asia on business and want to squeeze in an adventure, you might consider something relatively accessible from the city where you'll be. This book includes hikes that can be done in a long weekend, being a 2- to 4-hour drive from these major cities:

Almaty (formerly Alma Ata), Kazakhstan
Bishkek (formerly Frunze), Kyrgyzstan
Dushanbe, Tajikistan
Irkutsk, Russia
Khabarovsk, Russia
Khodzhent (formerly Leninabad), Tajikistan
Mineralniye Vody, Russia
Novokuznetsk, Russia
Petropavlovsk-Kamchatsky, Russia
Samarkand, Uzbekistan
Simferopol, Ukraine
Tashkent, Uzbekistan
Ulan Ude, Russia
Vladikavkaz (formerly Ordzhonikidze), Russia
Vladivostok, Russia
Yalta, Ukraine
Yuzhno-Sakhalinsk, Russia

You don't see the three biggest cities—Moscow, St. Petersburg, and Kiev—in the NIS on this list. Because this book focuses on travel in and around mountains, most of the areas described are on the continents' periphery, where the mountains are concentrated. Still, air and rail transportation make many of the treks a reasonable proposition in 5 to 10 days from Moscow, St. Petersburg, or Kiev.

Some people trace their roots to Russia. It can be interesting to make your way to the town or village your ancestors left 50 or 100 years ago. Whether or not you find any record of your relatives, you're still bound to have interesting adventures tracking down a historical society or sympathetic librarian, traipsing through overgrown cemeteries, or knocking on the door of an old lady who might have known your grandmother.

2 Preparing for Your Trek

Visas

In accounts of his journeys throughout Turkestan in the early 1870s (*Turkistan: Notes of a Journey in Russian Turkistan, Khokand, Bukhara and Kuldja*, 1876), Eugene Schuyler says his passport read, in Persian:

> To all Hakims, all Commandants of Forts, all Beks, all Amlakdars, and all Serdars: By this order be it known that one Russian American envoy with his people travels in our country for amusement, tomasha and pleasant pastime, therefore to this Russian, in every Vilayet and Kishlak where he may go, let nothing be done against the hospitality which is due to our guest, or against his wish, and let the hospitality be shown which is due to him, considering his position, and let masquerades not be made of him, and let improper words not be spoken to him.

If only visas to Russia and Turkestan were so eloquently simple now! Obtaining visas for travel to Russia (if you're not traveling with an organized group) has always been a bureaucratic hassle. While travel restrictions have eased so that you can go virtually anywhere now, the visa process became only more beastly after the breakup of the USSR.

Logic would dictate that the newly independent countries, desperate for foreign currency income, would minimize the hassles of visa procurement, making it easy for travelers to visit. On the contrary, each of the individual countries now requires authorization by their own Foreign Ministry, instead of the invitation from any business or organization (Russian or local) that used to suffice.

You can transit through Moscow without a visa if you're just changing planes and not overnighting. Foreigners still fly through special Intourist sections of large city airports, and it's still common practice to verify that your visa lists the destination city. If it's not on there, you may have a problem. What no guidebook or official source will tell you is that you *don't* have to have every town you visit listed on your visa if you're not traveling by air.

Some visa restrictions that no longer apply: You do not have to have advance accommodations in every city. You do not have to register your visa—although some of the old-guard or provincial hotels may still have this regulation on the books and will request your passport/visa overnight to put their hotel stamp in it. If you're not staying in hotels, don't worry about it.

There are "tourist" visas and "business" visas, theoretically depending on the purpose of your visit. In fact, you can travel around the country with either a tourist or business visa. Business visas can be issued in a shorter time, for higher fees.

HOW TO GET A VISA

To obtain a Russian visa, your application must be "supported" by a Russian organization, company, or individual. This invitation, faxed or telexed directly to the Russian embassy to which you send your application, must state your name, passport number, place and date of birth, the dates of your visit, and the cities to which you will be traveling. You should always get a copy of this confirmation to present as proof to the embassy.

Your visa application can also be supported by a friend in Russia. For this personal visa, you obtain two copies of the visa application from the Russian embassy, then fill these out and send both, with photos, to your Russian friend. He or she takes these papers to the local Visas and Registrations Office (UVIR) for an official stamp, and sends them back to you. Because of the unreliability of the Russian mails (see the Communications section in chapter 4, Traveling in Russia and Central Asia), it's much simpler to have your visa supported by an organization.

If you're going to be living in Russia or Central Asia, your residence permit must be "supported" by the organization under whose auspices you are there working or studying. Most organizations will not support your visa unless you are paying them for services. A few (including some travel agencies) will provide visa support for a fee.

You obtain a visa application form from the Russian embassy or consulate in your country of residence. (In the United States, besides the Embassy of the Russian Federation in Washington, DC, there are Russian consulates in San Francisco, Seattle, and New York.) The application must be filled out and returned with three photos and the visa fee. Allow at least a month for this process.

As of September 1993, most of the NIS have representatives in Washington, DC and issue their own visas independently of the Russian Embassy. In other countries, the Russian embassy still handles visas to some of the former republics.

The independent states—Armenia, Azerbaidzhan, Belarus, Estonia, Georgia, Kazakhstan, Kyrgyzstan, Latvia, Lithuania, Moldova, Tajikistan, Turkmenistan, Ukraine, and Uzbekistan—all have offices in Moscow. The *Russia Survival Guide* (see Bibliography) lists phone numbers and addresses for these embassies in Moscow and many of those abroad.

VISA REQUIREMENTS

The requirements for visas covering intra-NIS travel have changed so frequently since December 1991 that no information source older than a few months, including this book, can be considered current. If you're working through a travel agency or visa agency that deals extensively with Russia and Central Asia, your agent can probably update you on the visa situation. The *Russia Survival Guide,* revised annually, is another useful source (see Bibliography). It's also very helpful to talk to recent travelers and find out what visa regulations are actually being enforced. Contacting the Russian embassy or consulates, or the embassies of Kazakhstan or Uzbekistan, will get you the latest official version of the visa requirements, if you manage to get through by phone. Trying to get information from the embassies and consulates of the former Soviet Union may send you running to an NIS-savvy travel agent.

Both tourist and business visas can be double-entry, for an additional visa fee. This allows you to leave Russia during your visit and go, for example, to Uzbekistan (or Mongolia, Estonia, et cetera), then re-enter Russia on the same visa. Visa support received from Russian organizations now is only good for destinations within Russia, and will not get you a visa to Uzbekistan, for example. You must apply separately for a visa to the country you plan to enter from Russia.

If you're planning travel to Russia and several Turkestan countries, the fees for several different visas can add up: Ukraine currently charges $50, Kazakhstan $115, Kyrgyzstan $30, Uzbekistan $100, and Russia $20.

You may decide to get a visa good for the country where you're entering Russia or Central Asia, and then take your chances. In practice, traffic across most of the borders between Russia and the now-independent countries of Turkestan is treated no differently than when these were intra-republic borders of the Soviet Union. At most of these borders, there are no document checks and, in fact, travelers flying to Turkestan from one of Moscow's domestic airports do not go through the passport control procedure requiring that they relinquish their Russian entry visa as they would at the international airport. In other words, you can still get away with traveling to some of the Turkestan countries with only a Russian visa, if you enter from Russia.

This could all change overnight, so unless you want to gamble, it is essential to gather information from recent travelers. If you're not going through airport visa checks, your chances of not being checked are better. If you *do* end up having to pay for an additional visa, it probably won't cost more than if you had gotten it back home, and you're spared the hassle and expense of numerous faxes or telexes. Carry a few passport photos with you for such an eventuality.

Of course, it's simpler to arrange in advance a visa covering the entire route you plan to cover, but if you find yourself in Novosibirsk with an opportunity to make a side trip to the Altai, don't be deterred by the fact that your visa doesn't list Gorno-Altaisk. Especially if you are not traveling by air, no one is likely to check your visa.

On my first visit to Uzbekistan in 1985, I couldn't get a visa to anyplace outside the major "Intourist-route" cities. After hopping a bus to a village some distance from Samarkand, I was peering into the freshly fired kiln of an Uzbek potter when the frame of a large, uniformed man darkened the doorway. I acted innocently surprised. We sat in the potter's courtyard while the KGB man wrote up a "protocol" detailing how I had violated the Law on the Movement of Foreigners on the Territory of the Soviet Union. Then he drove me back to Samarkand and sent me packing to Leningrad. Fortunately, you don't have to worry about this sort of treatment anymore.

Getting to Russia and Central Asia

A few years ago, this was a very short discussion. Intourist, and Sputnik, its "youth travel" counterpart, were essentially the only ways to get in the door. Intourist, the monolithic State Company for Foreign Travel, is now defunct. In its place are a multitude of smaller, private companies. Many of Intourist's regional branches, now privatized, operate independently, and some of the hotels in the Intourist system are still called by that name. Otherwise, it's a whole new game.

The day has arrived when you can enter Russia or Turkestan from the west, south, or east. From the north it's a bit of a challenge, but theoretically also possible.

For an in-depth discussion of arriving in Russia or Central Asia by air on Aeroflot—booking flights, baggage restrictions, airport and airplane conditions, et cetera—see the Transportation section of chapter 4.

TO RUSSIA

By air. All of the major international airlines have direct flights from the European capitals to Moscow, Russia. Many also fly into St. Petersburg, Russia, and Kiev, Ukraine. Delta, TWA, and Aeroflot fly direct from New York. Aeroflot also flies to Moscow from Chicago; Miami; and Washington, DC. Traditionally, the cheapest international fares have been on the Eastern European carriers.

By train. You can take a train from Berlin, Germany, and Warsaw, Poland, into Kiev or Moscow. You can take a train from Helsinki, Finland, to St. Petersburg.

By car. It's possible to drive to Russia from Romania, Hungary, Slovakia, or Poland through the Ukraine. (For more detailed information, see Lonely Planet's *USSR—a travel survival kit*, in the Bibliography.)

From eastern Turkey, you can cross the border between Sarp and Batumi, Georgia, or between Kars and Leninakan, Armenia, and make your way by road north to the Caucasus. Check your country's state department travel advisories before considering travel through Georgia and Armenia, because of the local wars there.

By water. There are boats that run from Istanbul, Turkey, to Yalta, Ukraine.

TO CENTRAL ASIA (TURKESTAN)

By air. There are flights from Delhi, India; Islamabad, Pakistan; Istanbul, Turkey; Kabul, Afghanistan; United Arab Emirates; Berlin and Frankfurt, Germany; and Warsaw, Poland, to Tashkent, Uzbekistan. There are flights from Urumqi, China, and from Frankfurt to Almaty, Kazakhstan. Bishkek, Kyrgyzstan's airport is soon to open for international flights.

By car. There are overland routes from China: from Kashgar—road only—to Turgart, Kyrgyzstan, and from Urumqi to Khorgos, Kazakhstan.

TO SIBERIA AND THE RUSSIAN FAR EAST

By air. Some of these direct flights to Russia operate seasonally: From Anchorage, United States, to Magadan; from Niigata, Japan; Seoul, South Korea; and Anchorage to Vladivostok; from Anchorage; China; Pyongyang, North Korea; and Niigata, Japan, to Khabarovsk; from Nome, United States, to Provideniya; from Hakodate, Japan, to Yuzhno-Sakhalinsk.

By train. Trains that run to Russia are: from Ulaanbaatar, Mongolia, to Irkutsk; from Heihe, China, to Blagoveshchensk; from Harbin, China, to Khabarovsk; and from Suifenhe, China, to Vladivostok.

By car. Overland routes from China to Russia include from Manchuria to Zabaikalsk, from Harbin to Khabarovsk, and from Heihe to Blagoveshchensk. The overland routes from Mongolia are from Olgiy—road only—to Toshant and from Ulaanbaatar to Irkutsk.

By water. There are ships from Japan to Vladivostok (see the Ussuriland section of chapter 12, The Russian Far East).

Maps

Maps, probably the most important reference material for your trekking trip to Russia and Central Asia, are a sore subject.

Until recently, the only people in the Soviet Union who had decent topographical maps were pilots and, presumably, generals. These classified topos were so strictly controlled that hikers sketched maps from the descriptions of those who had previously explored an area. More than a few Soviet outdoorspeople perished on wilderness outings because of inaccurate hand-drawn maps.

Russia/Central Asia Travel Resources is working on making the previously pilots-only topographical maps (scale of 1:200,000) available for mail order in the United States (see Appendix A, General Resources). Included in some of the route descriptions in Section II are the quadrangles that cover that route in the Russian pilots maps series.

Soviet hiking and exploring clubs were required to prepare detailed reports—*otchyoty*—of an expedition's route (see A History of Backpacking and Mountaineering in Russia in chapter 1, Introduction). Now that the Soviet sports system is in disarray, these archives are not being maintained, but many excellent materials from Soviet expeditions are to be found in the Central Tourist Club of various cities. All in Russian, often handwritten, many of these *otchyoty* include painstakingly hand-drawn maps. Russian firms you contact may be able to help you obtain such information. Climbers also have traditionally produced meticulous diagrams and descriptions of alpine routes. These can be found in the collections of alpclubs, and sometimes at the KSP or "headquarters" of popular climbing areas.

Some hiking clubs and private cartography firms are now putting out topographical maps, but there is no reliable distribution system for them. If you arrange to trek in Russia through one of these clubs/firms, they should have maps.

The U.S. Defense Mapping Agency (DMA) satellite maps list, instead of hiking trails, a lot of smokestacks that have little interest for the hiker (but presumably did for intelligence agencies). Some of the roads, power lines, and other features they show don't exist. The Operational Navigation Charts (ONC) are on a scale of 1:1,000,000, and the Tactical Pilotage Charts (TPC) are on a scale of 1:500,000. The TPCs are not always available, but even if you can get them, the scale is too large to be of much use for the hiker. DMA maps can be purchased by calling the National Oceanic and Atmospheric Administration (NOAA, 301-436-6990)—have your credit card handy. Map retailers also sell these.

Equipment and Clothing

How much to pack? The lighter the better. It's important to be able to carry all your own stuff when traveling. (For high-altitude climbing expeditions, with all the extra gear and food required, this is not possible.) The trick is to pare down the load wherever you can. Don't take *everything* on the lists given later in this section. Take the essentials for what you're going to be doing.

The way many trekkers weigh themselves down is by taking many changes of clothes. You don't need more than two shirts: wear one while you're washing the other. Pants, too ... take *one* pair that looks good enough to wear in town and make sure they're *comfortable*.

This *does* work. I spent six weeks in Siberia with one T-shirt, one long-sleeved shirt, and one pair of pants. When my luggage was lost for two weeks, I discovered the second shirt was redundant—I got along fine with the clothes I had on. (This was actually the first time—out of more than 100 Aeroflot flights—that my luggage was lost, and then it turned up intact!) Still, it proved the value of the rule: wear on your back or carry in your carry-on what you absolutely need to have (contact lenses, passport, return plane ticket, et cetera).

Don't carry large containers of shampoo, lens cleaner, deodorant, et cetera. Go to the drugstore's "trial size" section. Leave the hair dryer, electric razor, and make-up at home. Go through your bag and pull out all the other items you can live without.

If you will be doing extended travel, you might consider establishing a "base" camp at a friend's home or a hotel in a location central to your journeys, and leaving some stuff there part of the time. Leave your business clothes at the hotel, or a bag at your partners' office, and head for the hills.

If you can't see dragging your own gear all around the world, consider renting some items from a Russian outdoor company (tent, cooking equipment, ice axe, sleeping bag, down parka). On some items for which fit is critical, such as your boots, bring your own. The Russians make good expedition-weight down parkas and other down products of reasonably good quality. Russian titanium ice screws have found their way to just about every corner of the world. They're always to be had, even in climbing camps, as are some other titanium-alloy items such as crampons, ice axes, and Friends (camming devices for rock climbing).

If you're going to have time to do some shopping around at the beginning of your trip, you can plan to get some of these items in Russia. This is not easy to do in Russia and Central Asia, where many supplies are not easily available. There is at least one climbing gear store in Moscow—Alpindustriya (near Izmailovo metro, tel. [095] 367-3183)—but the selection is far from complete, so you shouldn't count on being able to outfit yourself there. Various outdoor companies may have stuff to rent, but there is no system of outdoor equipment stores.

Russian baggage handlers are very rough on luggage. For this reason, airports have a special wrapping desk where, for a small fee, travelers get their

Soviet travelers have their suitcases wrapped for protection at the airport before they board their flights.

suitcases wrapped in paper and tied with string. Most Western-made luggage is sturdy enough to withstand even the brutal Aeroflot touch, but if you can get your pack wrapped (the "wrapper" may balk at doing this nonstandard-size item), you should—for a different reason: it makes your pack less of a target for thieves. I have a large, very lightweight duffle bag I stuff my pack inside when flying Aeroflot (an old seabag also works well). This spares the straps and belt buckle from getting snagged and torn off. Also, it makes it more challenging for a thief to get inside.

There are different schools of thought as to whether you should lock your duffle with a travel padlock. One holds that a lock suggests there is something inside worth ripping off. Many travel padlocks are easily smashed. Even with a good lock, a soft duffle is easy enough for a thief to slash with a knife. I think the best approach is to make your bag look as worn and undesirable as possible. Bright, shiny packs with lots of zippered pockets only invite pilfering.

EQUIPMENT

Ten Essentials

No matter what kind of trip you're planning, if you're going into the backcountry, pack the Ten Essentials:

1. Extra clothing—more than what's needed in good weather.
2. Extra food—enough so something is left over at the end of the trip.
3. Sunglasses—or goggles; necessary for most alpine travel and indispensable on snow.
4. Knife—preferably with can opener and scissors; for first aid and emergency fire building (making kindling).
5. Firestarter—a candle or chemical fuel for starting a fire with wet wood.
6. First-aid kit—see the detailed list in chapter 3, Staying Safe and Healthy.
7. Matches—carry in a waterproof container.
8. Flashlight—or headlamp; carry extra batteries and bulb.
9. Map—be sure it's the right one for the trip.
10. Compass—know how to use it, and know the declination, east or west.

Below is a list of recommended items to pack. What you take depends on what you will be doing, where you're going, and what season you're traveling in.

Pack—an internal-frame pack is most comfortable, and there's also less chance it will get wrecked as checked luggage

Sleeping bag (temperature rating appropriate to where you're going)

Sleeping pad

Tent

Repair kit—needle, thread, ⅛-inch nylon cord, ripstop repair tape, safety pins, et cetera

Stuff bags—assorted sizes and colors are helpful for organizing gear

Plastic resealable bags (various sizes)

Cookpots

Multifuel stove—the only fuel you can reliably come by is gas; Gaz canisters are not generally available and you can't fly with them

Water bottle

Plastic bowl, cup, and spoon

Water filter equipment and/or iodine tablets

Watch/travel alarm

Money/passport belt

First-aid kit—see the detailed list in chapter 3, Staying Safe and Healthy

Sun-blocking lotion and chapstick—glacier cream or zinc oxide are the best protection against high-altitude sun

Personal hygiene kit—soap, toothbrush, toothpaste, shampoo

Towelettes—on trains, buses, and airplanes—especially when your Aeroflot chicken is served—these are convenient for cleaning up

Toilet paper—yes, in out-of-the-way places it can be impossible to find toilet paper; take approximately one roll per week

Handkerchief—many bathrooms don't have paper towels

Feminine hygiene supplies

Gifts—When you get to know Russians and Central Asians and visit in their homes, they're likely to give presents and you will feel awkward if you can't reciprocate (for detailed information on gifts, see Cultural Considerations in chapter 4, Traveling in Russia and Central Asia)

Camera, lenses, and film

Film shield lead bag

Reading material

Writing material

Playing cards

Pictures of home, family, and friends

Musical instruments

Rubber sink stopper for sinks in hotels

Adapter for battery rechargers or for any electrical appliances—the 220-volt current in electrical outlets in Russia and Central Asia will fry Western appliances

Hot-water heating coil—if you can find one there, it will be most convenient because you won't need an adapter

Spare batteries

CLOTHING

Below is a list of recommended clothing for backpacking in Russia and Central Asia.

Shirt—if you're sun-sensitive, a light cotton long-sleeved shirt is excellent

Pants—for trekking, synthetic-blend, elastic-waist pants are comfortable and dry quickly; you'll also need wool, blend, or pile pants if you're going somewhere cold (side-leg zippers are helpful)

Hiking shorts

Long underwear, top and bottom (polypropylene or capilene)

Regular underwear

Swimsuit

Pile jacket or heavy sweater (for the mountains)

Bandana

Wool or pile hat (balaclavas are good)

Sun hat, or cap or visor

Weatherproof parka—for rain and wind (must fit over bulky clothing)

Weatherproof windpants

Wool mittens (or pile or polypropylene)

Overmitts

Thin liner gloves

Socks—several changes each of heavy-duty (wool or pile) and athletic type (cotton or synthetic)

Shoes—tennis or running shoes (with traction soles) and/or trekking shoes or lightweight boots; you might want a walking shoe or sandals for city travel

Towel, washcloth—I like the quick-dry, one-towel-does-it-all type that camping supply stores sell

CLIMBERS' EQUIPMENT

Along with any mountaineering equipment, such as rock-climbing gear, rope, et cetera, climbers should consider taking the following items.

Plastic double boots for snow climbing—it is possible to use a heavy leather mountaineering boot/supergaiter combination when climbing Mount Elbrus, but with plastic boots there is less risk of frostbite
Ice axe
Crampons—plastic crampon points or a carrying case keep the points from wrecking your pack or the stuff in it
Seat harness with locking carabiner
Ski goggles
Ski poles (optional)—telescoping poles are easy to pack
Gaiters
Down parka

SPECIAL CONSIDERATIONS

For Central Asia (Turkestan)

Long pants are perfectly acceptable for women. In the mountains, no one's apt to see you and shorts are okay. If you really *like* to hike in skirts, they're fine too, but you won't see Russian women hiking in skirts. As a rule, the only Asian women in the mountains are herders and they keep their bodies pretty well covered. If you prefer to wear a skirt in the city (they're cooler), keep it below the knees. Both women and men will probably feel uncomfortable in shorts in cities in Central Asia (even in Russia, only kids do this).

For Siberia and the Russian Far East

If you go in the winter, check out the average temperatures where you're going. Parts of Russia get colder than anything you've probably ever experienced (unless you live in Fairbanks, Alaska). Really **warm coats** (not short ski jackets) and good, **waterproof footgear** are essential. Sorrels (heavy, lined winter boots) are great; they'll also make you stick out like a sore thumb.

In parts of Siberia and the Russian Far East, mosquitoes, no-see-ums, and other insects can make you miserable (especially if you go before late summer) unless you take precautions. The bugs can do more than drive you crazy: In Ussuriland (Primorye) in the Far East, there is some mosquito-borne Japanese encephalitis. You can be vaccinated for this, but if you're going there for less than a month, you're probably better off trying to prevent mosquito bites (see the Health and Medical Problems section of chapter 3, Staying Safe and Healthy).

The most effective **insect repellents** have high concentrations of DEET—diethyl-meta-toluamide—but you shouldn't use 100 percent DEET repellents on your skin, only on clothing. **Mesh jackets, vests, and leggings treated with permethrin** are very helpful. You may be able to find these in hunting and fishing supply stores. A **head net** is funny-looking, but might save your sanity. Wearing a **permethrin-soaked bandana or hat** keeps ticks and other insects away from your head. You can also spray permethrin on your clothes. Permethrin (sold in a spray can as Permanone) is not approved for sale in some states. Definitely search it out and buy before you go. **Mosquito bed netting** is also worth its weight. Even if you're only staying in a city, the mosquitoes can drive you up the walls.

In tick season (spring and early summer), **long pants and long sleeves** with a tight fit around ankles and wrists are a must (see the discussion on tick-borne encephalitis in the Health and Medical Problems section of chapter 3, Staying Safe and Healthy).

For many Siberia treks, **rubber boots** are the perfect footgear. You should be able to buy a pair of these there. High rubber boots are useful for fording streams, rivers, and bogs; the tops can be turned down when not in active use. I hiked in rubber boots and found them more versatile than my hiking boots would have been, as we were constantly fording wet or muddy areas, or wading knee-high rivers.

Photography

A question I am frequently asked—"Can you take pictures in Russia?"—reminds me that many people outside the USSR don't realize how much has changed there. In the old days, under the watchful gaze of Intourist matrons, travelers were warned not to take pictures in airports, from airplanes, or of bridges, military installations, piles of garbage, or other things of state security significance. These days what you should be worried about is keeping an eye on your camera in cities like St. Petersburg, where every third teenager is a professional pickpocket. Take pictures of anything you want to. People are generally amenable to being photographed, as long as you're courteous about it. Most Russian children love to have their picture taken, while in Turkestan kids scatter at the sight of a camera.

Take plenty of film and spare batteries. Moscow and St. Petersburg are the only cities where you can count on being able to purchase film. Film may be on sale in tourist kiosks at airports elsewhere, but you're better off having your own supply. If you're an experienced photographer and at all discriminating about your film, by all means bring your own supply. Bring more than you think you'll ever use if you're going to Kamchatka.

For extended trips to different areas, it's good to have several speeds of film so as to be prepared for a variety of light conditions. There's so much light in Central Asia that 25 ASA film is usable. A polarizer filter is a must for mountain photography.

Outside of the capitals, you won't be able to develop your film. You'll have to carry your undeveloped film with you for the duration of your trip, or find a way to send it out of the country (with another traveler or one of the courier services mentioned in the Communications section of chapter 4, Traveling in Russia and Central Asia), if you're there for an extended period of time.

Pack the film in lead bags for putting through airport X-ray machines—even the ones that are labeled "Filmsafe" can't be trusted not to damage your film. You're taking a chance by carrying film in clear plastic bags and hoping to be allowed to pass it over the X-ray machine. The overseers of airport checkpoints relish the power invested in their offices and may well force you to put your camera *and* film through their machines—especially if you protest.

My experience has been that unless you're a serious photographer, heavy tripods or extra lenses don't justify their weight when traveling. Video cameras can be a problem, because you may have trouble finding places to recharge batteries. Polaroids are a fun icebreaker, and can be very practical.

One dusty, scorching afternoon in Mestia, we went from one cafe to the next; all were closed for lunch break. We walked into a store with the door ajar, and looked hopefully at the Pepsi bottles on the counter. The shopkeeper, visiting with a friend behind the counter, shook her head and nodded at the clock on the wall, indicating that she would sell us no liquid refreshment until 2 o'clock rolled around, a whole 20 thirsty minutes away. Ray, our group photographer, snapped a Polaroid of her and set it on the counter. She tried to ignore us and acted disinterested, but as the picture emerged, she got very excited. Dragging us into the back room of the store, which turned out to be her living room, she insisted that we sit down while her friend went for the daughter she wanted Ray to photograph. Out came not only Pepsi, but also good Georgian wine, and open-face sandwiches. Thanks to the Polaroid, we got "under the skin" of that town.

On another occasion, in the Pamir Alai, our Polaroid won over the herders who had initially balked at renting us burros. They got photos; we got burros. Everyone was happy.

Soon after Kamchatka and the Kurils were first opened to tourism in 1991, officials there began requiring permits for commercial photography or film-making. These permits were issued on a sliding fee scale, depending on who was filming and on what sort of budget, but were nonetheless outrageously expensive. If you are going to be filming with a conspicuous crew and equipment in these areas, you should inquire from a local organization about the current requirements. Otherwise you risk having your film confiscated. Kamchatka and the Kurils are the only places where I have heard of such avaricious "welcomes" for photographers.

3 Staying Safe and Healthy

Political Conditions

Some people are afraid to travel in the former Soviet Union because of "political unrest." Except for isolated hot spots, though, most of Russia and Central Asia are still very safe for travelers—safer than a good many other countries. In Russia and Central Asia, you don't have to fear terrorist violence because of your American passport, as in the Middle East, for instance. Even in the areas where there is violence, the hostilities are between neighboring ethnic groups. Hostility specifically directed towards Westerners is almost unheard of. This is not to say that you are immune to danger in areas where there is fighting; when the bullets fly, the warring factions don't check ID before they shoot.

Since the late 1980s, power struggles between competing factions in Georgia have erupted in bloody riots and, in north Georgia, violent clashes over territory continue between various ethnic groups living in this part of the Caucasus. It is probably optimistic to hope that the Georgian Caucasus will soon return to "normal." These lands have a history of warring factions and blood feuds. Abkhazians hate the Georgians. The Georgians hate the Russians. The Armenians hate the Azeris and vice versa. That is, those involved in the bloody territorial disputes hate each other—many Georgians are married to Russians, others want no part of the bloodshed. The war between Armenia and Azerbaijan sparked by the territorial dispute over mountainous Karabakh rages on. The period of communist rule, when peace was enforced in these parts, was one of the rare times of tranquility in its history. It is not safe at this time to stray into the Georgian Caucasus because armed bandits are robbing hikers. But watch the news. When it's safe again, go.

The southern Pamir in Tajikistan is also an area with a history of warring factions and blood feuds. "The frontier between Badakshan and the Kafir country [is] constantly violated by fierce inroads for slaughter and man-stealing from one side and the other...." wrote Henry Yule in *A Journey to the Source of the River Oxus*, describing the south Pamir in 1872. After the disintegration of Communist party rule, civil war broke out in southern Tajikistan. You should not go to southern Tajikistan, where it's too easy to take a bullet from a gun-toting youth crazed by drugs and killing. In fact, until the situation in Tajikistan improves, avoid traveling in isolated areas of this country without a speaker of Russian or Tajik.

These are pockets of ethnic violence in a country that has otherwise adjusted remarkably peacefully to radical political and social change. They are concentrated conflicts; while the potential exists for the violence to spill over into neighboring areas, this has not happened. The Abkhazian–Georgian battles have not affected the north side of the Central Caucasus, which is where most Western trekkers and climbers go.

Russians don't get very excited about politics anymore. During the August 1991 attempted coup, I was on Sakhalin Island in the Far East. Several groups of trekkers I had organized were in different parts of the country. Most didn't know anything was going on until it was all over. That potentially explosive moment came and went. The regions of Russia, and each of the Central Asian countries, continue to evolve into increasingly independent entities.

As for the intrigues in the Kremlin—even the October 1993 pitched battles between Yeltsin and communist hardliners—most Russians pay little attention to them and they should concern travelers even less. What's important is what's going on where you're headed.

In this part of the world where so much has changed in a few short years, it's important to gather information from current sources about specific areas. Before you travel, check with your country's state department (in the United States, 202-647-5226) to see if there are any travel advisories for places where you're considering travel. For instance, the U.S. State Department has separate "desks" for different areas of the NIS (e.g., the Western Slavic desk, the Trans-Caucasus desk) to which the U.S. ambassadors in each area report.

Travel advisories are often too global: state departments may issue a blanket advisory for the Caucasus without mentioning that certain parts of the region are quiet. Fax your embassy in Russia or the countries of Central Asia with specific questions. Try to find someone who's been to the area recently or has special knowledge of it (call your local university). Check the more current, in-depth reports in publications listed in the Bibliography in the back of this book. Read comprehensive newspaper and journal reports that mention specific place names.

Political conditions may add to the risks of travel in Russia and Central Asia. Throughout the chapters in Section II, I draw the reader's attention to any current political unrest that I am aware of. However, conditions change rapidly and you should research current events in the area to which you plan to travel. When you travel, you assume this risk, and should keep informed of political developments that may make travel unsafe or ill-advised.

Crime

Petty crime, unfortunately, has increased dramatically in the former USSR in recent years. Primarily, this consists of pickpockets in major cities; St. Petersburg reportedly is the worst because it attracts the most tourists. This is a city where tourists are frequently relieved of their wallets by time-told tricks like slitting their daypack pockets. Soviet luggage handlers have been known to pilfer bags, as have customs officials.

An explosion of lawlessness followed the opening of the Far Eastern ports. Petropavlovsk-Kamchatsky (often called simply Petropavlovsk) and Vladivostok in particular have earned a reputation as rough cities. These ports attract people looking for economic opportunities. Some of the commerce is illegal and those involved in it use violent means. The Mafia reputedly controls the lucrative market in used cars from Japan.

Is it more dangerous than New York or Miami? Probably not. The main thing is to use the caution you would in any high-crime city. Be careful about whose company you're keeping. Most foreign men traveling in Russia get hit up by hookers. And most Russian girls do not frequent foreign currency bars just to relax; it's a fair bet that the pretty woman in the short skirt and tall black boots at your hotel bar will be happy to lighten your wallet.

Take basic precautions to avoid your trip being spoiled by getting ripped off. Do not take items that are expensive or irreplaceable: leave your leather jacket and your heirloom jewelry home. Do not set your camera down or leave your purse lying around. It is a good idea to carry your rubles in one pocket and dollars in another, so that a taxi driver, for example, doesn't see you pull out a wad of dollars. Hold your handbag close to your body when walking in crowds and be aware of people around you.

Don't leave money or your passport in hotel rooms. *Do* carry a photocopy of your passport (separate from your passport and wallet) to speed reissue of your passport in case of theft. Also, carry the numbers of the companies that issued your credit card(s) so you can fax home this information for quick cancellation if your wallet is stolen.

Avoid potentially combustible situations, i.e., don't make disparaging remarks about Russian women in a bar full of drunken sailors. In general, exercise restraint when drinking with people you don't know well. Russians are accustomed to drinking very large quantities of alcohol (usually nothing weaker than vodka, and sometimes medicinal alcohol or Everclear, called *spirt*) and find it amusing to make nationalist contests out of drinking (see the Cultural Considerations section in chapter 4, Traveling in Russia and Central Asia).

Don't become a target for extortion; be very cautious in any transactions involving money. Know who you're dealing with, keep the terms clear and fair, and live up to your commitments. Embassies and police are little comfort if you get on the wrong side of people associated with crime rings.

Health Considerations

If you're going to be in the mountains or wilderness for more than a few days, carry a pocket wilderness medicine guide such as Stephen Bezruchka's *Pocket Doctor*. A mountaineering expedition should have along a reference guide such as *Medicine for Mountaineering* by James Wilkerson. Please don't rely solely on this chapter for preparation; I encourage you to consult books by medical experts on travel and wilderness medicine (see the Bibliography at the back of this book). Some suggested titles include *Travelers' Medical Resource* by William Forgey, *Travel and Tropical Medicine Manual* by Elaine Jong and Russell McMullen, and *International Travel Health Guide* by Stuart Rose.

IMMUNIZATIONS

No special immunizations are required for travel to Russia and Central Asia, but you should be current on routine immunizations such as tetanus/diptheria, measles, and poliomyelitis. You should also consider the following:

Hepatitis A. Protection against risk of acquisition of hepatitis A through potentially contaminated food and water, both in cities and rural areas, can be gotten from a single dose of 2-milliliter gamma globulin (immune globulin) the week before departure.

Typhoid fever. If a primary series was received more than three years ago, a booster dose is needed to renew immunity. A new oral typhoid vaccine has been released in capsule form. (This immunization is considered standard travel protection. There is no special risk of typhoid in Russia and Central Asia.)

Cholera. The risk of getting cholera through contaminated water and food, especially undercooked seafood, is best avoided by taking precautions with food and water. Cholera vaccine does not provide good protection; it is not recommended for routine travel by people in reasonable health. However, people on antacids or medication for stomach ulcers, or who have had stomach surgery, may benefit from vaccination. Consult your physician.

Tetanus/diptheria. Since 1990, there have been isolated outbreaks of diptheria in the former USSR. Routine immunization is protective and can be easily achieved with a booster vaccine, provided the traveler has received the primary series of immunization.

Encephalitis. Vaccination is the best precaution against tick-borne encephalitis, a concern only if you're planning travel in Ussuriland in the Russian Far East in springtime or early summer (see the Health and Medical Problems section later in this chapter). This vaccine is inconvenient for most travelers, as it's administered in three doses over the course of a year, and it's not available in the United States or Canada. The vaccine, an immune globulin serum specifically made for tick-borne encephalitis, is available only in Europe (made by Immuno, a Vienna company, the vaccine can be administered at the Frankfurt Airport; to make an appointment, call the Flughafenklinik at [069] 690 66 767). According to Immuno, "a single dose of intramuscular TBE immune globulin provides protection in 70 to 80 percent of cases for a period of four weeks. Two vaccinations of TBE vaccine, if given 10 to 14 days apart, offer protection over a longer period of time. The responder rate is 90 percent." Both TBE immune globulin and TBE vaccine are licensed in Germany. U.S. military personnel and others in government employ can sometimes get the vaccine stateside. Until it's approved by the U.S. Food and Drug Administration, however, it can only be dispensed in the United States by physicians participating in studies.

The immune globulin shots we get in the United States to prevent hepatitis A are probably of no benefit, since the people the serum is taken from are unlikely to have been exposed to tick-borne encephalitis. According to the Centers for Disease Control (CDC), based in Atlanta, Georgia, there is no evidence that TBE immune globulin, effective for tick-borne encephalitis in Central Europe, prevents "Russian spring fever." Neither does the CDC have any information about the Russian encephalitis vaccine. CDC doctors do not recommend one or the other for travelers to Siberia or the Russian Far East. However, most travelers and scientists spending extended time in the woods of southern Siberia or the Far East during the risk season try to get vaccinated.

FIRST-AID KIT

A first-aid kit is a must for adventure travel in Russia and Central Asia, whether you're planning extensive time in the wilderness or not. You should not expect to be able to buy *any* medical supplies in rural Russia and Central Asia. The capitals now have foreign currency stores and there are kiosks in some airports where you may find a narrow selection of supplies, but only Moscow claims full-service Western pharmacies.

Stocks in local Soviet pharmacies are unpredictable and you are unlikely to find any familiar brand names or products. Neither can you count on finding basic medications and medical supplies available in provincial clinics. Even if you are accompanied by a Soviet physician in the backcountry, he or she may have very limited medical supplies.

When you go into the wilderness or to the mountains, carrying a first-aid kit full of prescription drugs only constitutes preparedness if you know how to use them wisely. Your personal physician may be willing to prescribe medications for your first-aid kit, but unless your doctor also treks and travels, I suggest you consult a travel-medicine doctor before you go.

A doctor once prescribed diamox, decadron, and codeinated Tylenol for me when I was going on an expedition. I arrived at 13,000 feet (4000 m) with a bad cough and took the Tylenol with codeine to get some sleep. Not only did I not sleep, I spent the whole night feeling as though the swelling in my brain would explode my skull. The doctor who prescribed the drug did not warn me to never take sleep-inducing substances at high altitude if unacclimated, and I didn't know to ask.

If you find yourself needing advice on using your first-aid kit while in Russia or Central Asia, consult a Soviet medical professional before you self-treat, if at all possible. However, keep in mind that the Soviet doctor may be unfamiliar with Western drugs you're carrying. While penicillin-family drugs and some other medications translate directly into Russian, most physicians there don't know about diamox, for example, so you cannot always count on reliable diagnostic advice. Personally, I don't have qualms about taking medications prescribed by Soviet doctors. If you and the doctor don't speak the same language, however, you probably should not do this unless you have every confidence in the person translating your symptoms.

The following lists cover items you should consider for your first-aid kit.

Medications

Diarrhea treatment. For relief of symptoms of frequent watery stools and abdominal cramping, carry an antimotility agent (Lomotil or Imodium). For emergency treatment of severe diarrhea, carry an antibiotic (Bactrim, Doxycycline, Norfloxacin, or Ciprofloxacin). For treatment of giardiasis, carry Metronidazole (Flagyl).

Antibiotics. For skin infections and upper respiratory infections, carry Ciprofloxacin, Erythromycin, or Augmentin.

Allergies. Travelers with severe allergies to stinging insects should carry an Ana-Kit Insect Sting Treatment Kit or Epi Pen.

Pain relief and cough suppression. For severe headache, musculoskel-etal pain, or cough, carry a prescription pain medication such as Tylenol with codeine.

Miscellaneous Supplies

Antibiotic ointment—(Polysporin or Bacitracin) for minor cuts and abrasions

Antihistamine tablets—(Benadryl) for colds and hay fever

Aspirin, Tylenol, or ibuprofen

Bandaging—Bandaids, gauze pads, roll of tape, Ace bandage for minor sprains, sanitary napkins (can be used as a dressing—they're about the same size and thickness as an Army Battlefield Dressing, or ABD)

Blisters—Moleskin for preventing blisters, Second Skin for managing blisters

Decongestant—(Actifed, Sudafed, Contac, et cetera) for nasal congestion due to colds or allergies

Fiber supplement—(Metamucil, Citracel) for people prone to constipation when their diet is altered; you may also want a prescriptive stool soft-ener for extreme cases

Hydrocortisone cream—for relief of itching insect bites or sunburn

Motion sickness remedy—(Bonine)

Powdered electrolyte mix—(Exceed, Oral Rehydration Packets, et cetera) for fluid replacement and rehydration during severe diarrhea

Skin cleanser solution—(Betadine, Hibiclens) for cleaning minor cuts and abrasions

Syringes—Carry a couple of sterile syringes in case you end up in a Soviet clinic that doesn't have any clean needles

Vitamins—Even if you don't take vitamins at home, vitamin and mineral supplements are a good idea for travel in Russia; especially in the Far East and the north, it's hard to eat meals balanced with fruits and veg-etables much of the year

Superglue—Can be used to repair small lacerations that might otherwise re-quire stitches; clean the wound, pull the edges together, and apply glue.

HEALTH AND MEDICAL PROBLEMS

Check with the Centers for Disease Control (CDC), based in Atlanta, Georgia, for an update on medical concerns for travelers in Russia and Central Asia (404-332-4565).

Water Purification

Clean water is a much bigger problem in Central Asia than in Russia. Under no circumstances should you drink untreated water in rural Turkestan. You're prob-ably better off not drinking raw water in Asian cities also, although the only city documented to have contaminated water is St. Petersburg, where there's *Giardia lamblia* in the city taps. In cities, you can usually buy bottled mineral water, al-though some of the strains of *mineralniye vody* have an unpleasantly strong taste or are too salty. In the backwoods of Russia, there's little or no risk of bad water, but it's so easy to toss an iodine tablet in the water bottle, why not play it safe?

Nothing can ruin a trip faster than being laid low by diarrhea.

Don't let the thought of all the germs in this land of herders stop you from going, but do take every precaution to avoid ingesting them. Boiling water is the best way to disinfect it. If you have an electric water-heating coil, boiled water is as close as a water faucet and an electrical outlet. If you don't have that option, filter the water and iodize it, with either iodine tablets or a bottle of reusable iodine crystals dissolved in water.

But caution goes beyond purifying all the water you drink. I've seen trekkers who were fanatical about treating their water buy fruit in the bazaar and eat it unwashed, or wash the grapes in the water faucet at the bazaar and eat them....

Soviets will think all the caution about hygiene ridiculous. They may make fun of you or try to convince you the water's fine; stick to your guns. They've lived with the microbes all their lives. If you hire local guides or cooks, impress upon them that you're dead serious about boiling all water used in cooking and washing dishes. Explain *why*, and watch to make sure that it happens. It's so easy to get traveler's diarrhea in Turkestan that it's worth being extremely careful.

Cholera

In 1993, outbreaks of cholera were reported in Ukraine and in parts of Central Asia, but it is a danger primarily to natives living in poor conditions rather than to tourists. Food and water-purification precautions, especially avoidance of undercooked seafood, make the risk of contracting cholera remote. Fluid replacement and antibiotics are useful in treating cholera, which is much like travelers' diarrhea.

The incidence of cholera in an area can interfere with your travel plans even if you don't get sick yourself. When cholera broke out in Kazakhstan in August 1993, the area was quarantined and travelers were not allowed to cross from Kazakhstan to China. (Travelers also became marooned due to bubonic plague quarantines in Mongolia.)

Altitude Sickness

In Central Asia in particular, it's easy to "get high." Helicopters regularly fly people up to 13,000 feet (4000 m). You may have hiked and climbed at this elevation in Colorado without problems, but few people can fly from sea level to 13,000 feet and not suffer some symptoms of mountain sickness. Most people begin to feel normal after a day or two at altitude, but individuals more severely affected will have to descend to lower elevation and acclimatize more slowly.

Taking a cautious approach to acclimatization is *always* best. Headache, nausea, dizziness, difficult breathing, lack of energy, and lack of appetite are warning signs. If not taken seriously, these symptoms of acute mountain sickness (AMS) can progress to high-altitude pulmonary edema (HAPE) or high-altitude cerebral edema (HACE), which are sometimes fatal. If you are experiencing AMS symptoms, you should not go higher.

Acetazolamide (Diamox) helps some people acclimatize when taken prophylactically. This drug causes dry mouth and tingling in the hands. Unless you know from past experience that you have trouble adjusting to altitude, there's no good reason to take Diamox. Another drug, dexamethasone (Decadron), is sometimes used to *treat* people suffering from AMS. This drug can have dangerous, long-lasting side effects; it should be used only in extreme rescue situations. Never take Decadron to try pushing higher.

The "calcium-channel blocker" drug nifedipine has been used to treat HAPE with impressive results. It is a drug that is usually used for angina and to treat high blood pressure, but it also decreases the pressure in the pulmonary arteries, thereby limiting the degree of pulmonary congestion and pulmonary edema that can develop at altitude. The doses that have been used are 10 to 20 milligrams three times a day, although now it comes in a sustained-release form that can be taken once a day. It has also been used prophylactically in studies to prevent altitude sickness, although this remains controversial: the main concern is that it can lower blood pressure, although probably only transiently and probably not enough to be of concern in an otherwise healthy person. It appears to be better than Decadron for HAPE, and is certainly better than Diamox for treating established HAPE; descent, of course, remains the safest approach. Nifedipine has not been shown to be of significant benefit for cerebral edema (HACE). If evacuation from high altitude may be difficult, parties traveling above 4000 meters should consider having nifedipine in the expedition first-aid kit.

Russian climbers have a lot of experience with mountain sickness. Most of them know how to recognize symptoms and take it seriously. But their ideas about how to treat it don't always correspond to those accepted in the West.

Russians commonly carry very little water when climbing and may actually discourage you from drinking, saying it will "make you tired." This flies in the face of all Western medical research, which concudes that staying well hydrated minimizes the detrimental effects of high altitude. If you are taking Diamox, a diuretic, you should drink even more fluids than normal to stay hydrated. A gallon a day is not excessive.

A favorite Russian and Ukrainian food is *sala*—pork fat, eaten straight, or sliced and eaten on bread. They take this to altitude and swear by its "high-energy value." Most studies show that the body has trouble metabolizing fats and proteins under the stress of high altitude, and carbohydrates are the best food.

Likewise, Russians sometimes carry cognac to high altitudes, although the evidence is that alcohol heightens the oxygen deficit and further dehydrates you. Tea—which Russians are likely to drink in place of water, brewed very strong—is also a diuretic. Stick to electrolyte drinks to flavor your water.

Where everyone concurs is that you must go down if you're experiencing altitude problems. If you have a headache, feel nauseated, or are having difficulty breathing, don't try to "push through" for the sake of your party: you will become a much greater burden if they have to carry you down.

If you don't have previous experience with high altitude, it's essential you learn about it before pushing your altitude "threshhold." Reading up on mountain sickness may save your life. *Trekking in Nepal* by Dr. Stephen Bezruchka includes an excellent chapter on altitude sickness. You should also read *Mountain Sickness* by Dr. Peter Hackett and *Going Higher: The Story of Man and Altitude*, by Charles Houston (see Bibliography).

Rabies

Herders keep dogs that have been known to bite trekkers. You should be very careful to avoid these dogs, because of the potential risk of rabies. Don't approach a camp if people aren't present. If you encounter a herding dog on the trail, keep an eye on it and wield a stick.

Snake Bite

There are vipers throughout most of southern Russia and in Turkestan up to about 10,000 feet (3000 m). Although it's a relatively rare occurrence, be aware of the possible risk of snake bite. In case of snake bite, try to identify the snake, and get to a clinic as quickly as possible. Immediately after the bite, it may be helpful to try to suck out the venom. If help is hours away, tie a tourniquet above the area that was bitten; the tourniquet should be tight enough to occlude venous/lymphatic drainage, but not tight enough to cut off arterial flow. Try to limit your movement, especially of the bitten extremity, within the constraints of movement necessary for evacuation.

Tick- and Mosquito-borne Diseases

Ticks are a concern primarily for backcountry travelers in the southern portions of the Russian Far East. Ticks are a particular problem throughout Ussuriland (also known as Primorye) and endemic as far east as the Altai in Siberia. Local sources inform me there are not ticks as far north as Magadan, so you don't have to worry if you're going to Kamchatka or Chukotka.

The risk of getting bitten is much greater in spring and early summer. Caution is still warranted in July and August, and only in fall and winter is there no reason for concern about ticks.

Encephalitis, a viral infection carried by some ticks, can be fatal when not treated immediately. Dozens of people die every year in Russia as a result of tick bites. The first symptoms of tick-borne encephalitis can appear one to two weeks after a bite. They include headache and general weakness, a high fever in the evening, and a cold sweat in the morning. Victims can lose consciousness and die in another one to two weeks. If you are bitten, early treatment with TBE immune globulin injections can arrest tick-borne encephalitis if infection has taken place, according to Russian sources.

The best precaution against tick-borne encephalitis is vaccination. Russians living in Ussuriland (Primorye) who work or play a lot in the woods vaccinate annually. This vaccine is inconvenient for travelers, as it's administered in three doses over the course of a year, and it's not available in the United States or Canada. The vaccine (TBE immune globulin) is available only in Europe. For information on obtaining the vaccine, see the Immunizations section earlier in this chapter. If you're going for a short trip, it is probably sufficient to be very careful about exposure to ticks.

There is also some mosquito-borne Japanese encephalitis in the Russian Far East area of Ussuriland (Primorye). The risk of Japanese encephalitis is primarily in rice-growing and pig-farming areas; anyone who will be spending more than a month in these field conditions should get vaccinated.

Another reason to avoid ticks in the Russian Far East is Siberian (or North Asian) tick typhus, a disease similar to Rocky Mountain spotted fever, although it's generally not as likely to result in severe illness or death. Siberian tick typhus is caused by primitive bacteria (*Rickettsia sibirica*) that can only survive inside cells and are spread by tick bites. Symptoms are variable, but people almost always develop a 5- to 10-millimeter black scab at the site of the tick bite, usually three or four days afterwards, then become ill with a severe influenzalike illness. They may develop a near–total-body spotted rash. Doxycycline or ciprofloxacin are the antibiotics most likely to be useful against Siberian tick typhus, and are probably worth taking if a scap develops at the site of a possible tick bite.

Ticks, little black insects that burrow into the skin, prefer warm places on the body. To prevent them from finding their ideal habitat, wear long pants and long-sleeve shirts at all times in woods or grasses. Create a tight fit around ankles, wrists, and neck. Keep your shirt tucked in at the waist. Netting will not protect against ticks. Spray permethrin-based tick repellent on clothing (this is an insecticide that you can't use on your skin). Apply DEET insect repellent on areas of your skin not covered by clothing.

When in tick-infested areas, check yourself every one to two hours for ticks. Light-colored clothing makes it easier to see them. If you find a tick on yourself, it's important to remove it correctly. If you're near a town where there's a clinic, have it removed professionally.

Otherwise, there are several ways to get the tick out without leaving part of the possibly infected tick under the skin. Putting oil on the tick will sometimes make it back out. If this doesn't work, use tweezers. Grasp the tick as close to the skin as possible and pull with steady pressure. Do not crush or puncture the tick, as its body fluids may be infected. Try not to touch it with bare hands. After removing the tick, disinfect the area of the bite with alcohol or soap. Get to a medical facility as quickly as possible.

Folk Remedies

Many Russians have great faith in *narodnaya meditsina* (folk remedies). Almost certainly, if you get sick traveling there, or have a cut or burn, your friends will offer you *mumeo*. This smelly black paste is made from mountain rodent droppings, boiled down and cleaned.

Mountain people have known about *mumeo* (also called *Arkhar Tash*) for many centuries; Aristotle is said to have mentioned it in his writings. Throughout the heights of Asia, in Pakistan, India, Afghanistan, Nepal, and Tibet, *mumeo* is used as an ingredient in traditional medications.

In these countries, in the zone between high alpine meadows and the perpetual ice and snows, mountain mice eat a unique combination of hundreds of alpine plants, which their digestive process blends to produce *mumeo*, with its remarkable curative qualities.

Mumeo is applied topically to burns and cuts, which supposedly heal much faster than they would otherwise (my experience is that it works, although there is no scientific evidence). For a variety of sicknesses, *mumeo* is taken internally, dissolved in tea or honey. If you're shocked at the thought of mouse turds, remember: some drugs sold in fancy colored capsules use human and animal urine as a base.

While *mumeo* may be the most startling, it's only one of a wide range of Russian folk remedies. Other treatments include applying mustard poultices to the chest, breathing steam from a pot of boiled potatoes, and drinking tea boiled from a variety of herbs. Many of the "witches' cures" feature vodka: vodka with pepper, vodka with honey and melted butter, vodka with ginseng. Watch out for these: while a small shot of vodka may help your cold, significant amounts of the stuff will probably only exacerbate any conditions you have.

Otherwise, folk remedies are pretty innocuous and may even cure you—if you believe in them as strongly as the Russians do.

HOSPITALS AND OTHER HEALTH FACILITIES

Hospitals

The Kremlin Hospital (Athens Medical Center) near Moscow State University is the finest in the former USSR. If you have an illness or medical emergency requiring treatment or hospitalization elsewhere in the country, try to land in a *Chetvyortoye Upraveleniye* ("Fourth Department") hospital; these, the best-equipped, staffed by the most highly qualified medical personnel, were formerly reserved for the Party *nomenklatura* (elite).

Soviet hospitals and clinics used to treat foreigners for free, the same as with any Soviet citizen. Now, the likelihood is that some request will be made for payment, but there's no way to predict what your experience will be at a given place. The chances are that it's *kak dogovorishsya* ("however you cut the deal"), and that any attempts to clarify the cost *before* the doctor sees you will only invite requests for a larger payment. Meals are typically bad at Soviet hospitals, so you'll need someone to bring you food if you get stuck in one.

Steve Cunha, a geographer who studies the Pamir, is exceedingly grateful to Dushanbe surgeons who saved his life after he was shot by bandits in Tajikistan, but he offers this advice to climbers and trekkers:

> Be aware that unlike Nepal, Alaska, and much of South America, modern medical care is unavailable in large Central Asian capital cities. The ex-Soviet hospitals are far below Western standards. Most medical facilities throughout the former Soviet Union are critically short of medical supplies, overflowing with patients, and staffed by doctors and nurses with inferior and outdated medical backgrounds and equipment. There is also less concern for hygiene than in Western hospitals. The Dushanbe operating room had an open window, and excrement covered the bathroom floors.

Clinics

In Moscow there are a couple of clinics that treat foreigners: American

Medical Center (Shmitovsky Proyezd 3, tel. 256-8212), Intermedservice (Intourist Hotel, Tverskaya 3/5, tel. 203-9553), and International Health Care (Gruzinsky Per. 3, tel. 253-0703). The foreign missions also have clinics; on evenings and weekends they take turns being on call: American Embassy (tel. 252-2451), British Embassy (tel. 231-8511), and French Embassy (tel. 237-4655).

If you wind up in a provincial clinic, don't panic. There are many competent doctors, although they work in very limited facilities. For simple procedures like X-rays or a few stitches, they're probably fine. If at all possible, get out of the country or to Moscow for surgery or other invasive procedures.

Rescue and Evacuation Services

In the heyday of Soviet sports, mountain rescue groups were well organized and relatively well supplied, with helicopters in frequent use throughout the country and fuel for helicopters still cheap (see A History of Backpacking and Mountaineering in Russia in chapter 1, Introduction). Now, in the event an emergency evacuation is required, the alacrity of the response and whether you get a helicopter may depend very much on the circumstances.

If you're trekking with an organized Western group, under the auspices of a reputable Soviet agency, they should have radio contact and the clout to call in a chopper if necessary. If you're on your own, it's less likely that an SOS will be met by a coordinated rescue attempt. If a helicopter is requested, payment guarantees may be demanded in advance. This is not because Russians are mercenary or rapacious; it's a reflection of a system in nearly total disarray.

The government rescue services, now underfunded and poorly equipped, only respond in major disaster situations—such as the avalanche that swept away forty-three climbers on Peak Lenin in 1990. This is not Denali; there is no Park Service that will evacuate you at taxpayers' expense. Rescues are up to the commercial organizations hosting clients, some of which are reasonably well prepared for emergencies, others not at all. If you are "vagabond climbing," you take your chances on a team of good Samaritans coming after you should you get in trouble. If you're a client of a trekking/climbing agency, the likelihood of evacuation is best if you've gone through the organization that owns or leases helicopters in the region.

4 Traveling in Russia and Central Asia

Accommodations

A non-Russian–speaking foreigner traveling and staying in hotels is going to pay top dollar just about everywhere. If you have a Russian traveling companion, however, overnights can be arranged at more reasonable prices—between $5 and $15 a night, depending on your requirements. Even if you pay the way of your Russian escort, you will save money. You won't get away with paying "Soviet citizen" rates in Intourist hotels, or anywhere else you have to show your passport, but some hotels don't require this, and it's not necessary for apartment rentals. See also the Money section in this chapter.

The *Russia Survival Guide* (see Bibliography) lists current rates for big-city hotels, as well as contact numbers for bed-and-breakfast agencies.

HOTELS

Hotel room rates are different for Soviets than for foreigners. The bad news is that Western travelers are charged ten to twenty times more than Soviets. The good news is that the hotel may be turning away Soviet guests, but if you have hard currency in your wallet, they'll probably find a room for you.

In Soviet hotels, you *don't* get what you pay for. Hotel rooms for less than $40 are a thing of the past in major cities. Even in a $100 room, you're lucky to get toilet paper. If you find soap as well, consider yourself doubly blessed. The toilet may not flush. There may not be hot water all of the time. There's no guarantee you'll have a phone, or that the phone will work. The foreign-owned and -managed hotels springing up in cities frequented by tourists are a different story, but these are even pricier.

The travel agent booking your air arrangements can also book you a hotel in Moscow or St. Petersburg. As of this writing, hotels in other cities cannot yet be booked through airline computer systems. In the capitals, there are plenty of expensive hotels and few bargains. The bargains include the St. Petersburg Youth Hostel (3rd Sovetskaya Ul. 28, tel. [812] 277-0569, fax [812] 277-5102) and the Moscow Traveller's Guest House between Prospekt Mira and Rizhskaya (ul. B. Peryaslavskaya 50, floor 10, tel. [095] 971-4059). Outside of the capitals, Intourist hotels are usually the most expensive place in town. The rates may be twice as high as at the next rung of tourist hotels and the Intourist establishment usually doesn't provide significantly more comforts or conveniences to justify paying the higher prices.

Sometimes the best bargains are hotels belonging to various government ministries and institutes, for staff and associates on business trips. Most of them now cater to tourists as well. Called *vedomstvenniye gostinitsy*, these places tend to be clean and basic, but adequate.

This guesthouse at Djirgatal in the High Pamir promises more than just a bed. (Photo: Matt Hyde)

In the most remote rural areas, where the practice of squeezing foreigners' wallets hasn't yet taken hold, you may be able to find a room for a few dollars. Still, hotels in rural towns are best avoided if at all possible.

I stayed in a hotel in Dagestan where they set me up in what was clearly supposed to be the luxury suite: two large connecting rooms, elegant carpets, imported sofa. There was no bathroom. The outhouse was about 165 feet (50 m) away on an unlit path ankle-deep in mud. This squat-over-the-hole shack was so filthy, I didn't dare go near it even in the daytime. They locked the front door at night, so to get to the facilities, you had to wake up the "desk clerk." The only running water in the hotel was a single washroom for all the guests, with three cold sinks and paint peeling off the walls.

HOMESTAYS AND ROOM RENTALS

In the countryside, you may well be offered either to tent in someone's yard or to sleep in their house. The host may or may not suggest payment. *Especially* if payment is not requested, you should give them something: either some item in your pack that will clearly be useful to them (jackknife, sunglasses, baseball cap, et cetera), or the ruble equivalent of about $5. Russians are proud people and may refuse money; in this case, you should slip it into your host's pocket or leave it someplace where you know he or she will find it.

Most rural people in this country are poor; if you accept their hospitality without offering something in return, you're setting an example that will reflect badly on all foreign travelers, and on your country. By the same token, if you offer too much money—more than $20—you're also setting a bad precedent because that much will be expected from future travelers passing the same way.

The hospitality of Russians in cities is unlikely to extend to offering to take you in overnight. In part this is because people live in incredibly cramped conditions and simply don't have room for houseguests. Also, they are often ashamed of their living quarters and can't believe that the living room rug is good enough for a foreign guest.

In the capitals, the economical way to go is a prearranged homestay or apartment rental. A system of apartment or room rentals makes overnighting in private apartments a clean business arrangement in Russia. Traditionally in resort towns, and more recently in big cities, you can rent a room in an apartment, or a whole apartment for a night or an extended stay. English-language guidebooks to Moscow and St. Petersburg (see Bibliography) list phone numbers for the hundreds of agencies that arrange room or apartment rentals. In other towns, notices advertising rooms may be posted in airports or train stations. These range from $5 to $50 a night, depending on the town, location, size, and condition of the apartment or room. While these are more trouble to arrange than a hotel room, it's more convenient for a multiday stay because you have kitchen facilities.

In Central Asia, where this system is not widely accepted, it is slightly more awkward to arrange to stay in a private home: you can't ask to stay overnight in exchange for money for fear of offending your host, but have to wait for an invitation.

You can arrange homestays or room rentals before you go by contacting one of the bed-and-breakfast companies operating abroad. As the "bed-and-breakfast" label implies, some of these services include more than just a place to sleep, often providing meals, and possibly even being met at the airport or shown around town. This isn't cheap, but it can be an easy way to get your trip started in a big city. Also, the company setting up your homestay should be able to support your visa.

Transportation

For travel between cities, most people go by air or train; it is also possible to drive. Major cities often have local electric trains—*elektrichkas*—that take people out to their garden plots. In Central Asia travel between cities and towns is often by bus. Within cities, taxis and public transportation are the usual means of conveyance. There's no hitchhiking tradition; if you get a ride, it's expected you will pay for it. Don't be surprised at the vehicles that stop for you: I've been picked up by ambulances, Opals, and off-duty buses.

BY AIR

Aeroflot, until recently the largest airline in the world, is the most common form of transportation over the great distances between cities in Russia and Central Asia. Flying the Soviet airline, with its wretched or non-existent service, is an unforgettable experience. The planes are uncomfortable and smelly, the bathrooms disgusting. If you have normal-length legs, the person seated in front of you will probably turn around and snarl, "Will you get your knees out of my back!"

Often, though, by the time you actually get on the plane, you're so relieved to be there, you're oblivious to all the discomforts.

Fuel distribution problems have kept planes on the ground more and more frequently in the past several years, closing down small airports for extended periods of time and resulting in delays of hours or days at major city airports. It's difficult to get advance information from Aeroflot about delays, so you usually don't find out until you get to the airport that your flight has been cancelled or won't fly for hours.

As a foreigner, you at least get to wait out the delay in a spacious lounge—most major airports have separate Intourist sections where foreigners check in. These are insulated from the main hall of the airport where masses of tired travelers crowd waiting areas without chairs.

Intourist chaperones generally escort foreigners out to the plane separately, too. Then the free-for-all begins, as it's often festival seating, with the plane overbooked. Anything can happen when you fly Aeroflot. On one flight from Petropavlovsk-Kamchatsky to Moscow, we made an unscheduled landing in Yakutsk for refueling and were dumped out on the tarmac and left to wait there for four hours, with no updates about what was going on.

You can book Aeroflot tickets through a travel agent outside the country (which I recommend if you're only planning to transit through Moscow or whatever your arrival city is) or you can buy them once you get there, if your plans aren't set. You can book your tickets yourself in Moscow—in person only—at Inturtrans (ul. Petrovka 15), but it's easier to let a travel agent do it for you—and shouldn't be more expensive. For Aeroflot fares within the former USSR, call Aeroflot (in New York, 212-332-1050 or in Washington, DC, 202-429-4922 or 800-535-9877).

Unfortunately, even the official Aeroflot representatives abroad are often unaware of flights between smaller cities of the former Soviet Union. If you are told by an Aeroflot representative in New York, for example, that there is no flight between Magadan and Petropavlovsk-Kamchatsky, don't believe it. This is only one of the many flights that are not listed in Aeroflot's computer system. The breakup of Aeroflot into regional fiefdoms has only added to the confusion of this already unwieldy monster that was formerly the world's largest airline. Aeroflot USA cannot give you information about flights between Tashkent, Uzbekistan, and Frankfurt, Germany, because this route is flown by Aeroflot Uzbekistan. You can find out about these flights in advance from someone who travels there frequently, or you can wing it and buy tickets as you go.

Foreign passport-holders are required to pay for their tickets in dollars.

The rare exception where you may get away with paying rubles is if you are flying from a *very* remote airport where the accountant may not be set up to handle hard currency. The branches of Aeroflot in now-independent countries set their own fares, so it is no longer the case that it costs roughly the same amount to fly anywhere in Central Asia from Moscow. Unlike other airlines, there is no savings on Aeroflot round-trip tickets (i.e., round-trip fares are the sum of two one-way fares). Neither does advance purchase save you money.

Inquire about baggage weight restrictions and take them seriously. On most Aeroflot flights, passengers are allowed only 44 pounds (20 kg). Foreigners must pay for excess baggage in dollars (this rate seems to vary, but can be around $4 per kilogram over the weight limit). On small fixed-wing flights, even less baggage is permitted.

On international Aeroflot flights, there may be a cost savings to fly first class if you are way over the baggage limit. First-class passengers are generally allowed twice as much luggage and the additional cost of the ticket can amount to less than the excess baggage fees. On domestic Aeroflot flights, there is only one class of service, so this is not a consideration.

Your baggage is theoretically claimable at the Intourist area, if there is one. But it's not unheard of for it to come out in the proletarian baggage claim with all the other luggage on the plane. It's important to be vigilant, and check both places periodically until your bags appear. I have had the experience of taking a two-hour flight, and then waiting more than three hours to retrieve my bags.

You should arrange in advance to be met at Moscow airports or other major airports by friends, or representatives of a travel agency or the hotel you've booked; this is one case where trying to economize doesn't pay. If someone's meeting you, they may wait at the Intourist section and if you come off the plane into the main airport arrivals area with the Soviet passengers, your greeter may not find you. As with claiming baggage, check both areas for the person who's meeting you. Ironically, one of the most confusing airports is Moscow's Domodedova, through which more foreigners transit than any other airport, on the way to Central Asia, Siberia, and the Far East. Notes on Domodedova from my journal:

We arrive in the middle of the night from Almaty and wait in the separate Intourist building for our luggage. There are dozens of other foreigners waiting, having arrived on various flights. No information is posted about where bags can be claimed. Even as a Russian speaker, I can't get straight information from any of the staff about where the bags will be unloaded. After waiting more than an hour, I happen to go back outside where, in a dark area beside the building, our suitcases are stacked. No one announced the arrival of the bags from our flight; anyone could have walked off with them. The special Intourist building is about 300 meters from the main terminal building where our ride is supposed to be waiting for us (only ticketed passengers are allowed out to Intourist at Domodedova). The shuttle bus is nowhere to be seen, so we drag bags and skis through the freezing night across the snowy tarmac, wondering which of the many doors to go through to get to the hall where our driver should be waiting. There, the Intourist staffperson indifferently replies to our question about someone meeting the flight from Almaty: "Yes, a man was looking for you, but he left." She proceeds to try to set us up with a taxi driver who was visiting with her. In the meantime, our driver returns. He had been looking all over for us, having requested the desk clerk to tell us he'd be right back if we showed up!

Most of this is a comedy of inconvenience, but getting from the airport into town can be serious business. If it is not possible to have someone meet you, take a flight that arrives during the day and use public transportation. This is a much bigger hassle in Moscow than in smaller cities, involving transferring from bus to subway and then possibly bus again, which is not fun if you have much luggage. But the alternatives are less pleasant.

Especially in Moscow, taxi mafias control the traffic between the main domestic airports (Vnukovo and Domodedova) and international airport (Sheremetevo) and the city. As a foreigner, you are a target for these extortionist drivers. At best, you will be charged rates as high as Tokyo ($50 to $100 from the airport to the city). At worst, you could be robbed. Even the people who are supposed to be looking after foreign travelers' well-being are sometimes in cahoots with the driver mafia, like the Intourist clerk I described above.

Helicopters and Charter Flights

Many very remote places in Russia and Turkestan are accessible thanks to a marvelous machine called the MI-8. These helicopters, designed for the Soviet Army, are big, unwieldy birds that carry fifteen or more people and all their gear. The pilots adeptly fly through the extreme weather of the high Pamir and the low fogs of Kamchatka. A crew of three operates these birds: pilot, co-pilot, and navigator. Most of the pilots are veterans with a decade or two of rugged flying under their belts. Cautious professionals, they inspire confidence.

Chartering helicopters is best left to an intermediary, like a travel agency. Helicopters generally belong to the local Aeroflot affiliate, although they are sometimes leased to private companies and organizations. The going rate for choppers continues to climb, as fuel in Russia and Central Asia reaches world prices. Within the last year, I've heard quotes ranging from $120 an hour to $500 an hour. Like most everything in Russia, it's whom you strike a deal with. As a foreigner, you're at a bargaining disadvantage and the price will almost certainly be higher than if you have a Soviet arrange it. In many places, especially Kamchatka, there are now rules requiring the payment of higher rates if foreigners are on board.

Russian helicopters have been known to crash—one went down in 1993 on Chukotka, killing an international anthropologists' team. But this accident should not deter you from flying in helicopters there; helicopters are used throughout roadless regions of Russia and Central Asia much the way small fixed-wing planes link remote parts of Alaska; Russian helicopters have a good safety record. I'm more scared of riding with Russian drivers than flying in their helicopters.

In some areas where there are airports, it's also cost-effective to charter a small plane. The AN-2 carries ten passengers.

BY TRAIN

For travel within Russia and Central Asia, trains are still the best bargain. Officially, foreigners must pay hard currency for train tickets, but documents are not checked on trains so you should be able to travel with ruble tickets. You will have trouble purchasing a ruble ticket, though, if you don't speak Russian or have a Russian friend who can make the purchase for you. Even hard currency tickets are much less than travel on Aeroflot. The agency you're working with can purchase tickets for you, or you can buy them in advance at Inturtrans (they will charge hard currency) or at the station you're planning to train out from.

If you're planning a multiday train ride, you should be prepared for dirty conditions. Train bathrooms can be particularly disgusting and a thick layer of mud often blackens the windows. Carry plenty of premoistened towelettes to battle the filth.

Moscow and St. Petersburg have different *vokzaly* (train stations), depending which direction you're traveling. Moscow's train stations are: to the Baltics—Rizhsky Vokzal; to Belarus and Poland—Byelorussky Vokzal; to Central Asia, western Siberia, and the Urals—Kazansky Vokzal; to the Caucasus and Crimea—Kursky Vokzal; to eastern and northern Russia (the Trans-Siberian Railroad)—Yaroslavsky Vokzal; to St. Petersburg and Helskinki, Finland—Leningradsky Vokzal; to southeastern Russia—Paveletsky Vokzal; to the Ukraine—Kievsky Vokzal.

The most common way to get out of Russian cities is on the *elektrichka*, a local electric train that takes people out of town short distances to their *dachas* (country houses) and garden plots.

BY PRIVATE CAR

If you have a lot of time on your hands and like to drive, the most free-wheeling way to see Russia and Central Asia may be by car. Although it's possible to rent a car in Russia, this is expensive and not practical for independent travel. Neither is it practical to buy a car there. Automobiles, even Russian-made beaters, are expensive in the former USSR. It's best to pick one up in Europe and drive in.

It will be helpful if you have some auto-mechanic skills; Soviet roads are terrible, even in the cities. Outside of the capitals, there's no such thing as *autobahns* or interstates—in fact, there is precious little asphalt. The potholes will shake your car to pieces. Trying to get it serviced will test your patience; if you can find an auto mechanic, you'll have to make sure he doesn't exchange your battery for an older one.

You'll spend hours (and maybe days) waiting for gas. The more provincial you go, the bigger problem gas will probably become. You will be pulled over frequently by traffic cops, as foreign cars attract special notice. Russians rival Italians for crazy driving; especially in the cities, the accident rate is dismal. Personally, I have no patience for these sorts of challenges; I've never done an extended road trip in Russia.

After waiting in line several hours, drivers fill up with gasoline through a makeshift cardboard funnel.

Manfred, a German photojournalist I met, hired a Russian "companion" and hit the road for four months in his Jeep. When I ran into him in the Altai several months into his trip, he had already had fabulous adventures. His approach of taking a local escort is a good idea; this person can deal with the obstacles you run into and provide the added security of keeping an eye on your vehicle. Especially if you're traveling in a desirable four-wheel-drive foreign automobile, it simply isn't safe to leave it parked most places. Your windshield wipers, mirrors, tires, or all the above *and* the rest of the car may be stolen if you leave it in the wrong place overnight.

BY TAXI OR HIRED VEHICLE

Most taxis in Russia aren't cabs at all, but private cars that pick up passengers. Flag down cars by standing at the edge of the road with your right arm extended, hand open. For added effect, you can wiggle your hand up and down. The international thumb-up signal might get cars to stop, but that's not the local lingo.

When a driver stops, tell him where you're going and strike a bargain on the fare. It helps to know approximately what the current rate is for a ride across town (ask someone about this). Cabs often will pick you up only if they're headed the direction you're going anyway, so it may take awhile to get a ride. If you do get an "official" cab, the fare is still subject to negotiation. It's been years since taxi drivers would carry passengers for the fare on the meter.

While riding in these "gypsy cabs" has long been an accepted practice, it's not without risk. Again, as a foreigner you may be a target if you end up with a crook for a driver. Use your judgment; if you have a bad sense about someone, don't get in the car. Avoid cars with more than one person. Don't ride in private cars at night. Often these are the only "cabs" to be seen, so the bus or the subway are the only alternatives.

To get out of a city, it's often practical to hire an all-terrain vehicle, most easily arranged through a travel agency, or acquaintances.

BY BUS

Public transportation is the safest way to get around in cities, though crowded buses can be claustrophobic, and they're not as convenient as cars.

Many Russian vehicles are all-terrain vehicles. This bus fords rivers, too.

Bus service in all cities is pretty good. The major cities also have excellent subways.

In Central Asia, travel between cities and towns is often by bus. In fact, you haven't really "experienced" Russia and Central Asia until you've ridden a long-distance bus. David Koester, a six-foot-four–tall anthropologist who studies the native peoples of Kamchatka, describes one such trip:

> *I get a seat in the back perched over the spare tire, my knees at my chin. Pavement ends not too far outside of Petropavlovsk. Uncomfortable as we bound from rut to rut, I really feel sorry for the man in front of me who attempts to stretch out and sleep across the rim of the tire, his dog occasionally slipping off the seat into his face. After stopping for lunch in Milkovo, we bounce along for about an hour before the bus breaks down. I'm actually relieved: this means we can get out and stretch our legs. Four hours later, a new bus arrives to continue the journey and we finally reach Esso after midnight.*

These days, schedules and fares may depend on the driver's whim: Jonathan Bobaljik, a seasoned Russia travel guide, related to me that he arrived in Mineralniye Vody to find the afternoon bus to Baksan was "cancelled." The driver took 150 rubles from each person (the official fare was then 74 rubles) until he had a full bus and went anyway.

Marshrutny taxis are a cross between a taxi and a bus. These minivans carry eight to ten passengers on established routes within some cities and short distances between cities. Slightly more expensive than buses and much cheaper than taxis, they cost at most the equivalent of a couple of dollars.

Money

This book doesn't talk much about costs because prices change in Russia not from year to year but from week to week. In places, this book mentions what something should approximately cost in dollars because the dollar is a more stable gauge of price standards than rubles. Use these approximate costs only as a guide.

The ruble is an internally convertible currency: you can exchange dollars for rubles, and rubles for dollars, at Russian banks. Since 1992, there are no artificially set exchange rates. For up-to-the-minute information about the value of the ruble and what it will buy, see one of the English-language newspapers, such as *Commersant*, listed in the Bibliography.

The ruble floats free against foreign ("hard") currencies (technically, rubles may be accepted in the Baltics—Estonia, Lithuania, and Latvia—although these are not part of the CIS). Outside of the former Soviet Union, the ruble has no value; you cannot purchase rubles abroad, neither can you get rid of rubles once you've left the country. The countries of Turkestan have each introduced their own currency now, but these fledgling independent monetary systems may not last. Inflation also plagues these new currencies, and rubles continue to be accepted in Turkestan as this book goes to press. Everywhere in Russia and Central Asia, dollars are the preferred currency and people will always be trying to separate you from your dollars.

Theoretically, you can always change rubles back into dollars if you have documentation that you originally exchanged dollars at a bank. In practical terms, you may have trouble finding a bank open on the day you leave the country, or the bank may simply not have dollars on hand, or any number of other excuses. Especially if you exit Russia or Central Asia via an obscure border crossing, you may get stuck with rubles, so change small amounts of money at a time.

Many people expect that travel in Russia should be cheap because of the country's economic straits. But, while there are millions of Russians who live on $30 or less a month, for whom a few dollars is a lot of money, the attitude persists that foreigners can, ergo should, pay as though it were Paris. This stems, in part, from Russians' distorted popular image of Western life-styles. Russians reason that "if an American makes $200 a day, he should be able to pay $200 for hotel and meals." They often have little concept of realistic wages or the actual cost of living in the West.

Also, Russia and Central Asia haven't been exposed to the budget traveler; until very recently, the only tourists came through Intourist on package tours. As more students and world travelers make inroads, I think budget-priced services for this stratum will become more widely available.

The biggest problem is that the free market really hasn't caught on enough yet to create competitive rates for services. There's tremendous demand for economical accommodations, but few good bargain hotels. It's not for lack of entrepreneurs: The government offers no incentives and racketeers make it very difficult for private enterprise to survive. Hotels are the classic example of overpricing. Many firms and agencies offering tours or services will also try to milk you for dollars.

You can stretch your dollars a long way, though, if you're flexible and creative. The basic rule of thumb is: pay in rubles whenever you can get away with it. Officially, few services are offered to Westerners any longer for rubles; foreign tourists are seen as having pockets lined with gold and everyone wants some. But if you can avoid being an obvious tourist, the former Soviet Union can still be a travel bargain.

Speaking Russian helps, but if you don't, having a Russian friend or two who can do the talking when making purchases, getting hotel rooms, or ordering meals is the best bet. Traveling with Russian friends, or escorts, you can keep costs down by acting like a native.

In the old days, to look like a local you had to wear drab, Eastern bloc-made clothing and pack in ratty bags. It's easier now, because Western-made goods have flooded the Russian market. Many Russians wear bright, stylish clothes and foreigners blend into a crowd. Sloppy dressing (for women, especially) raises the "non-Russian" flag: avoid ragtag jeans and messy hair.

Watch your behavior to keep from having "foreigner" stamped on your forehead. Don't make eye contact or smile at strangers. Don't pause politely and let other people get ahead of you in line. *Do* be patient and docile if service is slow, rude, or non-existent. Especially in stores or agencies that are still state-run, making a fuss for quick service will only exacerbate the situation. In general, casual behavior in public—sprawling in chairs, feet on tables, chattiness—is not the Russian style. You don't have to copycat the natives to travel there. And you might not "pass" anyway. But if you're trying to get away with paying rubles whenever possible, these tips will help you keep your cover.

BRIBES

Russians, accustomed to the reality that paying people off is the only way to get things done, make sarcastic jokes about paying *dan* (tribute). There are interesting precedents in Russian history. In Kievan Russia, conquered peoples paid their conquerors tribute. The Tatars collected *dan* from natives when they swept the Asian continent. The Cossacks forced the natives to pay *yasak*, another form of taxation.

When is it appropriate to offer an extra "little something" to an official or a clerk? If you don't speak Russian, almost never. If you're traveling with a Russian escort who suggests that a bribe to a certain official whose help you need might smooth the way, let your companion handle it. It *is* the Russian way, and your friend will be much more effective than you. Vlad Klimenko, an American of Russian heritage who has worked in Russia as a foreign correspondent, relates from his travel journal:

> When we reach Lower Kul Sai, we're met by the local forest ranger. "Show me your documents," he orders. Our driver being already on his way back to Almaty, we're alone with the ranger. With his tatooed arms and harsh Jack Palance grin, he looks more like a recidivist on parole. Reluctant to show our American passports for fear a larger bribe will be demanded, I squat Central Asian style and let the minutes go by. The ranger doesn't seem too much in a hurry either. "How much?" I blurt out, finally. "One hundred rubles a day—or a bottle of vodka." Fifty U.S. cents a day didn't seem too steep, but pride forces me to haggle. "We don't have any vodka," I lie, "but I can offer you three hundred rubles for all of us." He agrees, with a final warning: "Leave your campsites clean."

For effective palm-greasing, it's important (1) to be sure the person receiving the bribe is in a position to do what you need and (2) to know approximately how much to offer. Too little and you may only insult them and sabotage your chances. Then there are a few public servants who are scrupulously honest and will be offended by the suggestion of a bribe.

Most foreigners don't have any way of knowing these things, so you should forget about bribes. Be diplomatic, polite, and patient. You can't go wrong striking up a friendly conversation and giving a token gift. Carry a supply of small items—baseball cap, nice pens, decorative pins, et cetera don't weigh much and can come in handy. If you're traveling alone, and feel you have exhausted all possible avenues for resolving a problem situation except bribery, keep these things in mind:

Be subtle. When you hand your passport to the agent who's insisting she can't get you a ticket on the flight you need, or to the bureaucrat who's refused to extend your visa, slip a $10 or $20 (or more, depending on how critical the situation is) into the passport. That way, if the clerk is honest, they can hand back the money and you can pretend you didn't know it was there. Or, they can slip it into their pocket without acknowledging the transaction. Especially if there are a number of clerks behind the same counter, don't be obvious about offering a bribe to one of them.

CASH, CREDIT CARDS, OR TRAVELERS CHECKS?

Credit cards are accepted by foreign currency stores. Some of these stores list prices in German marks or other currencies. When the charge comes through on your credit card, it will be converted into dollars according to the DM (Deutschemark) rate on the day of purchase. You can usually use a credit card at businesses that require foreigners to pay hard currency—Aeroflot, hotels, upscale restaurants. These places may require you to show your passport, because credit card theft has become widespread. Wherever you have the option of paying rubles (Russian stores, state-run restaurants, train tickets), you'll be charged more with plastic, if they even accept it. Cash advances from credit cards are easy only in Moscow and St. Petersburg, although a few of the independent Russian banks are now offering this service for a commission fee.

Travelers checks (TCs) are accepted when you buy rubles. American Express has offices in Moscow and St. Petersburg and will give you dollars for TCs, as will banks in some better hotels. Most banks, however, will not want to turn your TCs into dollars.

No one believes what an incredible hassle it is to convert plastic money or travelers checks into cash until he or she has spent a day going all over a Soviet city trying to find a bank that's open, has cash, and does these operations. You have to have cash. Carry mainly small-denomination bills ($5s, $10s, $20s, and a few $50s), for which it is easier to get change.

Every guide service or agency you work with wants cash. If you've arranged services in advance, they may agree to let you pay by wire transfer (especially if they have an account in a foreign bank), but not before they've begged for cash. If you're traveling independently, you'll have to pay cash for drivers, gasoline, rooms, meals, and anything else. Until TCs and credit card advances become more widely accepted throughout Russia and Central Asia, take enough cash to cover all of your anticipated expenses.

Cultural Considerations

It would be inaccurate to make sweeping generalizations about the people of a country numbering nearly 300 million (in 1991 after the Baltics split off, the population of the USSR was 284 million). This is a complex country encompassing vastly disparate life-styles and ethnic groups. The only thing that is certain is that if you travel in Russia and Turkestan, you will have encounters with people that will be surprising, touching, and eye-opening. While some people (especially in Siberia) resent foreign humanitarian aid, which they feel demeans their national pride, most are very eager to meet foreigners.

Trust your instincts about people. If you feel someone is insincere or is trying to take advantage of you, chances are you're right. Remember, there are many more who are genuine and honest, who would be happy just to meet you and exchange views with you. Seek these people out.

As you travel in remote places, people may be mystified as to your purpose. Many Russians don't understand adventure travel; to them, travel is a commercial venture (e.g., sell Zenith cameras in China, bring back leather jackets to sell in Irkutsk). You will find yourself explaining why you own a car and a house back home, but you are comfortable sleeping on the floor of a yurt. You will be questioned extensively about how people in your country live and how much things cost: how much is a kilo of beef? a month's salary? an airplane?

ECONOMIC DISPARITIES

Interacting with Soviets in the 1990s, it helps to be sensitive to the economic and social identity crisis many of them struggle with. Before the Gorbachev revolution, Soviet society was much more homogeneous. Although Soviet propaganda promoted the notion of an egalitarian utopia, Soviet society was not a classless society. A small upper class, sometimes referred to as the *nomenklatura*, enjoyed the privileges of membership in the Communist party: better apartments, special stores, the option of purchasing a wide variety of consumer goods, vacations at the best resorts, and sometimes even travel to Eastern Europe.

The vast majority of the population belonged to the middle class. Their standard of living was low compared to Europe, the United States, and other Western countries, but they didn't have contacts with people in these countries. They didn't travel abroad. The images the average Soviet had of the world outside the USSR were distorted by their only source of information: the Soviet mass media. They compared themselves to their neighbors and, overall, most people considered themselves neither rich nor poor.

In the short span of several years, under the chaotic new Soviet brand of free-market economics, a chasm has gaped open between the richest and poorest segments of society. A small percentage of people—mostly young entrepreneurs and old communist managers who retained their powerful connections and control of key enterprises and resources—has become fantastically wealthy, controlling millions of dollars. In Moscow and a few other major cities, another fraction of the population earns upwards of $10,000 a year.

The vast majority of the old Soviet middle class, however, has slid into poverty, getting by on a few hundred dollars a year. Not only have their meager government salaries lost most of their former buying power as a result of catastrophic inflation, but their social welfare net has evaporated. Now they compare themselves with other First World nations, and they realize they are poor. Many people, especially the older generation, are bitter at having spent their lives working for the perfect society, only to discover it was a lie. Their newfound poverty grates on them, and many people are painfully aware of the contrast in their situation to that of luckier foreigners. Some even suspect that foreign companies and governments are behind the rampant corruption that allows the most unscrupulous and ruthless Soviets to become extremely rich.

Other Soviets shoulder the heavy burden dealt them by social upheaval with almost unbelievable courage and good humor. Viktor Yudin, who has headed a Vladivostok institute for many years, epitomizes this grin-and-bear-it spirit. Viktor is one of the Russian Far East's most respected game biologists. Now that funding for scientific research has dried up, Viktor has been forced to move his institute's animals out to a farm several hours north of the city. It was here that I met him and his family. Notes from my journal:

> *Viktor meets us at the Spassk-Dalny station in the middle of the night in a vehicle that is a cross between a tank and a jeep. Crammed between our bags under a tarp in the curious rig, we bounce over a rough road for a few miles until Viktor pulls into his "compound." He leads us through a fence and two pairs of green eyes fix on us. The "toddlers," which weigh in at 130 kilograms and 110 kilograms, rise and stretch languidly. Viktor and his wife have been taking care of these abandoned tiger orphans for a year. Their dream is to move the animals out of the crowded enclosure of make-shift cages into a spacious refuge that would be open to the public. Viktor, a slim, steadfastly cheerful man with sparkling eyes, jokes about how the new economics have turned a leading scientist into a farmer. He rises early to catch fish to feed his animals. Wearing a threadbare jacket in the cold pre-dawn, he wraps his feet in rags, stuffs them into rubber boots, and strides off whistling.*

It is encounters with remarkable people like Viktor that renew my faith in Russia.

DRINKING

Especially if you make efforts to get to know people who are not in the tourism business, you will find Soviets hospitable and generous to a fault. Chances are, you'll be invited to someone's home and when that happens, there will probably be vodka. Drinking is the Russians' national pastime. Special occasions in particular are usually observed with large quantities of vodka, cognac, champagne, or all of the above.

Drinking carries the weight of social ritual there. As a guest, be careful to follow proper protocol. Toasts are the rule. Don't sip before the toast is finished. These can be elaborate, eloquent affairs—the Georgians, in particular are renowned for telling great toasts—or simply "to peace and friendship." When the toast has been said, everyone clinks glasses. Russians drink "to the bottom," draining their glasses at one tip and then immediately nibbling *zakuski* (snacks)—typically bread, cucumbers, sausage, or smoked fish—to lessen the punch. They don't drink tiny shots, either, but often down a half glass of vodka—straight—at a time. Even if you enjoy drinking, you will probably find it hard to keep up with Russians.

If you can't or don't like to drink, it can be a trying situation. You should never refuse when your host is pouring the first round. This could be interpreted as unsociable and insulting. Even if you don't drink, allow the host to pour you some vodka. Say *chut chut* ("just a little") and indicate that you want only a small amount by holding your index finger about a centimeter from your thumb. Then when everyone else raises their glasses, you can pretend to drink. It's easier for women to politely refuse subsequent rounds. If you're a man, about your only chance to save face and avoid offending your host is to claim liver problems.

Beware of drinking contests. If you're matching your Russian drinking partners shot for shot, things can get out of hand quickly. Russians are known to take a perverse pride in their ability to outdrink foreigners and unless you're a hard-core alcoholic (many Russians are), you will probably find yourself over your head and under the table. The same host who will be offended if you refuse to drink with him altogether may be equally disgusted to find you puking in the bathroom. Think of future generations of travelers before you lift that final, fatal shot of horrid Chinese cherry brandy to your lips.

If you're drinking in a safe place with trusted friends, and you don't mind spending the next day in a stupor, fine. Russians know how to have a good time and drinking with them can be very fun. Sometimes Russia just seems more bearable after an evening of liquor and laughs. I suggest a few simple rules to keep it safe:

Don't drink with strangers. Some people become ugly and vicious under the influence of alcohol and the convivial atmosphere can deteriorate to "You don't respect me...."

Establish your limit before you start drinking and don't exceed it, no matter how much you may be pressured.

If you have to get home to your tent, apartment, or hotel after the party, make sure you're accompanied by a friend who can look out for you.

Don't drive drunk and don't ride with drunken drivers.

GIFTS

Russians and Central Asians are generous folks. When you get to know people and visit in their homes, they're likely to give presents and you will feel awkward if you can't reciprocate. Until recently, it was hard to go wrong with any kind of small accessories or electronics items. Now, the Soviet market is flooded with Western products (even though many people can't afford these things) and it's more of a challenge to find special presents.

I suggest items that say something about the place you are from: postcards, decorative pins or patches, baseball caps, visors, T-shirts. Popular music tapes, elegant chocolates, gourmet food items, and children's toys are also appreciated; many of these you can now pick up in hard-currency stores in Russia, to keep your pack lighter. Gadgets (calculators, fancy pens, digital watches) that have your company's name on them may be handy for giving to officials and clerks you need to win over. If you've run out of gifts, there's one that is always appropriate: a bottle. As a foreigner, it looks better for you to give an imported brand (for sale everywhere) rather than *Moskovskaya* vodka. Your hiking companions will probably appreciate gifts of gear.

THE BANYA

A wonderful Russian tradition is the *banya*, or steam sauna. The Russians have raised the *banya* from a bath to an art form. Many Russians go to public *banyas* (bathhouses) in the city. In the mountains, the *banya* is often simply a canvas tent stretched over a wood frame. In the better-appointed base camps, it's a wooden structure.

There's nothing quite like *banya*-ing in the wilderness. The ritual goes like this: stoke the *banya* for several hours (in the high mountains, with propane) before anyone's allowed in. When it's roasting hot, get in and work up a wet sweat. When you're warm to the bones and glistening, slap yourself with fragrant *venniki* (cut and bound pine or birch boughs, soaked in hot water to soften them) so the pores open and all bodily aches and pains are drawn out. Dash for an icy stream. Begin again.

Food

The potato is *the* cornerstone of Russian cooking. Often it's the whole meal. Russians prefer them fried (usually in a lot of grease), but also eat potatoes mashed (called *puree*) or boiled. When you've eaten Russian home cooking and "trail meals" for awhile, it's amazing to think that until a couple hundred years ago they didn't have potatoes in this country.

Russians often don't consider outdoor adventure complete without a banya *(steam sauna). (Photo: Bill Dawson)*

They also like meat with their potatoes. The argument for "lite" food as a good diet has not yet caught on in Russia, where meat three times a day is a metaphor for the good life. Another favorite is *sala*—pure pork fat eaten raw, usually washed down with vodka. After weeks of contemplating fatty meat-balls (*kotleti*) and slabs of unidentifiable fried meat, you may find yourself obsessed with vegetables. There's little understanding of meatless diets. Vagabonding in the Soviet Union turned me, a militant vegetarian for a dozen years, into someone who eats anything. It's somewhat easier to manage a meatless diet in Central Asia; mutton plays a leading role in the local diet there, but there's also an abundance of fruits and vegetables.

The other staple Russian food is bread. Bread is to Russians what rice is to the Japanese. The price of bread is a barometer for judging quality of life, the values of socialism versus capitalism, and the popularity of Russia's political leaders. Most of the bread you find will not be that dark, heavy rye that is known in America as Russian rye. Outside of the occasional city bakery that bakes *chyorny khleb* ("dark bread"), the standard loaf is a chewy, coarse white bread—*bely khleb*. Quite delicious when freshly baked, this bread becomes tough and less appetizing after a few days. It lasts forever, though, and holds up well even when stuffed into a backpack.

In Siberia, you're unlikely to see many fruits or vegetables, but in late summer and fall, locals know how to harvest the bounty of the forest and transform it into a feast. Don't let your freeze-dried chicken keep you from enjoying the chicken of the woods; gorge on wild mushroom dishes, pine nuts, berry stews (*kompot*), and herbal teas.

In the Far East, you'll get to eat a lot of salmon. The Russians' favorite part of the fish is the eggs. They relish them straight, preparing them by blanching with scalding, salted water poured over the caviar in a cheesecloth bag—or even net stocking. Don't be put off by the idea of eating fish eggs. They're delicious. And you might go hungry if you don't eat them.

The items Russians consider trail food include: bread, potatoes, canned meat and fish, *sala* (raw pork fat), sweetened condensed milk, hot cereal, and tea. If you don't think you can hack this diet, bring your own lightweight freeze-dried or dehydrated food. Other things you might consider bringing from home include instant drinks, your favorite trail snacks, dried fruits (if you won't be in Central Asia, where you can get raisins and apricots), instant soups, cocoa, and vitamin supplements. For mountain expeditions or ex-tended backpacking, it's particularly important to bring some of your own lightweight food supplies.

You shouldn't be too insistent on eating Western food, though. Eating lo-cal food sometimes is part of the experience. Russians are great cooks and can present amazing meals when they have ingredients. In the woods, they're in-genious at turning limited supplies into tasty meals.

STORES

Now that the market economy is catching on, food supplies are much easier to come by. City groceries these days actually have food on the shelves,

Supplement staples with more flavorful foods purchased from street vendors, such as this woman selling apples, pears, cucumbers, and tomatoes.

in part because prices are too high for limited Soviet budgets. What you'll reliably find in grocery stories is bread, pickled cucumbers and tomatoes, and canned fish or meat; less reliably found are cheese, cottage cheese, fresh milk, sour cream, mayonnaise, eggs, butter, sugar, sausage, fresh meat, stale cookies, chocolate, apples, cabbage, potatoes, onions, beets, cream of wheat, rice, oatmeal, flour, and tea; only rarely will you find canned milk, yogurt, and caviar. In rural stores, you're lucky if you find the first four items on this list.

Then there's shopping "on the street." Peter Christiansen, who's been living in Petropavlovsk-Kamchatsky for several years researching Pacific fisheries, describes the kiosks, privately owned stores, and "commission shops" that have sprung up all over Russia:

> *These outposts of free enterprise offer a monotonic choice: Western candy bars and cigarettes, Chinese sportswear, and hard liquors, wines, and cognacs of unknown origin, most bought somewhere and then resold at a mark-up. It's as though the whole country has turned into a giant second-hand store. The hard liquors are particularly suspect, since they are often homemade and can contain anything from wood-grain alcohol to industrial spirits.*

Apart from these "luxury" products, the supply is very unpredictable. The odds of finding instant coffee, bottled juice, and beer are good. Other curious items appear for sale, like infant formula and German canned ham, labeled "EEC Humanitarian Aid."

Planning backpacking food can be challenging. In Moscow and St. Petersburg, there are now a number of small Western-style supermarkets. You'll find several of these in Intourist hotels. Others are listed in the Moscow Yellow Pages or in English-language newspapers you pick up at tourist hotels. These Western supermarkets are pricey, but if you must have peanut butter, you can find it there. Rely on the farmers' markets (called *rynok* or, in Central Asia, *bazaar*) for fruit, vegetables, and nuts.

It's a good idea to carry some snacks and instant coffee, tea, and soup. Most hotels will have an electric samovar, so you can get hot water. Better yet, travel the way Russians do, with a little electric water-heating coil. That way you're self-sufficient.

It's important to plan ahead and carry food when traveling on planes and trains. The availability can be hit and miss. Carrie Mackay, a student of Russian at Stanford, told me about her experiences riding the train in rural Khabarovskii Krai, where she was an intern:

> *At a busy train stop, Sasha hurries off to see what there is to buy, returning with potato dumplings and a jar of milk. The milk is bad and we dump it, washing down our dinner of bread, cheese, and sausage with tea brewed from the hot water kettle in the train car, and settle drowsily into the rhythm of the tracks. Next morning, we look for breakfast in the little town where we change trains. The only restaurant in town is serving hot cereal, buttered noodles, cucumbers, meatballs, and bread.*

For extended trips, it simply isn't feasible to carry a supply of dehydrated or freeze-dried camping food and it becomes necessary to rely on local supplies. The process of gathering food in rural Russia and Turkestan can be an adventure in itself. Most towns, no matter how small, have at least one store. But the store may well be locked and the clerk off watching the midmorning Mexican soap opera. One group of travelers that mountain-biked through the eastern Kazakhstan countryside reported that in the towns they knocked at every establishment that had opening hours tacked on the door, in hopes that it might be a store. The cans and jars gathering dust on the shelves of these rural stores are a mixed breed. When the mountain-bikers found some food item, they bought a sample and tasted it on the spot, before buying a supply for their panniers. One of them told me, "We just couldn't eat some of the canned stuff and we didn't want to haul it for days before we figured out it was inedible." You take what you get.

RESTAURANTS

In *all* hotels, getting meals can be a problem. Intourist hotels have restaurants, but often they require advance reservations. In Moscow and St. Petersburg, the best restaurants accept hard currency only. Outside of these major cities, though, most restaurants allow you to pay in rubles and the value is still good. Prices for meals vary wildly, but dinner ranges between the equivalent of $1 and $10.

Dan Waugh, a professor of Russian history who has been traveling to the

Soviet Union for thirty years, bemoaned the dismal service and complete lack of imagination in the menu at the Hotel Uzbekistan during a recent visit:

> *It is a cavernous and gloomy room with a mess-hall atmosphere. The waiters are surly. Evening dining is to the accompaniment of live "music," amplified to rock-concert levels. This is the menu served in state-controlled restaurants from Leningrad to Tashkent. It has the inevitable two or three kinds of beef dishes that have different names but are all variations on a theme: a small piece of unrecognizable meat that has been cooked to death and then covered with the pan drippings. Once you have eaten in the hotel for three days, you have exhausted the possibilities of the menu.*

Vedomstvenniye gostinitsy, smaller hotels, generally have only a "buffet"—if that—and these little snack bars don't serve much in the way of food. These "buffets," in hotels, theaters, or other public places, have okay food. Cafes also have sometimes interesting, though usually limited, menus. *Stolovayas* (cafeterias) are the ultimate greasy-spoon experience and are best avoided.

Communications

Getting in touch with guide services in remote parts of Russia and Central Asia is still one of the biggest challenges to planning travel there. Organizations involved in outdoor travel employ translators, so it's okay to send messages in English. Keep your messages short, use simple words and short sentences, and avoid slang expressions. For comprehensive, up-to-the-minute information about communications, check the sources in the periodicals section of the Bibliography.

TELEPHONES

Russians' phone manners in general tend to be curt, bordering on rude. Telephone operators are often downright surly; if they don't understand you, they're likely to hang up on you. The local operators are unlikely to understand English. The phrase you want when you call the operator is, for example, *"Zakazhite mne Yelizovo na 20:00"* (Please get me Yelizovo at 8:00 P.M.)—note that Russia uses the military system of telling time. The simplest way is to get help from a Russian friend, or a hotel reception desk, in making a long-distance operator-assisted call.

Overseas Calls

Making international calls to remote places in Russia, or cities where foreign telecommunications companies have yet to provide satellite overlays of the obsolete Soviet phone lines, takes patience. You may spend hours dialing over and over again, get recordings "the number you are dialing cannot be reached at this time in the country you are calling," be cut off, and finally get through to discover that you have reached a number that no longer belongs to the organization you're trying to reach.

Since the breakup of the former Soviet Union, it's possible to telephone direct from other countries to most major Russian and Central Asian cities. The country code (7) works for all the former republics. Contact the company that provides your long-distance phone service for information about international calls. Dial their international access code + 7 + city code + local number.

For example, placing a call from North America to Moscow through Sprint, you dial: 011 (Sprint) + 7 + 095 + Moscow phone number.

Local numbers are seven digits long for major cities. They can also be five or six digits long or, for small communities, four digits. The city code plus the phone number must equal ten digits. So, if you're trying to reach a five-digit local number, the city code should be five digits also. City codes for areas covered in this book are listed in parentheses before the number.

Some cities and towns cannot be dialed direct; for these you need to be connected by an international operator. Phone numbers for which direct dialing is not available generally (but not always) are less than five digits.

The international operator contacts a Russian operator in one of the cities through which international calls are routed, and the Russian operator connects you with your party. Since not all international operators know the ropes on calling in Russia, it helps if you have some idea through which city the place you're calling is generally routed—for example, calls to remote parts of the Russian Far East usually go through Novosibirsk.

If you have difficulty reaching a number in a city for which there's direct dialing, an international operator may have better luck putting your call through.

Several Far Eastern cities are now easier to dial direct through the Sprint network, using special city codes. Some of them require the (7) country code, others do not. If Sprint is not your long-distance carrier, you can access this service by dialing 10333. Check with Sprint for the most current information.

The only thing more frustrating than calling the former Soviet Union from abroad can be trying to call overseas from Russia and Central Asia. Don't count on being able to call out. If you can't place a call when you're passing through a city, you may be able to send a fax from a central post office or hotel. In an emergency, it will probably be easier to reach your embassy or consulate than to dial out to your country.

From Moscow, there are some direct satellite links in top-flight hotels. If you're callling from an ordinary phone, you can only dial direct between midnight and 9 A.M. and on weekends. Dial 8 + 10 + country code + area code + number. (The country code for the United States is 1.) At all other times, you have to "order" an international call from Moscow by dialing 8-194 (dial 8, wait for the tone, and dial 194) and requesting the country you want to call and the number. It can be very difficult to reach the operator.

In other cities, inquire about the number you have to dial to order international calls. Even from major cities like Irkutsk, Yalta, or Novosibirsk, it's common to be told there's a twenty-four-hour wait for an international line. In more remote places, the wait may well be several days long. Thanks to burgeoning international business activity in the Far East, it's becoming easier to call out of the country from Vladivostok and Khabarovsk than from many other parts of the country.

Calls Within Russia and Central Asia

If you're calling from one city in Russia or Central Asia to another, dial 8, wait for a dial tone, then dial the city code and local number.

If it's one of those operator-assistance–required numbers, dial 8, wait for the tone, dial 13, and request the number you want. Often, you may be required to wait—sometimes for hours— for the call you "ordered." You may, however, be able to order the call for a specific time in the next twenty-four hours, when the operator will contact you and connect you with your number.

Local calls from public phones used to be 2 kopeks, while special long-distance phone booths accepted 15-kopek coins. In Moscow, they've introduced a phone token, the price of which can rise with inflation. Some old Moscow phone booths and phones in other cities still operate on the 15-kopek or even 2-kopek coins. These are in short supply and, when you need to make a call in a pinch, no one will change you the coins you need. Check on what the phone booths are accepting when you get there and horde these valuable coins.

If your call doesn't go through at first, assume the phone booth doesn't work (especially if there's no dial tone) and try a different one. There's nothing unusual about having to try a half dozen phone booths to find one that works. To make a long-distance domestic call from a public phone, go to a *mezhdugorodny punkt*—an inter-city phone post. These are located in most post offices and airports. The ones in airports are coin-operated, so you have to stockpile a bunch of coins. In the post office, you "order" your call, prepay a certain number of minutes, and wait for the operator to get your party on the line and call you to a booth. It's much easier to make a call from a hotel room, or from someone's home, if you have the opportunity. If you can't dial long distance from your hotel room, or there's no phone, you can often place a call from the reception desk.

If "immediate" calls (*srochniye peregovory*) are available, you can usually get a call through in fifteen minutes to an hour. Request this service when you "order" your call. The improved service is worth the surcharge.

ELECTRONIC MAIL

By far the easiest way of communicating with Russia and Central Asia, if you have a modem, is via electronic mail (E-mail). If the organization you're corresponding with at that end also has E-mail access, you can exchange electronic messages. Otherwise, you can send faxes or telexes from your E-mail system. The convenience and cost-effectiveness of E-mail communication has many small companies there using "E-mail services," even if they don't have their own modem; for a fee they receive messages via someone else's modem.

Most E-mailing is done in English, or transliterated Russian. It's possible to send Cyrillic text as a binary file, but the receiver must have the same software to be able to read it when the information is downloaded. For more information about how to get on-line for communication with Russia, see Appendix A, General Resources.

Sprint has offices in the major cities of the Far East from which you can send E-mail messages. In Birobidzhan and Blagoveshchensk, you can E-mail from the local post office. (See Appendix A, General Resources.)

FAX

If you have a modem, sending a fax from your electronic mailbox is a great timesaver: your E-mail system will dial the number over and over again until the fax goes through. (If it's not a direct-dial number, though, you're still stuck with the operator.) If your E-mail system is unable to get the fax through, it could be the fax line is being used as a telephone line. Try sending your fax manually, so you hear what's on the other end of the line.

Acquiring an additional telephone line to plug in a fax machine is a very expensive problem for Russian organizations. Often one phone line has to do double duty as a telephone and fax. If you call a number listed as a fax, and someone answers, say you want to send a "fox": even if you get a Russian speaker, they should understand. You might need to call back after they plug the fax machine in or switch it on. If you dial a fax number and get an answering machine, even if you don't understand the Russian message, try sending the fax—it may well be a combination fax/answering device.

Other small companies borrow friends' phone lines for their fax machine, so the fax number changes frequently. Due to the poor quality of Soviet phone lines, faxes often do not transmit clearly. Sometimes they are so garbled as to be unreadable.

TELEX

If this is one of the more expensive ways of communicating with Russia and Central Asia, it's also one of the more reliable. If you're sending to a telex number ending in the call-back letters "*PTB SU*," this is a public telex number; it's important to indicate the name and phone number you're sending to.

You should give your Russian or Central Asian correspondent the option of replying to you via telex. Private mail services let you receive telexes in care of their telex number for a fee. If you are E-mail–connected, you can add a telex number to the services you receive.

MAIL

International Mail

The Soviet postal service is completely unreliable. Telephone, electronic mail, fax, telex, and telegrams are the only sure means of reaching Russia and Central Asia. In the old days, letters from abroad took weeks and usually had been opened before they were delivered.

My friend Bill Sumner lived for several years with his Uzbek wife in Chirchik, a town outside Tashkent, Uzbekistan. Bill's mail from America usually arrived preopened. Once he got a sealed window envelope, the kind where name and address usually show through the window. But the letter inside was blank-side-up in the window. The local postal "reader" had carefully resealed the envelope, but inadvertantly reversed the letter inside.

Now that the KGB isn't charged with reading everyone's mail, you would think things might have improved, but the mails seem to have only become more of a black pit. A letter might make it from North America to Moscow in two weeks. It might also take two months, or never arrive at all. Packages stand less chance of ever being delivered; anything larger than an envelope invites pilfering. If you must get mail through, send it with someone who's going, and have the person for whom it's intended pick it up.

When sending postcards or letters out of the country, check at a post office or hotel for the current rates. In small-town post offices, they may not even know the international postage rates. If they do know, they may not have any international stamps to sell you.

In the Altai in 1992, I tried five different post offices before I found one that had international stamps. Emboldened, I asked about the cost of mailing a letter to Petropavlovsk-Kamchatsky—domestic letters had been 5 kopeks for time immemorial, but I'd heard those rates had gone up. The postal worker replied, without looking up fom the book she was reading, "Has Kamchatka seceded from the Union now, too?"

Basically, it's best to stay away from Soviet post offices unless you're looking for comic relief. Forget about receiving mail while you're traveling there. Unless you're staying at one of the five-star, Western-operated hotels, you'll never see it. If you're a member of American Express, you can have mail sent to them for pickup (AmEx, ul. Sadovaya-Kudrinskaya 21-A, Moscow, tel. 095-254-4305; or AmEx, ul. Brodskovo 1/7, St. Petersburg, tel. 812-315-7487).

Mail Within Russia and Central Asia

Mailing within the country is somewhat more reliable, but a letter mailed from St. Petersburg can still take weeks to reach the Far East. If you want to receive mail from within the country, *do vostrebovaniya* (general delivery) to a post office sometimes works, but I've never heard of mail from abroad actually being delivered this way.

COURIER SERVICES

Courier services are the most reliable way to get important mail to someone in the former Soviet Union, although it's expensive. Check with your local couriers. Federal Express, TNT Express, and DHL all have international courier services. From the United States, the U.S. Postal Service and UPS also offer courier services, as do some airlines, including Aeroflot and Alaska Airlines.

TELEGRAMS

This is a communications means of last resort because it's very expensive, especially sending from abroad to Russia. However, telegrams get through when other communication means fail. Telexes and telegrams must be sent in English or transliterated. The only way to send (or receive) a telex in Russian is to substitute Roman alphabet for Cyrillic. From the United States, call Western Union.

5 Environmental Challenges

Governmental Mismanagement

As a people, Russians have a traditional love of nature that borders on the spiritual. Soviet government policy, however, was shaped by the attitude that conservation is unnecessary because Russia enjoys an inexhaustible supply of wilderness. During the communist era, the system of centralized planning that dictated agricultural and natural resource administration was a disaster for the environment. Local residents often had no control over dams, factories, and other industrial projects that affected their water supply and the air they breathed. Mismanagement on a massive scale produced inconceivable ecological disasters.

Intensive irrigation to increase cotton production in Central Asia diverted so much water from the region's two arteries, the Amu Darya and Syr Darya rivers, that the Aral Sea is dying. In many Russian cities, even in remote regions north of the Arctic Circle, terrible air pollution contributes to serious health problems and shortens life expectancy for their inhabitants. Chernobyl, the world's worst nuclear accident, contaminated the countryside for hundreds of miles around.

Until the late 1980s, ecological blunders were officially suppressed and voices of opposition were not tolerated. Chernobyl was not the first accident at a Soviet nuclear reactor; it was only the first to become public knowledge. Mikhail Gorbachev broke the Soviet whitewashing tradition when he acknowledged the seriousness of the ecological crisis in his country. Now there are numerous good books and articles on the environmental situation in the former USSR (see Bibliography).

Environmental activists enjoy close ties to the new Russian government. Svyatoslav Zabelin heads the Socio-Ecological Union, Russia's highest-profile environmental group. Zabelin is also an assistant to Aleksei Yablokov, Boris Yeltsin's ecological counselor. A number of Green Party members have been elected to Russia's Parliament. The new environmental awareness in officialdom is a positive change, but the race to save the environment there is a race against time, entrenched interests, and harsh economic reality.

As are all Russian governmental structures, the official environmental watchdog agencies are in flux. The USSR State Committee for Environmental Protection (*Goskompriroda*), created in 1987 to bring under one umbrella the myriad agencies with control over natural resources, was replaced in 1992 by a new Russian Ministry of Ecology and Natural Resources (Nature Use). The new ministry appears to be similar to the U.S. Department of Interior, Environmental Protection Agency, and National

Oceanic and Atmospheric Administration rolled into one.

Folks in the hinterlands are no longer silently taking orders from Moscow; now, the former Central Asian republics are sovereign countries. Even within Russia, the central government has lost much of its authority over regional matters. Local and regional officials assert their independent authority without consultation or approval from federal agencies. Some Siberian ethnic groups, such as the Yakuts and the Chukchi, are demanding political autonomy and economic control of the resources in the territories they inhabit. One observer noted that a village with a stand of timber can negotiate with a multinational corporation.

The breakdown of central authority has left the country's greatest wealth— its natural resources—up for grabs. All across the country, people and local governments are struggling to survive economically in the face of spiraling inflation and widespread unemployment. Raw resources are about the only thing Russia has to sell and foreign companies are eager for minerals, oil, gas, and timber. Laws regulating rights to land and resources are spotty and law enforcement is ineffectual, so this resource exploitation is subject to numerous abuses. Too often, environmental impact statements are skipped, doctored, or ignored with impunity.

Along with the lack of clear jurisdiction over natural resources and laws, corruption is rampant. Many government officials are on the take. Former Communist party officials remain in positions of power everywhere, controlling the sale or lease of property. Those responsible for managing resources often benefit directly from business deals involving the sale of gold or fish or metals. This goes far beyond what is known in the United States as the "revolving door" between business and government. In Russia, kickbacks are the rule, not the exception. An official may be an actual partner in a joint venture with a foreign company, or may grant the go-ahead on a project after receiving a generous contribution to his or her Swiss bank account. One Western businessman described how the manager of the factory he was negotiating to buy demanded a $50,000 personal bribe to win favor over other potential buyers. These officials in turn often have close connections with criminal rings.

Tourists and tour organizers frequently encounter demands for payment to enter a certain area, extracted by those in a position of granting permission or authorizing the hire of trucks or helicopter services. While these demands may be legitimate, most often they are simply palm-greasing (see the Bribes section of chapter 4, Traveling in Russia and Central Asia). Those who have political control over resources consider personal gain their due. So, resource use—including tourism—often benefits individuals more than communities or protected areas.

NATURE RESERVES

According to Sviatoslav Zabelin and Eugene Simonov in their article "New International Effort to Save the Zapovedniki," which appeared in the Spring 1992 issue of *Surviving Together*, the *zapovedniki*, or nature reserves, of the former Soviet Union are the primary component of an 80-year-old system for preserving biological diversity. There are 147 *zapovedniki*, housing an array of unique ecosystems typical of all the geographical regions, from the High Pamir to the deserts of Turkmenistan to the Far East's Pacific rain forests. No tourist or developmental activities are permitted in most *zapovedniki*; human activity is limited to maintenance and scientific research. Many are designed to protect Red Book–listed endangered species, like the goral mountain goat. A number of these areas are part of the United Nation's biosphere reserve program.

One of the first victims of the economic *perestroika* is the *zapovedniki*. Since government funding has traditionally been their only source of financial support, the very survival of the *zapovedniki* is threatened by the economic transition taking place in the former Soviet Union. The central government has drastically cut funding for "unprofitable" institutions such as the *zapovedniki*.

Now that central government support is shrinking, the control of natural resources is shifting to regional governments. And local authorities are showing less respect for the laws protecting the *zapovedniki*, expanding grazing, hunting, and logging activities in and around them.

The *zapovednik* system, administered in the latter part of the 1980s by the state agency *Goskompriroda* (State Committee for Nature), now falls under the umbrella of the new Russian Ministry of Ecology and Natural Resources (Nature Use). Individual *zapovedniki* have, along with critically insufficient funding, a less clear directive than ever before about how their reserves should be managed.

The managers of the *zapovedniki* are under pressure to open the reserves to foreign tourists to generate hard currency that would support personnel salaries, field research, ecological surveys, and anti-poaching patrols. More and more of them are opening their doors and joining the ranks of the few *zapovedniki* that have traditionally allowed recreational use, such as Teberda and Issyk Kul. Unfortunately, many think the only way to attract visitors is by building hotels and roads. They have no idea how to structure visitation that would provide the critical funding for park maintenance without impacting the natural environments the *zapovedniki* were created to protect.

The sad irony about the nature reserves falling through the cracks is that they cover only a small fraction of the territory of the former Soviet Union to begin with: only about 0.05 percent. There are several other less restricted designations. *Zakazniki*, of which there were nearly 3,000 in the former Soviet Union, are a type of semi-preserved territory with either temporary or permanent limitations, such as seasonal or restoration-period restrictions, on on-site economic activities, in the interests of natural resource conservation and wildlife reproduction. The several categories of *zakazniki* include zoological, botanical, landscape, hydrological, and geological. The majority of *zakazniki* are zoological, and have been set up to manage hunting, especially commercial hunting, but also attempt to conserve wildlife generally and expand the important game species, for example, bear or sable. Another form of protection for land is the *zapovedno-okhotnichye khozyaistvo*, or hunting preserve. National parks—protected land open for recreational uses—are a new phenomenon in the last decade. All of these systems together amount to less than 2 percent of land on which development is restricted to some degree.

LOGGING

The harvest of timber in the Russian Far East is another example of how the confusion over jurisdictions and the desperation for hard currency combine to sabotage sound environmental management. Until now, because of political restrictions on the Russian Far East and a limited transportation network, the forests of Siberia and the Far East have not been extensively logged. As the region has opened to the West in the past couple years, however, American, Japanese, and Korean timber companies have jumped at the chance to hack Siberia's forests.

The taiga—the mixed forest of larch, spruce, aspen, birch, fir, pine, poplar, and tamarack—stretches from the Baltics all the way to the Pacific. This boreal forest extends through the subarctic regions of Alaska, Canada, Scandinavia, and Russia, but it is the Russian taiga that constitutes the last big chunk of it left on the planet: a band as large as the whole continental United States. More than double the size of the tropical rain forests, the Russian taiga plays an important carbon dioxide–absorbing role in the global atmosphere.

Russian logging and processing practices are inefficient and wasteful; improved foreign technology could improve the yield without obliterating vast tracts of forest, causing soil erosion and destroying precious ecosystems. But so far, foreign companies have only been willing to clear-cut. Western clear-cutting operations denude the land much more quickly and efficiently than Russian workers with outmoded equipment.

Hyundai set the standard for irresponsible foreign timber harvesting. The South Korean corporation disregarded negative environmental impact statements and the opposition of the indigenous Udegei people to log the Pacific side of the Sikhote-Alin mountains, under the terms of a deal reached secretly with regional officials.

With the recent completion of the Baikal-Amur Mainline (BAM) railroad, which connects north Lake Baikal to the Pacific coast, the Siberian interior is also now accessible.

POACHING

The lifting of restrictions on travel in the Russian Far East was good for Russian people, giving them freedom to interact with the outside world and to determine their own destiny. But in some ways wildlife was better off under communism. Dozens of species of mammals and birdlife can be found only in the former Soviet Union, but some of these are on the verge of extinction. Topping the list of mammals and birds listed in Russia's Red Book of rare and endangered species are the Amur leopard (*Panthera pardus orientalis*), the Anatolian leopard (*Panthera pardus tullianus*), and the Siberian tiger (*Panthera tigris altaica*). The Turanian tiger, which once roamed the valleys of Central Asia, is now believed to be extinct.

The Botcha region of Primorski Krai is the transition between the boreal and temperate forest and the home of the Siberian (Amur) tiger. Already threatened by loss of habitat to clear-cutting, this rare cat (there may be as few as 200 of them left), the world's largest, faces a more formidable enemy in the poacher. Now that contact with foreigners is free and easy, poachers sell furs and animal parts (gall bladders, spleen, bones) for huge profits on the Oriental market. Customs officials, cut in on the spoils, turn a blind eye. Government officials are even in cahoots with poachers in some instances.

In 1992, at the scientific research camp Malta on southwest Lake Baikal, we ran into armed men. They said they were from the institute in Irkutsk to which the camp belonged and claimed the right to prevent us from venturing into the forest. We circumvented their camp and discovered the real reason they didn't want us around: they were playing host to Canadians hunting illegally. In addition, there have been a number of incidences of game wardens being killed by poachers.

Wilderness in the Balance

In Europe and the United States we came too late, in many ways, to the awareness that wild places improve the quality of our lives and have value preserved in their natural state. Russia stands at a threshhold. The countries of the former Soviet Union hold some of the last wildernesses on earth, especially in Siberia and the Far East.

There is still a chance for the *zapovedniki* to avoid the fate of many of America's parks: Yellowstone's highways and hotels, the air pollution and video parlors of Yosemite. Wild animals and birds found nowhere else on the planet could be saved from extinction. The Russian taiga, which totals more than 20 percent of the world's forests, could be harvested responsibly, with a minimum of disruption of fish and wildlife habitat.

But none of this is likely to happen of its own accord. To Russian officials, the value of forest as an air pollution filter, wildlife habitat, and recreation area hardly outweighs the immediate benefits of cash influxes to their strapped economies. Unless the foreign timber giants are forced to employ environmentally sound practices, and unless creative alternatives are found to develop the Russian economy, the taiga may be lost by the end of the decade.

ENVIRONMENTAL ACTIVISM IN RUSSIA AND CENTRAL ASIA

Even before *glasnost*, grass-roots groups challenged industrial projects, fighting long and hard (although ultimately unsuccessfully) in the mid-1960s to avert construction of the pulp mill on Lake Baikal. More recently, environmental activists and scientists have managed to stall the dam project slated for the Katun River and divert the northern rivers diversion project.

In the post-communist era, environmental groups have sprung up in cities all across the country, many of them presenting a strong challenge to entrenched political interests.

Without resources with which to organize, or an effective legal structure within which to work, Russian environmentalists have little hope of saving the taiga or the tigers. It will take an international commitment to the new environmental world order.

ENVIRONMENTAL INVOLVEMENT FROM ABROAD

We can't bring back the Colorado River's Glen Canyon or the virgin forests of the Pacific Northwest, but perhaps we can save virgin forests and unique natural environments elsewhere on our planet. You can find information on current Russian environmental issues in several journals (see Bibliography). *Surviving Together* is an invaluable quarterly with articles culled from the Russian and American press. If you're modem-connected, consider joining Econet, an on-line conferencing service and electronic mail network (see Appendix A, General Resources).

There are a number of environmental organizations working in areas covered in the chapters of Section II: Baikal Watch, Audubon Society, the Kuhiston Foundation's Tajikistan Parks Project, International Crane Foundation, Hornocker Wildlife Research Institute, Friends of the Russian National Parks, and Pacific Energy and Resources Center. Other environmental groups involved in projects in the former Soviet Union include The Wilderness Society, Association of State Wetland Managers, World Wildlife Fund, Sierra Club, and The Nature Conservancy.

You might want to learn more about and support some of the ongoing environmental projects in Russia and Central Asia sponsored by these organizations. Examine how directly their work benefits the Russian environment and aids Russian environmentalists. Some projects, unfortunately, eat up money in administrative expenses, publications, and staff salaries, with very few resources actually trickling down to alleviate basic environmental problems in the target region.

Several United States organizations in particular have advanced by leaps and bounds the abilities of environmentalists in the NIS to disseminate information and lobby on behalf of local environmental efforts. The Sacred Earth Network (SEN) and ISAR (formerly the Institute for Soviet–American Relations), working with the Russian Socio-Ecological Union (SEU), have distributed modems and PCs to individual eco-activists and organizations across the country, training them to use the equipment effectively in their work. ISAR and SEN have brought on-line hundreds of dedicated people. These individuals, who previously had no resources or means of communication—in some cases not even access to a typewriter or photocopy machine—now can network and share information with other activists there and abroad. Many of their E-mail addresses are listed under the Contacts heading of the information block for each section of the chapters in Section II.

WILDERNESS ETHICS

Sadly, during the years of Soviet rule, people were disenfranchised and cut off from the land. Many lost touch with nature. Many Russians seem relatively unconscious of personal responsibility toward the environment. They litter habitually, both in the city and the woods. Surprisingly, even outdoor enthusiasts often show little concern for the environment.

Many Russians consider tin cans biodegradable, and leave piles of refuse such as this at frequently used campsites. (Photo: Dennis Madsen)

Hikers, climbers, and river-rafters routinely throw cans in the campfire and leave them to rust. Since there is no specially packaged freeze-dried or dehydrated food, outdoorspeople carry mainly tinned food—fish, meat, jam, condensed milk. This means that in popular areas that see a lot of use, you come across large mounds of rusting cans, glass jars, and bottles. I find it paradoxical that the same campers who warn against picking wildflowers in a nature reserve think nothing of leaving piles of cans behind when they break camp in an area as wild as the reserve.

Eager river enthusiasts chop down trees for their rafts and poles, leaving the forest denuded in popular areas. Almost all camp cooking, except at high altitude where there is no wood, is done on campfires, so areas frequented by hikers are also marred by fire rings. Neither is it common practice to dig latrines, although Russians like to camp in large groups. Of course, it doesn't help the situation that popular campsites rarely have dumpsters or outhouses.

It's easy to be disgusted by the lack of environmental consciousness most (not all) Russians display in the outdoors. On the other hand, it's a good opportunity to set an example. Always observe low-impact camping rules.

Use designated or previously used campsites that are at least 200 feet (60

m) away from lakes, streams, and trails. Use a campstove for cooking. Do all food preparation and cooking at least 200 feet from any water source. Don't wash dishes or yourself in streams or lakes. Water used for washing (dishes or people) should be dumped well away from camp and at least 200 feet from any water source. If campfires are permitted and downed dry fuel wood is sufficient, burn your campfire in an existing fire grate or established ring of rocks. Burn only paper products if you burn garbage in your campfire. Carry a small trowel and bury human waste at least six inches deep and 200 feet away from any source of water. Burn your toilet paper carefully—don't set fire to dry brush or forest in your zeal to erase your trace—or pack it out. Don't throw food or garbage in streams or lakes. Carry out all your trash, maybe even somebody else's trash.

Also remember, however, that "packing it out" is only part of the problem with trash disposal. Many cities do not have adequate waste disposal facilities, so what you haul back from the mountains may well end up in an unsightly, unsanitary garbage pile in town. Nevertheless, this is a better place for it than in a backcountry campsite.

Even if your Russian companions laugh at you, you probably will have made a lasting impression. Russians are proud people. I have been told, in as many words, "No American is going to tell us where to shit." But they also respect Americans and in many ways want to emulate the West. A clean wilderness ethic is perhaps one thing we can share.

Most of the *zapovedniki* and some of the *zakazniki* and national parks in the regions covered in the chapters of Section II have no established system for dealing with visitors as yet. As a rule, they have no facilities, no established nature walk or trail system, no informational literature, and possibly not even any staff people who speak English. Many are in remote areas without telephone communications, where it could take months for a letter to arrive from abroad (for addresses of administrative offices, see Appendix A, General Resources). If you do manage to make contact with one of these parks or reserves, they may very well be confused about how to react to you. Remember, there is no tradition of independent travel in this country and the *zapovedniki* have primarily been off limits to all visitors.

It is essential that the *zapovedniki*, *zakazniki*, and parks be supported as protectors of wilderness and given a role in the developing wilderness tourism "new world order" in Russia and Central Asia. Most of them want to be involved in this process, while they may be unsure how to do so.

If you're planning a trip that will go into or near a reserve, make contact with the office. Pay your park entry fees. These fees, usually minuscule, are nonetheless important to keeping the parks alive. Also, if you have at least made a legitimate attempt to acquire a permit, it is less likely you will be hassled by a warden demanding payment in the backcountry. It is to be hoped that soon these protected areas will become better prepared for coping with visitors.

Overleaf: *Ash from Mount Koryakskaya enriches Petropavlovsk-Kamchatsky farmlands.*

THE TREKS, TRAILS, AND CLIMBS

Part 1

Western Russia

The western quarter of the former Soviet Union belongs to the European continent. Thus, geographers categorize the Caucasus as a European mountain range, and consider Mount Elbrus to be Europe's highest summit. Europe extends all the way to the Ural Mountains, with their spine stretching neatly south from the Arctic Circle; a snowfield melting on the east side of the Urals drains to Asia.

These are very different areas. The Crimea, Russia's best-loved resort coast, also offers moderate hiking through lovely highlands studded with ancient cave cities. In the Caucasus Mountains can be found spectacular alpine hiking and climbing on a par with the Alps, without the crowds—and without the comforts. The Urals are a wilderness experience, less traveled, and more difficult to travel, but interesting to those who want to experience the taiga. For those traveling from Europe, or using Moscow or St. Petersburg as a starting point, the Crimea, the Caucasus, and the Ural Mountains are all reasonably accessible by train, making them affordable even for a trip as short as a week.

Priut 11, on Mount Elbrus, claims to be the world's highest hotel.

6   Crimea

Only a narrow neck of land connects the Crimean Peninsula to the Ukrainian mainland. Steppes dominate the northern three-quarters of the peninsula. On the southern coast arc three ridges dividing the flatlands from the Black Sea. Inland on the southern part of the peninsula stretches a broad plateau studded with limestone formations. Although many of the valleys of these sweeping uplands are cultivated, the hills are still largely forested. The high, undulating inland landscape is expansive, and its climate is distinctly harsher than the subtropical coast. In winter, you can ski in the Crimean interior and sunbathe on a warm day in Yalta just a few miles away.

Human habitation of the Crimean Peninsula, historically known as Tavrida, is as old as recorded human history. Over the centuries, Scythians, Taurians, Greeks, Alans, Goths, Guns, Khazars, and Sarmatians all melted into the Crimean pot. By turns, Byzantine and later Mongol rulers brandished the Black Sea citadel.

Genoese merchants plied a thriving trade in the Crimea until the A.D. 1475 invasion of the Golden Horde. The Tatars, vassals of the Ottoman Empire, ruled until 1783, when Catherine the Great forced the last khan to abdicate. Tatar flavor still permeates the older parts of the coastal towns—stone walls and verandas overgrown with vines. Most Crimean place names are Tatar, although some have been replaced with Soviet names.

Stalin forcibly relocated most of the Crimean Tatars to Uzbekistan after World War II and now the population of the Crimea is predominantly Russian and Ukrainian. Only in the 1990s have some of the Crimean Tatars been allowed to return to their native peninsula, where they are now a landless, and dissatisfied, minority. The present population is primarily Russian, and Russian is the language spoken on the peninsula, although it has been administratively part of Ukraine since 1963 and has chosen to stay that way. In 1993, however, the government in Moscow has, however, passed a threatening resolution that Sevastopol will remain a Russian city, so the political winds may soon blow from the east again.

The Crimea's southern coast has been Russians' favorite vacation destination since the nineteenth century. This sunny corner of the country has also figured prominently in European history of the last fifty years. At Livadia Palace in Yalta, Churchill, Stalin, and Roosevelt carved up Eastern Europe. In August 1991, the world held its breath when Communist party hardliners took Mikhail Gorbachev and his family hostage at Foros for three days.

During the communists' heyday, Party functionaries and their families reveled at Miskhor, Artek, and other resorts on *putevki*—virtually all-expense-paid vacation vouchers. The Party elite constructed dozens of grandiose summer places in exclusive spots up and down the shore. The towns sprouted "sanitoriums"—vacation hotels—for workers and tuberculosis rest homes. Since the switch to a market economy, Crimean beaches, accessible only to Russia's nouveau riche, have thinned out somewhat. The most popular part of the coastline, around Yalta and Alushta, is very developed and still crowded in midsummer. But most tourists don't venture farther than their hotel and the beach; in the mountains, and especially in the "shoulder" seasons (spring and fall), you can get away from it all.

In spite of the resort atmosphere, the Crimea is a natural outdoor playground. The vast array of crags made it the USSR's rock-climbing mecca. Many Russian hikers cut their teeth on the easily accessible trails of the Crimean mountains.

I was surprised to find it so unspoiled, and troubled by the thought that a beautiful tract of land that has nurtured humans for thousands of years is in danger of being wrecked in this century. Much of the coast around Alushta and Yalta is littered with tasteless Soviet-era hotels, resembling a slum more than a resort. And now the post-communist land barons are grabbing land to build luxury vacation-home developments.

Simferopol, the Crimea's inland hub, is at the dividing point between the mountains and the steppes. Site of the ancient Scythian city of Neapolis, modern-day Simferopol lacks the appeal of other parts of the peninsula, but is the kickoff point for any travel there.

When hiking in the Crimea, you're never far from a town. Most places have a market where you can buy fresh fruit and vegetables, and the odd mishmash of products for sale in the private stands—Turkish candy bars and coffee, et cetera. The farther you get from the well-worn tourist path, the less variety you'll find.

Getting There

International boat passage from Istanbul, Turkey, to Yalta, Ukraine, is difficult to book in advance but can generally be arranged if your schedule is flexible.

From within Russia, there are several daily flights from Moscow and St. Petersburg to Simferopol (about 2 hours). The train from Moscow to Simferopol leaves from Kursky Vokzal (21 hours). From Simferopol, there is bus service to Alushta, Yalta, and Bakhchisarai, as well as many of the smaller towns. Another transportation option from the Simferopol airport to points on the peninsula are *marsurutny* taxis (see the By Bus section of chapter 4, Traveling in Russia and Central Asia).

For the **day hikes on the Crimean Main Ridge**, from Simferopol drive the Simferopol–Alushta highway for approximately 1 hour to Angarsky Pass.

For the **Perevalnoye-to-Vinogradnaya hike**, from Simferopol drive the Simferopol–Alushta highway to Perevalnoye, a town reached before Angarsky Pass.

Where to Stay

The Crimea boasts more hotels than anywhere else in the country. Most of these establishments, too numerous to list, serve the general public. Some are quite nice, but not cheap. Prices vary widely, ranging from $10 to $100 for a room. At the less expensive end are the many *turbaza*.

In Bakhchisarai, you can stay at the *turbaza* Prival at the east edge of town.

Along the route of the trek from Bakhchisarai to Yalta there are developed campsites and also a *turbaza* at Orlinyi Zalyot ("Eagle's Landing").

Along the coast, there are *turbaza* in Sudak, Novyi Svet, Ryibache, and Alushta. South of Yalta, at the Polyana Skazok, motel cabins are set on the hillside with a beautiful view. Alushta and Yalta both have several upscale hotels and dozens of sanatoriums. The sanatoriums, formerly reserved for private guests from particular ministries and factories, now open their doors to all paying customers. Tourism has long been the Crimea's economic base, and the system of room (or apartment rentals) from private citizens is well developed here. Rooms are widely available, especially in the greater Yalta area, between Yalta and Alushta (see the Accommodations section of chapter 4, Traveling in Russia and Central Asia).

When to Go

In May, June, September, and October, weather is generally warm and pleasant. Occasional rainy days are always a possibility in late spring and early fall. The sea is still cold for swimming in May, but it's warm into October. Colors are beautiful in late fall. July and August are hot (although this is a fine time for hiking too) and this is the busy season for the resorts.

Equipment and Supplies

The Crimea is particularly convenient for stocking up on provisions, since you're never far from a town and most have an open-air market.

The South Coast

At once lush and rugged, the Crimean landscape is its most flamboyant where it juts into the Black Sea, across the water from Istanbul, Turkey. About 200 miles of coastline snake from the coastal towns of Feodosiya to Balaklava, walled by the Crimean Main Ridge. The south coast doesn't run smoothly into the Black Sea; it squares off in sheer bulkheads that drop steeply into the sea.

The Crimean Main Ridge, 100 miles long, attains 5,069 feet (1545 m) at its highest point. It reaches as far as 5 miles (8 km) inland in places. Between its summits—Chatyr Dag, 5,010 feet (1527 m), Roman-Kosh, 5,069 feet (1545 m), Demerdzhi, 4,449 feet (1239 m), and others—roll lazy bluffs. This lovely, expansive Crimean version of the mountain meadow is known there as a *yaila*.

Caves riddle the Crimean Peninsula like mold in blue cheese. Chatyr Dag alone has more than 135 caves, some of which can be visited by tourists. Spelunking is very popular here. (See the Cave Cities section later in this chapter.)

Between the coastal towns, the hilly roads wind through apple orchards and vineyards with terrific views of the sea and the amazing 1,000-foot limestone garrisons hovering over it. Villages and towns rich in history nestle in bays between these limestone massifs. The relaxed pace has led some to call this the "Russian Riviera."

The climate on the southern coast is subtropical, the flora distinctly Medi-

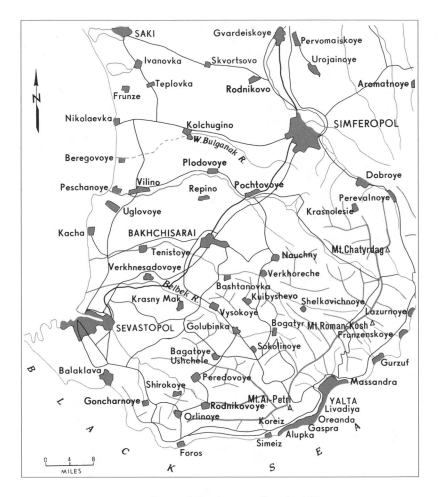

terranean: cyprus, magnolia, and acacias are all native. The grapes grown on the Crimea's sun-drenched hillsides produce wine prized by connoisseurs all over Europe. Crimean wines, considered to be Russia's best, were once cheap and accessible, but no more. In 1985, when Gorbachev launched his anti-alcoholism campaign, some of the oldest vineyards felt the axe. Now, you're lucky if you can find a *Pinogri, Vastarda*, or *Muscat Krasnovo Kameni* at any price, let alone champagne from the grotto of Novyi Svet. Most bottles find their way out of the country. Ironically, consumption of vodka and imported liquor has never been higher.

In the last century, Chekhov, Pushkin, Green, and other writers and artists flocked to the south coast for its balmy climate and inspiring landsape. The tsars and nobility built fairy-tale estates on the picturesque seashore.

Feodosiya was home to Aivazovskii, Russia's famous seascape painter. In

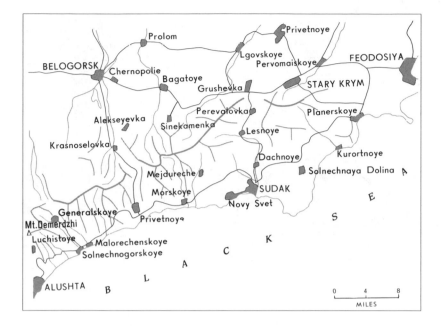

the local museum, you can see his stunning, monumental paintings of waves, sailors, and sailing ships. The gallery also has a good collection of Voloshin, another nineteenth-century Crimean painter (and poet) who captured in delicate watercolors the Black Sea's hues and the contours of the countryside.

The town of Sudak sharply contrasts old with new. The stone battlements of the Genoese fortress bricked into the cliff overlooking the sea are much more enduring than the decaying cement-block apartment houses and hotels built during the Khrushchev boom in the 1950s.

A side trip from Sudak, Novyi Svet ("New World") hides in a sheltered lagoon guarded by 1,000-foot cliffs. In Russia, Novy Svet is synonymous with fine champagne. Only a few centuries ago, passing galleys were raided by pirates from their encampment on a promontory south of town. Scramble down to the water to discover the secluded "Tsars Beach." Along the way, you pass the grotto where Shalyapin performed for Nicholas II. Like other Crimean beaches, the Tsars Beach has more rocky outcroppings than sand.

Alushta is the second-biggest resort center, and one of the least appealing places on the coast. Between Alushta and Yalta, however, you'll find several charming hamlets, Gurzuf and Massandra, with Tatar-era houses and winding streets. You also pass Ayu-Dag (Bear Mountain), resembling a bear bending over the sea.

Yalta climbs the hill steeply from the edge of the Black Sea, walled by the natural fortress of Ai Petri at its back. The principal city on the south coast, Yalta is like a floor of fine hardwood that has been painted over too many times. Each era of Black Sea history has left its mark on Yalta, whose old

Along the Crimean coast are great back roads for bicycling. (Photo: Keith Gunnar)

town still hints at faded glory, although concrete-block vacation resorts choke the waterfront. The pace here is relaxed and it's a fun place to wander for a day or two, taking in Livadia Palace (site of the Yalta Conference) and the Chekhov Museum, and just admiring the sailors' snappy uniforms.

Beyond Yalta, the traffic thins again, the road dipping down to more coastal towns, picturesque Koreiz and Simeiz. Alupka Palace, built for Count Vorontsov, takes you back a century. Stone lions face the sea at the front door of this English-style castle, while the view from the back captures the soaring Ai Petri cliffs.

Balaklava, a primordially perfect lagoon, bears battle scars from the Crimean War, and the sinister secret of a present-day submarine moorage. Sevastopol, home of the Black Sea fleet, remains "officially" closed to tourists at this writing.

This scenic country is ideal for day hikes or multiday adventures. Because of the proximity to the coastal highway and towns, you have endless options for mixing and matching trails; you can essentially start hiking and come out of the mountains anywhere you want to. At the same time, in the mountains you are completely removed from the crowded vacation resort scene on the coastline.

It's also good cycling country. Crimean roads are among the best in the country—the national cycling team trains here. Avoid the main drags (Simferopol–Yalta, Alushta–Yalta, and Sevastopol–Simferopol highways): on the back roads, between Bakhchisarai and Ai Petri, or along the coast between Feodosiya and Sevastopol, you'll find great riding. Most places, several roads embroider the coast, so you can generally find a smaller one with minimal traffic.

DAY HIKES ON THE CRIMEAN MAIN RIDGE

From **Angarsky Pass**, 2,467 feet (752 m), either **Chatyr Dag** or **Demerdzhi** summits can be reached in **a day**.

PEREVALNOYE TO GENERALSKOYE

This is a **3- to 4-day hike**. From Perevalnoye, hike to **Krasny** ("Red") **Caves** in **1½ hours**, where there's nice camping.

Hike via Lyisyi Ivan mountain to **Demerdzhi Peak** and the **Dolina Privedeniya ("Valley of Ghosts")**. From here, it's an **8- to 10-hour** hike to **Djurdjur Waterfall**, so it's best to camp somewhere in between.

The trail then drops along the river to Generalskoye, on the highway about 6 miles (10 km) northwest of Solnechnogorskoye. Solnechnogorskoye is on the bus line to Alushta. From Alushta, there are frequent buses to Simferopol.

Cave Cities

Halfway between Simferopol and Sevastopol lies the ancient city of Bakhchisarai, seat of power of the Tatar khans. *Krim Girai: Khan of the Crimea*, a nineteenth-century account by Englishman Theodore Mundt, vividly describes life in the capital of the last khan. It's easy to imagine the scenes in this historical kiss-and-tell when you tour the Khan's Palace, with the harem upstairs still decorated in period style.

Between Bakhchisarai and Yalta, in the lower-elevation (1,150 to 2,450 feet [350 m to 747 m] above sea level) Second and Third Ridges of the Crimean Mountains, a series of "cave cities" fans out. Concentrations of hundreds and thousands of chambers carved into the limestone stratifications, these relics dating from the fifth and sixth centuries impressed me more than any museum I've ever seen.

Archaeologists presume they were built by the Byzantines to defend their inland settlements from marauders who frequently landed on the coast. Several of them were monasteries. Most of the cave cities were abandoned after the Tatar take-over of the peninsula in the fifteenth century. In some of the churches, you can see traces of frescoes on the walls. And you can scramble around the multilayered mazes of storerooms, livestock pens, winepresses, and other utilitarian chambers, all empty and silent, yet seemingly alive and teeming with stories.

The easiest cave city to find is Chufut-Kale, on the hill just outside Bakhchisarai. Chufut-Kale, meaning Jewish Fortress, is named for the Karaites, a Jewish sect that last inhabited it. In earlier incarnations it was called Kryik-or. This city was not only a fortification but a trading center, whose overgrown streets you can still trace.

Chufut-Kale is somehow too close to civilization and too easy to find; much more intriguing are the cave cities you unearth in the hills south of there. Also on the outskirts of Bakhchisarai, the Uspensky Monastery hangs over the cavity of the valley below, cells chipped into the cliff. The trek from Bakhchisarai through the cave cities and the Big Crimean Canyon takes you on an incredible jaunt back through time. A little book in Russian, *Cave Cities of the Crimea*, by Gertsen and Makhneva, has maps and goes into the history of each particular cave city.

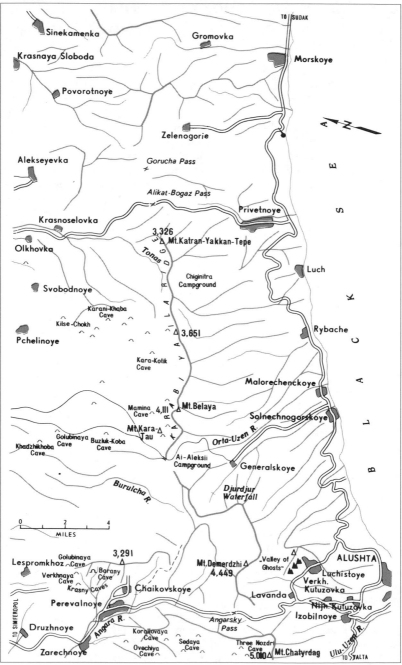

The Khan's Palace in Bakchisarai harks back to the days when the Tatars held sway over all Crimea.

BAKHCHISARAI TO YALTA

This **7- or 8-day trek to cave cities and the Big Crimean Canyon** takes you along a frequently traveled path and is not a wilderness experience, although it goes through some beautiful terrain. You can really make this trek into any length, as it takes you through towns and within a couple hours' walking distance of the road at all times. It's easy hiking on well-traveled trails. There are also several short side trips. Route finding is simple: trails in the Crimea are among the few Russian trails that are actually marked. This trail is posted as **route 212-0554 (93)**.

Head southeast out of Bakhchisarai on a stony road, leaving the slopes of Kordon-Baur on the right, toward the foot of Mount Beshik-Tau (Cradle

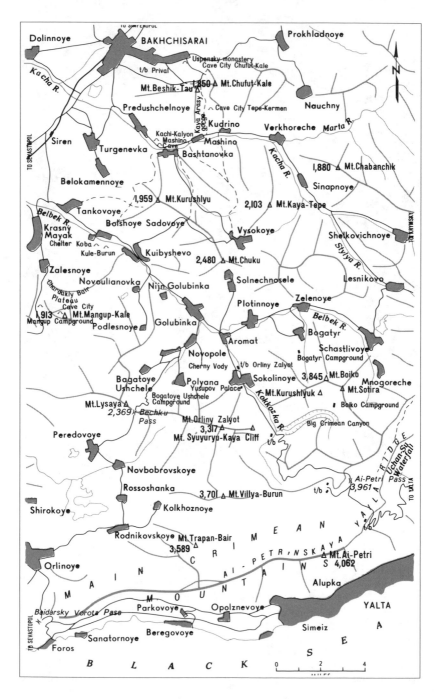

Mountain). In about **1 mile (3 km)**, you'll pass a small springs with a gazebo in the juniper and hawthorne woods. From here the path takes a turn to the right, south through a walnut grove. At the edge of the grove, the path divides, going left to Mashino through the Kaya Arasy gorge, or straight on to Kachi-Kalyon monastery and Predushchelnoye. Take the left path toward **Mashino**. A few kilometers north of Mashino is a fascinating cave city, Tepe-Kermen. (You can also hike to Tepe-Kermen by circumnavigating Mount Beshik-Tau.) Hiking toward Bashtanovka, for a short while, you follow the Bakhchisarai–Sinapnoye highway. Then, cross the Kacha River and keep it on your right as you walk through orchards. There is a campground on the outskirts of **Bashtanovka, 5 miles (8 km), 2 to 3 hours**.

On the hill above Bashtanovka are settlements from the Middle Ages. Probably founded by Byzantine monks in the late eighth century, the Kachi-Kalyon monastery has more than 120 caves. Winemakers and potters lived here from around A.D. 500

From the Bashtanovka Campground, cross the stream and a big field and follow the sign "kuibyshevo 6 km" up a little pass. Descend the slopes of Mount Kurushlyu to the Belbekskoi Valley below. Pass through the village of **Kuibyshevo** and cross the Belbek River. Turn right onto the path to **Maloye Sadovoye**. (You can also reach this village on the Bakhchisarai highway.) On the rocky promontory of Kule-Burun are the ruins of the Syuirensky Fortress, and farther west on Ai-Todor is the cave monastery Chilter-Koba. From the foot of Ai-Todor promontory at the southern edge of the village, the road leads up to the Chardakly Bair Plateau. Cross the plateau to the southwest to the village of **Zalesnoye** in the Karalezsky Valley. Turn left from the village onto a road through the woods to **Mangup Campground, 11 miles (18 km), 5 to 7 hours**.

Imagine visiting New York 200 years after the last resident deserted the city. Although never the size of New York City, Mangup boasts a long and illustrious history. Archaeological digs have revealed Copper Age and Stone Age habitation, and Taurians lived there 3,000 years ago. Byzantine defense structures date from from the fifth and sixth centuries. In the eighth century, the city was captured by Khazars, and was burned in the tenth. Mangup was the seat of government of the Feodoro dynasty, which reigned from A.D. 1200 until 1475. During those years, the Feodoro princes challenged the Genoese on the coasts of the Crimea and kept at bay the Tatars occupying the steppes of the Peninsula. Today at Mangup, you can see the ruins of the citadel, palace, church, and main fortress gate.

Also near Mangup (to the west) are ruins of two cave monasteries, Shuldan and Chelter. Chelter, the larger, comprises more than fifty caves. These, and other Greek Orthodox monasteries, were subsidized by the Moscow princes, who were interested in cultivating support among the pockets of Christianity in this Muslim-controlled sea.

From **Mangup Campground**, descend to the Dzhan-Dere gorge and south, then right through a stand of pine mixed with oak scrub. The path crosses the Adyim-Chokraksky Valley. Follow markers carefully; there are many diverging paths. A steep ascent leads out of the valley floor, into a beech forest. In this forest, follow a gravel road, passing hayfields. Where the road goes downhill, turn right onto the path. Before the descent to Bechku, Mount Lysaya is off to the right. From this summit, you get great views of the Main Ridge of the Crimean Mountains. The path leads to the Golubinka–Peredovoye highway near **Bechku Pass**. Turn left and head down this road about 500 feet (150 m) to pick up the path to **Bogatoye Ushchele Campground**, **11 miles (18 km)**, **5 to 7 hours**, on the shore of the Bechku River.

The forest here is mixed with spindly birch, scrub oak, juniper, and rosehip, the woods light enough for thick grass cover. There is little virgin oak left on the peninsula, as it was long popular for building houses, ships, furniture, and farm implements, and the bark was used in tanning leather. As you reach the higher elevations—Mount Lysaya is 2,369 feet high (800 m), you get into groves of beech. In the mountains of the Crimea, Asian beech mixes with European beech, producing some interesting hybrids. The thick canopies of these trees block out most light, so you hike along the trail thick with beech leaves in a half-gloom.

After leaving **Bogatoye Ushchele Campground**, about 1,000 feet (300 m) along the forest path you arrive at the **Golubinka–Peredovoye highway**. Turn left and go 325 feet (100 m) on this road, then turn right into the forest toward a little lake and the village of **Polyana**. Near Polyana (formerly Markur) are remains of two settlements from the Middle Ages, and on the summit of nearby Sankyik-Kaya rise the ruins of an eighth- or tenth-century fortress.

At the edge of Polyana, turn right and walk past rose fields and a two-story building called Chyorniye Vody (black waters). The waters of this spa are believed to cure arthritis and rheumatism, among other ailments. For about 650 feet (200 m), follow the paved road toward **Novopole**, then turn right and continue through the village. The road passes through tobacco fields and roses. Crossing the Kokkozka River, you come to the village of **Aromat**, named for the predominant industry of the area: roses. On the Yalta–Bakhchisarai highway where there's a war monument it's only 1 mile (1.5 km) toward Sokolinoye to *turbaza* **Orlinyi Zalyot**, **7.5 miles (12 km)**, **3 to 4 hours**.

An optional shorter route from *turbaza* Orlinyi Zalyot to Boiko Campground also takes you to the scenic Big Crimean Canyon, 6 kilometers from the *turbaza*. Walk through Sokolinoye, passing the Yusupov Palace on your right (the nobleman's hunting estate is now a boarding school). The main road through the village gradually turns into a trail, also named after Yusupov. After about an hour, the trail leads you to the remains of a big, burned oak in a field, where it divides. To the right, the trail leads down to the highway to Yalta. To the left it leads to the Boiko Campground, along the right side of the canyon. Straight ahead leads to the Big Crimean Canyon.

For the longer route to Boiko Campground, from *turbaza* **Orlinyi Zalyot**, cross the Kokkozka River and turn right on the trail, which ascends to an open area with views of the Orlinyi Zalyot massif, Syuyuryu-Kaya Cliff, and, in the distance, Mount Boiko and Ai Petri. The path winds through mixed dwarf oak and birch. This member of the birch family (*grabinnik* in Russian) is widespread in the subtropical climate of the Crimea. Pass through a field with a triangular marker, then turn right toward **Nagornoye**, which you walk through

At Tepe Kermen and other nearby cave cities, thousands of chambers carved into the limestone stratifications attest to the Crimea's long habitation by humans. (Photo: Keith Gunnar)

to get to the **Bogatyir Campground, 5 miles (8 km), 2 to 3 hours**.

From the Bogatyir Campground, cross the Boiko ridge, over **a pass between Mount Boiko and Mount Sotira**. The ninth-century Spasa Cathedral you pass suggests that people have appreciated this special place for a very long time. Descend a steep trail through shady woods to the **Boiko Campground** on the far side of Yokhogan-Su River, **4.5 miles (7 km), 2 to 3 hours**. About 0.6 mile (1 km) downstream from the Boiko Campground is a 40-foot (12-m) waterfall.

From the Boiko Campground you can do an optional 4.5- to 5-mile (7- to 8-km) day hike into the Big Crimean Canyon. About 0.3 mile (0.5 km) from the campground, a trail takes off up the right bank of the canyon. The 1-mile-long (2-km-long) canyon is 1,050 feet (320 m) deep in places. The Auzun-Uzen River cuts through it, decorating the canyon bottom with rapids, waterfalls, and natural pools. In addition to groves of dwarf birch, beech, maple, and linden trees, the canyon cultivates unusual species of flora including rare ferns and orchids. In the canyon, a *zakaznik* (semi-protected reserve), picking flowers, woodcutting, and camping are not allowed.

To continue the trek, from the **Boiko Campground** cross back to the other side of the Yokhogan-Su River and head to your right into the forest for a while, before dropping down to and crossing the **Kuru-Uzen River**. The path climbs to 4,200 feet (1274 m), wandering over the grassy Ai Petri uplands, eventually coming out on the **Yalta highway**. Turn left on the highway and follow it for 1 mile (2 km) to the weather station, near where there's a **hut, 8.5 miles (14 km), 4 to 5 hours**. You may camp on the Ai Petri heights, or descend to Yalta.

From this panorama, much of the beautiful southern coast spreads before you. The 3,000-foot (900-m) towering cliff of Ai Petri, topped with jagged aretes like battlements, presents an awesome backdrop to the seashore south of Yalta. Often wrapped in fogs, Ai Petri has its own microclimate. The temperature is significantly lower up here. In fact, in winter, there's often good skiing on Ai Petri, when it's warm in Yalta just about 3,400 feet (1050 m) below. Near the top of the Ai Petri cliffs (just above the top tram station) is a stand of dwarf birch and beech and to the northwest are some yew trees more than 1,000 years old.

From the **Ai Petri hut**, go along the highway (toward Bakhchisarai), and in about 500 feet (150 m) turn right onto the gravel road. After another **15 to 20 minutes**, go right again onto the path, which drops steeply down the hillside to the **Uchan-Su Waterfall, 5 miles (8 km), 2 hours**—literally, "flying water" as the Tatar name translates, 300 vertical feet (90 m) of it—and the road to Yalta. This road is heavily traveled by buses and cars, so you can make your way either to Yalta or back to Bakhchisarai.

7   Urals

Many Americans' first thought when they hear "Russian mountains" is the Urals. The Urals are old mountains, probably the least dramatic that you'll find anywhere in the country. Some refer to the range as the "gray-haired Urals." The Urals stretch more than 1,200 miles (2000 km) from south to north, and people living from Chelyabinsk to the Arctic Circle proudly talk of living not in Siberia but *na Urale* (in the Urals).

The Trans-Siberian cuts across the middle of the Urals, where the mountains are at their lowest. This rail line connects the region's major cities, Perm and Ekaterinburg (formerly Sverdlovsk), with Moscow and Siberia. Russian towns in the Urals date back to the late 1600s, when early prospectors mined copper on what was then the eastern frontier. While Russians and Ukrainians are the principal ethnic group in the Urals, in the southern Urals there are large concentrations of Turkic peoples, whose presence recalls the period between the thirteenth and fifteenth centuries, when the Mongols were the supreme power in the land. Two of these Mongol-descended ethnic minorities, the Tatars and the Bashkirs, have political status as Autonomous Republics.

The Urals Region, rich in metals and minerals, makes its living primarily from heavy industry and mining. It manufactures a large share of Russia's steel and heavy machinery. During the Soviet period, the Urals' metallurgical and chemical plants were geared overwhelmingly toward military production. As a result, the Urals were closed to foreign travel, and many cities were such closely kept secrets that they didn't even have names, but were assigned numbers.

It is not the mountains in the Urals that impress, but the expanses. Taiga blankets most of the Urals. The mountains are rocky pimples jutting up from the forest. In fact, in these parts, a mountain is called *kamen*—meaning, simply, "rock." In the north, near the Arctic Circle, the taiga forest gives way to mountain tundra.

Away from the industrial population centers, you may see wolves, bear, and gamebirds like capercaillie, a large grouse common to the taiga. Several nature reserves are dedicated to the preservation of species found in the forests of the Urals. These include the Ilmen Zapovednik and the Bashkir Zapovednik in the southern Urals. In the western foothills of the northern Urals is the Pechora-Ilych Zapovednik.

Northern Urals

This is a rugged, continental climate: January temperatures get down to -23°C.

For some interesting Urals sightseeing, stop in Verkhoturye on your way to or from the hikes to Konzhakovsky Kamen or Denezhkin Kamen if you have some extra time. Fourteen Orthodox churches in various states of decay bear witness to the history of what was once the most important religious center in Eastern Russia, its main cathedral the largest in the country after St. Isaacs'. Tsarinas who fell from favor were exiled here. Set in pretty pasture-

Taiga blankets most of the Urals, the mountain range that divides the continents of Europe and Asia.

lands on the Tura River, Verkhoturye is a quiet place, unless you happen to land there on a weekend, when most of the population gets drunk (as they do in most towns across Russia).

Ekaterinburg (formerly Sverdlovsk), the major city of the Northern Urals, seems to be famous for little more than being one of Russia's most industrialized cities, as well as the place where the last tsar and his family were murdered and, a few decades later, the Soviets shot down Gary Powers' U2 spy plane. Neither is a very appealing reason to visit the place, but I found myself liking this city.

Downtown Ekaterinburg is a pleasant place to stroll in summer, with broad tree-lined avenues and squares. People I encountered there struck me as a true salt-of-the-earth breed. In spite of desperate belt-tightening in this region, whose economy was almost entirely dependent on military production and is now rebounding from the Cold War, people's attitude is determined: "We'll get through this, too."

Getting There

You can reach Ekaterinburg from Moscow by air or by an overnight train from Moscow's Yaroslavsky Vokzal.

To reach the **Shunut Kamen** hike, from Ekaterinburg take the electric train to Revda (1 hour). From Revda take the bus to Krasnoyar (1 hour).

To reach the **Konzhakovsky Kamen** hike, from Ekaterinburg take the overnight train to Karpinsk. From Karpinsk, take the once-daily bus to Kytlym. Get off at the Serebryanka River (1½ hours).

To get to the **Denezhkin Kamen** hike or ski trip, from Ekaterinburg take the train to Krasnoturinsk, then go by bus to Severouralsk.

To get to the **Vesyoliye Gori** hike, from Ekaterinburg take the train to Nizhniye Tagil (4 hours); from Nizhniye Tagil, take the bus to Visim (3 hours).

Where to Stay

Ekaterinburg was a closed city until 1991, so it wasn't until recently that Intourist unveiled plans to build a hotel. The other Ekaterinburg hotel options are pretty limited.

In Karpinsk, which is near the Konzhakovsky Kamen hike, there's a *turbaza*, but you're better off camping.

When to Go

Outdoor enthusiasts consider February and March the ideal time for getting out in the Urals. On skis, on the wings of the snow, you can travel twice as far. In May and June encephalitis-bearing ticks, while not as widespread as in the Far East, can be a problem (see the Health and Medical Problems section of chapter 3, Staying Safe and Healthy). July through September are good hiking months in the North Urals.

Equipment and Supplies

Rubber boots are the footgear of choice, even for climbing Konzhakovsky Kamen, because water stands in the low areas on the ridge.

Stock up on supplies in Ekaterinburg.

SHUNUT KAMEN

There's a **hot springs** at Shunut Kamen, 2,162 feet (660 m). From Krasnoyar, a logging road leads to the Shunut Kamen trail. It's a **4-hour** hike to the summit.

KONZHAKOVSKY KAMEN

This is a **2- to 3-day loop hike** that can be shortened by just going in and out on the same trail.

The road from Karpinsk to Kytlym, a swath cut straight through the taiga, keeps you awake as you bounce and jolt as if on a carnival ride. A passenger on our bus noted that it's more dangerous in rainy weather, when a vehicle can disappear into one of the potholes and never be seen again. Just where there's a hint of hills in the distance, get off the bus at the Serebryanka River (1½ hours).

Three rivers drain the Konzhakovsky Ridge to the south: the Serebryanka, Konzhakovka, and Katyisher. Trails ascend along all three rivers to the ridge. The Konzhakovka River trail sees the most use. The route given here takes you up the Serebryanka and down the Konzhakovka. The disadvantage of this is carrying full packs up and across the ridge. If a loop isn't preferred, you can also go in and out the same trail, along any of the three river trails.

On the north side of the Kytlym Highway, to the right of the bridge over the

Serebryanka River, the trail heads into the birch woods. There's no trailmarker at the trailhead, although up the trail somewhat higher a sign indicates it's the way to Serebryansky Kamen. The trail may well be muddy, or even underwater in places. Six miles (10 km) in, **3 to 4 hours**, having climbed about 800 feet (250 m), the slopes begin to steepen toward Serebryansky Kamen. Here, on the left riverbank, is one of the last places where there's good camping. Higher up, dense forest and boulder flows choke the steep slopes.

From **Serebryanka campsite**, follow the trail along the stream through thick woods that are mossy underfoot. The trail's faint in places, but it's easy to orient oneself from the stream. Just above the campsite, the Serebryanka River branches, the right branch leading more directly to **Serebryansky Kamen**, **2 to 3 hours**, with little waterfalls and pools at its head. Where the trail runs out in the moraine tongues, you can already see Serebryansky Kamen, 4,281 feet (1305 m) high. Pick your way through boulders and patches of forest toward the far right side of the ridge. The ridgecrest, barren and studded with rocky outcroppings, deceives. Although it's not clear from below, the high point is toward the east edge of the ridge. The trees run out; the last 1,000 feet (300 m) of climbing is on boulders.

You can see the smokestacks of Karpinsk in the distance and, down below, Kytlym, a closed military town where missiles reputedly still nestle in their underground silos. To the west stretches a string of barren hills, the last bump

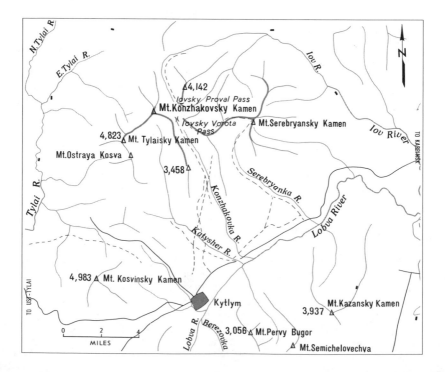

being Konzhakovsky Kamen, the highest on this ridge. To the southwest are Kazansky Kamen and several other summits in the ridge known as the Bugri ("Moguls"). Waves of hills lap the fading horizon in all directions. Although we saw four other people the day we hiked this ridge, the pervasive feeling of being quite alone in a vast expanse never left me.

For bearings from Serebryansky Kamen to **Konzhakovsky Kamen, 4 to 5 hours**, go by the sun or by your gut feeling. The rocks are so magnetic the compass needle whirls like a top. In clear weather, route finding up here is a cinch. The blank ridge is dotted with "summits"—piles of rocks that stick up high enough that you have to climb over or traverse around them. Between these high points, the grassy permafrost plateaus can be wet. The sense of openness and isolation on the ridge is exhilarating. While traversing, we surprised a couple of ptarmigan and, near the summit of Konzhakovsky, a large hare.

On the ridge between Konzhakovsky Kamen and Iyov Peak (really just one of those rock piles), Konzhakovsky Pass is the saddle from which you drop down to the **Konzhakovka River, 2 to 3 hours**. If you get lucky, you'll stumble onto the trail leading down the hillside. Otherwise, just follow the drainage down the slope of boulders and brush until you reach the stream. Again, where the grade flattens out, you'll find good camping.

From Konzhakovka River to **Kytlym Highway, 2 to 3 hours**, the trail through forest follows the stream. Again, it's likely to be muddy. This is a popular trail: chances are you'll see other people, or at least signs of them. Along with people sign, you'll also probably see bear tracks.

Near the road, the Konzhakovka River joins the Katysher. You come out again in sleepy fields with haystacks on the road from which you started, 3.75 miles (6 km) closer to Kytlym. The bus comes by once a day headed back to Karpinsk.

The hills on the south side of the road (the Bugri and Kazansky Kamen) look like they might be interesting if you could find a reasonable trail to them. We found only a swamp full of spiders, slugs, and hordes of mosquitoes.

DENEZHKIN KAMEN

The climb of Denezhkin Kamen resembles that of Konzhakovsky Kamen, but, unlike Konzhakovsky Kamen, Denezhkin Kamen stands by itself in the taiga. It's also possible to ski from Konzhakovsky Kamen to Denezhkin Kamen in 11 days or so.

VESYOLIYE GORI

The Vesyoliye Gori ("Happy Hills") are a day away from Ekaterinburg, near Visim. In winter, you can ski right over the top of **Starik Kamen**, 7,014 feet (2138 m), one of the peaks in the Vesyoliye Gori—about a **3-day** trip. Just follow the power lines to Korpushikha. From Korpushikha, get a ride to Nevyansk, and train from there to Ekaterinburg.

Polar Urals

The Polar Urals are generally considered the most interesting part of this range. These mountains are truly "out there." Few foreigners have made acquaintance with the deer, elk, wolves, bear, and foxes who roam these northern woods. Those who *have* been to the Polar Urals rave about the clear rivers and exquisite sunrises, sunsets, and fall colors. Underfoot, it's not uncommon to find beautiful quartz and amethyst crystals.

Just south of the Arctic Circle, the boundary cleaving the continents of Europe and Asia runs across the Ural's highest summit, Narodny, 6,217 feet (1895 m), far north in the Polar Urals. Hard-core adventurers like to cross-country ski here. Winter ski trips are serious undertakings because, in bad weather (a frequent occurrence), you can find yourself stuck a long way from population points. These mountains are so far from anywhere that approach hikes can take days. Some people like to shorten these approaches by floating the rivers. It's also possible to helicopter in.

Getting There

Take the train from Moscow's Yaroslavsky Station toward Vorkuta, getting off at Pechora on the Pechora River (this takes the better part of 2 days). You can also fly to Vorkuta from Moscow. From Pechora, take a hydrofoil up the Pechora River to Aranets.

Where to Stay

You can probably arrange to stay with someone in the village of Aranets.

When to Go

Summer doesn't last long in these polar regions; go in July or August, or else wait for winter and go on skis.

Equipment and Supplies

Aranets has a small store, where you should be able to find bread, cereals, and maybe some tasteless candy. It's preferable to lay in supplies in Moscow.

ARANETS TO KOS-U

This is a **9- to 10-day** trek that takes you on through several mountain

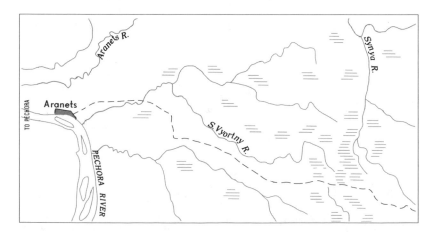

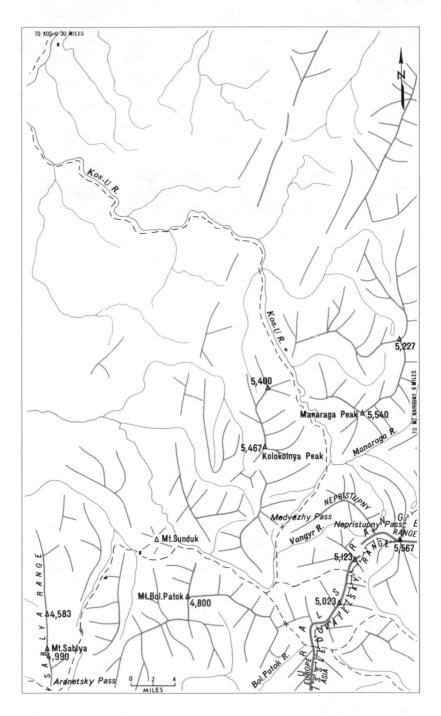

Late-summer hikers in the Urals forest

ranges and river drainages, with the option of climbing any of several peaks en route. Some of the peaks require technical rock climbing skills and equipment.

Aranets, the starting point, is a typical Urals village with wooden houses and streets full of dogs. The taiga and the swamps encroach on the fringe of town. At the east end of town, a trail leads to the **Sablya Mountains—4 days** away. In summer, your feet may be soaked the whole time. You can cross via easy **Aranetsky Pass** or climb Mount Sablya, 4,990 feet (1435 m). Steep rock walls shear from most of the summits in the Polar Urals; the east face of Mount Sablya is one of these—a challenging technical rock climb.

Beyond Aranetsky Pass, there's good camping on the **Sed-Yu River** (*yu* means "river" in the Komi tongue). The hike up the **Sablya Ridge** along this river takes **another day**. Out of this flat watershed, the trail heads northeast. Continue over the hills and valleys toward the **Vangyr River**. On the left, views of the Sunduk massif and ahead of you the mountains of the central Polar Urals—Nepristupny ("Inaccessible") and Issledovatelsky Kryazh ("Investigator's Ridge"). The Vangyr, a good trout (*kharius*) stream, is easily crossed higher up.

The climb to **Nepristupny Pass** is **another whole day**'s hike. From here you have the option of descending east toward the Ob River and Asia, descending west to the Manaraga River, or traversing along Issledovatelsky Kryazh to Narodny Peak. This last option is the hardest—and the most interesting: a 3-day trek through alpine meadows above tree line.

To make the loop trek to Kos-U, descend west to the **Manaraga River**. From a base camp on the Manaraga River, you can do climbs of several premier Polar Urals peaks: Narodny, Manaraga, and Kolokolnya. Jagged, seven-headed Manaraga Peak, 5,540 feet (1820 m), requires rock-climbing gear and experience. Below Manaraga are cabins, making this a viable alternative for winter touring also.

To get back to civilization, take a good trail along the scenic **Kos-Yu River**, with its many rapids and good fishing. From the Manaraga massif to the **Kos-Yu railroad station** takes **3 to 4 days**. The Vorkuta–Moscow train stops here.

8   Caucasus

Geographers consider the Caucasus the dividing point between Europe and Asia. That makes Mount Elbrus, at 18,510 feet (5643 m) a gentle-sloped volcano in the Central Caucasus, the top of Europe. The jagged profile of the Caucasus may resemble the Swiss Alps, but everything here is higher by several thousand feet. Elbrus and another volcano, Mount Kazbek, 16,512 feet (5033 m), anchor the main ridge of the Caucasus. The Main Caucasus is divided into three sections: west, central, and east, with the Western Caucasus falling west of Elbrus and the Eastern Caucasus to the east of Kazbek.

The Western Caucasus is noted for luxuriant forested valleys and hillsides, with snowy, turreted peaks. The hiker finds more contrast here than in any other mountain area—the Western Caucasus ranges from high glaciated alpine to the subtropics near the Black Sea.

The Central Caucasus contains the highest, most challenging alpine summits of the Caucasus Range. Between Elbrus and Kazbek swarm dozens of 15,000-foot and 16,000-foot (4500- and 4800-m) peaks. There are only twenty non-classified passes through the Central Caucasus (see the Soviet Mountain Pass Rating System section in chapter 1, Introduction). Glaciation here is much more extensive than in the east and west of the range. Elbrus and Kazbek are nearly completely covered by glaciers. The three "chains" of the Central Caucasus—the Svanetian, Digorian, and Ossetian—link many famous, beautiful peaks. The sharp pinnacles of Shkhelda, 14,331 feet (4368 m), and Ushba, 15,420 feet (4700 m), are as beautiful as the legends about them.

South of Kazbek, the Eastern Caucasus continues to Dagestan and the Azerbaidzhan Mountains on the Caspian side. I was more taken with Dagestan than perhaps any other place I've traveled in Russia and Central Asia. Hiking in Dagestan, "Land of Mountains," resembles the Nepal experience of trekking from one high village to the next, surrounded by stunning alpine scenery. Much of Dagestan and neighboring mountainous Georgia is studded with villages and towns.

The Western Caucasus' Black Sea coast is humid and subtropical. On the eastern end of the Caucasus, where this range fades to a virtual desert, the continental climate is dry, with hot summers and short winters. In the mountains, the climate is cool and wet. Winter lasts for seven months. The average temperature in July is 24°C to 29°C in the foothills, 14°C at 6,500 feet (2000 m), and 8°C at 9,800 feet (3000 m). In January the foothills are -5°C on the north side, 3°C on the south side, -7°C at 6,500 feet, and -12°C at 9,800 feet. Snowline is about 9,800 to 10,200 feet (3000 to 3100 m) in the Western Caucasus, 11,000 to 11,700 feet (3360 to 3560 m) in the Central Caucasus, and 12,100 to 12,500 feet (3700 to 3800 m) in the Eastern Caucasus.

Elbrus stops the wet air coming off the Black Sea, making the Eastern Caucasus drier than the Western or Central Caucasus, although there are many foggy days in Khevsuretia and summer rainstorms with hail are frequent. Autumn begins in the Eastern Caucasus in September.

Indigenous women sell beautiful hand-knit sweaters, made from locally dyed and spun wool, in the open-air market near Mount Elbrus.

British and German alpinists were the first to explore the Caucasus Mountains (in the nineteenth century). Many have compared the breathtaking mountain scenery of the Caucasus to the Alps. Douglas Freshfield, who explored the Caucasus Mountains in the 1860s, wrote:

> *Undoubtedly the difficulties of everyday travel in the Caucasus exhaust much of that energy which finds vent in Switzerland in scaling the highest peaks, but ... it is quite impossible to convey in words any idea of the beauty of the landscape, or grandeur of scale which placed the scenery beyond comparison with any of the show-sights of Switzerland.*

The similarities stop there. Outside of the Central Caucasus' Baksan Valley, headquarters for Mount Elbrus, no trams screech up the hillsides. Tourists don't venture beyond the few developed recreation areas; a fraction as many people hike and climb in the Caucasus as in the Alps. The Caucasus are more hiker-friendly than when Freshfield passed through more than a century ago, but there are still plenty of obstacles to traveling there. You'll find few of the comforts of the Alps here: no convenient mountain huts where you can rent a bunk and buy a meal, no well-organized guide services or outdoor gear and food stores.

To Russians, *Kavkaz* (Caucasus) means more than mountains. Mineralniye Vody—Min Vody—is the hub of a cluster of resorts where tourists come to "take the waters": Pyatigorsk, Kislovodsk, Yessentuki, and Zheleznovodsk. On the north shore of the Black Sea, a string of Caucasus resort towns have traditionally rivaled the Crimea in popularity with vacationing Soviets. At the end of a climbing expedition, many climbers like to hike across passes from the north and end up on the Black Sea. Sanchara, 8,530 feet (2600 m), Marukh, 8,989 feet (2740 m), Klukhor, 9,239 feet (2816 m), Donguzorun, 10,371 feet (3161 m), Tviber, 11,745 feet (3580 m), and Gezevtsek, 11,368 feet (3465 m), have long served as gateways to the Black Sea.

The Western Caucasus is the most accessible part of the Caucasus for hikers wishing to avoid steep ice and rock. Uzunkol, a popular rock climbing area with an *alpbaza*, also offers excellent moderate hiking nearby. The nearer you go to the Central Caucasus, the more technically challenging the terrain becomes, and it is seriously alpine by the time you reach Dombay.

Best known among foreign mountaineers, and most popular with Russians, is the Central Caucasus—especially Prielbrusye (the area around Elbrus) and neighboring Dombay just to the west. Dombay and Prielbrusye attract mountain enthusiasts year-round. Compared to the Alps or the Rockies, their ski areas have limited terrain and poorly groomed runs. But for the sheer adventure of it, the Caucasus is a fun place to ski. The backcountry skiing is superb. Few Russians own mountaineering ski equipment, so the slopes are virtually untracked, even in close proximity to the ski areas. The top Caucasus ski resorts are in Georgia, at Bakuriani and Gudauri, both not far from Tbilisi. At Gudauri, developed and operated by an Austrian company, you can stay in a European-class hotel. Heli-skiing has also caught on in the Caucasus, primarily among Europeans. A French company, Yak & Yeti, runs heli-ski tours out of Krasnaya Polyana.

This band of glacier-draped peaks bridging between the Black Sea and the Caspian now claims triple citizenship: in these mountains Russia borders Georgia and Azerbaidzhan. Unfortunately, the Caucasus have suffered some of the bloodiest ethnic conflicts to break out since the Soviet era ended. The Georgians rebelled against Russian rule. The ethnic groups of north Georgia—the Svans, Abkhassians, Cirkassians, and others—formed the Army of Autonomous Mountain Peoples and have been battling the Georgian army in areas neighboring the Caucasus Black Sea coast. The Georgian side of the Caucasus (the south side of the range), a fascinating area scattered with picturesque villages, cannot be recommended as safe for hiking and mountaineering at this time. The general breakdown of authority in the mountain regions of Georgia has unleashed criminal activity unheard of during Soviet rule, including muggings of mountain travelers and the looting of their camps.

Parts of the Eastern Caucasus have been caught up in local unrest in the past couple of years, but this is a vast region and other areas are peaceful. While Ingusheto-Khevsuretia and Checheno-Tushetia have seen their share of ethnic strife, and war continues in Azerbaidzhan, Dagestan remains unaffected by the violent currents. When I pore over maps of the Caucasus, a trek from Georgia across the mountains to Upper Dagestan cries out to be done, but until things in Georgia settle down, this is not a reasonable proposition.

The alpine recreation centers of the Central Caucasus—Elbrus and Dombay, at the edge of the Western Caucasus—have not been affected by the outbursts of violence that occur elsewhere in the Caucasus. Administratively, these areas are part of Kabardino–Balkaria, in the Russian Federation. For travel outside of the north side of the Central Caucasus, it's essential to gather current information about stability, law, and order in specific areas. The situation changes so frequently there that no source older than a few months can be considered current. See the Political Conditions section of chapter 3, Staying Safe and Healthy.

The Caucasus are the most accessible big mountains in the former Soviet Union, with an established (if not always simple) system of transportation and hotel services. You can drive there in several days from Germany, or fly in two hours from Moscow. There are roads to within spitting distance of many of the high valleys and major concentrations of peaks. And with a long, illustrious history of climbing and hiking, routes in the Caucasus are well established and documented. The Caucasus offer hundreds of fabulous climbing routes, of various technical difficulty.

Numerous adventure travel companies—both foreign companies and Russian outfits—offer trips to Mount Elbrus. Prices are very competitive. Your chances of actually *climbing* (as opposed to spending your time trying to overcome logistical problems) are much better if you hire an experienced hand to make the arrangements for you. It's the responsibility of the tour agency to make sure there's a place for you at Priut, the "base-camp" hotel high on Elbrus (there's no way for individuals to book rooms in advance at Priut). Another good reason to have an escort or two is to keep an eye on your stuff at Priut. Theft is unlikely from your room, but if you're camped outside near Priut, your tent might be raided while you're climbing.

If you go through a company, compare prices, check carefully what services are included, and look at their track record. In guided group trips, what you pay is not necessarily what you get. Most of the guide companies organizing trips in Prielbrusye are based in Moscow or St. Petersburg. Locals seem to have less idea how to facilitate mountaineering expeditions.

You don't need a permit to climb Mount Elbrus. So why not go on your own? No reason not to … if you're very flexible, thrive on uncertainty, and have endless patience. It may or may not save you money over an organized, guided trip.

If you choose to go on your own, be prepared to negotiate a lot. This may be Europe, but many of the services at Prielbrusye (chair lifts, hotels, Priut) operate the Asian way: if you get in touch with the right people, who are on good terms with the local Kabardin and Balkar chieftains, everything will go your way.

At the very least, unless you're a very experienced mountaineer with high-altitude ascents under your belt, hire a guide at the mountain. Guide fees are still low ($10 to $50 a day). Enough climbers congregate at Prielbrusye in the summer that it should be relatively easy to hook up with a guide once you're there, although this requires networking, as there's no organized guide service. If you find someone you trust and get along with, you can probably talk him or her into showing you around some other alpine routes.

Two separate groups share responsibility for rescue services on the mountain. Ostensibly, the KSP is responsible for climbers and the KSS for "hikers" (see the Rescue and Evacuation Services section of chapter 3, Staying Safe and Healthy), but the distinction is murky. Neither group has a helicopter, although supposedly the KSP can radio for one in case of emergency. Also, purportedly you can buy rescue insurance before climbing, which would cover the cost of a helicopter or other rescue operations. This sounds like a nice idea, but given the way things work at Prielbrusye, I'm skeptical about its reliability.

Western Caucasus

In the Western Caucasus, the Dombay area is at least as scenic as the Central Caucaus' Baksan Valley, and probably more pleasant because it is not as crowded. It's also known for its mild climate and large number of sunny days. From this valley at 5,250 feet (1600 m), where the wild rivers Dombay-Ulgen, Amanauz, and Alibek converge, you can see the chain of the Main Caucasus.

Another 3 miles (5 km) beyond Dombay, on the Alibek River road, is Alibek Gorge. From the climbing camp, in a grove of firs, a variety of summits and hikes are at your doorstep. This is a year-round facility, which serves skiers in winter. The top chair lift at Dombay deposits skiers at the summit of Mount Musat-Chitara. A top-to-bottom run averages 3 miles (5 km). The skiing here at Dombay is reputed to be better than at Cheget in neighboring Prielbrusye, which is steep and moguled. Beyond Teberda, you are in the Teberda *zapovednik*. Easy climbs from around Dombay include Bolshaya Marka, 12,329 feet (3758 m), Sofrudzhu, 12,421 feet (3786 m), and Sulakhat, 11,184 feet (3409 m).

Getting There

You can reach the Dombay region from either Min Vody or Cherkessk.

To reach Min Vody, there are flights from Moscow, St. Petersburg, and some other Russian cities; there is train service from Moscow, Kharkov, and Rostov. From Min Vody, the bus to Dombay takes 5 to 6 hours; the bus reaches the resort of Teberda first, then Dombay ½ hour later.

To reach Cherkessk, take the Moscow–Vladikavkaz train, which stops in Cherkessk. From Cherkessk the bus to Dombay via Teberda takes 2 to 3 hours.

You can reach Sukhumi, on the Black Sea coast, by Aeroflot service from major Russian cities. You can also drive to the Caucasus, through Rostov. From there, take the bus to Min Vody and follow the above instructions from Min Vody.

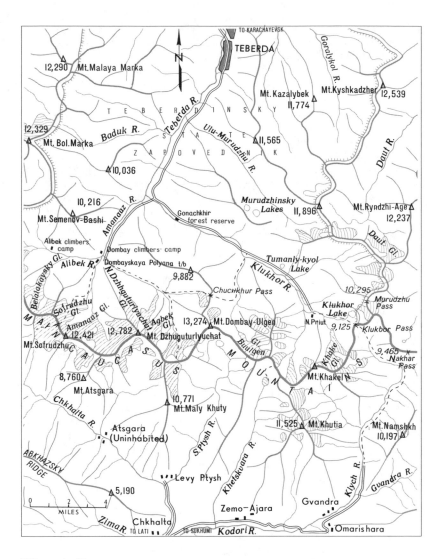

Where to Stay

In Dombay, the best hotel, called the Dombay, boasts an Olympic-size indoor pool and two discos. The most attractive place to stay is the turreted Gezag, a log fortress. Other lodgings include the Sputnik hotel, the climbers camps *alpbaza* Dombay and *alpbaza* Alibek, and *turbaza* Dombayskaya Polyana. There are also hotels in Teberda.

When to Go

June through September are most reasonable, with your best shot at good weather being July and August. After early September, the weather deteriorates and becomes colder.

Equipment and Supplies

The crowd that goes to American ski resorts Vail or Aspen for shopping will be disappointed with Dombay, which lacks all of the luxuries and most of the amenities of the typical ski village. Whether it's ski gear, climbing equipment, or camping supplies, bring your own. Food can generally be purchased from one of the hotel restaurants, to augment what you find at the market. You may end up with some surprising combinations.

DOMBAY TO SUKHUMI

This **2- to 3-day hike** goes from the north side of the Caucasus over Klukhor Pass to the south side. **Maps:** Karachaevsk K-37-VI.

From **Dombay**, hike back down the Teberda highway to as far as Gonachkhirsky gorge, then turn right onto the Sukhumi–Military Track. Hike through this scenic valley to **Lake Tumanly-Kyol**, which is a good place to camp.

Beyond the lake are pine woods; the trail follows the moraine to the **North Priut**, at about 6,500 feet (2000 m), from which the trail ascends through snowfields to the top of **Klukhor Pass**, 9,125 feet (2781 m). Just before the top of the pass is a lovely lake, Klukhor Lake. It's a steep snowfield down the south side of the pass, with the trail leading off from the lower left edge. This trail crosses numerous streams before coming out on the trail through Klych gorge. Then the descent through the woods takes you to the **South Priut**, where there's an organized campground. From the North Priut across the pass to the South Priut is **18.6 miles (30 km)**.

The trail traverses hillside slopes cut by the Klych, Chkhalta, and Kodori rivers. From the village of Gvandra, a bus runs along the Kodori River. The road passes through the village of Lati and skirts the Bogatsky cliffs to reach **Sukhumi**.

Central Caucasus

The double-breasted summit of Mount Elbrus—the 18,441-foot (5621-m) East Summit and the 18,510-foot (5642-m) West Summit—can be seen from mountain passes for miles around, looking like an adopted child in a family of rugged alpine peaks. This benign giant drains into both the Black Sea and the Caspian Sea. A nontechnical snow climb, Elbrus attracts mountaineers from all over the world aspiring to the Seven Summits club, or just wanting to push their personal altitude record. The perpetually white bulk of Elbrus (its name is of Persian origin, meaning "Snowy Mountain") lords over the Baksan Valley, a breathtaking alpine setting defaced by several slummy towns with dilapidated apartment buildings and a string of cement-block hotels that make the area resemble a seedy Chamonix. The less time you spend in the Baksan Valley proper, the more you'll appreciate Prielbrusye ("Elbrus area").

In the market at one end of the Cheget hotel parking lot, local women gather to gossip and sell gorgeous hand-dyed, -spun, and -knit sweaters and scarves. Kiosks outside the market are probably the only spot in the valley

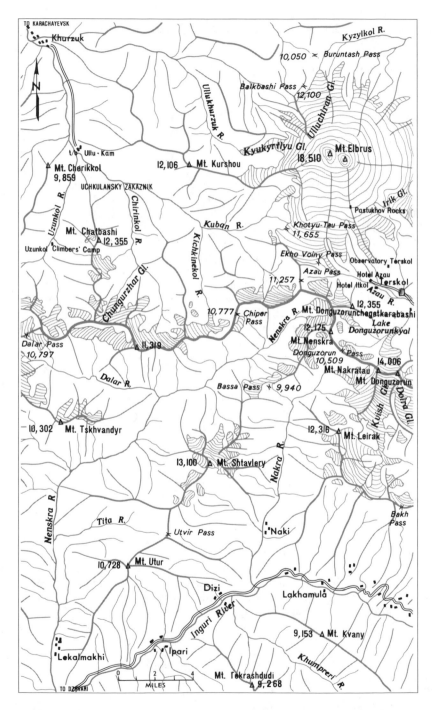

TO KARACHAYEVSK
Khurzuk

N

Kyzylkol R.
10,050 Buruntash Pass

Balkbashi Pass
12,100

Ullukhurzuk R.

Ulluchiran Gl.

t/o Ullu-Kam
Mt. Cherikkol
9,859

12,106 Mt. Kurshou

Kyukyrtlyu Gl.
18,510 Mt. Elbrus

UCHKULANSKY ZAKAZNIK

Irik Gl.
Pastukhov Rocks

Uzunkol R.

Chirinkol R.

Kuban R.

Mt. Chatbashi
12,355
Uzunkol Climbers' Camp

Khotyu-Tau Pass
11,655

Kichkinekol R.

Ekho Voiny Pass
Azau Pass
11,257

Observatory Terskol
Hotel Azau
Hotel Itkol Terskol
Azau R.

Chungurzhar Gl.

Dalar Pass
10,797

11,319

10,777 Chiper Pass

Nenskra R.

Mt. Donguzorunchegetkarabashi
12,355
Lake Donguzorunkyal
12,175
Mt. Nenskra
Donguzorun Pass
10,509
14,006
Mt. Nakratau
Mt. Donguzorun

Dalar R.

Bassa Pass 9,940

Kuish Gl.
Dolra Gl.

10,302 Mt. Tskhvandyr

12,316 Mt. Leirak

Nakra R.

13,100 Mt. Shtavlery

Nenskra R.

Tita R.

Utvir Pass

Naki

Bakh Pass

10,728 Mt. Utur

Dizi

Inguri River

Lakhamula

9,153 Mt. Kvany

Lekalmakhi

Ipari

Khumpreri R.

0   2   4
MILES
TO DZHVARI

Mt. Tekrashdudi
9,268

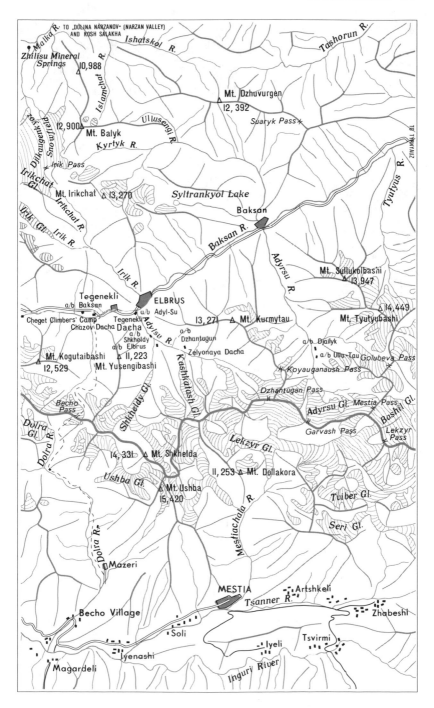

Mount Elbrus, 18,510 feet (5642 m), is the highest summit in Europe. (Photo: Pat Morrow)

where you can find postcards of Elbrus and wine for sale, though the kiosk's hours are mysterious. Inside the hotel is an espresso bar; the walls have pictures of an avalanche that buried the second-story windows.

Unlike the Alps, trails in the Caucasus are not usually marked. Hikes on the south side of Elbrus see many hikers during the summer season, so the trails across popular Becho Pass and Nakra Pass, for example, are hard to miss. Local herders also use the trails, going back and forth from the towns to the high meadows. Yusengi, Nakra, and Dolra valleys are usually full of sheep, so you should purify your drinking water diligently.

Getting There

You can reach the Central Caucasus from Mineralniye Vody (Min Vody), Nalchik, or Vladikavkaz (formerly Orzhonikidze). To reach these towns, there are flights from Moscow, St. Petersburg, and some other Russian cities. You can also reach Min Vody, Nalchik, or Vladikavkaz by train from Moscow, Kharkov, and Rostov. You can also drive to the Caucasus—through Rostov. Once you are in the Caucasus, you can travel between towns by bus.

To reach the southeastern approach to Mount Elbrus—**Prielbrusye**—take the bus from the Min Vody airport or Nalchik to the Baksan Valley; Terskol, the end of the road at the foot of Mount Elbrus, is 3 to 4 hours from Min Vody. Bus ticket windows are to the left when you emerge from the Min Vody airport. Watch for people with backpacks and climbing gear and follow them. (Prielbrusye is closer from Nalchik.) You can get off the bus anywhere along the way in the Baksan Valley. If you don't find a bus going to Prielbrusye, you can usually strike a deal with a private car going that way.

To reach one of the northern approaches to Mount Elbrus—**Khurzuk**—take the Moscow–Vladikavkaz train to Cherkessk, and take the bus or drive from Cherkessk to the village Khurzuk via Karachayevsk.

To reach another northern approach to Elbrus—the **Narzan Valley**—bus or train from Min Vody to Kislovodsk. From there you'll probably have to hire private transportation, preferably an all-terrain vehicle. The road is reasonably good as far as the tourist camp Dolina Narzanov in the Narzan Valley. The road ends at the Kharbaz River, a tributary of the Malka, but it is very rough. It will keep you alert as you consider the prospect of being plunged to the depths below. There are no villages in the area, although you may see Balkar herders' camps. Because the area is undeveloped, wild mountain goats and bear are sometimes sighted.

To reach the **Bezengi Valley**, follow the above directions to Nalchik; from Nalchik take the Nalchik–Vladikavkaz highway, then head into the mountains following the Urvan River. At the confluence of the Urvan and Cherek-Balkarsky rivers, the road continues along the churning Cherek-Balkarsky and up the Bezengi Valley. From the town of Bezengi (3 to 4 hours from Nalchik), 20 steep winding kilometers bring you to Bezengi climbers camp.

To reach **Kazbegi**, from Min Vody or Nalchik, take the bus through Vladikavkaz to Kazbegi. There is also a bus to Kazbegi from Tbilisi, Georgia. There are direct flights to Tbilisi from Vienna, St. Petersburg, and Moscow.

Where to Stay

In **Prielbrusye** (the area around the southeast side of Elbrus), the road from Tirnyauz follows the Baksan River through the villages Verkhny Baksan, Elbrus, Tegenekli, and Terskol. The Adylsu River road branches off to the southeast just past the town of Elbrus; scattered along this road are a series of climbers camps: Adyl-Su, Shkheldy, Elbrus, Dzhantugan. These, and another camp just past Tegenekli—Baksan—formerly belonged to the Trade Unions Sports Organization (VCSPS). In the good old days, they were crowded with young climbers (see the A History of Backpacking and Mountaineering in Russia section in chapter 1, Introduction). Now that the VCSPS system has unraveled and young people can no longer afford to go to the mountains, many of these camps are empty. You may be able to stay at one of them inexpensively. They're basic, ranging from dormitory-style to double rooms. Meals are the mess-hall kind. You can generally hitch a ride to the climbers camps Elbrus and Shkheldy. Dzhantugan, at the very end of the road with little traffic going that way, is a long walk. However, it's in a scenic spot with good access to hikes and climbs.

Another camp, Ullu-Tau, is up the Adyrsu valley (not to be confused with Adylsu), a gorgeous hideaway surrounded by jagged Peaks Jailik-Tau, Adyr-su Tau, and Mestia Tau, and dwarfed by the 13,123-foot (4000-m) wall of Ullu Tau. The road up to Adyr Su takes off south out of the village of Verkhny Baksan. Where it's blocked by a cliff, a vehicle elevator connects the upper and lower sections of road. The trail goes around the side.

Typically, foreign climbers stay in one of the hotels on the main drag: Itkol, Cheget, or Sokol. Another hotel at the foot of the moutain, the Azau, has been closed for remodeling for several years.

The luxurious way to go—and not necessarily more expensive than the cockroach-infested hotels—is one of the *dachas*. The beauty of the Central Caucasus wasn't lost on Communist party bosses and they had a number of chalets in the valley. The Zelyonaya Dacha, Chazov Dacha, and Tegenekli Dacha now accept foreign guests. These places have well-appointed private bedroom/sitting rooms and bathrooms. The Zelyonaya Dacha has an elegant dining room, lovely sauna, and—for a price—several three- and four-room deluxe suites. Another nice lodge, Djailyk, is up the Adyrsu valley. These places may or may not be accepting individual guests, as they are generally booked by organizations.

The world's highest hotel, a quonset hut at 13,780 feet (4200 m) called Priut Odinnadtsati ("Refuge of Eleven"), houses 120 people. Three successive chair lifts reach almost to Priut. Due to the easy access, Priut is often overcrowded in summer. Many people come up just to enjoy the spectacular view and spend the night at the world's highest hotel. At the most crowded times, people vie for space on the floors, though permission to do even this requires bribes to the appropriate administrators. An alternative is to bring your tent and camp in the rocks a couple hundred yards from Priut. The facilities, including kitchen, common area, and a filthy outhouse with a very airy view down, are just as accessible. You may even sleep *better*, as Priut can be noisy at night.

On the north side of Elbrus, near **Khurzuk**, there is the *turbaza* Ullu-Kam and, farther up the road, the Uzunkol Climbers Camp. In the **Narzan Valley**, there is the tourist camp Dolina Narzanov.

In the **Bezengi Valley**, there are cabins at the Bezengi Climbers Camp.

In **Kazbegi**, the Intourist hotel rates two stars, but it might be worth an overnight if you've been awhile without a shower.

When to Go

For climbing and hiking in the Central Caucasus, June through September is most reasonable (although Mount Elbrus does get climbed year-round), with your best shot at good weather being July and August. After early September, the weather deteriorates and becomes colder.

Equipment and Supplies

As with Dombay in the Western Caucasus, you can't count on finding ski or climbing gear for rent or sale in the Central Caucasus, although these are world-class alpine centers. Some of the seasonal kiosks offer an unpredictable selection of items, but even basics such as sunscreen or sunglasses are not reliably available. Here again, your best bet for purchasing food for outings is from the hotel restaurants, which have much greater variety than the few stores.

For the **ascent of Mount Elbrus**, special equipment is required. See the

Mount Elbrus Ascent section below. For the **Ullu-Tau-to-Mestia trek**, you will need a rope and ice screws—and the ability to use them.

DAY HIKES AROUND PRIELBRUSYE

The name **Zelyonaya Gostinitsa** ("Green Hotel") describes the way these inviting meadows at the top of the Adylsu valley feel to those returning from the several rugged alpine climbs this trail provides access to. From *alpbaza* Dzhantugan, the walk is about **1½ hours**. Like many valleys in the area, it begins with a steep section, but most of the walking is along a well-trodden trail with gentle elevation gain. To extend your day hike, there are good campsites not far from the lower ends of the glaciers.

Yusengibashi/Becho Pass is a scenic **3- to 4-hour round-trip** hike up a steep valley opening into scenic meadows at times reminiscent of the Alps. The trailhead is easy to find: going up the main road from Tegenekli village, it leaves to the left (south) just before the first bridge (over the Yusengi River). For 1½ hours, the obvious path climbs steeply through a wooded valley alongside the cascading river, suddenly opening into meadows at about 8,000 feet (2400 m). The trail is a well-worn dirt path, used fairly regularly by local herders tending flocks up the valley. If it has rained recently, the trail may get muddy and slippery on the steeper sections. For rock climbers, someone has put in a few bolts on some boulder problems along the trail. The meadows appear quite suddenly and the trail levels off. A wet plain spreads out where the meltwater meets from the slopes of rugged Yusengibashi and Becho peaks directly ahead. This trail continues through the valley to cross Becho Pass into Svanetia (see Svanetia Circuit, below), but the hike to the meadows and back is one of the nicer day hikes in Prielbrusye.

In winter, **Mount Cheget** becomes the Baksan ski scene, with its very moguled hill. In the summer, the chair lift sometimes takes tourists up for spectacular views of the valley and of Mount Elbrus. An unpleasantly steep trail winds its way up under the **first chair lift** (**1- to 2-hour walk**). From there a disused service road continues up **another hour** past the top of the **final chair lift**. Another **40 minutes** on rocky trails to a series of **false summits** rewards the hiker with breathtaking views of Elbrus to the northwest and Donguzorun-Tau to the east. The Number 7 Glacier, named for its distinct shape, clings to the face of Donguzorun, making this mountain look incredibly foreboding. The trails fade out at an obvious false summit. You can scramble a bit farther to a second or third false summit, but to continue to the actual summit of Cheget is a technical climb on a ridge of mixed rock and snow. The base of the chair lift at Cheget is just over 6,600 feet (2000 m) and the false summit at the trail's end is just under 11,000 feet (about 3350 m). It's an excellent training day for those going on to climb, but the views are just as worthy if you take one or both of the lifts up to 10,500 feet (3200 m) and walk from there. Unfortunately, the bare ski hill slopes are less attractive in the summer when snow no longer hides the skiers' litter.

The **Donguzorun/Nakra Pass** trail under the shadow of massive Donguzorun-Tau leads up from the parking lot at the base of Mount Cheget, past the hotel and chair lifts. **Two hours** of steady uphill walking leads to

Donguzorun Lake, fed by glaciers on two sides. Just past the lake are the ruins of Severny Priut ("North Refuge").

MESTIA-TAU ASCENT

This is a **class 1B climb** of 13,550-foot (4130-m) Mestia-Tau, which can be climbed in a day; it's **5 hours from Mestia Pass**. Basic alpine gear is required: ice axe, crampons (though you may not need them), rope, and a few ice screws just in case.

Traverse the Mestia Plateau (hidden crevasses) under the southwest slopes of Mestia-Tau and ascend a snow and ice slope to the saddle between Mestia-Tau and Pik Miit. From the saddle, ascend the broad snow and ice ridge (cornices) for 800 feet (250 m), then climb a 130-foot (40-m) rise onto a shoulder. From here, ascend the broad snow and ice slope of the southwest ridge to a rocky step. Ascend its easy, broken rocks (loose stones, belay) to the south ridge. Now turn left and follow the ridge to the summit. (This description of the Mestia-Tau climb is reprinted with permission from *Classic Climbs in the Caucasus,* by Friedrich Bender.)

MOUNT ELBRUS CIRCUIT

Exodus Expeditions contributed this description of the trek they do circling Mount Elbrus counter-clockwise from the Baksan Valley in **7 to 10 days**:

From the village of Elbrus, hike up the steep path through alpine meadows and pine groves high above the Irikhat River. It's best to camp a couple thousand feet below **Irikhat Pass**.

Once over Irikhat Pass, 11,950 feet (3640 m), there's a short but steep descent to the Djikaukengyoz Snowfield, which you cross to reach a wide moraine. **Two hours** beyond the moraine is good camping on a braided gravel fan with spectacular views of extinct volcanoes, black basalt walls, and multi-colored cliffs. From here hike on down to the **Irikhitsyrt Plateau** at about 9,500 feet (2900 m).

Following the Kyzylkol River, climb the valley past Buruntash Pass, 10,050 feet (3063 m) to camp below **Balkbashi Pass**, 12,100 feet (3688 m). Balkbashi Pass has been used for centuries for transporting local products to markets in the Malka Valley.

To reach Balkbashi Pass, after crossing the Kyzylsu River, follow the well-trod path to the saddle, where there are good views of Elbrus's west summit. Follow the easy, gradual descent along the Ullukhurzuk River, through pine forests. Cross the river several times over well-constructed bridges before entering the picturesque village of **Khurzuk**, at the confluence of the Ullukhurzuk and Ullukam rivers. Nearby is a small watchtower dating back to the twelfth century and Tamerlane.

A climbers' side trip: 13.6 miles (22 km) from Khurzuk is the Uzunkol Climbers Camp, in the Uchkulansky *Zakaznik*. Around Uzunkol are numerous challenging rock climbs, including the famous rock fortress Dalar, 13,054 feet (3979 m). (If you want to reach this area without hiking the Mount Elbrus circuit, you can bus or drive to the village Khurzuk from Cherkessk via Karachayevsk.)

Hike up the beautiful Ullu-Kam Valley. Climb **several hours** and camp below Khotyu Tau Pass, 11,630 feet (3545 m).

From the saddle at Khotyu Tau Pass, the huge Khotyu Tau snowfield stretches out to the base of the south face of Elbrus. Cross the small Azau Glacer to attain the pass Ekho Voini ("Echo of the War"), 11,250 feet (3430 m), and descend the steep slope to camp on a sandy ledge overlooking the Baksan Valley.

Hike over loose boulders to the snout of the glacier, past the basalt cliffs on Elbrus's southwestern slopes to the lower cable station at Hotel Azau near Terskol.

MOUNT ELBRUS ASCENT

An ascent of Elbrus is not a trek. The mountain's easy accessibility makes many underestimate it. Like any mountain bigger than everything else around it, Elbrus makes its own weather. On a day when the rest of the Caucasus basks in sunshine, high winds can batter the summit of Elbrus and the weather may deteriorate rapidly.

While the standard route on the mountain presents little objective danger, in a whiteout you can easily get off route and wander into a crevassed area. Additionally, because the hotel high on the mountain, Priut, can be attained so quickly (in one day from sea level), climbers are often tempted to push for the summit without taking enough time to acclimatize.

High altitude and big-mountain weather combine to pick off climbers: each season people die on Elbrus. Attempt it only if you have experience with snow climbing techniques and have previously climbed to at least 14,000 feet (4000 m)—see the discussion of altitude sickness in the Health and Medical Problems section of chapter 3, Staying Safe and Healthy. Crampons are generally used, at least until the sun comes up and softens the snow, and are essential in the event that sections of the route become icy. Ice axes should be carried, although they are sometimes unnecessary. Plastic climbing boots are good protection against frostbite on Elbrus (see the Climbers' Equipment section in chapter 2, Preparing for Your Trek). The angle is gradual all the way to the top of Elbrus and many climbers find ski poles helpful in maintaining balance and forward momentum. Elbrus is commonly climbed unroped, although a party should be prepared to rope up should a storm impair visibility. For those who'd rather hike than climb, there are many nice day and multiday hikes in the area.

The keys to success on Mount Elbrus are physical conditioning and careful acclimatization before the climb, and good pacing during the ascent. Rest step to victory! Many strong climbers are turned back even in perfect weather because they underestimate the mountain and don't acclimatize enough.

Elbrus's nearly symmetrical cone was first climbed in 1829 by Killar Khashirov, the Kabardin guide accompanying a company of Russian soldiers under the command of General Emmanuel. They ascended **from the north**, along the Malka River. Nowadays, virtually all climbers ascend from the south, ignoring the North Elbrus valleys where "Narzan," a reddish liquid reputed to be the best mineral water in Russia, springs from the ground. At the head of the Malka River, the Zhilisu Mineral Springs are a popular camping spot. There are no buildings, but there is a crude hot springs tub.

A climb of Elbrus via routes other than the standard southern one is a serious mountaineering endeavor: no chair lifts, no hotels, no flagged trail. You are much farther from the possibility of help if you need it. Depending on exactly where the snowline is on the Irakhik Plateau, you'll have 7,000 to 8,000 vertical feet (2000 to 2400 m) of snow climbing, much of it crevassed. If you want to descend to the south—a shorter, safer descent route—you'll have to carry all your gear as far as the saddle between Elbrus's east and west summits.

The overwhelming majority of climbers go up the **south (Baksan Valley) side** of Mount Elbrus. While the summit day itself is long and exhausting because of the high altitude, the climb of Elbrus from the Baksan Valley offers more comforts than that of any other big mountain. In addition to the hotels in Terskol, there's the world's highest hotel, Priut Odinnadtsati.

Three successive chair lifts reach almost to the Priut, although at any given time at least one of these is usually out of service. A snowcat operates on the last several hundred meters from the top chair to Priut. The second cablecar crashed in 1992, killing one Russian passenger and seriously injuring several others. (To avoid riding these ill-maintained chairs—and to gain better acclimatization—you may want to hike all the way up to Priut along the rough road left from construction of the cablecars.)

A **typical ascent** of the mountain takes **4 days**, after several days' acclimatization on day hikes in the valley (some of the more popular ones are described above). If you have the time, it's better not to push this fast. Giving yourself a couple days of leeway improves your chances of summitting in case you're unlucky with the weather.

The **first day** is spent going up from **Terskol to Priut**, 13,780 feet (4200 m), **6 to 7 hours**, and settling in. The **next day**, most climbers go only as far as the **Pastukhov Rocks**, 15,748 feet (4800 m), an obvious rock band about **2 hours** from Priut, and **return to Priut**. On **summit day**, with a pre-dawn start, the climb via the Pastukhov Rocks and the saddle, 17,160 feet (5230 m), between the east and west summits takes **6 to 10 hours**. The climb from Priut is all on snow, without any crevasses on the standard route. Dozens of people climb Elbrus every day at the height of summer, so the route is well trodden. The **descent** is another **3 to 5 hours**. Most climbers overnight again at Priut before descending.

DOLINA NARZANOV TO BAKSAN

This is a **4-day trek** across Mount Elbrus' north flank. It is described here from north to south, but it can also be done from south to north (Baksan to Dolina Narzanov)—just reverse the description.

From **Dolina Narzanov** in the Narzan Valley, an all-terrain track goes most of the way to Zhilisu (which, if driven, would shorten the trek by two days). However, you can hike from Dolina Narzanov, keeping off roads. Moderate forest trails lead to the open grassy ridges of Balkaria. There are panoramic views of the Central Caucasus and especially Mount Elbrus staring you in the face. A carpet of lobelia, daisies, and forget-me-nots stretches as far as the eye can see.

The track winds up to the Bichesyn Plateau, with the Malka flowing in a deep canyon on the left. Easy **Kayaeshik Pass**, 8,200 feet (2500 m), leads into the basin of the Malka headwaters. Drop down to the *kosh* (herders' summer camp) in the Kyzylkol River valley, **Kosh Salakha, 11 miles (18 km), 4 to 6 hours**.

From Kosh Salakha, head east up the obvious stream valley. After about **1.5 miles (2 to 3 km)**, turn south, paralleling the stream uphill to the edge of the Malka Valley, with views of the canyon below. Descend for about **1.25 miles (2 km)** into mixed woods and meadows. **About 4 miles (6 or 7 km)** of flat hiking along the Malka Valley brings you to the **waterfall Karakash**. Cross a footbridge and ascend **another hour** along herders' paths to **Zhilisu, 7.5 miles** total from Kosh Salakha **(12 km), 6 to 7 hours**. The Zhilisu Mineral Springs are just lukewarm, but the setting makes up for it. A raging torrent called "The Cirque" tumbles down directly over the hot springs. Two other waterfalls, the Karakash and Sultan, are within easy walking distance from camp.

The easiest way to hike to the Baksan Valley from Zhilisu is across Kyrtykaush Pass. You can also cross steeper Irikhat Pass or take the long way around to the west (see Mount Elbrus Circuit, above). Follow the good horse trail east, ascending the Islamchat terraces and then climbing through ancient moraines to the Islamchat Valley. The summits Karakaya and Balyk protect this valley from Elbrus' romping glaciers. The hike to **Kyrtykaush Pass (6 to 8 hours)** is long and gradual. It translates from Balkar as the "pass to which one walks up grassy slopes," and is the main thoroughfare for herders. You can camp right on the pass, where you'll find water.

From Kyrtykaush Pass, descend scree slopes down the other side to the Kyrtyk Valley, where there's another *kosh*. The trail zigzags down along the Ullusengi River toward where it converges with the Kyrtyk, in the hanging valley Ullusengi. A couple hours lower is another *kosh*, where the Zugullu River feeds into the Kyrtyk. The trail leads you into the north edge of the village **Verkhny Baksan (6 to 8 hours)**. (If you're doing this hike from south to north, at the bridge across the Syltransu, take the trail to the *right*.)

SVANETIA CIRCUIT

One mountain pass separates Kabardino–Balkaria from the ancient kingdom of Georgia. Top either Becho Pass or Nakra Pass and you'll find yourself in Upper Svanetia, Georgia's remote, mountainous northern province. To visit Svanetia is to step into another century. The trek described here, from the north side of the range in Baksan to the south side of the Central Caucasus, is a truly world-class one that is, however, risky as long as the war continues in north Georgia. See the introduction to this chapter.

Upper Svanetia, squeezed between some of the most savage peaks of the Caucasus in the upper reaches of the Inguri River, is something of a natural fortress. Roads and modern communications reached Mestia, the region's administrative center (population 3,700), relatively late. Even today to get there by car from Zugdidi, the nearest major city, takes more than 4 hours and, especially in winter, is a hazardous trip due to avalanches that frequently wipe out stretches of road. The inaccessibility of the region has helped to preserve traditional ways among the people of Svanetia.

These watchtowers of Svanetia, a province of northern Georgia, serve as a reminder that the contentious relations between neighboring ethnic groups in this region can be traced back many centuries. (Photo: Vadim Gippenreiter)

The Svan people, who speak their own language, are one of many ethnic groups in Georgia. Throughout history, the Svans have fought off invasion by the Kabardins, Balkars, and other tribes of the northern Caucasus. The four-story stone watchtowers the Svans built as a defense still stand today—more than 200 of them in Mestia alone. On the opposite side of the river from town, a classic Soviet *turbaza* detracts from Mestia's medieval character, but otherwise the town is charming. The *turbaza* may also be the only place to stay and get a shower.

For the most part, tribes who live in the mountains do not climb mountains; Svanetia is the exception to the rule. Not only is Svanetia popular with mountaineers—some of the classic climbs in the Caucasus are here—but Svanetia produces fine alpinists. Misha Hergiani, considered in his day to be the Soviet Union's foremost alpinist, hailed from Mestia. Hergiani died climbing in Italy in 1969; today his house, one of the watchtowers, is a museum.

While most climbers use modern synthetic clothing, locals cross Becho Pass in standard shepherd garb. (Photo: Pat Morrow)

The cultural experience of Mestia is icing on the cake; the scenery in Svanetia is reason enough to go backpacking there. Although you can do this **loop from the Baksan Valley** in **4 days**, you should really plan on a day or two in Mestia. The trails to Becho and Nakra passes from the Baksan see a lot of hikers and should be easy to find. In several places it may be necessary to ford rivers. **Map:** Mestia K-38-VII.

Approach Becho Pass from the **Yusengi Valley**. The trailhead is easy to find: going up the main road from Tegenekli village, it leaves to the left (south) just before the first bridge over the Yusengi River (see Day Hikes Around Prielbrusye, above). Hike about **3 hours** on a dirt trail. This trail passes through part of the Kabardino–Balkar High Mountain *Zapovednik*. Above the meadows, the path ascends the moraine to the glacier. On the glacier, where there are usually no open crevasses, traverse right (about **1 hour**), then climb up the snowfield to the rocky **Becho Pass**. You'll be hiking in snow for approximately 2 hours (the last few hundred feet) even in summer, though crampons are not necessary. From the top of the pass, 10,581 feet (3225 m), you're rewarded with fabulous views of Mount Ushba and Mount Shkhelda.

From Becho Pass, descend steep scree slopes toward the **Kerunda Glacier**. The trail follows the left edge of the glacier through a saddle. In places where the going is steep, you may find a fixed handline. Drop down over numerous moraine ridges to the lush **Dolra Valley**, a logical place to camp. If you don't stop here, it's a very long day from Baksan. From this beautiful valley, you can see the last icefall of the Dolra Glacier. Notes from my Caucasus journal:

> *Perched on a rock in the Dolra Valley, hugging my legs from the cold. My companions not yet awake. Mist veils the green hillsides and the surrounding peaks—a shroud that gives the whole scene a surreal quality. Nothing moving in the valley. Even the black cows, which the Svan milkmaid drove up at first light, stand stolidly immobile as boulders. The shepherd woman sits on a rock waving distance away, knitting. The physical and metaphysical seem miraculously connected.*

The trail follows the Dolra River down through the forest. Emerging from the woods into the broad Becho Valley, it turns into a road, reaching the village **Mazeri** in **2.5 miles** (**4 km**), then **Becho Village** in **3.75 miles** (**6 km**), **8 to 10 hours** more from Becho Pass. From Becho Village, you're on the highway and are better off trying to get a lift into **Mestia**. There's lodgings in Mestia, and it's worth visiting the town for a day or two.

From Mestia, get the bus to **Dizi**. (If you can arrange a ride, it's better to go as far as the village of Naki and avoid walking the dusty road.) From Dizi, the road climbs steeply, passing through the village of Shtakeri before Naki. **Naki village**, a settlement of houses scattered over 3 miles (5 km), is the last community.

Your guide back into the alpine is the **Nakra River**, fed by majestic Mount Nakratau. Follow the churning white water upstream, starting out through forest, which transitions to bushy undergrowth and finally meadows. Higher up, where you hike through the **Nakra Valley**, this wild mountain river is just a stream, swallowed up in places by the abundant wildflowers. The **meadows several hours below the pass**, above the Nakra River, are a good place to camp. The scenery is stupendous.

The trail winds right toward the **pass, called variously Nakra and Donguzorun**, through luxurious alpine meadows. You'll be in snow near the pass, **12 to 14 hours** from Naki. Drop down the north side to **Donguzorun Lake and Cheget, 2 to 3 hours**.

ULLU-TAU TO MESTIA

Donguzorun/Nakra Pass is an easy way to hurdle the spine of the Main Caucasus from north to south. But going over Mestia Pass and down the Lekzyr Glacier is a beautiful, wild, and **challenging 3-day alpine crossing** into Svanetia. It requires a rope, ice screws, and mountaineering skills. Again, while there is strife in north Georgia, this area is unsafe for travel.

From **camp Ullu-Tau** in the Adyrsu River valley southeast from Baksan village, ascend the path up the left bank of the Adyrsu River to below Triangle Peak and the site of the **Mestia Bivouac**, 2 to 3 hours from camp. Continue up the left lateral moraine of the Adyrsu Glacier to the glacier snout. Traverse this to the right to the scree of a rock island. Turn at the island on the left and continue up a path to the top of the island and **Mestia Hut, 3 to 4 hours** from camp. The hut sleeps about a dozen people.

From the hut, descend to the Adyrsu Glacier and cross, then ascend 230 feet (70 m) over a steep snow and ice rise on the right side of some rocks onto a plateau. Traverse this and climb up over a steep 165-foot (50-m) rise between rock islands. Then turn right and ascend the snowfields and slopes of the Adyrsu Glacier, crossing two wide crevasses by snow bridges, onto the snow plateau between Ullu-Tau, Sarikol, and **Mestia Pass**, 12,660 feet (3859 m). This is a possible bivy site, 3 to 4 hours from Mestia Hut. (This description from Camp Ullu Tau to Mestia Hut is reprinted with permission from *Classic Climbs in the Caucasus*, by Friedrich Bender.)

From the pass rises a 30-degree slope that can be ice by late summer. To the right of this slope is a moraine you can get onto where it turns the corner from south to west, then flattens out. The trail follows the moraine skirting the edge of the glacier. Where the glacier flattens out, you should walk it west towards the "Lekzyir Cross." Three tongues converge into the south-flowing **Lekzyr Glacier**. You need to descend the center of this ice dragon.

Lower down, the route is over moraines to the left edge of the glacier, cliffy in places. At the bottom of the glacier is an insurmountable icefall. Get off on the left by crossing the stream, or, if there's too much water, look for a snow bridge higher up. Below the icefall, a trail appears along the left bank of the **Tuiber**. Passing through meadows and forest groves, this path eventually turns into a rutted road leading into **Mestia, 8 to 10 hours** from Mestia Hut.

From Mestia, the road follows the Inguri River on steep hillsides of cherry-laurel, chestnut, and walnut, passing picturesque Svan villages. From Mestia to Zugdidi, it's a 4- or 5-hour drive. At Zugdidi, you can catch a train to Batumi, Tbilisi, or Sochi, Georgia.

BEZENGI ASCENTS

East of the Baksan Valley, at elevation 7,200 feet (2200 m) near the biggest glacial system in the Caucasus—the Ullu-Shiran-Bezengi—are some of the most superlative views and hardest climbing anywhere in the Caucasus. The **Bezengi Wall** is a test piece for even very experienced mountaineers. The 7.5-mile-long (12-km-long) wall is punctuated from east to west by challenging 15,000- and 16,000-foot (4500- and 4800-m) summits.

Isolated routes on these peaks range from grade 2B to 5B (see the Soviet Climbing Route Rating System section in chapter 1, Introduction). The traverse of the whole wall is considered one of the hardest routes anywhere. In the vicinity of

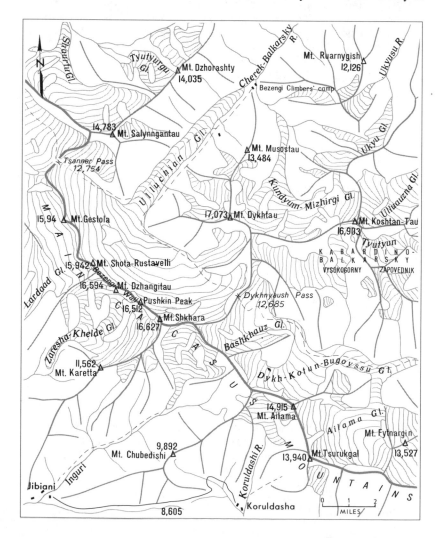

the Bezengi Wall are other world-famous summits, including **Dykhtau**, 17,073 feet (5298 m), **Koshtan-Tau**, 16,903 feet (5151 m), **Pushkin Peak**, 16,512 feet (5100 m), and **Mizhirgi**, 16,486 feet (5025 m).

MOUNT KAZBEK ASCENT

The Kazbek region is located at the eastern end of the Central Caucasus and is an almost independent mountain system. The region is made up of several prominent mountain ridges, which spread out like the fingers of a hand northward into the Dagestan Highlands and only in one place, at the watershed of the two big rivers of Ardon and Terek, link up with the Main Ridge of the Caucasus. Here, between the upper stretches of these rivers, rise numerous important 4000ers. Close to the prominent 15,882-foot (4780-m) Mount Dzhimara rises the dominating volcanic cone of Kazbek, at 16,512 feet (5047 m) the highest peak in the region.

The mountain was first climbed in 1868 by a party led by Douglas Freshfield. In those days there was no information and the Georgian Highway was still only a rough track, yet the pioneers penetrated this mountain world with their heavy equipment, enduring unimaginable hardships. Nowadays, a good motor road leads very comfortably to the village of Kazbegi below Gergeti, traditional starting point for the very rewarding ascent to the summit.

Irrespective of the lack of technical problems on this and other routes, one

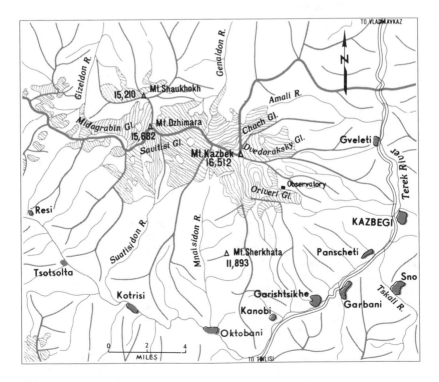

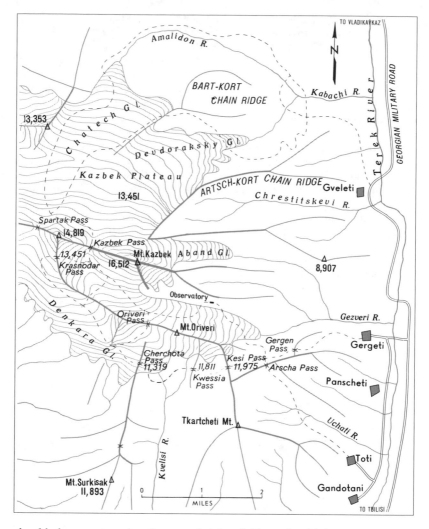

should always remember the great height of this peak with its propensity for dangerous changes of weather. In the automatic meteorological measuring station, which is quite low in elevation, temperatures down to -47°C in summer and -70°C in winter have been recorded.

The customary **1-day ascent** goes from Kazbegi village to the Observatory at 12,073 feet (3680 m), a big concrete meteorological station that was built in 1933; from there the climb follows glaciers and snowfields. **Maps:** K-38-XV Per. Krestovy, K-38-IX Ordzhinikidze.

From the **village of Kazbegi**, 5,577 feet (1700 m), ascend the track right of the hairpins along a former stretch of railway until immediately opposite the Gergeti Church, 5,906 feet (1800 m). Now ascend the valley on the left or, better still, on the right side, cross a ridge and follow a well-trodden path to the edge of the glacier. From here the **Observatory** is already visible and is reached easily by a route straight up the Gergeti Glacier, **4 to 6 hours** from Kazbegi village.

From the Observatory, go west along a well-trodden path to an unmanned meteorological measuring station. Now continue below the southwest face in a northwesterly direction or, better still, get on to the glacier near the measuring station. Ascend the middle of the glacier around Kazbek, gaining height until the notch of the double summit is visible. Now make a long steady climb straight up the snow and ice slopes to the notch and then over more or less (according to the weather) icy, easy slopes to the summits, **6 to 8 hours** from the Observatory.

(This description of the climb of Mount Kazbek is reprinted with permission from *Classic Climbs in the Caucasus*, by Friedrich Bender.)

Eastern Caucasus

Dagestan is a remarkable mountain kingdom in the Eastern Caucasus famed for illustrious carpets, silver crafts, and pottery. The Bogossky Range, in northeastern Dagestan, offers a chance to trek in lovely mountain country through villages left by the wayside during the industrial revolution, with no roads and no electricity. The scenery is exotic, arid, and alluring. The foothills, which rise almost directly out of the principal city of Makhachkala, are cut with a dusty ribbon of road that winds through vineyards and cornfields.

Persian writing decorates tombstones in Dagestan, a Muslim province of the Eastern Caucasus.

The tunnel to the village of Gimri, a 2.5-mile (4-km) plunge into the bowels of the earth, spits you out into a striking mountainscape. Long ridges banded accordion-fashion with cliffs suggest a colorful fortress of steep slopes and ravines. The colors are all earth tones; there are no trees. Sunflowers lining the road shoulder turn their smiles south.

Climbers consider Southern Dagestan the most interesting corner of the republic. The Yeredag *alpbaza* just outside Kurush, Europe's highest village at 11,500 feet (3500 m), offers access to many climbing routes. From here you can climb Bazardyuzyu, 14,650 feet (4466 m), Dagestan's highest summit, and nearby Shalbuzdag, which legend holds to be a sacred mountain.

Among the traditional *auls* (as villages are called in Dagestan) is Gimri, birthplace of Shamil, the nineteenth-century Dagestani hero. Shamil led the resistance to the Russians for more than thirty years. His small band of militants used their familiarity with the forbidding geography of the mountain fastnesses to hold the Russian troops at bay, surrendering only in 1859 when Shamil was betrayed and surrounded.

Dagestan is an ethnic mosaic. Its mostly Muslim population of 2 million speaks thirty-two different languages (newspapers are published in seven of these languages): many of these tongues are unintelligible to inhabitants of neighboring towns. These linguistic defenses, and the towns built in the most geographically formidable places, all reflect the history of invasions that people in these parts have suffered over the centuries.

Today, Russian is the lingua franca. Makhachkala, where Russians are in the majority, is not particularly interesting. Outside Makhachkala, most of the towns have preserved traditional ways. One of Dagestan's main ethnic groups, Avartsi, live mostly in Upper Dagestan, speaking their own dialect of the Avarsky language.

Kubachi and Bolshoi Gotsatl are two *auls* celebrated for local artisans' silverwork, where these craft traditions live on. In Bolshoi Gotsatl, more than 300 silversmiths decorate jewelry, vases, and swordcases with elaborate *chern*—blackened silver inlay. In some others, like the famous pottery town of Balkhar, very few masters are left. Utsunkul is reknowned for its wood inlay craftsmen.

The people of Dagestan, growers of pears, peaches, plums, and apricots, have always been relatively well off because fruit is an expensive luxury in Russia's cold northern reaches. The Dagestani houses, two-storied affairs fronted by enclosed verandas completely glassed in with hundreds of tiny panes, are evidence of Dagestan's economic well-being. The tightly clustered towns perch precariously on the steep hillsides, some distance from the orchards down in the river valleys. Fruit-growing extends all the way to the village of Agvali.

Legend holds that he who summits seven times on the mountain Shalbuzdag supposedly earns a place in Mecca. And if you happen to be a "she"? Forget about Mecca. Islam in Dagestan appears to be little more egalitarian than Islam anywhere else. Women aren't allowed into services at the mosques, which are enjoying a revival after decades of religious repression under the Soviets. Women shadow men in public life, serve them at home. All women, even very small girls, cover

A Dagestani woman carries hay to her livestock.

their heads with scarves. Women do most of the hard labor, from carrying water in metal jugs slung across their backs with scarves, to hauling huge loads of straw, stooped beneath which they are barely visible.

Dagestan remains part of Russia, and has until now avoided the ethnic conflicts splintering neighboring Georgia and other regions of the Caucasus. Like other Caucasus peoples, Dagestanis have earned a reputation for being patriotic, passionate, proud, and overwhelmingly hospitable.

The cultural diversity, combined with striking mountainscapes, makes this a fascinating place to travel, if not an easy one. There is no tourist infrastructure, and not even fluent Russian—let alone English—will do you much good in most of the outlying areas. On the other hand, people are very friendly and not resistant to photographs.

The Dagestan roads are indescribably bad. Even the republic's major arteries cannot be called highways—most of them are unpaved, heavily potholed, hairpin zigzags up steep mountainsides. By road, it's a full day's travel from Makhachkala to Agvali, where the trek described below begins. Don't make the mistake of imagining an all-day bus ride the perfect opportunity to catch up on your sleep—you will spend those eight hours clinging to your seat and praying the driver holds most of the bus wheels from the precipice. The last four hours' drive from Tindi is along the river, where the road is still rough but not as harrowing.

Getting There

The starting point for this area, Agvali, can be reached from the cities of Makhachkala, Grozny, or Vladikavkaz (formerly Ordzhonikidze). To get to these cities, there are flights from Moscow, St. Petersburg, and some other Russian cities. You can also take the train from Moscow, Kharkov, and Rostov to Vladikavkaz. From Makhachkala there is currently a daily flight to Agvali (as well as flights to Sovetskoye, near Ratlub), and a bus from Makhachkala to Agvali (8 hours). You can try hitchhiking, but there's relatively little traffic on these roads, and this is unlikely to be faster than the bus. From Grozny or Vladikavkaz, it's possible to drive to Agvali.

Where to Stay

Outside of Makhachkala, local hotels are best avoided. And in the mountains, there simply aren't any. If the weather isn't suitable for camping, your best bet is to find someone who will take you in for the night and pay them the equivalent of $5 or so. Private homes tend to be spacious. Plumbing conveniences are usually lacking, facilities being the outhouse and the public bath. Most homes get their water from springs. There are lots of cattle, sheep, and goats, so be wary of water sources.

When to Go

June through September is the best time to go. The winter rains begin in late September. Mosquitoes are generally not a problem here.

Equipment and Supplies

While TV and Soviet culture have affected the more accessible villages, the life-style is still traditional, and quite conservative. Neither female nor male trekkers are advised to wear shorts in the towns or villages. It does get hot here in the summer, making it uncomfortable to hike in long pants. You might want to bring a pair of loose-fitting cotton or nylon pants that you can pull on over your shorts when you come to a settlement.

A campstove is an absolute must; in the mountains people burn dried cow dung. They collect it throughout the summer, plaster the *kizyak* (cowpies) onto the side of the house to dry and then stack it like firewood for the winter.

In Dagestan, cowpies are dried, then stored in sheds for later use as fuel during the cold mountain winters.

Meat and dairy products are the mainstay of the diet: a salty homemade cheese, curds, kefir. At home, people bake delicious *lepyoshki* (rounds of bread) and a Dagestan dish called *chudu*—dough stuffed with potatoes, meat, or cheese—is very tasty. There's no peanut butter here, but the locals make a spread (called *urbech*) from ground apricot pits, hemp seeds, and honey that's even better. I tested their theory that *urbech* provided enough energy to keep you hiking for hours, and wasn't disappointed. You can buy fruit and vegetables in the market in Agvali.

AGVALI TO GOCHOB

This 75-mile (120-km), 7- to 9-day trek crosses the Bogossky Range between the Andiisky Koisu River and the Avarsky Koisu River. It can be shortened to a 43-mile (70-km), 5- to 7-day trek. Route finding is generally easy. This trek follows major river drainages, named for the communities they go through (Angida, Ratlub). In the mountains, donkeys are readily available, usually equipped with saddles for load carrying. **Maps:** Bogossky section, K-38-XVII Khunzak, K-38-II Khabsavyurt, K-37-V Gantiadi; South Dagestan section, K-38-XXIV Akhty.

From **Agvali** catch a ride up the hill toward **Khushtada** and get dropped off just before the Pioneers' Camp. Head up the ridge not far from the TV tower and watchtower ruin. The trail traverses the hillside, winding up and

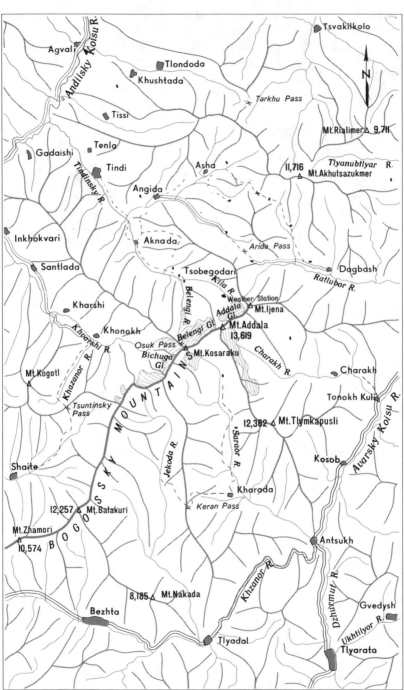

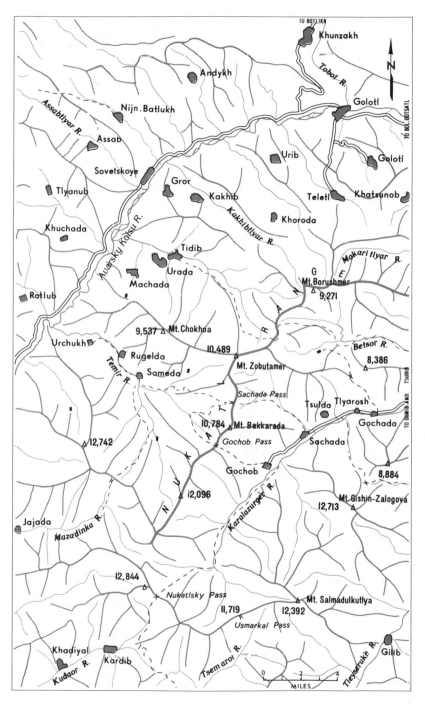

TO BOTLIKH

Khunzakh

Tobot R.

N

Andykh

Golotl

TO BOL. GOTSATL

Nijn. Batlukh

Assabllyar R.

Assab

Urib

Golotl

Sovetskoye

Gror

Kakhib

Khatsunob

Teletl

Tlyanub

Khoroda

Kakhiblyar R.

Khuchada

Tidib

Mokari tlyar R.

Avarsky Kolsu R.

Urada

G

Machada

Mt. Borushmer

E

Ratlub

△ 9,271

R

N

9,537 △ Mt. Chokhoa

Betsor R.

Urchukh

10,489

8,386

Temir R.

Rugelda

Mt. Zobutamer

△

TSURIB

Someda

TO GUNIB AND

Sachada Pass

Tsulda

Tlyarosh

T

10,784 △ Mt. Bakkarada

Gochada

△12,742

Gochob Pass

Sachada

U

12,096

Gochob

8,884

K

Mt. Gishin-Zalogova

Jajada

12,713 △

N

Kardlazurger R.

Mazadinka R.

12,844

△

Nukatlsky Pass

△ Mt. Salmadulkutlya

11,719

12,392

Usmarkal Pass

Khadiyal

Tleyserukir R.

Gilib

Kardib

Kudaor R.

Tsemaror R.

0   2   4

MILES

over several spurs. Past the village of **Tissi**, the trail drops down to the river and then climbs again into the forest. After you cross a low pass, and a couple more rises, the villages of **Tenla** and Tindi come into view, as well as the peaks of the Kad Range.

Tindi (**3 to 4 hours** from Agvali) resembles a house of cards, or rather a whole town of card houses, one built on top of another, the whole thing balanced on the cliff. Beyond Tindi, snowy summits wink. This is the end of the road.

There is no main street in Tindi or, really, any streets to speak of. You make your way through the stone labyrinth, ducking beneath porches and strolling across roofs. The path leads out of town, across the stream, and up the hillside opposite town. Threads of herding trails wind up the hill through pastures. In 1991, electrical wires pushed their way to Angida. This detracts slightly from the remote feeling of the place, but makes route finding very simple. Beyond the *kosh* partway up the hill, bear right toward the forested slopes for Angida (go straight if you're headed to Asha).

Follow the wires to the high point at about 8,200 feet (2500 m), where you're rewarded with panoramic views of the glaciated summits of the Bogossky Range, the highest being Mount Addala, 13,619 feet (4151 m). The trail drops gradually along the south side of the ridge to **Angida** (**2 to 3 hours**).

The unrelenting migration to the cities leaves mostly the old people in these villages buried in the mountains. Only twenty year-round households remain in Angida, and seven or eight in Asha. Many of the stone houses that climb the narrow buttresslike steps are deserted. The children and grandchildren return in summer and fall to help with planting, harvesting, and carrying the locally produced salty cheese, curds, and butter to Tindi on burros. (The electrical lines mark the trail another half hour out of Angida, then turn northwest to Asha, at the confluence of the Asha and Angida rivers.)

From Angida cross the Asha River and head uphill along the trail on the north side of the Angida River. A lone family dairy farm on this hillside, just above stone ruins, is noted on the map as Otsiberi. The trail traverses the hillside for a mile or so (a couple of kilometers), climbing very gradually, until you cross the Angida River. From this point, you can see Arida Pass, 10,200 feet (3109 m).

The trail follows the right bank of the river until the river bends to the left. There are good places to **camp in the valley** if you want to save the pass for the next day. Pick your way through scree up to **Arida Pass** (**4 to 5 hours**). Here, views of the Nukatl Range peaks radiate, and you can see Dagbash and the other villages ahead on your path. The pass is traveled mainly by herders, although the folk of Angida might cross it for a wedding, funeral, or other event in Dagbash. Burros do fine on this pass.

The descent from Arida Pass is somewhat steeper, about 1,300 feet (400 m) on scree. The trail is clear all the way. Small streams on this hillside chase each other into the Ratlub River, which the trail crosses over and over again for the next 12.5 miles (20 km). Sometimes the bridges wash out, but this doesn't present a major problem; it's not critical which bank of the river you

Dagestani burros usually carry cheese, curds, and butter to the market; they do a good job with backpacks, too.

follow and the fords are easy. The trail follows the Ratlub most of the way, with occasional detours into the forest. On the right rise the peaks of the Addala massif: snowy Addala itself and Ijena, whose steep slopes drop right to the river. A side stream from this massif flows into the Ratlub on the right.

Continue following the main drainage down. Before you reach Dagbash, forested slopes appear on the right. This band of forest continues all the way to Ratlub and beyond, one of the relatively rare patches of woods remaining in these mountains, which have been denuded by centuries of woodcutting and grazing. Along the way are *kosh* and *letovki* (summer camps) where cheese, butter, and curds are produced.

Dagbash (**3 to 4 hours**), not visible as you descend from Arida Pass, reappears, pinned to the hillside above the river. You can climb 1,000 feet (300 m) up the hill to the village, or bypass it by staying low alongside the river. This is a slightly smaller community than Tindi, although both towns have schools through the eighth grade.

Past Dagbash, the trail crosses the river and follows the right bank all the way to Ratlub, 5 miles (**8 km**) with a 3,300-foot (1000-m) elevation drop, veering off into the woods in places. Before Ratlub, you come to a series of abandoned villages. **Ratlub** (**2 to 3 hours**) retains fewer of the traditional hill-houses than Tindi.

Theoretically, Ratlub is on the highway, but the road is very rough and not many vehicles actually make it all the way up here. If you don't find a ride, hike out either side of the Ratlub River to where it meets the **main road**, **1.25 miles** (**2 km**) along the Avarsky Koisu River. (If you're planning to end your trek here, the bus to Makhachkala comes through here once a day from Tlyarata, via Sovetskoye—the major town in the region, which will probably be, or already has been, renamed. You may be able to find out in Ratlub what time the bus comes.) Continuing from Ratlub takes you into one of Dagestan's most scenic regions, the mountains of the Charadinsky Zakaznik. It may be possible to catch a ride from Ratlub as far as Someda, where the road ends; otherwise, follow the trails from village to village. From the highway the trail to **Someda** (**4 to 5 hours**) rises gradually in and out of the woods, following the Temir River.

In 1.5 miles (2.5 km) beyond Someda, ascend the hillside to the left. The trail traverses a boulder slope that is steeper than Arida Pass, to gain **Sachada Pass** (**3 to 4 hours**).

At the high point on Sachada Pass, follow the ridge to the right for **3 miles** (**5 km**) to **Gochob Pass**, 9,200 feet (2800 m), through high alpine meadows where herds graze. The panorama opens to glacial cirques, with Mount Bakkarada on your right, and the village of Gochob below you. It's a gradual descent down to the town, hillsiding up and down a series of spurs. After dropping down to the river, go over a rise to the left to reach **Gochob** (**5 to 6 hours**).

This cluster of ancient dwellings set in the crown of the Nukatl peaks seems like the very edge of civilization. It's well worth the tough hike across the pass to reach this fabulous place. There's currently no bus service to Gochob, only a rough road out to Charoda and Tsurib, where the bus to Makhachkala (a 10-hour trip) passes by.

There are numerous alternatives for making this an even longer trek. A couple of them: **Gochob to Tlyarata** via Nukatlsky Pass (**4 to 5 days**); and **Tlyarata to Tindi** and then returning to Tindi (**8 to 10 days**), via Bezhta, Mount Zhamori—an easy alpine summit with 2,600 feet (800 m) of elevation gain, Shaitle, Tsuntinsky Pass, Khazanor River, Khonokh, Kvarshi, and Inkhokvari.

Shorter alternative treks in this area include: **Tindi Circuit,** going to Aknada and Angida (**2 to 3 days**) and then returning to Tindi; and **Khushtada to Assab** (**4 to 5 days**), via Kvanada, Gimerso, Tlisi, and Akhvakh. From Assab, there's a road to Sovetskoye.

MOUNT IJENA ASCENT

This is a **2- or 3-day hike** that includes an ascent of Mount Ijena. There are a number of routes up Mount Addala, all technical. Mount Ijena, to the east of it, can be done without technical gear. Mount Tunsada separates Ijena from Addala.

From **Angida**, follow the line of houses down the ridge. The trail continues dropping until it hits the river. There you hang a right and follow the Angida River down to its junction with the Kila River. Cross the wooden footbridge and head upriver to the left. Just before you come upon Aknada's remaining houses, a cliff juts into the river, the giant chunk bitten out of it forming a sort of entrance arch to **Aknada** (**2 hours**). In Aknada, in the stone ruins of the mosque, we found a cupboard stuffed with parchments covered in curling

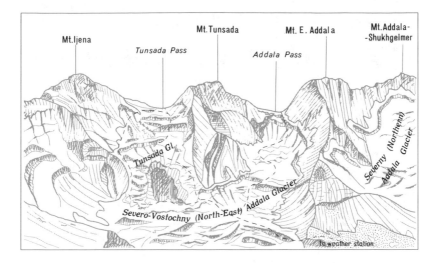

Arabic letters. (For a day hike, you can turn around here and return to Angida.)

The path beyond Aknada follows the Kila River (also sometimes called Kologoda River), climbing along the slopes of the Kad Ridge. You pass several *kosh*, including **Agoch** and **Atabala**.

From the ruins of **Igotsatli** *kosh*, you can see Mount Addala, 13,619 feet (4151 m), the highest summit around, where the Bogossky and Kad ridges knit together. Crossing the Kursanagi River, the trail climbs through scree all the way to **Tsobegodari** *kosh*. The lush grass of the *kosh* is welcome after the boulder ascent. From Tsobegodari, cross a bridge over the Kila onto a rocky promontory, washed on the left by the Belengi River, on the right by the Kila. **Campsites** on this promontory provide views of the valleys, Osuk Pass, and the Belengi Glacier.

Now the path rises through birch and underbrush, leaving the river below. Climb to the grassy spur from where you can see high above you the Sulak weather station, 9,700 feet (2952 m), and the path to it. Ascend to the **weather station**.

From the weather station, cross the **Severo-Vostochny ("Northeast") Addala Glacier** to its east edge. Crevasses should be open and reasonable to cross unroped. Climb scree slopes along the left edge of the **Tunsada Glacier** to **Tunsada Pass** and scramble from there to **Ijena**'s summit (**7 to 8 hours round-trip from weather station**).

Retrace your steps to **Angida**. Or you can cross Ijena Pass and descend from there to Dagbash; for directions from Dagbash, see the Agvali-to-Gochob trek, above.

Part 2

Central Asia (Turkestan)

The geographical term "Central Asia" actually defines a region which includes countries other than those in the former Soviet Central Asia, which
are the countries that Part 2 of this book describes. Soviet Central Asia—
which was formerly known by the traditional name Turkestan—comprised
present-day Uzbekistan, Tajikistan, Kyrgyzstan, Turkmenistan, and southern
Kazakhstan. (Northern Kazakhstan is considered more Russian than Central
Asian.)

Turkestan is a highly mountainous area where the great Asian cordillera is
fused by the Pamir Mountains. Geologists call it the Pamir Knot: from here,
the Himalaya sweeps south and east in its grand crescent, the Hindu Kush
southwest, and the Tian Shan northeast. Half of the Tian Shan and most of the
Pamir are the domain of Turkestan.

The Pamir is the second biggest mountain range in the world. Tectonic
forces are still at work in the Pamir, which grow about 2.25 inches (6 cm) every year. Many of the glaciers are also on the move. The Tian Shan encompasses a vast range of climatic and geographic zones. There are said to be
7,800 glaciers in the Tian Shan, many of them advancing.

At the center of Turkestan, the borders of Tajikistan, Uzbekistan, and
Kyrgyzstan intertwine in these huge mountains like the pieces of an intri-
cate jigsaw puzzle. Several chunks of Uzbek territory are, in fact, completely landlocked within Kyrgyz domain. Likewise, Vorukh is an island
of Tajik land within the landmass of southwestern Kyrgyzstan. The borders of these republics were carved out more or less along ethnic lines,
with the Uzbeks, Tajiks, Kyrgyz, and Kazakhs the majority ethnic group
in their respective nations. Still, each nation is populated by a mix of
these—and other nationalities, including almost 50 percent Russian populations in the major cities.

Ruled by khans until the Russians conquered first Samarkand, then Bukhara
and Khiva, in the second half of the nineteenth century, the dissolution of the
Soviet empire has left the people of Turkestan faced with democratic self-rule
for the first time in recent recorded history.

The Uzbeks have for centuries been settled people, engaged in agriculture.
Contemporary irrigation of the cotton fields has decimated Turkestan's two
main rivers, the Syr Darya (Jaxartes) and Amu Darya (Oxus). The Syr Darya
no longer flows to the Aral Sea, and the Aral has become a highly concentrated saline pond from which dusty winds blow, poisoning the people who
live in the region for hundreds of miles around.

The Kazakhs, Kyrgyz, and Turkmens, however, are traditionally nomadic
horsemen and were forcibly collectivized. While the nomadic life-style is
mostly a thing of the past, many of these people summer in high camps, grazing their sheep in the valleys of the Pamir and Tian Shan. They summer pri-

Kyrgyz woman felting; even in their mountain camps, these people create beautiful blankets and embroidered tapestries. (Photo: Vladimir Maximov)

marily in brush-wood stockades, less commonly in Mongolian-style yurts. These camps, usually consisting of a large extended family, are called *kosh*. The mountain people are usually very friendly and hospitable, offering trekkers bread or *airan* (kefir). They tell tales of snow leopards, bears, and wolves.

The region is an ethnic melting pot, with the basic stock flavored by centuries of Turkic-Mongol influence. Unlike the Uzbeks, Kazakhs, Kyrgyz, and Turkmens, the Tajiks trace their ethnic and linguistic roots to Persia. They are lighter skinned than their Turkish-Mongol neighbors, and many blue-eyed Tajik beauties supposedly trace their bloodlines to Alexander the Great.

The towns of Turkestan are a curious mix of the old—dazzling turquoise minarets with elegant Persian motifs—side by side with tasteless Soviet-era architecture. In the Uzbekistan cities of Samarkand, Bukhara, and Khiva—the showcase "Silk Road" cities—palaces and monuments dating from the time of Timur and before have been restored, and mosques rebuilt. Other ancient cities—Osh, Kyrgyzstan; Khodzhent (formerly Leninabad), Tajikistan; Kokand, Uzbekistan—are less illustrious, but not overrun with tourists. The capitals—Tashkent,

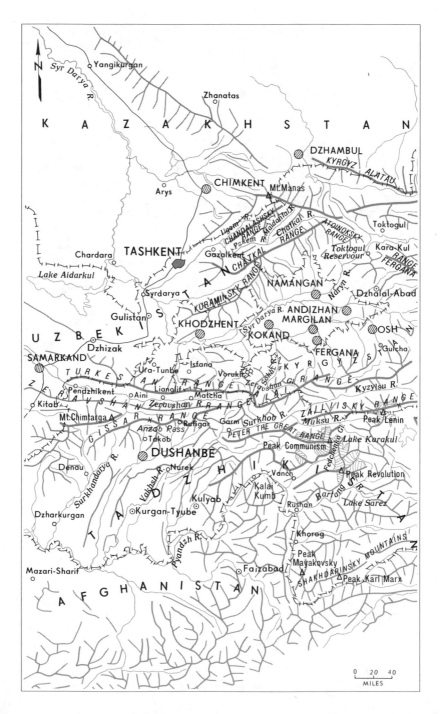

The Kazakh and Kyrgyz peoples traditionally led a nomadic life-style; this girl is still at home on a galloping horse. (Photo: Vladimir Maximov)

Duck into one of Samarkand's side streets and imagine that you have been transported back in time to the days of Timur.

Uzbekistan; Dushanbe, Tajikistan; Bishkek (formerly Frunze), Kyrgyzstan; and Almaty (formerly Alma Ata), Kazakhstan—don't warrant a special trip, but are interesting to poke around in for a day en route to the mountains.

In the cities, everyone knows Russian, but some Asians are not eager to speak it; a popular way of asserting independence after decades of Russian dominance has been the passage of language laws requiring the local language to be used in government, schools, and the media. In the smaller villages, many speak only rudimentary Russian. Outside of the villages, you will meet herders and hunters who speak only their native language.

I confess to an inexplicable, persistent passion for the land of Pamir. Inexplicable, because as a young woman traveling alone in Uzbekistan in the mid-1980s, I found the gawking men very wearing. These are Islamic lands: Asian women avert their eyes in the street and, in general, aren't much in evidence because they're at home taking care of families that average five children. Men trail Anglo women with frank, unabashed stares.

The decades of Soviet rule have created a hybrid Muslim culture. Literacy among women and the number of women working as professionals are higher than any other Islamic country. The women of Turkestan don't wear the veil, although most *do* wear traditional clothing: brightly patterned silk dresses, with silk trousers. Girls wear their long black hair braided in dozens of plaits falling to their waists. They have lived side by side with Russians, so European customs are familiar, and some of these customs have been adopted. Yet the towns and people of Turkestan remain distinctly Asian. One saying Russians like to quote: "Asia—it's a subtle question."

Time moves slowly in Turkestan. Many hours of the day are spent sipping hot tea in the hot afternoons. Conversation tends to be unhurried. In fact, everything is unhurried. If someone's promised to meet you at two, don't be surprised to see them at four. If your driver was to meet you Tuesday morning and doesn't show until Tuesday night, be grateful that he got there at all. If you can get into it, the Turkestan pace is delightfully relaxing. If you can't get into it, better to stay away.

Asians can be as generous with their hospitality as with time. Take opportunities to meet local people (something that's easier to do in a small town or village) and you'll likely find yourself seated in the shade of a grape-draped courtyard, at a table piled with nuts, sweets, melons, and other fruit. Your host pours the *pialo* (a special little ceramic bowl) half full of green tea over and over again; to pour the cup full would be a sign the guest was not welcome. This Asian hospitality can also reach extremes that are hard to deal with. Notes from my Uzbekistan journal:

In Rashid's home, carpets cover the floor and walls. The only piece of furniture is a TV. He does not introduce me to his wife or any of the children who wander in and out. With Rashid's friend, we sit on the floor and sip tea. "Now we will have plof," *my host announces. An hour goes by, then another. I am anxious to make the last bus back to Bukhara. He won't hear of me leaving without dinner. I don't have a clue how to get back to the bus station on my own. After three hours have gone by, the* plof *appears. My host dips two fingers into the* plov *piled on the communal platter, pinches it with his thumb and drops it in his mouth. My efforts at getting the greasy rice to my mouth are not as successful. I decline the vodka, but Rashid pushes it on me, insisting, "If you don't toast my daughter, she won't get married." Dutifully, I down the vodka. The toast is followed by another, then another toast. There is no refusing to toast: it turns out Rashid has seven daughters,*

Throughout Turkestan, men while away scorching afternoons in teahouses.

all unmarried. By the time I make it back to the bus station, the last bus is long gone.

Central Asian place names are particularly confusing. Kyrgyz, Kazakh, and Uzbek are all Turkic languages with many words that closely resemble each other from one language to the next. (Tajik is a Persian language.) Geographic names in Turkestan often describe what the place looks like, what colors things are, or distinctive features: *Ak* (white), *Su* (water), *Chon* (big), *Tash* (stone), *Kok* (blue), *Kara* (black), et cetera. There are dozens of rivers and streams here—and in China—called *aksu* (white water), *karasu* (black water), *koksu* (blue-green water). *Kent* or *Kand* is a town.

All the Central Asian cities have markets (*bazaars*) where vendors sell all manner of fruits and vegetables. William Eleroy Curtis, in *Turkestan: The Heart of Asia*, describes the Samarkand bazaar in 1911:

> *The Samarkand Registan is ... enclosed on three sides by some of the most majestic examples of Saracenic or Arabian architecture ever erected. The fourth side is open and occupied by ramshackle booths ... it is a sort of a ragbag of a place, a hotch-potch, but is attended by some of the most serious and serene men of Oriental type that you can imagine. They wear garments of brilliant colours, yellow, green, purple, and scarlet, in stripes and plaids and their intellectual-looking heads are crowned with snowy turbans, but their legs and feet are bare. They squat with their legs crossed in little narrow booths, sip coffee, smoke cigarettes, gossip with each other and scrap with customers over the price of their wares.*

The *bazaar*, which is now off to the side of the Registan, has changed little since Curtis was there. A visit to the bazaar is a good way to feel the pulse of an Asian town. In season, the fruits and vegetables are wonderful. Chances are you've never seen so many melons in one place as at the *bazaar*.

Like the *bazaar*, the teahouse is a ubiquitous Turkestan tradition. The *chaikhana* (*chai* means tea) may be indoors or outdoors: the patrons sit on low platforms that resemble nothing so much as four-poster beds. In his memoirs of Turkestan travels in the last century, Eugene Schuyler recounts that in the *chaikhana* "nothing but tea is sold ... the natives bring their own bread and raisins, tied up in the folds of their girdles, which when spread out serve as their table-cloths." Not much has changed.

Melons and the abundance of other fruits and vegetables in the outdoor bazaars make August and September a tasty time for trekking.

Travel to mountain areas of the southern Pamir in Tajikistan is risky at this time. There have been incidents of hikers, including foreigners, getting shot. The Pamir Alai, at Tajikistan's northern edge (much of it actually falls in Uzbekistan and Kyrgyzstan) is still safe at this writing. Travel in the High Pamir is still safe because there are no towns or villages above about 11,500 feet (3500 m) and you don't have to worry about armed bandits assaulting the base camp at Peak Communism. You should, however, check the conditions in towns along your expedition's access route. The Tian Shan is not affected by Tajikistan's strife. It is important to obtain current information about this region. (See the Political Conditions section of chapter 3, Staying Safe and Healthy.)

Try to get a local guide (i.e., ethnic Uzbek, Tajik, Kyrgyz, or Kazakh) when traveling in these parts. Hostility toward Russians is more in evidence in Uzbekistan and Tajikistan, but just about everywhere the welcome is warmer when the locals find out you're not a Russian.

You can sometimes rent burros or horses from the herders, although unless you're on an extended climbing trip and have a lot of gear, it's hardly worth the trouble. Herders usually don't want to let their animals go very far off. You may have the understanding that you're hiring animals for a week, and then it turns out three days into the trek that the burros have to leave because a truck has arrived a valley away delivering sugar. The donkeys themselves are a dubious blessing; they can be ornery and obstinate. Pack your gear in plastic bags inside your pack in case the donkeys fall down and deep-six your gear in the river.

If you *are* hiring animals, it's important to have an experienced handler along, as improperly loaded or overloaded animals don't last long. Vodka and rope are the preferred currency for bargaining with the herders. The herders keep dogs that are fierce and have been known to bite trekkers, so if you're passing a *kosh* and don't see the herder, carry a rock or stick and be on your guard. Riding burros or herders' horses, unless you're very experienced, is not recommended (there are reports of Dushanbe doctors amputating arms broken in spills from livestock).

In the mountains, especially in high melt seasons (through July), the rivers are to be reckoned with. Mountain rivers can easily rise a foot or more between morning and evening. Most trails follow drainages, and the sheer number of mountain rivers makes it practically impossible to avoid fording rivers. If you can't ford late in the day, try at first light.

In Turkestan, there are climbers' hostels in several of the cities. Called *alpbaza*, and often named after a climbing camp, these are transit places for climbers enroute to camps. They have traditionally been the cheapest accommodations in town. Some are very basic—outhouses and one water faucet for the whole establishment, cooking on campstoves—while others actually have private rooms with bathrooms.

In the capital cities of Tashkent and Dushanbe there are Intourist hotels, as well as a variety of other hotels. *Alpbaza* Varzob is on the outskirts of Dushanbe (see the High Pamir and the Eastern Pamir/Pamir Plateau and Western Foothills sections in chapter 9, The Pamir Mountains). In the smaller towns, the availability of hotels is spotty, but if you ask around and there's no hotel, you may be invited to stay with a family.

In the capitals—Tashkent, Dushanbe, Bishkek, and Almaty—there are agencies that arrange for travelers to rent a room or an apartment. These are the most economical lodgings in cities. You need a basic command of Russian (or the local language) or travel with a Soviet to take advantage of these. (See also the Accommodations section of chapter 4, Traveling in Russia and Central Asia.)

Turkestan home cooking is excellent, with vegetables spiced a variety of delicious ways. Restaurant and cafe meals can be on the greasy side, with fairly limited menus. Be careful about eating salads or raw vegetables in restaurants: remember, if they've been washed in water that's not purified, you may have problems. Rare is the traveler to Turkestan who manages to avoid diarrhea, but taking precautions can save you miseries. (See also the discussion on water purification in the Health and Medical Problems section of chapter 3, Staying Safe and Healthy.)

Plof, rice cooked with mutton, grated carrots, and onions, is standard Turkestan fare. *Shurpa* and *lagman,* both spicy soups with noodles and mutton, are other common items. They eat two varieties of meat-stuffed dough (like potstickers): *manti* are steamed, *samsa* are baked. Any of these dishes are served with the omnipresent tomato and onion salad. It's hard to avoid the mutton.

They love *halva* (a confection made of crushed sesame seeds and honey) in Turkestan. If you let your local guide do all the shopping for your trek, you may end up with so much *halva* you'll never want to see it again in your life. Another "snack" to beware of is rock-hard sour milk balls sucked to avoid thirst. You definitely have to develop a taste for these.

Stock up on dried apricots, raisins (*kishmish*) and nuts at the bazaar. Even small *kishlaks* (villages) may have markets, but the selection is much more limited. Throughout the region, you can buy *lepyoshki*—wheels of chewy bread. These are unbelievably delicious when soft and freshly baked—especially if you are famished. They get hard after a few days, but they keep for a long time and travel well in the pack when they dry out a bit.

Bring your own freeze-dried and dehydrated food from home. You can pick up cheese, sausage, peanut butter, and other such staples in Moscow if you fly through there. In the near future, such things will probably also appear in stores in the major cities of Turkestan (in particular Tashkent and Almaty), but don't count on a selection of Western products. Candy, juices, and beer (actually, just about every kind of alcohol imaginable) seem to be the first products to flood the country.

Carry fuel for cooking everywhere in the mountains of Central Asia. Especially in the high mountains, there are no trees. In the valleys at the lower elevations, although some locals (and some Russian hikers) do burn the ancient junipers, trees are too scarce for trekkers to burn them.

9 The Pamir Mountains

The Pamir Mountains, called the "Roof of the World" by geographer Raphael Pumpelly at the turn of the century, perforate the sky at the Himalaya's northwest reaches. This quadrangle of high ridges and snowy peaks rises to its greatest heights in eastern Tajikistan. Stretching from Samarkand, Uzbekistan, in the west through Tajikistan and Kyrgyzstan, the Pamir Mountains extend east to the Fergana Range in Kyrgyzstan, where they merge with the Tian Shan.

To the east of Dushanbe rise the Pamir's Western Foothills. The Peter the Great (called Peter the First in Russian), Darvaz, Vanch, and Yazgulem ranges rise from the Tajik Depression to their abutment with the Academy Range where the Pamir reaches its zenith at over 23,000 feet (7000 m) in the High Pamir. Soviets generally refer to the peaks along the Pyandzh River, on the Afghanistan border, as the Southwest Pamir (although southeast would be technically more correct). Kara Kul Lake and Sarikol Lake sit in the barren Pamir Plateau, which stretches southeast to China. Along with the canyons east of the High Pamir, this is known as the Eastern Pamir. North and west of the High Pamir lie the mountains of the Pamir Alai, which some geographers consider a subrange of the Pamir.

The 500-mile-long (800-km-long) Pamir Alai mountain system can be thought of as the seam joining the Pamir Mountains to the Tian Shan. Up to 155 miles (250 km) wide in places, the Pamir Alai links a series of ranges between the Samarkand oasis and the Fergana Mountains. The Pamir Alai includes the Fanskie Gori and the Turkestan, Gissar, and Zeravshan ranges.

The point where the ridges of the Pamir Alai merge is called the Matcha Mountain Knot. At its core, Pik Igla and Matcha Pass stitch together the great wall of the Alai Range to the southeast, the Turkestan Range riding westward toward Samarkand, and, south of the Turkestan Range and paralleling it, the Zeravshan Range. South of the Zeravshan Range, wedged between it and the Gissar Mountains (which lie just north of Dushanbe, Tajikistan), are the popular Fanskie Gori ("Fan Mountains," pronounced "fon").

The western High Pamir consists of four parallel ranges—the Peter the Great, Darvaz, Vanch, and Yazgulem—which rise abruptly from the Tajik Depression just east of Dushanbe. These ranges extend east until they merge with the High Pamir (Academy Range). Farther south in the Southwest Pamir, just north of the Pyandzh River (which forms the Tajikistan border with Afghanistan), the Shakhdarinsky Mountains are another spectacular range that has long been a test piece for Russian mountaineers. Peak Karl Marx, 22,057 feet (6723 m), is reputed to be the toughest face in the country. Nearby Peak Engels and Peak Mayakovsky are no less impressive.

The central area of the High Pamir is also called the Northwest Pamir and the Academy Range. Of the former Soviet Union's four summits higher than 23,000 feet (7000 m), three cluster in the High Pamir: Peaks Communism, Lenin, and Korzhenevskaya (the fourth is Peak Pobeda, in the Tian Shan).

From the east side of Peak Communism, the incomparable Fedchenko Glacier runs south all the way to Peak Revolution, 22,880 feet (6974 m), a challenging, technical peak in the same Academy of Sciences Ridge. This glacier may be the biggest icecube between the Alaska–Yukon glaciers and Antarctica (though some opt for the Baltoro group in northwest Pakistan).

In the Eastern Pamir, Kara Kul (Black Lake) sits in a high-altitude desert, 13,000 feet (4000 m), a couple of miles (a few km) from China. The Pamir Plateau extends east to the Fergana Range, and east of the Fergana is the Tian Shan. South of Kara Kul, Soviet Officers' Peak, 20,450 feet (6233 m), tops the Muzkol Mountains near Sarez Lake, formed by a massive mudslide in 1911.

Most of the big peaks of the Pamir, 105 of them more than 20,000 feet (6000 m), are rarely or never climbed, except for the three popular 23,000-plus-foot (7000-plus-m) peaks. Until the late 1980s, the Pamir was closed except to Western climbers on expeditions to Peaks Lenin, Communism, and Korzhenevskaya. (Most place names glorifying communism and communist heros were renamed after 1991, so don't be surprised if many of these peaks also get relabeled.) Now that the restrictions have fallen, the principal obstacles to access are the remoteness of the High Pamir and the tumultuous political situation in Tajikistan.

When the Union collapsed, bloody struggles for political control of the republic erupted between Islamic fundamentalists and the old communist factions. Gorno-Badakshan, the mountainous eastern half of Tajikistan, was an "autonomous district" under the Soviet system. In 1992, Gorno-Badakshan declared its independence from Dushanbe, the capital city of Tajikistan, and fighting spread village to village. Gorno-Badakshan recently recanted the independence declaration, but the political roots of the conflict have been obscured as the isolated battles escalated into a tragic civil war that's claimed between 20,000 and 40,000 lives.

Most of the fighting has been concentrated in southwestern Tajikistan, along the Pyandzh River, west of Kalai Kumb. There has been extensive fighting in and around Dushanbe also. The entire border with Afghanistan is potentially very dangerous, especially during low water, when the Afghans come across.

The most interesting areas for recreation and adventure travel (including Kara Kul Lake, the East Pamir canyons, and the Pamir Plateau) have not experienced any fighting and are relatively safe at this writing. It is important to obtain the most current information about safety before venturing into any part of Tajikistan; this key situation changes from month to month. Steve Cunha, a University of California Davis geographer who studies the Pamir, warns against solo travel without a companion who speaks Russian or the local language, for the simple reason that you will not understand current warnings from honest local people. He adds:

> *The Soviet dismemberment and accompanying civil strife in Central Asia (Tajikistan, Armenia, Afghanistan, et cetera) has dislocated thousands of people. Severe economic uncertainty and the influx of weapons from Afghanistan compound the problem. This is a real ethnic caldron with lots of desperate people and little law enforcement. Though most*

travelers will have no problem, vagabonding by significant numbers of travelers remains untested in Central Asia. I urge you to err on the side of caution.

When Stalin carved Turkestan up into Soviet Socialist Republics, he drew the borders such that ethnic tensions still bubble. Samarkand, historically a Tajik town, became part of Uzbekistan. Khodzhent (called Leninabad under the Soviets) was given to Kyrgyzstan. Many Tajiks continue to reside in these areas that the Pamir Alai spans, alongside Uzbeks, Kyrgyz, and Kazakhs who for centuries have herded the vast expanse of the Pamir Plateau south into what today is Western China. The mountain Tajiks are the most defiantly fundamentalist in observing the Islamic traditions. One of the poorest parts of the USSR, this region had long boasted the country's highest birth rate; since the onset of the Tajik Civil War it can now claim the highest mortality rate as well.

Pamir Alai

The 500-mile-long (800-km-long) Pamir Alai mountain system links a series of ranges between Uzbekistan's Samarkand oasis on the west and the Fergana Mountains on the east. To the north is the Fergana Valley of Kyrgyzstan and to the south is Dushanbe, capital city of Tajikistan. The central point of the Pamir Alai is Matcha Pass, what's known as the Matcha Mountain Knot. From here, the Alai Range sweeps to the southeast to the Fergana Range; the Turkestan Range extends west to Samarkand; and the Zeravshan Range also runs west, just south of the Turkestan Range. South of the Zeravshan Range is the Gissar Range, and wedged between these two are the Fanskie Gori.

Many Pamir Alai peaks have never received a human footprint; while most of its summits clear 13,000 feet (4000 m)—thirty-five of them are more than 16,000 feet (5000 m)—they don't have the "macho" appeal of the 23,000-foot (7000-m) High Pamir peaks, and only the most accessible of them have been climbed. What they do have is "Matcha appeal."

Squeezed between the Fergana and Zeravshan valleys, the Turkestan Range continues west from Matcha Pass at Pik Igla, where the Alai Range leaves off. A road across Shakhristan Pass cuts down the center of the range. This string of narrow, steep-sided hanging valleys and awe-inspiring glacial cirques is called by the traditional name for the cluster of countries known in this century as Soviet Central Asia: Turkestan. The glaciers have carved out the Turkestan Range so dramatically you feel like you are in the midst of an ongoing work. Granite faces pushing 18,000 feet (5500 m) surround you. In midsummer, the valleys are carpeted with forget-me-nots, geranium, bistort, and many other wildflowers.

The Tajik–Kyrgyz border snakes along the crest of the Alai and Turkestan ranges. These mountain landscapes are too high for villages, but the herders (*chabani*) keep their sheep here in the summer. Kyrgyz nomads have herded here for centuries. And Fedchenko himself, the great explorer of the Pamir, passed this way in 1871. The valleys, hydrated by robust glacial rivers, are prime agricultural land. Orchards and weeping willows shade the riverbanks in this hot, dry belt. Trekker David Burbee describes a visit with herders in the Uryam Valley of the northern Turkestan Range:

> *Bottle of vodka tucked under my arm, Sasha and I head off to visit the herders. We step through the doorway into the yellow lamplight into a single large room with benches covered in sheepskins, carpets and an incongruous red-checkered tablecloth in the middle of the floor. We remove our shoes and sit on the floor, several broad, brown faces gazing on us. Sasha translates. "Where are you from," I'm asked first. The men cutting melon and mutton pause their knives in mid-air when they hear "American." Next question: "How many children do you have?" "None," I respond, "I'm not married." As this answer's translated into Russian, several pairs of black eyebrows fly up in unison. This brings on the next question of my age; the response "thirty-five" creates more alarm. By Kyrgyz standards, this is not a healthy situation.*
>
> *Melon and a platter of mutton are served. Next I'm questioned about my salary. My monthly salary is first converted into rubles, then into the local currency: sheep. I make somewhere in the neighborhood of four to five sheep a month. After learning how much schooling I have, it's determined that I really should be making more, uh, sheep.*
>
> *Our discussions continue through the night. As we prepare to return to our camp, the old man speaks. "We will never forget the night the nice American came to visit. Now you must go back to America and ask your boss for more sheep, and find a wife."*

The Zeravshan—"Strewer of Gold"—River flows out of the Zeravshan Range and through Samarkand, Uzbekistan, petering out farther west at Bukhara. Wedged between the Zeravshan Range and Gissar Mountains, the Fanskie Gori are more than foothills of the Pamir. Steep, rugged peaks— eleven of them higher than 16,500 feet (5000 m)—punctuate the ridges in this corner of the Pamir Alai. While fruit trees, poplars, birch, rosehips, and barberries grow at lower elevations, the Fani are sparsely vegetated, with only the wizened juniper braving the higher reaches. This striking, arid landscape evokes images of Mongol raiders charging mountain passes. The heavy snows for which the Fani are known feed rivers that rush through narrow ravines. These major rivers—among them the Archmaidan, Pasrud, and Iskander Darya—often obliterate bridges and whole sections of trail on the steep hillsides, making it necessary to make wide detours to find a ford.

In the Pamir Alai, the cold, wet period lasts from November to April. Between May and October there are lots of sunny days. In the mountain towns, temperatures average -2°C in January and 25°C in July. At up to 5,000 feet (1500 m) in the summer the weather is warm or hot (10°C to 30°C). At the same time of year, during the hottest months of the summer (July and August), at above 9,800 feet (3000 m) it rarely gets above 10°C to 15°C.

Several of the treks described below are accessible from Samarkand, Uzbekistan. On the road from Samarkand to the Fanskie Gori, Rudaki is the last town. Named for the Tajik poet who lived between A.D. 858–941 (you can visit his mausoleum), Rudaki gives you an inside glimpse of a Central Asian village. The residents live in traditional earthen homes built into the hillside, most of them making their living from livestock and agriculture. Residents of *kishlaks* in the Fani foothills spend summers at mountain *kosh*. Some of them keep burros and it may be possible to arrange to hire a pack animal. But there is as yet no such established practice, so it's best to not count on it.

The Fanskie Gori, less than three hours' drive from Samarkand, are the most popular part of the Pamir Alai. The opportunity to see Samarkand, the easy access, and the abundance of hiking and climbing routes combine to make the Fanskie Gori popular with both climbers and hikers from all over the former Soviet Union. You will not have a wilderness experience in this area; these groups have burned much of the little wood there was in the lake basins, often desecrating the junipers in the process. They also leave behind heaps of trash at frequented campsites. Be careful to purify water everywhere in Central Asia, but in particular in the Fanskie Gori, where water supplies are extensively contaminated by animal and human use. This is one price you pay for the proximity to Samarkand. The trails, however, are well marked by frequent travel, and there will almost always be someone to ask directions of if you are uncertain.

Getting There

For the four treks described below, access is from Tashkent or Samarkand, Uzbekistan, or Dushanbe, Tajikistan.

International flights to Tashkent include Lufthansa's new Frankfurt–Tashkent routes; Aeroflot flies to Tashkent from Delhi, India; Islamabad, Pakistan; Istanbul, Turkey; Kabul, Afghanistan; and some cities in the Middle East. Air Uzbekistan, which has branched off from Aeroflot, also flies some international routes, including service from Frankfurt, Germany. It's difficult to book these flights, because they are not listed in travel agents' computer systems.

From Russia, there are flights from Moscow daily and St. Petersburg to Tashkent, Khodzhent, and Dushanbe. Direct service from Moscow to other Turkestan cities, such as Fergana and Samarkand, is spottier. You usually have to fly into one of the capitals and get a connecting flight.

The train from Moscow to Tashkent takes almost three days. (The Central Asian trains' only reputation is that of a long, dirty ride. If you choose this route, *do* take a container of baby wipes for keeping the grime at bay; *don't* take anything you mind losing if bandits sweep your train.)

The journey to the starting point of the **Lyanglif-to-Kan trek** begins in Samarkand; plan on a 3-day vehicle trip to the start of the hiking (see the trek description below). The hiking ends at Kan, with another day's ride to Kokand. Kokand is about 100 miles (160 km) from Tashkent, on the busline to Fergana, 56 miles (about 90 km). Under the Soviet empire, Aeroflot flew regularly from Moscow to Fergana; these days, you may have to fly via Tashkent. Trains also run between Margilan (near Fergana) and Tashkent.

For the **Aksu Valley Loop**, begin and end in the Aksu Valley via the village of Isfana in the Fergana Valley. There's an airport at Isfana, but good luck finding a flight to it. From Tashkent, Isfana is a 4-hour drive; from

Khodzhent it's a 2-hour drive, but the air connections from major cities to Khodzhent are more difficult. From Isfana, hike 4 hours up a rough road to the Aksu Valley. You may be able to hire a car in Isfana and avoid hiking the dusty road up the mountainside to the Aksu Valley, but some years it washes out and is passable only in a four-wheel-drive vehicle. A better bet is to try to hitch a ride with one of the truckloads of climbers headed up the road in July or August. This road is where the trek ends as well, so just reverse the directions to get back to Isfana.

For the two treks in the Fanskie Gori, **Artuch to Lake Iskanderkul** and **Margazor Lake to Lake Iskanderkul,** first get to Samarkand. From Samarkand, drive southeast on the road to Pendzhikent, which crosses from Uzbekistan into Tajikistan. At Sudzhina, the road branches south toward the Margazor Lakes, the left fork continuing east toward Rudaki and Aini. For the **Artuch** trailhead, continue to Rudaki; past Rudaki, the road becomes a rough track, petering out at the climbers' camp of Artuch. Bus service from Pendzhikent to Rudaki is irregular; you're better off hiring transportation. Artuch can also be reached from Dushanbe, by driving 3 or 4 hours north over Anzob Pass. For the **Margazor Lake** trailhead, from Pendzhikent head due south along the Magiandarya River. Driving through the Shing River valley, the road dwindles to tire ruts to Gushor Lake (3 or 4 hours from Samarkand). Gushor is the first of a series of lovely mountain lakes. You'll pass Nofin Lake, Khurdak Lake, and, finally, Margazor Lake. The end point of both treks, at **Lake Iskanderkul,** is on the Khodzhent–Dushanbe road; Dushanbe is 87 miles (140 km) away via Varzob climbers' camp and Anzob Pass. Anzob Pass, 11,000 feet (3372 m), is only open summers from about the end of June, when the last snow melts out. There is no reliable bus service, but there is enough traffic on this road that you should be able to hitch a ride.

Where to Stay

In Samarkand, there's Alpbaza Artuch (Pos. Aeroporta—KSP, 703009 Samarkand, tel. 52236) and Osh Alpbaza (tel. 53496). In Isfana there's a guesthouse. In Tashkent and Dushanbe, there are Intourist hotels; Dushanbe also has *Alpbaza* Varzob. The small towns often have *alpbazas*; in the capital cities, room rentals can often be arranged.

When to Go

It's reasonable to go into the Pamir Alai from mid-June to mid-September. There may still be snow in the passes in June, and by early September it will be getting quite cold. In July and August, the temperature is generally pleasant, but not hot because of the high elevation. There can be extended periods of rain even during these months.

For the Fanskie Gori, the season is June through mid-October because this range enjoys a milder microclimate: it is drier and warmer than at similar elevations in other parts of the Pamir Alai. All the same, in a heavy-snow year, snow may linger in the passes through June. In summer, sudden afternoon showers and lightning storms are common. These mountains are hot during the day in July and August. Temperatures drop considerably at night.

Equipment and Supplies

You can stock up on supplies in the *bazaars* of Samarkand, Tashkent, Kokand, Khodzhent, or Dushanbe, depending on the trek you choose and the route you select to get there. Smaller towns like Isfana have more limited offerings, although there is generally a market of some sort.

For the **Lyanglif-to-Kan** trek, be prepared for glacier travel and steep snow—possibly ice—slopes. Also, be prepared for the possibility that you will see few or no other people for more than a week and help is very far away in case of emergency.

LYANGLIF TO KAN

The journey to and from this mountaineering trek takes you from one old Silk Road city to another, via the Zeravshansky Glacier. The road portion starts in Samarkand, which celebrated its 2,500-year anniversary in 1970, takes you to the trailhead in Lyanglif, then from trees' end to Kan, and the remaining road journey winds up in Kokand. The *khans* ruled from Kokand in the eighteenth and nineteenth centuries; it was a center of Uzbek learning long before then and you can still visit the *madrassas* (Islamic schools) and mosques. Nearby Margilan, today the headquarters for the Fergana Valley's silk industry, is another ancient city. Fergana is actually a new part of Margilan.

This **16- to 19-day trek** goes to the heart of *Kohistan*—"mountain country." While this trek doesn't cover the entire distance between Samarkand and Kokand on foot (it's actually a very long drive at either end), it is still a long hike (12 to 14 days of hiking, plus 4 or 5 days of travel by vehicle). Approached via the

Scenes like this evoke the Silk Road lore of these mountains. (Photo: Bill Sumner)

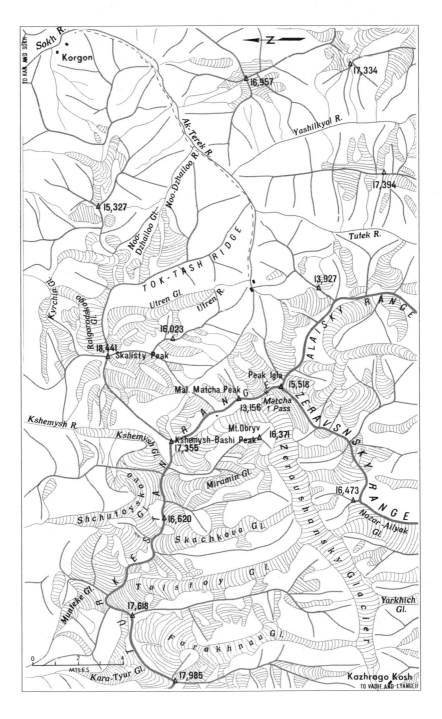

Zeravshan River valley, the route traverses the length of the Zeravshansky Glacier—15.5 miles (nearly 25 km)—into the Matcha Mountain Knot, then crosses
Matcha Pass and drops down to the Alai Mountains-fed Sokh River in the Kokand
oasis. It is a **hard-core and remote** high-alpine adventure. This is challenging
backpacking, requiring **mountaineering skills and equipment**, including
crampons, ice axe, and rope.

For the start of the trek, drive from **Samarkand** through Pendzhikent to
Aini (1 day). (Aini also can be reached from Dushanbe, Khodzhent, or
Tashkent.)

From Aini, continue the drive upvalley to the *kishlak* Lyanglif at the head
of the Zeravshan Valley. Likely it will take the better part of **2 days** to reach
Lyanglif from Aini.

The road doesn't go much beyond the *kishlak* of Lyanglif, although there
are small settlements farther up the Zeravshan River. Lyanglif is where you
begin hiking. There may be bridges over the river beyond Lyanglif, but
keep to the left side of the Zeravshan River, because the path on the river's
right is often covered by slides. Beyond Vadif there are no more bridges
and the river is dangerous or impossible to ford right up to the snout of the
Zeravshansky Glacier. It's a **3- or 4-day** hike from Lyanglif to reach the
Zeravshansky Glacier. The glacier is challenging to get onto on the left
side. Seracs, crevasses, and a moraine ridge block the way. It's better to
cross over to the right side, where there's a *kosh* called **Kazhrago** at the
Zeravshansky Glacier's edge.

From here, 300 or 600 feet (100 or 200 m) up the glacier there's a trace of a
trail that navigates through the jumble of rocks and ice. This trail continues,
climbing along slopes and on and off glacial moraines, to the point where the
Tolstoi Glacier runs into the Zeravshansky about halfway between the foot of
the Zeravshansky and Matcha Pass. Here (a **2- or 3-day hike**—with heavy
packs—from Kazhrago) is a flat, green area with several small tarns.

Farther along, it's convenient to follow the center line of the moraines.
Numerous glaciers feed the mighty Zeravshansky Glacier, which is a half
mile (1 km) across at its foot and nearly twice that at its widest point. Big
tributary glaciers from the Turkestan Range on the north include the Tolstoi,
the Skachkova, and the Miramin; from the Zeravshan Range on the south,
tributary glaciers include the Nazar-Ailyak and Bely Akhun. These tributaries
carry broken-up material to the main flow, creating a flat stripe down the
middle. Snowline on the bordering slopes is around 12,800 feet (3900 m).

The glacier flows south from below Kshemyish-Bashi Peak in the
Turkestan Range, then wraps around Mount Obryv and continues southwest.
The upper section is almost always snow-covered, and the slope is very moderate, with two minor icefalls before you reach Mount Obryv. Where the glacier turns the corner, there are deep crevasses, some of which may be open in
late summer.

It's best to camp on the moraine below **Mount Obryv (1 day from Tolstoi
Glacier)**. This is a spectacular camp, with hanging glaciers on either side. On
the Zeravshansky Glacier side, Peak Igla drops off in steep cliffs about 4,900
feet (1500 m) long. North of Igla are the Peaks Malaya Matcha and Matcha.

Peak Igla is actually a ridge of rocky aretes extending about a half mile (1 km) to the southwest from Matcha Pass.

Two passes are called Matcha: Matcha I Pass (Soviet Mountain Pass rating of 2A; see the Introduction) lies between Igla and Malaya Matcha. Matcha II Pass (Soviet Mountain Pass rating of 2B) lies north of Matcha. This trek takes you over Matcha I Pass. To reach Matcha I, climb from the base of Obryv up the snow-covered glacier—about a 35-degree angle. Roped travel up this is recommended, because there may well be hidden crevasses. From the 13,156-foot (4010-m) pass, you can't see down to the Ak Terek Valley, hidden around the corner. Head down the 45-degree snow slope, watching for rock-fall from Malaya Matcha Peak. Continue down on snow to your right until you reach the Matcha Glacier, then keep to the moraine's sharp ridge. Descending the glacier, the left side is more easily traversible, the right more broken up with large crevasses by the icefall that drops into Ak Terek Valley. Herders come up as high as the glacier and you may find signs of them here. Follow the herders' trail down the Matcha Glacier moraine to a small lake at the base of the Igla Glacier, walled by the cliffy, snowy slopes of the Alaisky Range and the Ak Terek massif. A 2,600-foot (800-m) ice wall rises from the lake. The path goes around the lake, then drops toward woods about 1,600 feet (500 m) below. Look for a *kosh* **or a campsite** in this area (**1 day** from the other side of the pass).

The trail picks up the Ak-Terek River heading east. Where it crosses the **Utren River**, there's a *kosh* in the lush Utren Valley. This campsite is **1 day** from the campsite just this side of the pass.

If you've got the time, the Utren, North Tutek, or Yashilkyol gorges make beautiful side-trip hikes, the riverbanks overgrown with willows, birch, and aspen. The North Tutek and Yashilkyol rivers flow into the Ak-Terek on the right, and the Utren and Noo-Dzhailoo on the left.

In places, the Ak-Terek takes over the trail and you may have to ford in water up to your knees. Below where a mudslide cut off the valley, forcing the Ak-Terek into a side canyon, you come to the remains of the *kishlak* Korgon. Thirty minutes farther down the trail is **Zardaly** (**2 days** from the Utren River *kosh*). This 6,500-foot (2000-m) village, set in the Ak-Terek's cliffy crown, bustles with apple- and apricot-growing activity in the summer, but only a couple families winter here. Near Zardaly, two sturdy streams dump into the Ak-Terek: the Archabashi and the Khodzhaachkan. Together, these three make the Sokh River.

From the green fields of Zardaly, the path leads into a narrow canyon, then plunges down a steep hillside, clinging to the cliff high over an abyss. Glaciers line deep valleys on either side of the sunny Ak-Terek Valley, fingers of ice reaching down below tree line. From Zardaly through the Sokh River valley to **Kan**, a *kishlak* of neat, well-kept houses shaded by fruit trees, is about **18.5 miles** (**30 km**), **1 day** from Zardaly. For the last 7.5 to 9 miles (12 to 15 km) of this road (from *kishlak* Kyzyltash) you may be able to get a ride by truck.

From either Kyzyltash or Kan it's a dusty 4- or 5-hour drive to the town of Sokh in the south Fergana Valley. From here, you can drive to Shorsu,

Khodzhent, Kokand, or Fergana. Sokh to **Kokand** (via Rishtan) is about a 5-hour drive (**1 day** from Kan).

AKSU VALLEY LOOP

This is a **7-day loop trek** on the northern flanks of the Turkestan Range which can be shortened to 4 days by cutting out three day hikes (which is not recommended, because you would pass up some incredible scenery) or lengthened by linking up with a trek into the Assan Ussan area. If you do the latter, you can come out the Karavshin River to Vorukh. Otherwise, you'll begin and end at the mouth of the Aksu Valley, a 4-hour drive from the Fergana Valley town of Isfana. Isfana, like the other dusty Central Asian villages en route from Tashkent, is very much a Third-World settlement. The road from

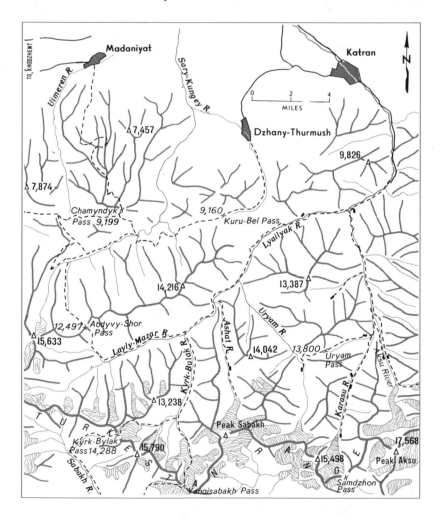

Isfana ends at 9,200 feet (2800 m) in the lush, green Aksu Valley, nestled between the granite giants peaks of Aksu, 17,564 feet (5355 m), Blok, 17,155 feet (5230 m), and Iskandr.

Three high mountain valleys parallel each other: Aksu, Uryam, and Ashat. In the course of this trek, you cross two high passes and, on optional side trips, explore the cirques at the heads of the valleys. Each successive valley is more wild than the last. The area was virtually undiscovered (by nonlocals) until Russian climbers started coming here in the early 1980s. Now, in midsummer the Aksu Valley proper is crowded with climbers from all over the former Soviet Union, but there's plenty of room to camp. Many climbers, most of whom are Russians, speak some English.

There is a *kosh* in the Aksu Valley and if you want to hire a guide, you may be able to find someone in one of the climbers' camps who speaks some English and will be happy to work. But be careful—the climbers concentrate on routes in the vicinity of the Aksu Valley and they may not have been across Uryam Pass themselves! A guide really isn't necessary, because the trails in this area are reasonably good and the topography is dramatic enough that it's

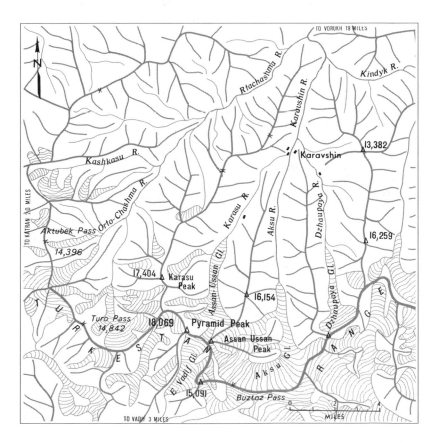

This climbers' base camp, with imposing Aksu looming in the background, is the starting point of the Aksu Valley Loop trek. (Photo: Bill Sumner)

difficult to lose your way. You just follow the narrow, steep-walled valleys, any one of which leads you down to civilization.

A **day hike** from the **Aksu Valley** *kosh* to the cirque at the base of the **Aksu face**, 11,000 feet (3300 m), is a good way to acclimatize for the trek. A **6-hour round trip**, the trail follows the valley floor most of the way and then goes along the moraine, between the boulder fields at the foot of Blok Peak, named for the Russian poet Alexander Blok. You get a close-up look at the sheer granite walls and jagged northwest summit ridge of Aksu.

To begin the trek, from the **Aksu Valley kosh**, hike across Karasu Valley until you meet the trail up to **Uryam Pass**. The trail climbs gradually to the pass, 13,800 feet (4200 m), and the footing is good. Drop 1,500 feet (450 m) to Uryam Valley. The descent from the pass is through shale higher up and, lower down, the trail crosses and recrosses a creekbed. Lower down there are some meadows that are good for camping, but the **best camps are in the Uryam Valley (4 to 6 hours)**. The valley abounds with mushrooms: if you know your edibles (or are with someone who does), you'll eat gourmet here.

Take a leisurely **day hike** to the **head of Uryam Valley (5 hours round-trip)**. The path snakes along the Uryam River through meadows ever deeper and deeper in wildflowers. Each bend in the river reveals a new still-life of green valley, glacial boulders and water cascading from rocks. The trail peters out in a boulder field below a breathtaking glacial cirque panorama.

From your campsite in the Uryam Valley, the path zigzags up steep hill-sides sparsely dotted with junipers to Sabakh Pass, 14,042 feet (4280 m), the high point of this trek. This trail is less pronounced than the Uryam trail, but you can see the pass clearly from the valley floor and it doesn't really matter how you reach it. Plan on **3 or 4 hours to Sabakh Pass**. From 12,500 feet

(3800 m) on, the hiking is on scree. Standing atop the pass, for as far as the eye can see are row upon row of unclimbed peaks over 16,000 feet (4800 m). The **2-hour descent** to **camp in Ashat Valley** is down scree slopes, without much of a trail. It's recommended that you camp two nights in Ashat Valley.

Another recommendation is to do a **day hike** up to the **cirque**, about **3 hours round-trip**. Hiking along the Ashat River, you're dwarfed by the massive granite faces of Parus and Sabakh. The Ashat Valley and Ashat River are also sometimes called Sabakh. The Ashat River converges with the Lyallyak River, which the Uryam also flows into downstream.

Descend the Ashat Valley to the confluence of the Ashat and Lyallyak rivers. The first part of the hike is dusty scree on steep hillsides with boulders, above a gorge that cuts deep into the earth. The trail drops down to the ravine bottom, crossing and recrossing the Ashat River on bridges built by the herders. These bridges, which sometimes look marginally solid for livestock, are usually substantial enough for trekkers. Camp at the little oasis at the **confluence of the Ashat and Lyailyak rivers** (**5 hours**).

Leave behind the U-shaped valleys to continue down the narrow gorge for about **3 hours** on a path that brings you to the *kosh* **on the Uryam River**. From here, follow a jeep track for **3 miles** (4.9 km) until you hit the **main road** from Isfana to Aksu—you have now completed the circle. There's a grove of apple and apricot orchards **along the river** that makes a good camp. Back in Isfana, with a little luck you may be able to get a shower and a beer, but don't count on it until you get back to Tashkent or Khodzhent.

ARTUCH TO ISKANDERKUL LAKE

This is a moderate **5- to 6-day trek** that goes from an elevation of 6,500 feet (2000 m) to 9,800 feet (3000 m) from villages between Samarkand and Dushanbe. The route leaves from Artuch and skirts the northern edge of the Fani, passes through the Kulikalon and Alaudin lakes district, then goes across Kaznok Pass to Iskanderkul Lake. (The second trek in the Fani, Margazor Lake to Iskanderkul Lake, below, is somewhat easier but longer, arcing down through the Margazor Lakes and Dukdon Pass. It can be done in reverse and combined with this trek for a 2-week-long loop. The Artuch-to-Iskanderkul Lake trek can also be done in reverse, originating in Dushanbe, and combined with the second Fani trek for a 2-week-long loop in the other direction.)

The trail from **Artuch** to Lake Kulikalon is a good one, winding gradually up 1,500 feet (500 m) through junipers. **Two and a half miles** (**4 km**) from Artuch brings you to **Kulikalon**, the first of the thirty azure lakes that stud the Fani. A plunge into one of these frigid alpine lakes makes you forget the heat in short order. You have your choice of campsites all around here.

From Kulikalon, it's about **4 hours** to climb the 3,000 feet (1000 m) to the top of **Kulikalon Pass**, where you are rewarded with a view of sparkling Lake Alaudin on the other side. The two lake basins (Kulikalon and Alaudin) are at approximately the same elevation; descend to **Alaudin Lake** (**2 hours**). Camping at Alaudin, you are in the very heart of the striking high summits of the Fanskie Gori.

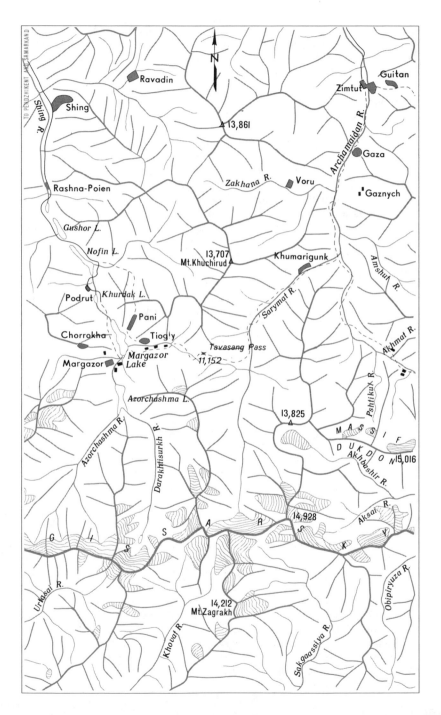

Ravadin

Shing

Shing R.

TO PENDZHIKENT AND SAMARKAND

△13,861

N

Guitan

Zimtut

Archa maidan R.

Gaza

Rashna-Poien

Zakhana R.

Voru

Gaznych

Gushor L.

Nofin L.

13,707
Mt. Khuchirud

Khumarigunk

Amshut R.

Podrut

Khurdak L.

Sarymat R.

Pani

Chorrokha

Tiogly

Tavasang Pass

Margazor
Lake

11,152

Akhmat R.

Margazor

Pshtikut R.

Azorchashma L.

13,825
△

Azorchashma R.

Darakhtisurkh R.

M A S S I F
D U K D O N
15,016

Akhbashir R.

14,928

Aksai R.

G I S S A R S K Y

Urlasai R.

Obipiryuza R.

14,212
Mt. Zagrakh

Khovat R.

Sakgaassiya R.

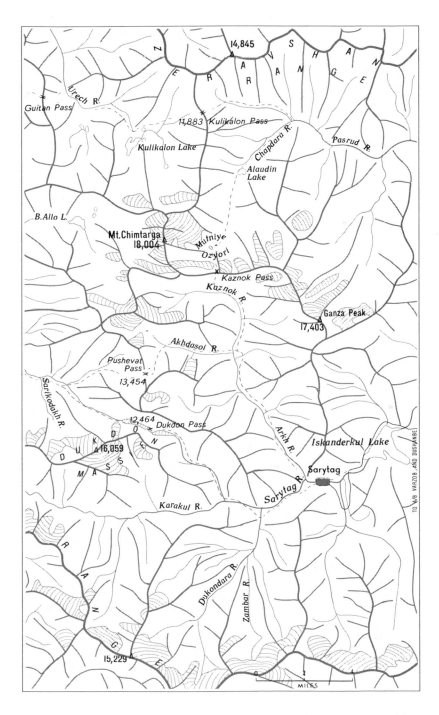

On the southern wall are Peaks Maria, Mirali, Energiya, and Chimtarga. Opposite is Chopdara. Each of these well-defended fortresses offers numerous challenging technical rock routes. Some, like Chopdara, have no easy way up. Mount Chimtarga, the highest summit at 18,004 feet (5489 m), is a relatively nontechnical climb. It can be done in 2 or 3 days from the Mutniye Lakes (farther on this trail), or from the Zindon (west) side.

From Alaudin Lake, a gradual 1,500-foot (500-m) rise over a trail through a glacial moraine, much of it on shale, takes you to the **Mutniye Lakes**, **3.75 miles (6 km)**. The Mutniye Ozyori, "Murky Lakes," have a higher concentration of glacial silt than the lower tarns. The camping here, mostly on scree, is more barren than at the lower lakes.

From Mutniye Ozyori proceed to **Kaznok Pass**, **6.25 miles (10 km)**. Kaznok Pass, at 13,251 feet (4040 m) and a Soviet Mountain Pass rating of 1B, is a bit too steep to be burro-able. The **2-hour descent** from the pass brings you to the valley of the **Arkh River**. There are good camps in meadows along the river.

Follow the Arkh River **3 hours** to a birch grove, where you hook up with the **road leading through the *kishlak* Sarytag to Dushanbe**. Few vehicles travel this road, but **12.5 miles (20 km)** east on the road, you come to **Iskanderkul Lake**, on the Khodzhent–Dushanbe road. The road goes along the edge of the lake, whose surface mirrors Mount Dozhdemerny. Iskander, the local translation of the name Alexander, lingers prominently, more than two millenia after the conqueror's passage here. Popular as a boys' name, Iskander also labels many geographic features in Asia.

From here, there are likely to be plenty of cars and trucks, and chances are you can get a ride the 87 miles (140 km) across Anzob Pass to Dushanbe. Anzob Pass, 11,063 feet (3372 m), is only open summers from about the end of June when the last snow melts out. En route, you pass through Varzob Climbers' Camp.

MARGAZOR LAKE TO ISKANDERKUL LAKE

This is a **68-mile (110-km) trek of 6 to 8 days**. As mentioned in the previous trek, Artuch to Iskanderkul Lake, this trek can be reversed and combined with the Artuch-to-Iskanderkul Lake trek—or you can reverse the Artuch-to-Iskanderkul Lake trek in combination with this trek and hike the opposite direction. Either way, the two combined are about a 2-week-long trek.

At this trek's starting point at **Margazor Lake**, the last lonely *kishlaks* of Pani and Tiogly cling to the steep slope of the Angarimosh Valley. Hike on scree up toward **Tavasang Pass**, 11,155 feet (3400 m). Over this easy pass, descend the steep, tiresome hill to the valley of the **Sarymat River**, where there's an old mining town—abandoned concrete-block Soviet buildings clashing with the local adobe. While hiking this valley overgrown with *oblepikha* (buckthorn), birch, and rose willow, you'll cross and recross the river several times.

Continue on toward the Sarymat's confluence with the Archamaidan River, passing more Tajik summer encampments. The trail crosses the Archamaidan and tracks the stream south for about half mile (1 km), before climbing high above the river. Only the occasional *yurt* is to be seen glued to the hillside.

Pass tributaries to the Archamaidan, Kochkut, and **Akhmat rivers**.

Continue upstream on the Archamaidan. Beyond its confluence with the Sarikhodakh and Pushnevat rivers, ramble upward through **edelweiss meadows** dwarfed by the Dukdon massif.

Climb steadily up until you reach the scree line of the West Dukdon Glacier moraine. Cross **Dukdon Pass** on snow, 12,467 feet (3800 m), Soviet Mountain Pass rating of 1A, and drop steeply into the picture-pretty **Karakul Valley**.

Reach *kishlak* Sarytag just past where the Arkh River, rushing down from a bundle of snowcapped 16,000-foot (5000-m) Fani summits, joins the Karakul and creates the Sarytag River. An azure ribbon, the **Sarytag River** meanders through a broad, tree-lined floodplain, with nice rock pools and birch groves for bathing and siestas.

Soon the trail turns into the road to Iskanderkul Lake. For directions from the lake to Dushanbe, see the previous trek, Artuch to Iskanderkul Lake. (The Margazor Lake-to-Iskanderkul Lake trek was contributed by Exodus Expeditions.)

High Pamir

The High Pamir is the core of the Pamir Mountains, containing three of the four highest peaks of the former Soviet Union. This is an area of huge summits, enormous glaciers, and extreme mountain weather. Most people who travel here do so to climb these peaks.

The former USSR's highest summit, 24,590-foot (7495-m) Peak Communism, hunkers at the junction of two major ridges: the Academy of Sciences Range and the Peter the Great Range. Peak Communism is a massive mountain, dwarfing the surrounding peaks—many of them over 19,000 feet (6000 m)— with its imposing north face, a sheer headwall. To its north, across the Moskvina Glacier, the former Soviet Union's fourth-highest summit, Korzhenevskaya Peak, 23,310 feet (7106 m), counterbalances Peak Communism's bulk with its elegant fluted lines. In between these two giants and slightly east of them is the smaller Peak of Four, 20,992 feet (6398 m). At the southern end of the Academy of Sciences Range is Peak Revolution; the huge Fedchenko Glacier extends from Peak Communism to Peak Revolution.

Northeast of Peak Communism, in the Zaalaysky Range, Peak Lenin, 23,405 feet (7134 m), straddles the Tajik–Kyrgyz border. This mountain is the former Soviet Union's third-highest peak. (The second-highest mountain, Peak Pobeda, is located in the Tian Shan; see chapter 10.)

On the north side of the High Pamir is the Alai Valley, a major corridor scattered with dusty villages. This valley is visible even from the slopes of Peak Lenin. Lukovaya Polyana ("Wild Onion Meadow"), the last outpost before entering the moraines, glacier, and snowy slopes of Peak Lenin, is an inviting, grassy plain. A summer storm can leave the Polyana, almost always bare and dry by July, knee-deep in snow. The red-toned foothills—even the High Pamir are rich in color—hem these meadows.

The climate of the High Pamir, as one might guess from its position embedded deep in the Asian landmass, is extreme continental. In the foothills south and east of the High Pamir, Dushanbe is a roaster in July when the thermometer hovers around 28°C, while in January temperatures average 1°C. In the High Pamir at the height of the late-summer climbing season, it can range between 5°C and 25°C during the day, and get down to -20°C—or even -50°C above 23,000 feet (7000 m) at night.

Centuries ago, the area to the north of the High Pamir, the Alai Valley (with the Surjov River Valley), was an important branch of the Silk Road.

Peak Communism was first climbed by Soviet mountaineer Abalakov in 1933 and was named in honor of Stalin. Later changed to Peak Communism, this mountain is probably due for another incarnation soon. (Russians' tastes in geographic names—and monuments, architecture, and socio-ideological experiments—tend toward the grandiose.)

Two incidents in particular fix Peak Lenin in the annals of mountaineering tragedies. In 1974, an eight-woman team led by Elvira Shataeva was caught by a storm high on the mountain. The women, determined to prove that an all-women's expedition could succeed, did not descend immediately. The wind shredded their flimsy Soviet tents. They perished, one by one, to the last woman, maintaining radio contact with base camp until the end.

More recently, on July 13, 1990, an earthquake-triggered avalanche swept the Skovorodka ("Frying Pan"), a flat area at 16,700 feet (5100 m) on Peak Lenin, dumping tons of ice and snow into the icefall below it. Skovorodka, long a popular camp, was home that Friday to forty-four climbers. One survived. Searchers found one body in the icefall, but no trace of the remaining forty-two climbers, sixteen of them foreigners. Of the Russian climbers who were lost, several had extensive Himalayan climbing experience; half were from St. Petersburg (formerly Leningrad).

Most travelers reach the High Pamir by way of the northern foothills, through the towns of Osh or Djirgatal. Djirgatal, an indolent Tajik hamlet, parts the Pamir foothills at just over 6,500 feet (2000 m). The pace in Djirgatal moves so slowly, one thinks it's a small village, but in fact several thousand people call it home. It is as difficult to tell the population of a Central Asian town as to guess the age of their women. You'll share buses and planes with portly Tajik gentlemen in *tyubeteika* (the square black cap embroidered with white stitching worn throughout Turkestan) bringing watermelons and other crops to market; you'll be shadowed by curious Tajik children who dart away shyly at the sight of a camera. Djirgatal has a market, a hotel, and a *chaikhana* (teahouse), whose walls are painted with lovely Pamir landscapes.

In 1990, there was only one public telephone in Djirgatal. I waited three hours to place a call to Moscow. None of my companions in the line complained or seemed the least bit impatient about the long wait. When I finally got through to Moscow, my call was cut off within a few minutes. I decided there was no point trying to call anywhere farther.

Djirgatal is a good place to acclimatize before heading for the High Pamir. It's an even better place to decompress post-expedition. After weeks in the land of snow and ice, as you drop down over the lush, rolling Pamir foothills to this valley where the Surkhob River braids its sandy delta, you may make you think you've gone to heaven. Definitely you'll think so looking back on it

Colonies of these family-style tents spring up every season at popular climbing base camps in the Pamirs and Tian Shan. The view from this tent is of the north face of Peak Communism

from hot, dirty Dushanbe—or Chicago, or Los Angeles. It is unlikely the advent of the free market will replace the age-old traditions of the high mountains with modern efficiency. So chances are you'll have some time—a few hours or a few days—to enjoy the *chaikhana* in Djirgatal.

Some travelers find Osh a more authentic old Turkestan town than Samarkand, largely because it was left off of the main Intourist circuit. Osh retains its large, traditional *bazaar*, and the central part of town is largely unsullied by Soviet block architecture; the monolithic apartment buildings cluster on the outskirts of the city.

The *chaikhana* (teahouse) tradition is still alive and well here. In fact, the *chaikhana* is about the only way to escape the midsummer afternoon heat in this town of few trees. Osh belongs to Kyrgyzstan, but historically it's an Uzbek town. Most of the population of about 200,000 are Uzbek. In recent years, there has been friction between the ethnic groups in this divided city; in 1990, these conflicts erupted in bloody riots.

As mentioned in the introduction to this chapter, travel in the High Pamir, and access from its northern foothills towns, is largely undisturbed by the battles in southern Tajikistan. Access through Dushanbe, however, may represent a risk, due to extensive fighting in and around that city in recent years. Be sure to obtain the most current information about safety before venturing into any part of Tajikistan.

The climbers' camp at Peak Lenin, Achik-Tash, was built by the IMC (see the A History of Backpacking and Mountaineering in Russia section of chapter 1, Introduction) and was run for many seasons by Muscovites. In 1992, Achik-Tash came under Kyrgyz management. Bekbolot Koshoev, formerly Communist party boss in Osh, has claimed the camp, the mountain, and all access to it and has installed his family members at Achik-Tash camp to extract fees from hapless climbers venturing into their web. The Koshoev clan has no connection whatever to mountaineering and their coup has seriously undermined safety and rescue operations on the mountain. Other companies and guide services continue to run expeditions to Peak Lenin, circumventing the Koshoev gang, but the political maneuvering has driven up the cost of a climb here and made it difficult to predict the climbing environment from one season to the next.

Climbers usually helicopter in to the peaks. Theoretically, each expedition charters its own helicopter flight, but when bad weather keeps the choppers from flying for several days, it is often the case that several groups are waiting for a ride and the scene turns into a free-for-all. Helicopter transport to and from these base camps distinctly resembles riding city buses in Russia: as many people cram on board as possibly can and still get the door closed. Getting on the helicopter ahead of other waiting climbers depends primarily on whether your sponsors have clout with the pilots. Sometimes, even clout won't get you on the chopper. In 1992, the Dushanbe airport ran out of fuel and the helicopters were grounded for more than a week. (See the By Air section of chapter 4, Traveling in Russia and Central Asia.)

These frequently climbed mountains are not a wilderness experience, so it's better to wait until the climbing camps fill up with High Pamir veterans who can advise you about the routes, and help break trail through deep snow. On a month-long expedition, chances are you'll find yourself tent-bound for at least 3 or 4 days. Hopefully, this will happen to you in base camp and not high on the mountain. Climbers' biggest foe is the winds that frequently blow at up to 50 to 70 miles an hour in the High Pamir.

Getting There

The capitals of Tashkent, Uzbekistan, and Dushanbe, Tajikistan, are the main points of access to the High Pamir; they serve as hubs, with air, train, and bus connections to smaller cities such as Djirgatal and Osh.

International flights to the capitals of Turkestan are limited, but the picture's improving. Lufthansa has a new Frankfurt–Tashkent route; Aeroflot has international flights to Tashkent from Delhi, India; Islamabad, Pakistan; Istanbul, Turkey; Kabul, Afghanistan; and some cities in the Middle East.

Within the NIS, Aeroflot has daily flights from Moscow and St. Petersburg to Tashkent and Dushanbe.

The train from Moscow to Tashkent takes almost three days. (The Central Asian trains' only reputation is that of a long, dirty ride.)

During the climbing season, helicopters transport climbers in and out of the popular High Pamir base camps, sometimes making several trips a day to or from Osh, Djirgatal, or Tashkent. The base camps are **Fortambek** climbers' camp and the base camp on **Moskvina Glacier**, near Peaks Communism and Korzhenevskaya, and **Achik-Tash** (Pamir Climbers' Camp), near Peak Lenin. Detours can be arranged into other areas.

Access to **Peak of Four, Peak Communism, and Peak Korzhenevskaya** is from Djirgatal. You can get to Djirgatal from Dushanbe by truck or other vehicle (most Soviet cars are treated as four-wheel-drives, whether they are or not) over a rough track winding along the Vaksh River, taking the better part of a day. Or you can take the "commuter flight" and get there in about an hour. Dushanbe's commercial flights came to a standstill in 1992 during a fuel shortage and have been erratic ever since.

Djirgatal's little airstrip does double duty as the helicopter landing pad for expeditions. Climbers usually helicopter from Djirgatal into Fortambek below Peak Communism, or to Moskvina on the north side of the mountain, the base camp for both Peaks Communism and Korzhenevskaya (about 45 minutes). It has not been possible to get advance flight reservations out of Djirgatal. After one expedition, we actually secured tickets to Dushanbe the same day we reached Djirgatal, only to be bumped by a gaggle of local Communist party dignitaries, awkard in their ill-fitting black suits, dispatched to Dushanbe for the funeral of an official.

Access to **Peak Lenin** is usually from Osh, east of Fergana. Many climbers bus to Achik-Tash (Pamir Climbers' Camp) from Osh, but the helicopter is a much easier way to go. The bus ride is a 9- or 10-hour ordeal, described by Dan Waugh, chairman of the University of Washington's Russia Studies Department and an avid Turkestan climber:

> *...the roads have no guard rails, and a brake failure could easily send one over the edge and thousands of feet to the valley below. Our bus overheats well before we reach the pass, but somehow the driver coaxes it to the summit. The real miseries begin when we leave the paved road two hours before reaching Achik Tash, to bounce across the rutted track that gradually ascends toward the snow and ice.*

The helicopter trip from Achik-Tash, base camp at Peak Lenin, to Moskvina, base camp at Peak Communism, takes 25 to 30 minutes.

Most climbers leave Peak Communism the same way they got there: by helicopter. It is possible, however, to trek out. Hiking out from Moskvina to civilization is a rugged 5- to 7-day walk. You end up at the Navruz Company's base camp on the Muksu River, near the village of Devshir. From Devshir, the occasional truck makes the rough drive to Djirgatal and Dushanbe. It's also possible to walk out to the Muksu River from Fortambek climbers' camp.

Where to Stay

In Dushanbe there's *Alpbaza* Varzob (Pos. Luchob, tel. 240403, 245064, or 345914); this climbers' hostel on the outskirts of town has the same name as the climbers' camp Varzob. There are also several tourist hotels.

Tashkent has a variety of hotels.

In Djirgatal, climbers frequently camp out in the little fenced-off birch grove next to the airstrip. A dormitory nearby has been converted to a guesthouse for travelers.

In Osh, in addition to the Osh *Alpbaza*, there's at least one hotel.

When to Go

The high-altitude climbing season is July and August. Mountaineers begin trudging up the Pamir giants in the second or third week of July. If you go earlier than that, you may have the place to yourself, but will have to contend with unstable weather and high avalanche hazard.

Snowstorms blow through the High Pamir even in mid- to late summer. Moskvina, Fortambek, and Achik-Tash base camps, all snow-free most of the time, may be buried under a foot or more of snow after a summer storm. Winds frequently blow at 50 to 70 miles an hour high in the Pamir. Wind flags are particularly common over the summit pyramid of Peak Communism. Korzhenevskaya Peak, only a few miles away, enjoys more temperate weather and is often climbable when high winds batter Peak Communism.

Equipment and Supplies

When you go on an expedition to the High Pamir, it's standard practice to let the guide service or travel agency that's arranging your trip shop for the food. If you're shopping for yourself, stock up on fresh things in the market in Tashkent or Dushanbe, where there's a great variety of fruits and vegetables in the summer.

Bring all your own climbing gear. The only climbing equipment you can count on being able to buy is Russian-made titanium ice screws. There are individuals in the high mountain base camps who have these to sell. (See also the introduction to Part 2, Turkestan.)

PEAK COMMUNISM ASCENT

There are two standard routes on Peak Communism: Suloeva begins from Fortambek climbers' camp; Borodkin begins from Moskvina. The **Suloeva Route** is the easier of these two routes. From the Fortambek Glacier, it gains the Big Pamir Firn Plateau, which extends approximately 1.75 miles by 7.5 miles (3 km by 12 km) at 19,000 feet (5790 m). From the plateau's eastern edge, the standard route climbs satellite summit Peak Dushanbe, 22,800 feet (6950 m), crossing from there to the summit pyramid of Peak Communism.

From Fortambek, you can also climb **Peaks Abalakov**, 21,150 feet (6446 m) and **Suloev**, which rub shoulders with Peak Communism on the Peter the Great Ridge.

The **Borodkin Route** on Peak Communism's north side is approached from the Moskvina Glacier. This route attracts many climbers because a base camp at Moskvina, 14,000 feet (4000 m), gives you the option of climbing both Peaks Communism and Korzhenevskaya.

This route, which requires crossing below an icefall and then climbing some technical rock sections, ascends the Borodkin Ridge to 20,000 feet (6096 m), then drops 1,000 feet (300 m) to the Big Pamir Firn Plateau. From there, the route is the same as from Fortambek.

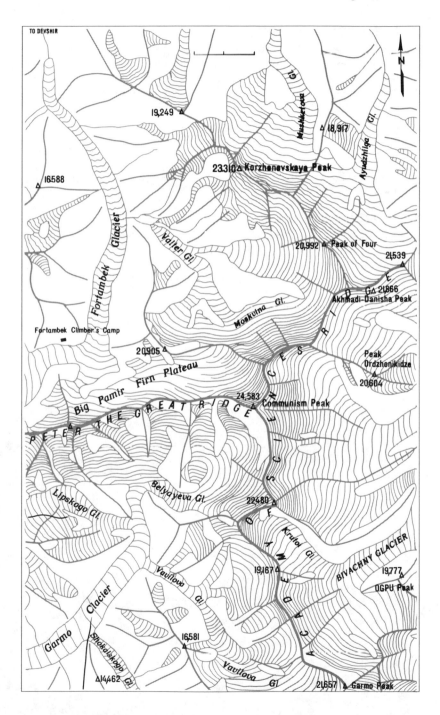

PEAK OF FOUR ASCENT

In the High Pamir, Peak of Four, 20,997 feet (6400 m), between Peaks Korzhenevskaya and Communism, is a good nontechnical acclimatization climb. From Moskvina base camp, it can be done in several days, heading up the glacial moraine as if to the Borodkin Route, then left up the distinct broad ridge at the cirque's head.

PEAK KORZHENEVSKAYA ASCENT

This peak is climbed from the base camp at Moskvina Glacier. The route from Moskvina is via a scree slope, then ascending a steep knife-edged ridge, the center one of the three prominent ridges leading to the summit. Most of the climb is on snow.

PEAK LENIN ASCENT

This mountain, with its reputation as a high-altitude walk-up, is on the short list of most-climbed 23,000-foot (7000-m) peaks in the world. While many mountaineers gain high-altitude experience climbing Peak Lenin, dozens of experienced alpinists have also died on the mountain.

The established base camp at Achik-Tash offers most of the comforts of home. Neat rows of "Polish cabins," orange and green stand-up–room tents on platforms, alongside a couple of buildings that house the kitchen, mess hall, and camp administration, give the place a military sense of order. The best part is the *banya*, next to a pond reflecting the summit of Peak Lenin on a clear day.

Trekking along the trail toward Travellers' Pass, Peak Lenin in the background (Photo: Matt Hyde)

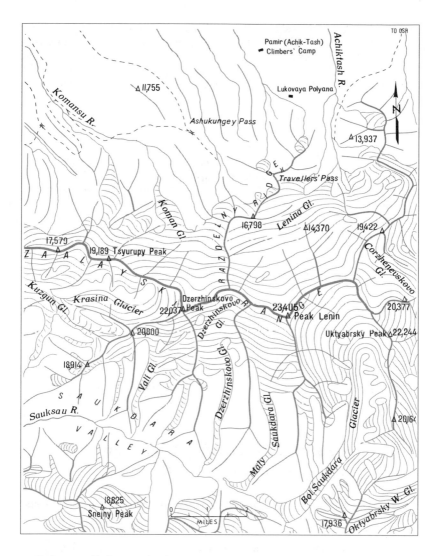

Lukovaya Polyana, the last outpost before entering the slopes of Peak Lenin, is several hundred feet above Achik-Tash. Expeditions from all over the former Soviet Union traditionally put down roots for the season on Lukovaya Polyana, each erecting a mess tent and pitching their base-camp tents in a circle around it.

From Lukovaya Polyana, the path leads over the small, steep **Travellers' Pass**, across a stream that becomes a river by midday, and over several miles of moraine to the edge of the glacier. Another mile of glacier walking brings you to the glacier's head at about the 14,000-foot (4267-m) level. This is a frequent place for **Camp I**.

The mountain is shaped something like a great armchair; at this point you are situated in the middle back of the seat. The right "arm," as you face it—the Razdelny Ridge—is a long snow slog with few crevasses. On a fine day in late July, the track up to this ridge, the most frequently climbed route on the mountain, can look like the line outside a Moscow vodka store. Notes from my Peak Lenin journal:

> *Camped at 19,800 feet, planning to go to the summit tomorrow. We burrow deeper into our bags and try not to hear the wind. In the morning, though, a summit attempt is out of the question: tall wind flags stream from the summit. Weather watch continues, reason tainted by desire. Around noon, we convince ourselves the wind is dying down—in fact, all that's changed is there is finally some visibility. Far below, the Alai Valley stretches its dusty length east to west, untouchably close.*
>
> *Gena kick-steps directly up the hill to the clavicle where our east ridge knits together with the summit ridge. The wind rises as steadily as we do; we've only come up 1,600 feet, but the wind has already sapped my strength and will. I'm happy to crawl into the false yellow warmth of the tent. When light finally comes at seven, we're beyond self-deception. The night has been an eternity—altitude headache throbbing to the nightmare humming of the wind. In a torpor, we strike the tents and start down the ridge. My head feels like it will split open with every step.*
>
> *We've descended 7,000 feet. The last little uphill, Travellers' Pass, looms before me. I march heavy-footed up the rise; my metabolic reserves have been reading empty for a couple of hours already. Disbelieving, I take in the green velvet carpeting the slopes, the marmot poking his chubby golden bulk out of the earth, and the riot of wildflowers surrounding our base camp in the Wild Onion Meadow.*

Eastern Pamir/Pamir Plateau and Western Foothills

By Steve Cunha

The deep, dark canyons of the Eastern Pamir and the undulating Pamir Plateau lie a stone's throw west of China and north of Afghanistan. Numerous unclimbed 19,600-foot (6000-m) summits lord over this 13,000-foot (4000-m) extension of the Tibetan Plateau. In addition are many gorgeous lakes, where most of the treks in this section take you.

Kara Kul ("Black Lake") Lake is an immense inland saline sea embedded east of the High Pamir and south of the Pamir Alai. The Sarikol Range juts upward from its eastern shore, forming the international frontier with China. An important bird-nesting habitat, Kara Kul Lake is accurately named when the dark waters reflect the tempestuous weather generated around the surrounding peaks. The sweeping views, ever-changing weather, and salty odor are an unforgettable scene.

Sarikol Lake, 99 miles (160 km) south of Kara Kul Lake, is a gem in an emerald setting, positioned at the southern margin of the Pamir Plateau. Hiking in this open scenery provides dazzling vistas of manifold 19,600-foot (6000 m) glaciated peaks of the Hindu Kush, and the rolling grasslands of the Pamir Plateau. Walking is limited only by your imagination and the streams that usually go underground by early July.

Sarez and Yashikul lakes lie slightly west of and about halfway between Kara Kul and Sarikol lakes. Sarez Lake is imbedded in the Eastern Pamir canyons, while Yashikul Lake fills Pamir Canyon just west of the Pamir Plateau. Both were formed after massive earthquakes shook loose earthflows that dammed their canyons. The 1911 Sarez quake annihilated *kishlak* Usoy, and left the Murgab River with no outlet. The lake level rose 785 feet (240 m) in three years, inundating 46.5 miles (75 km) before a subterranean channel burst thorough the center of the earthen dam and reestablished the river. Numerous Russian and Tajik scientists fear that earthquakes may trigger a dam failure that will send the waters of this 46-mile-long (75-km-long) lake caroming down the Amu Darya basin from Sarez Lake to the Aral Sea. The shores of Sarez Lake are almost totally barren, creating a desert lake scene that bears a striking resemblance to artificially created Lake Powell in Arizona.

The Western Foothills of the High Pamir are four parallel ranges—Peter the Great, Darvaz, Vanch, and Yazgulem—that rise abruptly from the Tajik Depression just east of Dushanbe, and follow east until merging with the High Pamir (Academy of Sciences Range). The terrain of these western outriders of the High Pamir closely resembles the North American Rocky Mountains, though the rivers are larger and the High Pamir looms to the east. Much of this region lies within the Gorno-Badakshan Autonomous Oblast, which has been forbidden terrain since the Bolshevik Revolution for all but a few shepherds, farmers, and the Soviet Army.

The beautiful Sangvor triangle, nestled between the Peter the Great and Darvaz ranges, offers some of the best hiking in the Pamir. At Sangvor, footpaths radiate from the confluence of the Obi Mazar and Obi Hingu rivers. Two or three Russian hiking clubs stage annual outings here. Although this is a fraction of the number of visitors to other parts of the Pamir—in particular the Fan Mountains—it represents a sharp increase since communist-era travel restrictions. Logistical difficulties, strenuous terrain, and difficult river crossings discourage many from entering this domain.

On the Pamir Plateau, the summers are short and cool, and snowfall occurs in all months. Despite cold summer nights and omnipresent morning and evening winds, you can expect plenty of warm and sunny afternoons. Keep a sweater handy though, as the temperatures plummet when clouds block the sun.

The cold crystalline waters of alpine Sarikol Lake have nourished explorers, traders, scientists, and soldiers since antiquity. These headwater uplands were an important Silk Road corridor. Marco Polo slept here en route to the court of Kublai Khan. Five centuries later, British Naval Captain A. E. Wood verified Polo's description.

Today, Kyrgyz nomads and Russian soldiers are about the only ones allowed into this sensitive geopolitical zone where three empires meet. Travel in a large group with a local guide is preferable to solo jaunts. However

tempting, be mindful that the Afghan Hindu Kush is *terra incognito* until officials can ascertain personal safety.

Several contemporary border disputes preclude trekking in the Sarikol
Range at the present. This is strictly enforced on both sides of the border! A
10-foot-high (3-m-high) barbed-wire fence follows the base of the Sarikol
Range in Tajikistan for more than 62 miles (100 km).

Assuming an end to civil hostilities in Tajikistan (a *big* assumption), the
possibility for transfrontier trekking into the Tashkurgan Nature Reserve
(China), Khunjerab National Park (Northern Pakistan), and the Wakhan Corridor (Northern Afghanistan) may become a spectacular reality. In addition,
there is the planned Sarikol National Park and Wildlife Preserve.

Unlike elsewhere in the Pamir, trekking in the Kara Kul Basin is easy on
both the feet and the mind. The well-defined routes are simple to navigate.
Aside from tremendous winds and sudden outbreaks of rain and snow, the
only significant concern is the lack of fresh surface water, which can present
problems for those who fail to plan ahead.

Getting There

The cities of Tashkent, Uzbekistan, and Dushanbe and Khodzhent (formerly Leninabad), Tajikistan, are the main points of access to Western and
Eastern Pamir/Pamir Plateau; they serve as hubs, with air, train, and bus connections to smaller cities such as Osh.

International flights to the capitals of Turkestan are limited, but the
picture's improving. Lufthansa has a new Frankfurt–Tashkent route; Aeroflot
has international flights to Tashkent from Delhi, India; Islamabad, Pakistan;
Istanbul, Turkey; Kabul, Afghanistan; and some cities in the Middle East.

From Russia, Aeroflot has daily flights from Moscow and St. Petersburg to
Tashkent and Dushanbe.

The train from Moscow to Tashkent takes almost three days. (If you
choose this route, *do* take a container of baby wipes for keeping the grime at
bay; *don't* take anything you mind losing if bandits sweep your train.)

From Dushanbe and/or Tashkent, travel to the Trans-Plateau Highway,
which traverses east from Khorog (on the Khorog–Dushanbe highway) to
Murgab, Alechur, Kara Kul Lake, and Osh. Much of this two-lane road is
paved and in fair condition. Traffic is sparse and the vehicles are stuffed to the
gills with people, animals, and cargo. Travel in eastern Tajikistan is an adventure in itself. Ask the drivers to fill and transport large drums of fuel in the
rear of the vehicles. It is preferable to travel with at least two vehicles, because rivers frequently intersect the remote and unsigned dirt tracks. Hire local guides as you go.

For the **two Kara Kul Lake hikes**, travel to the Trans-Plateau Highway.
From Dushanbe, travel the road to Khorog (on the Pyandzh River adjacent to
Afghanistan) to the Trans-Plateau Highway and take it east to Kara Kul Lake.
Or from Tashkent, travel to Osh, Kyrgyzstan; from Osh, travel the Trans-
Plateau Highway south to Kara Kul Lake.

For the **Sarikol Lake-to-Langar hike**, travel to the Trans-Plateau Highway as described in the preceding paragraph, and proceed to Sarikol Lake,

about 100 miles south of Kara Kul Lake.

For the **Sarez and Yashikul lakes hikes**, from Dushanbe take the Dushanbe Khorog highway to Rushan; from Tashkent, travel to Osh; from Osh, travel the Trans-Plateau highway south to the Dushanbe–Khorog highway and take it to Rushan. You can do the hike in reverse direction, starting out at Yashikul Lake; reach Yashikul Lake by taking the Dushanbe–Khorog highway from Dushanbe to Khorog and from there taking a rough dirt track to *kishlak* Alechur, halfway between Khorog and Kara Kul Lake (1 day). At *kishlak* Alechur, cross the Alechur River east of the marsh and drive the rough dirt track along the north side of the lake until the trail is reached at a point 5 miles (8 km) below the earthen dam that marks the west shore of Yashikul Lake (1 day). Alternatively, from *kishlak* Alechur you can follow the dirt track along the north shore of Yashikul Lake to the Karabyoomer River, where a footpath follows the lakeshore to the Sarez Lake turnoff, 12.5 miles (20 km), 1 to 2 days.

For the **three Sangvor hikes**, take the Dushanbe–Khorog highway from Dushanbe to *kishlak* Tavildara; inquire in Dushanbe about road conditions first. Frequent washouts, triggered by heavy rains and seismic activity, often close this road above the turnoff at the Obi Hingu River for weeks on end. From *kishlak* Tavildara, continue another 15.5 miles (25 km) to where the road crosses the Obi Hingu River; bear straight at this point and continue to Sangvor, at the confluence of the Obi Hingu and Obi Mazar rivers (10 to 14 hours). The bridge over the rivers is just below *kishlak* Sangvor, which is located on a river terrace 300 feet (100 m) above the rivers.

Where to Stay

In Dushanbe there's *Alpbaza* Varzob (Pos. Luchob, tel. 240403, 245064, or 345914); this climbers' hostel on the outskirts of town has the same name as the climbers' camp Varzob. There are also several tourist hotels.

Tashkent has a variety of hotels.

In Osh, in addition to the Osh *Alpbaza*, there's at least one hotel.

When to Go

July through September is the best time to go.

Equipment and Supplies

As with the rest of eastern Tajikistan, you will need to bring all of your supplies, stocking up in Dushanbe, Khodzhent, Osh, or whatever major city you use as your starting point. With the notable exception of bread, you cannot rely on the markets for any consumer goods, even in the Murgab and Khorog administrative centers. The barren market stalls and shelves attest to the mountain Tajiks' and Kyrgyz' disdain for retailing. Severe fuel shortages and a Russian exodus since declaration of Tajikistan's independence compound the problem. Carry fuel; firewood and dung are scare commodities, and remember to bring extra cord, tinned meat, and sunscreen to give to Kyrgyz and mountain Tajik hosts.

In the western foothills, there are no supply points or *kishlaks*. Carry extra food to share with sheepherders. Carry small gifts (e.g., tobacco, cord, first-aid supplies) for local Tajik farmers (along the Obi Hingu) and sheepherders who may invite you for tea and bread.

KARA KUL LAKE CIRCUMNAVIGATION

Allow **one week** to circumnavigate Kara Kul Lake. Steep slopes on the southwest shoreline, several marshes, and a lack of fresh water complicate the hike. Carry a 3-day supply of water, cooking fuel (no wood is available), and adequate clothing to cover temperatures that oscillate between 0°C and 33°C within a single day.

The badlands immediately surrounding the lake are composed of glacial loess and old lacustrine deposits. The soft and almost totally barren surface provides excellent footing. Move inland from the lakeshore when marshy ground impedes walking.

Cross the **Muzkol** (south end), **Akdzulza** (southeast end), and **Karaozulsa rivers** (north end) by either wading, swimming, or using a small dingy or raft. These rivers and several "dry" streambeds—burrow 1.5 feet (0.5 m) into the sand—provide potable water.

A short gain in elevation rewards the hiker with stunning views of the immense lake surface and surrounding glaciered peaks. This cold lake is fine for swimming, and the high salt content increases buoyancy.

KARA KUL LAKE CIRCUIT

This hike takes between **6 and 8 days**, and the ridgetop views are spectacular in all directions. The tributary Muzkol, Akdzulza, and Karaozulsa rivers are easy corridors into the looming High Pamir east of Kara Kul Lake. Foot and stock trails follow wide floodplains before ascending to the high pastures at the foot of the Pamir glaciers. You will have no end to trekking options and spectacular scenery, shared only with mounted Kyrgyz pastoralists and their stock. Rivers provide the one nagging nemesis; judge fords carefully and respect the powerful currents of these meandering streams. Carry fuel, because wood is either nonexistent or in short supply.

This interesting loop trek samples the unusual juxtaposition of ice and floodplain, marshland and desert; walk from the **south end of Kara Kul Lake** into the Eastern Pamir foothills. Follow the **Akdzulza River** northwest from the Akdzulza Delta, gradually making your way over the watershed divide and dropping down to the **Karaozulsa River** (**2 or 3 days**).

Hike downriver to the confluence with the **Karatash River**, where you can swing due south toward **Peak Severny**, 17,867 feet (5446 m), (**2 or 3 days**).

A prominent canyon northwest of this peak makes for a somewhat strenuous crossing back to the shores of **Kara Kul Lake** (**1 day**). Follow the shoreline (**2 to 3 days**) back to your beginning point.

SARIKOL LAKE TO LANGAR

This spectacular **8- to 10-day trek** covers **62 miles** (**100 km**) as it retraces the Silk Route along the Pamir River from Sarikol Lake to the small border town of Langar. This is an **easy hike** across reworked glacial sediments. The

Entire families summer in the high-mountain herding camps of Turkestan.
(Photo: Lee Mann)

terrain is wide-open, affording breathtaking views of the Hindu Kush and Pamir ranges. Most of this route follows the meandering **Pamir River**, a feature that marks the international frontier with Afghanistan. There are no extraordinary camping spots or unusual detours; simply hike downriver—water is available along the entire route—and camp whenever necessary.

The entire region is devoid of trees. Winds will be your companion every morning and afternoon. Rainfall is rare, and the side streams are easy to cross; so is the Pamir River, for that matter. Camels, ibex, and Marco Polo sheep are frequent companions. Simply follow in Marco Polo's footsteps (the old Soviet boundary markers also work) across the wide floodplain in the shadow of the Afghan Hindu Kush.

A jeep track follows the entire length of the Tajik side of the river, though in places this rough track is 6 to 9 miles (10 to 15 km) from the river. In 1991, only two vehicles per month traveled this route. There are army posts at Sarikol Lake and about halfway between the lake and Langar. You will likely see Kyrgyz nomads on the Tajik side and feral camels on the Afghan side.

Just below Langar, the river descends into a 3,300-foot-deep (1000-m-deep) canyon before merging with the **Wakhan River** (the combination forms the Pyandzh River). The town of **Langar** is a good stopping point for your trek, though you could also continue **one more week to Ishkashim**.

SAREZ LAKE CIRCUIT

Plan at least **one week of strenuous hiking** for the round trip to Sarez Lake from any direction. Note that the presence of large lakes and icy rivers can be deceptive—this is a severe high-elevation desert! You must be in excellent physical shape, and able to carry all of your food and two days' worth of water (in case of a mishap or wrong turn).

To reach the trailhead, leave the Dushanbe–Khorog Highway at **Rushan** and negotiate up the rough track that follows the **Bartang River** for 75 miles (120 km); a high-clearance vehicle is necessary. This can also be a very interesting hike, with very little vehicle traffic after the initial 25 miles (40 km). The road ends 3 miles (5 km) past *kishlak* **Padym**, where construction crews may be camped.

Plans call for continuing the road to Kara Kul Lake, though financial problems associated with the declaration of independence may delay completion. If the crew is in residence, be sure to advise them of your plans—they dynamite several times a day!

From the road end, follow the footpath along (and sometimes through) the scenic **Bartang River** to the confluence with the **Murgab River at *kishlak* Barchand, 10 miles (16 km), 1 or 2 days**.

The path climbs sharply above the Murgab River, affording magnificent view of glaciered peaks above and the deep blue river below. The trail eventually drops to the river, **5.5 miles (9 km)**, affording idyllic **camping on gravel bars** colonized by willlows.

From here, the easiest way to reach Sarez Lake is to follow the footpath up a **steep side canyon** that joins the Murgab River 1,500 feet (500 m) *downstream* from a series of impressive cataracts (if you see the cataracts, you have gone too far). The trail climbs unmercifully to a prominent overlook, then travels laterally up the canyon to the **giant earthflow** that created Sarez Lake, **5.5 miles (9 km)**.

Follow the trail until the radiant turquoise color of **Shaday Lake** is visible. Continue a few steps more for a view of Sarez Lake in the distance. The turnoff to reach Sarez Lake is not well marked, and the penalty for missing it is severe, given the state of the earthflow. There is a somewhat dilapidated wooden "nature reserve" sign about 650 feet (200 km) before the turn. The turnoff to reach Sarez Lake is just before both these lakes are visible. The rough trail cuts across the debris and provides excellent views of this chaotic scene before dropping to Sarez Lake. This is some of the most hauntingly spectacular country that I've ever seen.

Alternatively, you can ascend to the lake by following the Bartang River. However, this leads you into the heart of the debris flow, where the intense summer heat, dark rock, lack of landmarks, and total absence of water can take a quick toll on even the most fit hiker.

Return the way you came, or continue to Yashikul Lake, described below.

SAREZ LAKE TO YASHIKUL LAKE

This **10-day hike** through the Eastern Pamir involves deep canyons, enormous freshwater lakes, interesting *kishlaks*, breathtaking passes, and the endless vistas of the Pamir Plateau. The **48-mile** (**78-km**) hike can begin at either point, but is described starting from Sarez Lake (see the preceding hike to reach the lake).

From the earthen dam at Sarez Lake, the beginning of the long climb around the shores of the lake are marked by a **scientific station** between Shaday and Sarez lakes. Ascend **Mardzana Pass** to a large plateau with a magnificent view of Sarez Lake and the Muzkol Range. The relatively easy descent to **Sarez Lake** contours above a large inlet that ends where the **Lanzar River** enters the lake, **11 miles** (**18 km**), **2 days**.

The west shore of Lake Yashikul is a 37-mile (60-km) walk from this point along a well-marked path. Follow the **Langar River** through a narrow canyon for **12 miles** (**20 km**), **2 days**. The trail moves up and down the steep slopes, but always stays in sight of the river. Water is available in this otherwise desert country. When the canyon opens up, swing due east, keeping with the main Langar River. Within a short distance, 2.5 miles (4 km), the first of three large lakes appears.

Continue beyond these lakes until you come to a good place to break up the hike: a 15,187-foot (4629-m) pass that crosses the Alechur Range (and separates the Yashikul and Sarez drainages). Glaciers and melting snow provide reliable water throughout the year, but carry water up the pass if there are no signs of snow. A well-beaten footpath makes its way up the desolate canyon to the **pass, 9.25 miles** (**15 km**), **1 to 2 days**.

After you come down the other side of the pass, continue until you reach the **Goonm River**, just below Lake Yashikul, **15.5 miles** (**25 km**), **3 to 5 days**. From the Goonm River, the path continues to **Lake Yashikul, 5 miles** (**8 km**).

Alternatively, several routes split from the main Sarez–Yashikul path, and pass spectacular alpine lakes that dot the Alechur Range. It is possible to reach the southeast shore of Sarez Lake by crossing the divide into the **Pamaev drainage**. This involves some steep climbing, and you should have a good topographic map and be comfortable with off-trail hiking. Water is available. A fine footpath along the **Kamamardshanau River** and a 14,000-foot (4300-m) pass across the **Alechur Range** provides a feasible, though strenuous, route to the northeast shore of Lake Yashikul via the Alechur River.

SANGVOR TO BADAKSHAN CHECKPOINT

Kizikul Lakes are on the western boundary of the proposed Pamir National Park. These two glacial lakes are a beautiful stopover on your way across Peshoy Pass and the Darvaz Range in the western foothills of the Pamir.

There are few established trails here, just days worth of fine walking and exploring in several directions. The canyon bottoms are excellent places to seek shelter during storms. Water is plentiful and, in many cases, devoid of glacial silt. Wood is plentiful along the main rivers, but very scarce elsewhere. This may well be the finest hiking country in the Pamir.

Exercise extreme caution during all stream crossings. Inquire in Sangvor about the status of bridges. The cable bridge near *kishlak* Sangvor is usually the more reliable.

From **Sangvor**, cross the **Obi Mazar River** and hike downriver to the confluence with **Kyzykul River**. Alternatively, you can cross the **Obi Hingu River** near *kishlak* Sangvor, which is smaller and 7.5 miles (12 km) downriver from Sangvor, and walk upriver to the confluence with **Kyzykul River**. From either starting location, you pass the ruins of *kishlaks* depopulated during the 1940s under Stalin's reign.

In the lower canyon, an enormous landslide forces the river underground for 1,500 feet (500 m). You will notice waterfalls flowing from a cavern in the upper portion of the landslide. The trail becomes indistinct in the marsh above this point. Bear right (west) and regain the track where it switchbacks up the next steep hillside. Saturated wildflower-strewn meadows break the steep ascent to Peshoy Pass. Note the changing vegetation from oak-lined terraces of the Obi Hingu to mid-canyon juniper stands, subalpine, and finally alpine plant meadows near the pass above the upper lake. **Kyzykul Lakes**, the two delightful alpine lakes, reward your effort. They are loaded with fish and are frequented each evening by Asiatic brown bears, mountain sheep, and fox. Look for their tracks and scat along the sandy lake shores. The meadow-lined valley between the lakes is delightful.

From the upper lake, ascend to the meadow above the lake and continue up to **Peshoy Pass**, 12,600 feet (3847 m)—and the proposed Pamir National Park boundary—into the Pyandzh River drainage. Scale the pass either to the left or right of the snow cornice. (From the upper lake, you have the option of exploring a side canyon to the east before ascending the pass.)

The view from the pass is spectacular, but it's even more so if you ascend a short distance in either direction. The western Pamir fall away on either side, and the massive Hindu Kush of Afghanistan looms to the south. The rolling alpine uplands of the Darvaz Range afford hiking reminiscent of the San Juan (Colorado) and Wrangell (Alaska) mountains. Sheep trails run in all directions; the verdant grasses attract thousands of domestic stock animals throughout the summer.

From the pass, a walk of **several days** puts you at the **Badakshan checkpoint** on the Khorog–Dushanbe Highway. This can also be an excellent starting point for doing this hike in reverse direction.

SANGVOR TO VANCH

From **Sangvor**, a well-worn trail/road follows the western foothills river Obi Mazar's canyon to the pilgrimage site, **22 miles (35 km), 2 to 3 days**, of **Hazarati Burg**, a Muslim cleric said to be buried in a somewhat time-worn shrine. During the height of the summer pilgrimage, up to twenty-five Tajik men trek to the burial site each day. Camping is delightful along this river. Riparian willow and birch forests grow in dense stands. Fish abound and the hillsides harbor significant bear and sheep populations. Side streams offer pure water as an alternative to the silt-laden Obi Mazar. Only one family farmed this drain-

When the snow melts, the mountain people of Turkestan head for the highlands with their sheep. (Photo: Lee Mann)

age in 1992, thus the rest of the canyon and all the tributaries are wilderness.

An easy walk to the **Mazar Glacier**, **6.25 miles** (**10 km**), puts you in a lunar landscape characteristic of active glacial outwash plains. A frigid katabatic wind flows down this glacier every evening. Numerous tributary canyons beg exploration, each affording unique combinations of waterfalls, alpine meadows, horned ridges, and small cirque glaciers.

Adventurous types can cross the upper Obi Mazar (difficult, rope required), or the terminus of the Mazar Glacier, and backtrack to the **Darsharbak River**, where a large glacier canyon offers wilderness seclusion and spectacular scenery. A **strenuous 3-day hike** crosses the **Darvaz Range** into the Badakshan administrative town of **Vanch** near the Afghan border.

SANGVOR TO MUKSU RIVER

This hike in the western foothills takes you to one of the overland access routes to the High Pamir: the Muksu River, which leads to either Fortambek Climbers' Camp or the Moskvina Glacier base camp. The larger Obi Hingu River drainage is more challenging and numerous routes cross the divide between it and the Obi Mazar River. The easiest way to reach the Obi Hingu is to start at **Sangvor** and ascend the road/footpath up to the last settlement above *kishlak* Arzink, a couple days' walk from the headwaters of the **Obi Hingu River**, below Mount Agassiz. This is a wilderness trip and no provisions are available.

Just above Arzink, the valley widens as several glacial outwash streams coalesce to form the Obi Hingu. From a tiny settlement, it is possible to cross the various channels and enter the wilderness of the upper drainage. Use extreme caution crossing the rivers. It might be prudent to arrange a horseback ferry with local Arzink residents. Alternatively, one can cross the Obi Hingu on a footbridge a couple of miles (several km) below Arzink. However, enormous landslides on the south side of the canyon may complicate reaching the upper drainage from this approach.

In either case, the ridges that divide the various glacial canyons offer superb views of the High Pamir, while birch thickets in the sheltered canyons invite camping. A 1-day walk up any canyon brings you to the terminus of a large Pamir glacier (which often facilitates a safe—though tricky—passage to the opposing riverbank).

From the last tiny settlement above Arzink, bear north (left) and follow the narrowing flood plain until two large glacial streams diverge in opposite directions. From the obvious split, a strenuous days' hike leads across a pass and into the Muksu River drainage. The somewhat undefined route follows the lateral moraine on the north side of the canyon to the base of the Devloxan Glacier. Cross the river below the glacier (carefully) or pick your way across the rubble overlying the glacial ice. Use extreme caution in either case. Walking below the 650-foot (200-m) face of this glacier is daunting!

Continue up the moraine until a 10-foot-high (3-m-high) glacial boulder marks the route to the 13,845-foot (4220-m) **pass, 3 miles (5 km)**. If you reach two elongated small lakes nestled between the moraine and the canyon wall, you have gone too far. Ascend a long and steep scree valley until a low dip in the ridge appears to your left. The view from the summit is spectacular—the contorted Pamir Knot fills every angle of sight. Immense pyramid-shaped Mount Agassiz, 19,282 feet (5877 m), and Peak Moskva, 22,261 feet (6785 m), dominate in the distance.

If you decline the strenuous climb to the pass, remember that numerous side canyons throughout the upper Obi Hingu beg for exploration; many are reminiscent of high meadow-strewn cirque basins of the European Alps and North American Rocky Mountains.

The precipitous drop down a scree slope to the Sugran Glacier is more difficult than dangerous. Descend the glacier to the outwash plain and walk **2 or 3 days** to the **Muksu River**, where a ride to Dushanbe or Djirgatal may be arranged.

10   The Tian Shan

Nearly half of the 1,500-mile-long (2500-km-long) Tian Shan (Chinese for "Celestial Mountains") lie in Turkestan (formerly Soviet Central Asia), most of this in Kyrgyzstan. The northern fringe extends into Kazakhstan and the southeast edge reaches into Uzbekistan. Like the Dzhungar Alatau and Pamir Alai mountain systems bordering it, the Tian Shan marches on east–west lines. Sometimes Tian Shan is written "Tien Shan." "Tien" is the older romanization of Chinese, which isn't in general use anymore because it was confusing and Anglocentric.

Hemmed by the Iliisky Valley to the north and the Fergana basin on the south, the Tian Shan encompasses a vast range of climatic and geographic zones. The verdant valleys and fruit-tree oases of the Western Tian Shan are a world away from the Central Tian Shan's frigid, rugged, and starkly beautiful high peaks.

The Tian Shan enjoys long summers, with July temperatures in the foot-hills averaging 25°C, and 15°C to 20°C at elevations between 6,500 and 9,800 feet (2000 and 3000 m). January averages -5°C at elevations below 3,200 feet (1000 m), with the mercury dropping about another 10°C for every 3,200 feet (1000 m) of elevation gain. In general, there's much less precipitation in the high Tian Shan than on the periphery. Dzhergalan in the Central Tian Shan foothills gets 32 to 40 inches (80 to 100 cm) a year, and the Engilchek Glacier less than half as much. Snow volumes vary greatly from ridge to ridge. There's very little snow on the west side of Lake Issyk Kul, while 33 inches (85 cm) pile up at Dzhergalan. The snowline in the Tian Shan lies generally between 11,500 and 13,000 feet (3500 and 4000 m). Snowline in the Kyrgyz Alatau and Talassky Alatau ranges from 10,500 to 11,500 feet (3200 to 3500 m); in the Muztag it's up around 14,700 feet (4500 m).

The Celestial Mountains are the bastion of the snow leopard. Rarely ob-served, this beautiful, elusive cat (*Panthera uncia*) stalks the high ridges of Kyrgyzstan and Kazakhstan. Kathleen Braden, in her article "The Outlook for Snow Leopard Protection in Four New Countries of Central Asia" published in the *International Snow Leopard Trust Bulletin* (vol. X, no. 2, 1992), says there are about 450 of them in the Tian Shan, almost 60 percent of the total snow leopard population.

According to U. Grachev and A. Fedosenko of the Almaty Institute of Zo-ology, there are three areas where snow leopard populations are still stable. The Northern Tian Shan's Alma-Ata *Zapovednik* and the junction of the Zailaiisky and Kungei Alatau ranges is one; the Western Tian Shan's Aksu-Dzhabagly Nature Reserve and the adjacent Maidantal and Ugamsky ridges is another; and the Dzhungarski Alatau's Lepsinsky and Tokhtinsky *zakazniki* is the third.

Until recently, snow leopard pelts could be found in the *bazaars* of Central Asian cities for a few hundred rubles. Now that the cat is protected by being listed in the Red Book of endangered species, the skins are not sold openly, but locals still shoot snow leopards to keep them from killing livestock.

According to Braden, the snow leopard is also threatened by encroachment on its territory. Cattle grazing decreases the numbers of wild goats and sheep—the snow leopard's major prey—and reduces its habitat.

For Kyrgyzstan, Kazakhstan, Uzbekistan, and Tadjikistan as a whole, land that is suitable for snow leopard habitat is also under protected status, totaling less than one-half of one percent of the countries' territory.

In the past, umbrella legislation and agencies working out of Moscow, such as *Goskompriroda*, provided some attempt at inter-republic coordination. Despite the USSR's dismal environmental record, much of the investment and human resources for preserving the snow leopard in Central Asia came from the central government in Moscow and the Russian ethnic population in the region. Under the USSR, strong educational systems, such as branches of the Academy of Science, were established in all the republics. Conservation education through schools and and zoos, the publication of regional-level Red Books, and popular journals on conservation all brought these issues to the attention of the general public.

Republic-level ministries, academic and research organizations, and environmental organizations do therefore exist in the four countries of Turkestan. One issue for these newly independent countries may be where the fledgling governments will find funds to support conservation agencies. Another concern is inter-republic coordination of environmental programs now that the convenient tool of the central government has been lost.

Snow leopard ecology is a good case in point, with its ranges overlapping political jurisdictions throughout the Tian Shan and Pamir Mountains of the four eastern Turkestan republics. The main source of employment in Kyrgyzstan, Uzbekistan, and Tajikistan has been agriculture, with domestic herding a prime occupation. Nonindustrial economies in the region actually threaten the snow leopard's existence: as Central Asia is deprived of economic subsidies from the central government, the people turn to expanding their herds and agricultural croplands, encroaching further on the snow leopard's already diminishing habitat. Braden argues that the fate of the wild snow leopards here may depend on what paths for economic development and societal values are open to the human populations of Kyrgyzstan, Kazakhstan, Uzbekistan, and Tajikistan.

For more information about efforts to protect snow leopard habitat, contact the International Snow Leopard Trust (see Appendix A, General Resources).

Western Tian Shan

From Mount Manas, the highest point at 14,705 feet (4482 m) in the Talassky Alatau on its northern edge, the Western Tian Shan drops off west to disappear in the great sands of Asia. In between, it weaves in the Chatkal, Chandalashsky, Pskem, Maidantal, Ugam, Fergana, Kuraminsky, and Atoinoksky ranges.

Walnut, maple, hawthorn, birch, apple, and honeysuckle all grow at the lower elevations. In the river valleys, travel sometimes requires bushwhacking through a thick snarl of wild berry bushes: barberries, raspberries, blackberries, and bright orange buckthorn berries.

At higher elevations, much of the Western Tian Shan is high-altitude steppe. Once I rode along in a helicopter with a meteorological crew that was placing snowfall measuring sticks on high points of the Chatkal, Pskem, and Ugam ranges. (In the days when fuel prices were artificially suppressed, weathermen could afford to hire helicopters....) We set down on ridge after ridge, each tall in waving grasses and yellow-spotted with wildflowers. These ridges usually lose their snow early on in the hot, dry summers and they rolled away green as far as the horizon, studded with rocky buttresses.

Average temperature in July is 20°C, but it can get as hot as 30°C to 40°C. In January, it's -5°C on average, but -20°C in the high mountains.

Overall, the mountains of the Western Tian Shan are mild and hiker-friendly, but be prepared for heat, bushwhacking in some of the valleys, and, if you explore far from established paths, wild rivers and steep, cliffy talus slopes. The big rivers of the Syr Darya basin—the Chatkal, Pskem, and Naryn—defy fording anywhere in the mountains.

Getting There

While you can access the fringe of the Western Tian Shan in a few hours from Tashkent, to get into really wild, beautiful country it's best to venture a bit farther, using Namangan or Andizhan farther east as a kick-off point.

International flights to Tashkent include Lufthansa's new Frankfurt–Tashkent routes; Aeroflot flies to Tashkent from Delhi, India; Islamabad, Pakistan; Istanbul, Turkey; Kabul, Afghanistan; and some cities in the Middle East. Air Uzbekistan, which has branched off from Aeroflot, also flies some international routes, including service from Frankfurt, Germany. It's difficult to book these flights, because they are not listed in travel agents' computer systems.

Within Russia, there are flights from Moscow daily and St. Petersburg to Tashkent. Direct service from Moscow to other Turkestan cities, such as Namangan or Andizhan, is spottier. You usually have to fly into one of the capitals and get a connecting flight.

The train from Moscow to Tashkent takes almost three days. (The Central Asian trains' only reputation is that of a long, dirty ride. If you choose this route, *do* take a container of baby wipes for keeping the grime at bay; *don't* take anything you mind losing if bandits sweep your train.)

For the **Alyam Pass Loop**, drive 2 hours from Tashkent to Chimgan; from Chimgan, drive ½ hour more to the Koksu River. (While buses run from Tashkent to Chimgan, you may have problems hiring a vehicle in Chimgan, so it's best to arrange for transportation from Tashkent all the way to the Koksu.)

Where to Stay

There are numerous hotels in Tashkent and on down the line. In Tashkent and the other capital cities, there are also agencies that arrange for travelers to rent a room or an apartment. Outside the city, in more remote towns, this is not an accepted practice, although if you ask around and there's no hotel, you may be invited to stay with a family.

There's an *alpbaza* in Chimgan.

When to Go

There's no perfect time to go to the Western Tian Shan: you have to choose between rain or heat. Generally it's best from May to October. There's high danger of avalanches between October and May. April and May are the season when the region gets most of its annual rainfall. Fewer than half the days are sunny during these months. Nonetheless, many Russians choose to hike here in spring when things are still green and blooming, to avoid the heat that sets in later in the summer. September is optimal for hiking temperature-wise, but by this time all the vegetation at the lower elevations is brown.

Equipment and Supplies

Stock up on food at the market in Tashkent, or en route in Chirchik. Some horses are kept at Chimgan and it may be possible to hire pack animals.

ALYAM PASS LOOP

Two hours' drive from Tashkent is a large reservoir (Charvaksky) and recreational settlement called Chimgan. Chimgan's biggest local draw is its ski hill, but it's also popular with climbers and hikers in the summer months. The little community takes its name from the mountain, Chimgan, 10,745 feet (3309 m), which has routes of varying difficulty (Soviet Climbing Route ratings of 1B to 4B). The crags where local rock climbers boulder are also here.

The Alyam Pass Loop is a **moderate, 4- to 6-day trek** easy to reach from Tashkent. This trek follows the north side of the Koksu River to Alyam Pass, 6,336 feet (1932 m), crossing Keng-Dzhailoo Ridge, then back to Chimgan along the Chatkal River. Both the Koksu and Chatkal are technical mountain rivers (class IV to VI), carving through narrow ravines, so much of the time on this hike you are restricted by the canyon walls. The trail is poorly maintained in places, but is passable by horses. **Map:** 1:200,000 quadrangle K-42-XXIII.

Begin on the road from Chimgan, at the Koksu River. The path along the **Koksu River** ascends gradually for **10 to 12 hours** northeast until below Alyam Pass. If it hasn't been washed out by spring river torrents, there's a **bridge** across the Koksu just before the pass. From here to the pass the trail gains 1,500 feet (450 m) in elevation, about a **2-hour scramble**. From **Alyam Pass**, descend a loose scree slope. There are good camps at the base of the pass, on the **Chatkal River**.

It's a **10- to 12-hour hike** from here to **Chimgan** on the trail alongside the Chatkal River, passing camps of beekeepers. Most of the trail along the Chatkal is actually in Kyrgyz territory.

Northern Tian Shan

The Northern Tian Shan consists of the Kyrgyz Alatau in the west and the Zailiisky Alatau and Kungei Alatau in the east, south of which is Lake Issyk Kul. The Kyrgyz Alatau straddles the Kyrgyz–Kazakh border west of Kyrgyzstan's capital city of Bishkek (formerly Frunze). The Zailiisky and Kungei *alataus* are tightly squeezed together due south of Kazakhstan's capi-

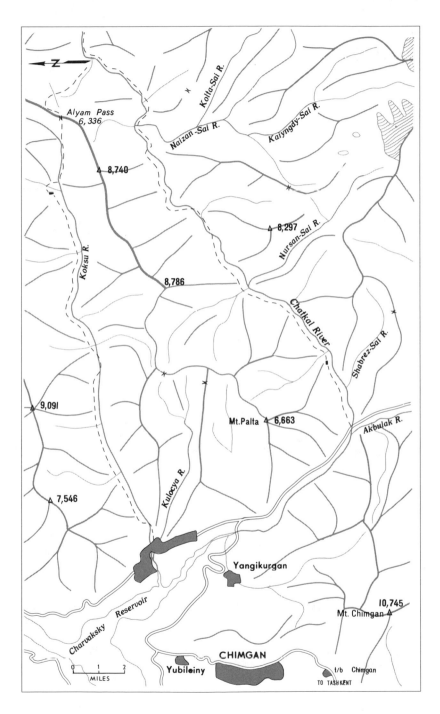

N

Alyam Pass
6,336

△ 8,740

Kolta-Sai R.

Naizan-Sai R.

Kaiyngdy-Sai R.

△ 8,297

Nursan-Sai R.

Koksu R.

8,786

Chatkal River

Shabrez-Sai R.

△ 9,091

Mt.Palta △ 6,663

Akbulak R.

△ 7,546

Kulocya R.

Yangikurgan

Charvaksky Reservoir

0 1 2
MILES

Yubiloiny

CHIMGAN

10,745
Mt. Chimgan △

t/b Chimgan
TO TASHKENT

tal, Almaty (formerly Alma Ata). The huge Lake Issyk Kul lies in a basin south of these two ranges.

Alatoo (or *alatau* in Kazakh) means literally "colorful rocks." In effect, it is synonymous with mountains. One Kyrgyz friend suggested that in Kyrgyzstan, a country of mountains, people had no need for a special word describing mountains. Another explained that in local lore *tau* refers to mountains with rocky slopes and green valleys suitable for grazing animals, while *bel* are mountains covered year-round with ice and snow.

The Northern Tian Shan still evokes its history of felt-clad horsemen galloping across high valleys. This is the traditional mountain homeland of the Kyrgyz and Kazakh people, although these tribes are not limited to the northern Tian Shan: The Kazakhs' range extends through the Altai into present-day Mongolia and the Kyrgyz have relatives as far south as the southern Pamir in Xinjiang province. The Kyrgyz and Kazakh peoples were wanderers until this century, and cities are recent innovations in the northern Tian Shan. Bishkek, called Frunze through the Soviet period, was a minor settlement known as Pishpek before the Russians' coming. Almaty grew out of the Russian fort of Verny; the city's population still has a Russian majority.

Two of the longest ridges in Turkestan are the Zaiilisky Alatau and Kungei Alatau, which band the north shores of Lake Issyk Kul. The Tian Shan's tectonic origins still make themselves felt in the numerous earthquakes that shake the Zailiisky Alatau, literally, "the mountains that lie beyond the Ili River." The region also gets giant mudslides, especially on the north side of the Zailiisky Alatau. In these two ranges, Tian Shan fir march up the mountainsides from the river valleys. The forests of these tall native trees, perfectly Christmas-tree shaped, seem straight out of a fairy tale. Mountain lakes abound.

In fact, hundreds of tarns sparkle among the ridges of Kyrgyzstan. Lake Issyk Kul, at 113 miles (182 km) long and 36 miles (58 km) wide the largest of seven major lakes in Kyrgyzstan, is a significant blue spot on any world map. The expanse of Issyk Kul resembles an ocean until the morning fog lifts, revealing the fringe of snowy peaks of the Terskei Alatau and the Kungei Alatau, which sandwich the lake. Issyk Kul has no outlet. This mountain-locked pool is only lightly salinated, but it doesn't freeze in winter, in spite of the 5,250-foot (1600-m) elevation.

In the Kyrgyz Alatau, Zailiisky Alatau, and Kungei Alatau, summertime temperatures average 15°C to 25°C during the day and 5°C to 10°C at night. There is frequent rain in early and late summer. The average winter temperature in the mountains is -29°C. Lake Issyk Kul enjoys a pleasantly mild climate: 17°C is average for July on the lakeshore, while the temperature hovers around 0°C in the winter.

The town of Karakol, at the east end of Lake Issyk Kul, appears on most maps as Przhevalsk, which it was called in honor of Nikolai Przhevalsky, the nineteenth-century explorer. Przhevalsky actually spent more time "discovering" Ussuriland, Mongolia, and Xinjiang than he did roaming Kyrgyzstan. But he had the misfortune of succumbing to his last illness here at Issyk Kul, where he's buried.

Tall, stately firs colonize a Terskei Alatau valley. (Photo: Vladimir Maximov)

The mountains of the Kyrgyz Alatau are Bishkek's playground, and the mountains of the Zailiisky Alatau are in Almaty's backyard. Thanks to this accessibility, the northern Tian Shan offers many fine hikes on well-used trails.

A short drive from Bishkek, the capital of Kyrgyzstan, you can find the full range of winter and summer activities in the high snowy peaks and alpine meadows of the Kyrgyz Alatau. Ala Archa and Alamedin valleys offer easily accessible yet remote mountain fun. Ala Archa and Alamedin awe with their Yosemite–like walls that frame the valleys and the rivers that thunder down from faraway glaciers. The Ala Archa Valley is a national park where recreation is actively encouraged.

In summer, day and multiday hikes along the Kyrgyz Alatau's Ala Archa Valley floor or on the many side trails lead to scenic vistas of the region's many 14,000-foot (4300-m) summits. White-water kayaking is popular on the Ala-Archa River. Within a day's hike of an alpine lodge near the trailhead are climbing routes to challenge the big-wall climber or peak-baggers. The rope tow in the glacial cirque at the head of the valley is one of a half dozen little downhill ski areas where Bishkek residents play in winter.

Few major cities anywhere can boast a backyard mountain range like the Zailiisky Alatau. Only a half hour from Almaty you come to Medeo, where there's a world-class competition skating rink and the Medeo hotel/sports complex. A few miles farther—the road rides the top of a unique dam slung across the valley in hopes of preventing mud slides from crashing through town—is the best ski area in Central Asia: Chimbulak.

Laced with good trails, the Zailiisky Alatau and Kungei Alatau are easily accessible from both Almaty and Bishkek. In summer, the snowline's around 12,500 to 13,500 feet (3800 to 4100 m). If you're off an established trail, remember that there are bridges across the wild rivers only in the lower elevations where there's herding activity.

The most direct—and most popular—routes between Almaty and Issyk Kul are given below. Due to their frequent use, the trails are easy to find. Unfortunately, you'll find previous travelers' trash at campsites all along the way. Trails to the east and west of Ozerny Pass are much closer to the wilderness experience. There have apparently been some instances of younger herders—sometimes armed—robbing hikers in these mountains (see chapter 3, Staying Safe and Healthy).

Lake Issyk Kul is a popular vacation spot, its north shore developed with a string of vacation hotels, several of the most luxurious built by the Communist party. A road circles the lake, but much of the south shore is wild. It's faster to reach Karakol (at the east end of the lake) on the highway along the northern perimeter. Issyk Kul is a "kul" place from which to kick-off or conclude forays into the Northern Tian Shan.

Getting There

The access points for the Northern Tian Shan are Bishkek, Kyrgyzstan, and Almaty, Kazakhstan.

There is an international flight to Almaty from Urumqi, China. Bishkek's airport is not yet an international airport, so from outside Russia and Central Asia you must first fly to Moscow, St. Petersburg, or another Turkestan capital such as Almaty or Tashkent, Uzbekistan.

From inside Russia, there are flights from Moscow daily and St. Petersburg to Almaty and Bishkek (4 hours). You can also fly to Bishkek from Tashkent (30 minutes). Or you can drive from Almaty.

For the **four hikes in the Ala Archa and Alamedin valleys**, from Bishkek, it's a 1½-hour drive to Ala Archa lodge or the Warm Springs Sanitorium in the Alamedin Valley. Public transportation is unreliable, and will drop you a mile short of Ala Archa and 9 miles short of the Alamedin trail. On Sundays, it's easy to find a ride back to Bishkek with groups returning from a weekend in the mountains.

For the **Chimbulak-to-Mutnoi River hike**, drive or take the bus from Almaty (½ hr) to the Chimbulak Ski Area. From Turistov Pass it's a 1½-hour drive back to Almaty.

For the **Aksai River-to-Alma-Arasan hike**, drive or ride the bus from Almaty to the Aksai River canyon, about 12 miles (20 km) southwest of town (1 hour). The drive back to Almaty takes about an hour from Alma-Arasan.

For the **Ozerny-to-Lake Issyk Kul hike**, drive south from Almaty 12.5 miles (20 km) to Bolshoi Alma-Atinksy Lake, elevation 6,890 feet (2100 m), and continue to below Ozerny Pass. From Grigorievka, the drive west to Bishkek (along Issyk Kul's north shore) takes 3 to 4 hours. Bishkek to Almaty is another 3 hours by car.

For the **Kul Sai hike**, drive southeast from Almaty through mile upon mile of monotonous Kazakh steppe, which offers little in the way of scenery. Scores of half-submerged pillboxes add variety to the terrain as you come within 60 miles (97 km) of the Chinese border. Drive past the town of Saty and up the Kul-Sai River to the lowest of the three Kul-Sai lakes (7 hours from Almaty).

Where to Stay

In Bishkek, the Dostuk Hotel is the most expensive ($60 and up) and least desirable lodgings. The Intourist hotel Alatoo, near the train staion, is a better deal. About ten minutes from downtown, the Issyk Kul is a Western-class hotel with rooms for about $45.

The Ala Archa lodge, elevation 8,000 feet (2440 m), accommodates up to 180 people in summer, 80 in winter. Arrangements are best made in advance, although small parties usually have no trouble getting rooms. The cafeteria serves breakfast and dinner, but most visitors cook on campstoves outside. Bathroom facilities are primitive, with no showers. Accommodations at Alamedin are limited, but there are a few double rooms available at the Warm Springs Sanitorium, especially midweek.

Hotels in Almaty, just like everything else, are more expensive than in Bishkek. There are several tourist hotels in downtown Almaty, where rooms start at $80. There are also some small guesthouses with much simpler accommodations at a fraction of the price. One, called the Uyut, charges $5 a night.

Only a half hour from Almaty, in Medeo, there's the Medeo hotel/sports complex. A few miles farther is the ski area Chimbulak with another hotel.

When to Go

The adventure season in the Kyrgyz Alatau, Zailiisky Alatau, and Kungei Alatau is year-round. You can travel in the Ala Archa and Alamedin valleys any time of year. Swollen rivers may complicate approaches and trails in the spring, and there is frequent rain in early and late summer.

The season for the Kul-Sai region is June through September. Mid-September is an ideal time to hike in the Kul-Sai region. Most of the summertime hikers are gone. So are the shepherds who come here with hundreds of sheep, "protected area" or not. In late summer there are still raspberries and wild mushrooms.

Equipment and Supplies

Water filters are mandatory in summer to strain the glacial silt out of the river water. In summer, pack animals are available from the herdsman who lives at the Alamedin trailhead.

Stock up on fresh produce, meat, and bread in Bishkek and Almaty.

ALA ARCHA VALLEY

This is an **easy overnight hike**. The Ala Archa Valley extends 9.25 miles (15 km) beyond the Ala Archa lodge to a cirque dominated by peaks between 12,000 and 13,500 feet (3600 and 4000 m) high. The trail takes off on a washed-out road from the lodge for 1.25 miles (2 km), then moves onto meadow, talus, and then moraine farther up the valley, **6.25 to 7.5 miles (10 to 12 km)**. The trail crosses the Ala-Archa River three or four times on bridges, although these can be washed out in the spring and early summer. It is possible to reach the head of the Ala Archa Valley in **a long day**. The trail is good through the meadows, although swampy in places. There are some good **campsites** in the moraine at the **head of the valley** near the ski school. In summer, you can use one of the **stone huts** at the school **for cooking** and there's a **small dorm** that sleeps up to twenty people in relative comfort. The school is untended in the summer, so it's first-come, first-served.

AK-SAI GLACIER

This is another **easy overnight hike** in the Ala Archa Valley. The Ak-Sai River valley is the basin of big walls: Korona, Free Korea, Semyonov Tianshanskovo. Total elevation gain from the trailhead to the glacier at the head of the valley is 2,460 feet (about 750 m) over 4.25 miles (7 km).

The trailhead diverges from the main Ala Archa Valley track right at the *alplager* Ala Archa. The trail heads immediately southeast up and over a small shoulder and into an alpine meadow. It rises with a constant steep gradient for 1.75 miles (3 km), with about 1,600 feet (500 m) elevation gain, then levels out for another 1.75 miles (3 km) to the base of a waterfall, where it ascends into the Ak-Sai cirque.

With heavy loads, it takes **4 to 5 hours** to reach the **waterfall**, then another **3 or 4 hours** to reach the foot of the **glacier**. There's decent **camping at the waterfall**. At Ratzek Camp on the moraine at the foot of the **Ak-Sai Glacier**, a small, two-story **stone hut** sleeps ten people, and there are good **campsites** nearby.

ALA ARCHA VALLEY TO ALAMEDIN VALLEY

This is a **3- or 4-day strenuous hike**. A local guide is a good idea on this one; the route finding can be tricky. Carry lots of water, because you won't find any from the time you leave the Ak-Sai River until you reach the Chon-Kurchak River.

About 2.5 miles (4 km) up the Ak-Sai River trail from the trailhead, a little feeder stream comes in from the east. From here, a side trail turns and goes up over Sharkiratma Pass, 13,500 feet (4100 m). This route is very steep, somewhat exposed near the top, and sometimes washed out in places. The views from this pass and the shoulder of nearby Peak Uchitel, which this trail crosses, are spectacular, looking down onto both the Ak-Sai and Chonkurchak glaciers. **Elevation gain to Sharkiratma Pass** is roughly **4,900 feet (1500 m)** over **5 miles (8 km)** from the *alplager*.

From the pass, descend about 1,000 feet (300 m) to the **Chonkurchak Glacier** on a trail that's steep and loose at the top. There's a **small hut** at the foot of the glacier. From here on out the trail's easy, although it's essentially cross-country travel. Cross the **pass north of the glacier**, to the **Kurchak-Tyor River**, which you can wade across, and over another **unnamed pass** to the **Chichar River**. This brings you out right at the Warm Springs Sanitorium in Alamedin.

ALAMEDIN EAST PASS

This is a **leisurely 4- to 6-day round-trip hike** that goes up the Alamedin Valley to Alamedin East Pass, and then back. Starting from the Warm Springs Sanatorium at about 7,500 feet (2300 m), the valley ascends in a series of steps about **12.5 miles (20 km)** to the **Tyuk-Tyor Glacier** at about 11,000 feet (3350 m). The steps are fairly even, averaging 1.25 miles (2 km) of flat meadow, interspersed with short risers. As you make your way up the terraced valley, you'll have lots of opportunities for radial day hikes from alpine-meadow camps on the Alamedin River. See great eagles soar, hunting for lemming and mountain partridge.

The trail is unmarked as it winds up the eastern bank of the river through

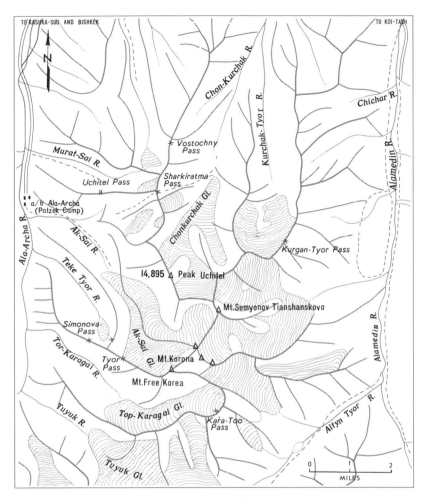

pasture, meadow, talus, and dry riverbed. There's good **camping all along
the way** to Ashu-Tyor. Through the summer, the river is too high to wade and
there are no bridges, although with horses you can ford almost anywhere.
You'll have to ford several side streams, tributaries of the Alamedin. There's
a bridge over the Salyk River, but not the Achyk-Tash, Kyok-Sai, or Altyn
Tyor rivers. Where the trail splits at the foot of **Mount Aman-Too**, 14,997
feet (4572 m), head east to Ashu-Tyor cirque. (For an optional side trip, you
can cross the river and continue straight up into the Tyuk-Tyor Cirque.) This
fork is not marked, so keep an eye on the map, or have a guide. Both trails
ascend steeply from this point.

To follow the **Ashu-Tyor River**, climb **650 feet (200 m) over 2.5 miles (4
km)** to **three small lakes**. Then the trail gradually rises to just below
Alamedin East Pass, where you get on the snow-covered glacier for the final

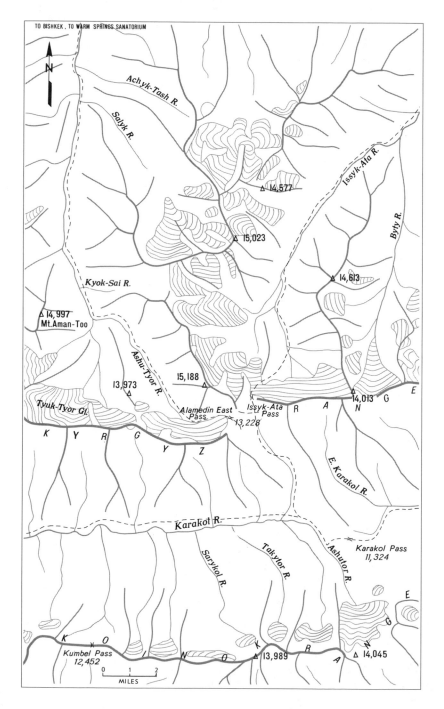

TO BISHKEK , TO WARM SPRINGS SANATORIUM

N

Achyk-Tash R.

Salyk R.

Issyk-Ata R.

Byty R.

△ 14,577

△ 15,023

Kyok-Sai R.

△ 14,613

△ 14,997
Mt.Aman-Too

Ashu-Tyor R.

15,188 △

13,973
△

Tyuk-Tyor Gl.

Alamedin East
Pass

Issyk-Ata
Pass

R   A

△ 14,013 G
N   E

K   Y   R   G   Y   Z

13,228

E. Karakol R.

Karakol R.

Sarykol R.

Takytor R.

Ashutor R.

Karakol Pass
11,324

E

G

N

△ 14,045

K   O

W   O

K

R   A

△ 13,989

Kumbel Pass
12,452

0   1   2
MILES

650 feet (200 m) of elevation gain to the pass. You can **camp in the valley** and do **Alamedin East Pass**, 13,228 feet (4033 m), as a day hike, glorying in the whole southern Kyrgyz Alatoo.

CHIMBULAK TO MUTNOI RIVER

The **3- or 4-day easy hike** from Chimbulak Ski Area to Turistov Pass and down to the Mutnoi River is just one of many fine hikes, scrambles, and climbs accessible from Talgar Pass.

From the base of Chimbulak at 7,200 feet (2200 m) to the top of the ski hill, **Talgar Pass**, at 10,500 feet (3200 m), is a **1.75-mile (3-km)** hike when the chairs aren't running (**2 to 2½ hours**).

From Talgar Pass, descend **20 to 30 minutes** on a good, albeit steep, trail to **Sauruksai River**. The river is shallow at this point and only 10 or 13 feet (3 or 4 m) across, so you can cross on rocks. From the river, hike the grassy, northeast slopes of Pik Chkalova to the **Levi Talgar River (1 to 1½ hours)**. Head up the Levi Talgar **2 to 2½ hours** to a **broad meadow**. There's **good camping** here or 1 hour farther where the Turistov River flows into the Levi Talgar (total hiking time from Chimbulak is 5 to 7 hours).

Head west up the Turistov River through the pretty, forested Talgar Valley. You're hiking along the boundary of the Alma-Ata *Zapovednik*, which takes in Talgar Peak (the highest summit in Zailiisky Alatau) and the main knot of these mountains. Below Turistov Pass, hike around the lower moraine and bottom of the glacier. To get up to the pass, ascend first on scree, then climb a snow-ice slope that's about 20 degrees steep and 130 to 200 feet (40 to 60 m) long (**4 hours from meadow**). Descend scree and snow slopes (15 to 20 degrees) to the southwest and then follow the Mutnoi River until you come to the road.

From the road, you can either head back to Almaty, or continue across Ozerny Pass to Issyk Kul (see the Ozerny-to-Lake Issyk Kul hike, later in this section).

AKSAI RIVER TO ALMA-ARASAN

The Aksai River canyon, about 12.5 miles (20 km) southwest of Almaty, was the epicenter of the devastating 1911 earthquake. This is an **easy hike of 3 or 4 days** over about 25 miles (40 km) without difficult fords.

Hike up the **Aksai River** to the **confluence of the Karasai** and Aksai rivers, **5.5 miles (9 km), 3 to 4 hours**.

Hike from the Karasai River through woods and meadows, across a **11,500-foot (3500-m) pass**, to the **Kargalinka River, 7.5 to 8.5 miles (12 to 14 km), 7 to 8 hours**.

Hike to the **Prokhodnaya River** and descend to **Alma-Arasan**, where there's a small hotel, **10 to 12 miles (17 to 19 km)**.

OZERNY TO LAKE ISSYK KUL

This is generally an **easy, nontechnical 3- to 6-day hike**; in late summer, crampons and an ice axe may come in handy if there are sections of bare ice at the passes.

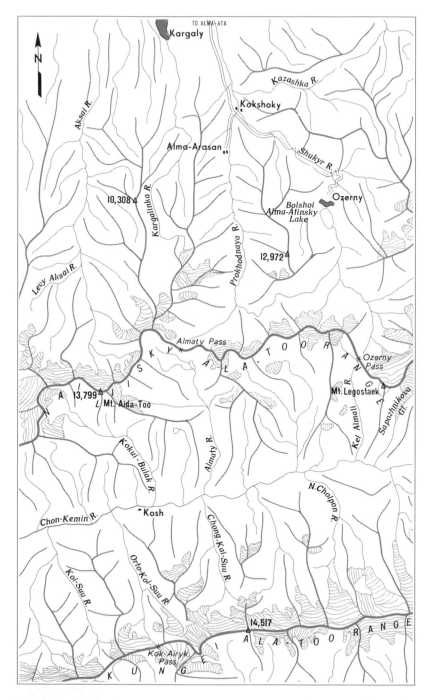

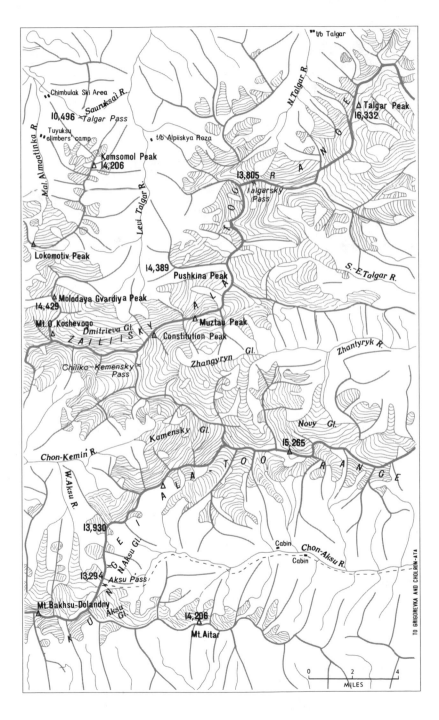

A Kazakh boy frolics on his pony at Kul Sai.

From Ozerny at **Bolshoi Alma-Atinksy Lake**, hike through forest and alpine meadows toward Ozerny Pass. The top section before the pass is a snow
slope (to 20 degrees). The last 10 to 15 minutes could be ice in late summer.
Ascend 11,838-foot (3609-m) **Ozerny Pass** (**2 to 3 hours**). Make a quick descent on scree from the pass, then hike along the **Kel Almali River** 30 minutes to where it flows into **Chon-Kemin River**. There's good camping here.
The descent from the pass to this point takes another **2 to 3 hours**; total hiking
distance from the trailhead is **9.25 miles (15 km)**.

Head up the Chon-Kemin River **2 to 2½ hours** to the **Aksu River** just below Zhasyk Kul Lake. There's good camping here or on the moraine near the
lake.

From **Zhasyk Kul Lake**, hike up the Aksu River trail to below the **Aksu
Glacier** (**4 hours**). From here, the paths diverge and you have a choice of
ways to Lake Issyk Kul:

1. The longer way is across **Aksu Pass** and down Chon-Aksu River to
Grigorevka (**3 days**). Head up the moraine on the left side of the Aksu Glacier. Ranged at the top of the glacier are North Aksu Pass, South Aksu Pass,
and East and West Bozteri passes, in that order. You want to go across **North
Aksu Pass**. The trail climbs first along the moraine, then up scree (**2 to 3
hours from glacier to pass**). Descend to the east to the Chon Aksu valley 30
to 40 minutes on scree, then down grassy slopes to the river. Cross as high as
you can to the right side of the river and stay right, where the trail is best.
There's **good camping** at the edge of the forest, **2 to 3 hours from the pass**.
It's another **1 or 2 hours' hike** down to the road. It's possible to drive from
here to **Grigorevka**. Walking, it takes **6 to 8 hours.**

2. The shorter route is across **East Bozteri Pass** to **Bozteri** (**2 days**). Proceed up the glacier to the pass, as in the route above. Head due south up the center of the Aksu Glacier toward **East Bozteri Pass**. Ascend the pass on gradual snow slopes of 15 to 20 degrees. From the base of the glacier to the top of the pass is **3 to 4 hours**. Descend scree to the glacier on the other side, then down the moraine. Below the moraine is another scree section. It's **1 hour down from the pass** to where a number of streams flow together. Hike **4 hours** to the village of **Bozteri**, just east of Cholpon Ata.

LOWER KUL-SAI LAKE TO LAKE ISSYK KUL

By Vlad Klimenko

A less direct route to Issuk Kul from the Almaty area of Kazakhstan is via Kul Sai and across Sarybulak Pass. Kul Sai is the collective name for three small mountain lakes located in the Zailiisky Alatau a 7-hour drive southeast of Almaty. This is an easy **3- or 4-day hike**.

From the trailhead at **Lower Kul-Sai Lake**, the trail to Middle Kul-Sai Lake, the second major watershed, runs parallel to the stream connecting the two lakes. The trail goes through stands of tall Tian Shan pines. Visibly etched into the ground by hoofprints, the trail is a reminder of the nomadic civilization that's existed in these parts for ages. At **Middle Kul-Sai Lake** (**6 to 9 hours**), meadows open along the southern bank. This is a **good camp** from which to explore the surrounding mountains and valleys. The down side of

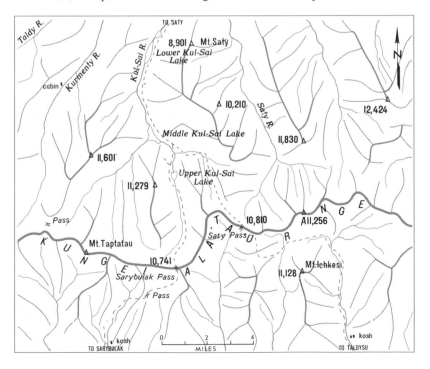

camping at Middle Kul-Sai are the piles of rusty tins left by previous campers.

One good **day hike** is the trail to **Upper Kul-Sai Lake**, the trail climbing the steep incline around the east bank of the middle lake.

From Middle Kul-Sai Lake to Sarybulak Pass the trail heads south, with the lake gradually receding on the left. The trail passes through a large open pasture that offers a good general perspective of the surroundings. At the far end of the pasture, the trail dips into a creek that can be crossed on logs or forded.

From there the trail zigzags up an embankment to a smaller clearing. At that point it makes a sharp right and continues hugging the northwest slope for approximately an hour. The creek that it crossed remains below, on the right. With the creek remaining on the right, the path gradually curves to the left (south) as the slope broadens out, bringing a parallel set of ridges into view on the right. At this point the trail ends up being close to a smaller streambed that divides these two ridges at the base. Several rough corrals and wooden tent-frames indicate that this is a **favorite high camp** for hikers. Looking north past the increasingly hazy-colored shades of each successive ridge, you see the edge of the yellow-brown steppe.

Evidence of rockslides abounds; in some places hiking is exclusively over large rocks and boulders. Perpendicular to the direction of the walk stands the sharp-toothed ridge that marks the border of Kyrgyzstan as well as the Issyk Kul basin. To reach Sarybulak Pass, veer left up a gradual incline instead of heading directly toward the face. The incline takes you right up to the base of the ridge; from there you can see a small pond and, beyond it, another gradual incline heading to the right. This is **Sarybulak Pass**, elevation 10,741 feet (3275 m). From here you get a spectacular view to the north (toward the steppe) as well as an impressive perspective on Lake Issyk Kul and the main body of the Tian Shan beyond it.

From Sarybulak it's **a half day** to the road that runs along the banks of Issyk Kul. The descent is rapid and very scenic. There's quite a bit of grassy pastureland, but most of it is steeper than on the Kazakh side. Follow the streambed down for **2 hours** until you reach a **fork**, designated by a small ridge that splits the descent route. From here it's **45 minutes** to a local collective **farm**—a good rendezvous point to meet your pickup vehicle if you've arrranged for one.

Central Tian Shan

The Tian Shan reach their zenith at Kyrgyzstan's eastern border with China. To geographers these mountains are the Central Tian Shan, but in local lore this knot of high, formidable mountain ranges is known as the Muztag, or "Ice Mountain." More than an ice mountain, the mighty Muztag is an impregnable ice citadel, fortified by the Tengri-Too, Engilchek-Too, Kokshaal-Too, Meridionalny, Saridzhasky and Kaiyindy ranges. Peak Pobeda, 24,405 feet (7439 m), and Khan Tengri, 22,949 feet (6995 m), crown the Muztag. Many of the surrounding peaks are over 19,600 feet (6000 m).

Two of the Soviet Union's top five peaks shadow the South Engilchek Glacier. Peak Pobeda, or "Victory Peak," sits astride the disputed Kyrgyz–

Khan Tengri showcases the sheer grandeur of the Central Tian Shan, one of the world's premier big-mountain citadels.

Chinese border itself. There is easily enough of this mountain for the Kyrgyz and the Chinese to share. The high point in the Kokshaal-Too (the highest range of the Tian Shan), Peak Pobeda's massive bulk abuts the Zvyozdochka Glacier with a 1.75-mile (3-km) vertical headwall.

Khan Tengri is as delicate in shape as Pobeda is bulky. This elegant pyramid, with its fluted ridges, has the aesthetic appeal of Ama Dablam and a handful of other peaks of perfect lines. The mountain's upper third is marble that glows red in the dark, making the mountain seem illuminated from its very core.

Even the passes of the Muztag are high—many too high for a helicopter to fly over. The helicopter pilots snake along the great glaciers that course the corridors between ridges, burying the mountains' feet in ice reputed to be up to a mile deep in places. Flying into the Central Tian Shan, you see a panorama of sharp summits strung together like shark's teeth into serrated ridges. These mountains seem not to have been pushed up by tectonic forces, but carved out by a sculptor. They have an elegance of form unusual in such massive peaks.

There are said to be 7,800 glaciers in the Tian Shan, many of them advancing. Mightiest of them all is the Engilchek (variously spelled Inilchik or Inylchek). The 38.5-mile-long (62-km-long) Engilchek Glacier wraps around the Tengri-Too Range like a tuning fork. The Engilchek Glacier feeds the Engilchek River, flowing west into the Sarydzhaz River, where it turns south through deep canyons and waters China's Tarim Valley.

Near the junction of the two arms of the Engilchek Glacier, on the North Engilchek Glacier, a unique ice-locked lake submerges the glacier's surface. Named for a German explorer, Lake Merzbacher is actually two separate lakes. While the shockingly blue (and shockingly cold!) waters of upper Merzbacher Lake are ice-free, icebergs choke the lower lake. Once a year, usually between August 10 and 20, but occasionally as early as the end of July, the lower lake swells and ruptures the glacial walls containing it, forcing water into the glacier's chasms. The glacier spews icebergs torn from the foot of the glacier onto the silt bed below, raising the water level in the Engilchek River. Those who've observed this phenomenon describe the thunderous noise of the ice lake bursting its bonds.

A traversable moraine runs most of the length of the North and South Engilchek glaciers, broken in places by icefalls. Between these two arms of the glacier are packed some of the most awe-inspiring peaks anywhere: Khan Tengri, the blood-red mountain, elbowed by Chapayeva, Gorkovo, and Petrovskovo— sheer walls of rock dropping thousands of feet to the glacier. And between them course some of the most massive glaciers in the world, many of them advancing. A trip up the Engilchek Glacier is like stepping back into the last ice age. It's comforting to see this ice dragon thumbing its nose at global warming.

Overall, the Central Tian Shan is an excellent place to go if you are seeking perspective on the human condition. Watch an avalanche roar down a mountainside, a white tornado taking 8,000 vertical feet (2400 m) in a few seconds, then swooping across the glacier's surface, depositing tons of rock and ice debris. The frequency of these avalanches leaves many of the mountain faces perpetually bare, displaying the striking effects of geologic forces—variously colored layers tilted at dizzying angles.

In the centuries before sailing ships opened trade routes by sea, merchants transported their goods between Europe and Asia on horseback and in camel caravans. These routes, defined by the high peaks of the Pamirs, Tian Shan, and Karakorum, as well as other natural obstacles like the Taklamakan Desert, came to be called the Silk Road. Turgart Pass, in the Central Tian Shan on the border with China, was one of the few ways through the Tian Shan. In central Kyrgyzstan one encounters reminders of the bold travelers who traced the Silk Road through treacherous terrain hundreds of years ago; one such reminder is Tash Rabat, the fifteenth-century fortress and caravanserai south of the town of Naryn.

The earliest European exploring parties made their way into the Muztag along the Engilchek River and up the Engilchek Glacier. It was the Tyup River Valley that Petr Semenov traversed in 1857 when he plunged into the Central Tian Shan, the edge of the known world to Europeans at the time. An approach that takes 45 minutes by helicopter today required several weeks in 1857 when Semenov and Przhevalsky headed into this vast unknown on horseback. For his efforts on behalf of the Russian Geographical Society, the tsar bestowed on Semenov the honorary suffix Tian-Shansky.

Khan Tengri was first climbed in 1931 by M. Pogrebetsky. When Soviet alpinists Sidorenko, Yitman, and Ivanov made the first ascent of Peak Pobeda in 1938, they thought it was under 23,000 feet (7000 m). Only later was the peak discovered to be the second-highest peak in the Soviet Union.

The other peaks in the Muztag—including two striking mountains toward China, Pogrebetskovo Peak, 21,408 feet (6527 m), and Peak of Military Topographers, 22,543 feet (6873 m)—are climbed much less frequently than Pobeda and Khan Tengri. In general, however, the military restrictions prevented exploration of this mountain fastness and many major summits are unclimbed, while many others have not been repeated since the first ascent.

Politics have obstructed access to this territory even more than extreme conditions; the Central Tian Shan was at the center of the border tug-of-war between the Soviets and the Chinese in Central Asia. Near Turgart Pass, you can see the military bunkers from 1982 when the Chinese army crossed this border but was turned back. The paranoia that made the KGB and Soviet Army close vast areas of the country seems particularly ironic in the frozen reaches of the Muztag, but it effectively excluded adventurers from the region for most of the century. Special military permission was required for Soviet mountaineers to go on expeditions to the Central Tian Shan. Foreigners were not allowed here at all until 1989.

There are few villages in mountainous central Kyrgyzstan, although the traveler passes numerous settlements of yurts. Naryn, the biggest town, is a dusty, nondescript place. Unless you need to stock up on fresh fruit and vegetables there, you may want to bypass it and stay in the pristine high country.

Many find glacier walking monotonous and tiring. Others revel in the other-worldly aspect of it, and the endless challenges of finding the best way around crevasses. I suggest heading up a big glacier like the Engilchek only if you've done enough glacier strolling to know you enjoy it. As there are plenty of gaping crevasses at the Engilchek's upper end, you should be comfortable dealing with these beasts.

The Central Tian Shan is a harsher environment than the Pamir, colder and more precipitous. Experienced climbers say the effects of altitude are felt more acutely because of the northern latitude and compare it to 26,000 feet (8000 m) in the Himalaya. These are not mountains for aspiring high-altitude climbers to cut their teeth on; experience is a must. (See the Climbing section of chapter 1, Introduction.)

Peak Pobeda, the most northerly 23,000-foot (7000-m) peak in the world, may also have one of the highest death tolls of any mountain: the "standard route" on this mountain, a 2.5-mile (4-km) traverse above 23,000 feet (7000 m) on the west ridge, picks off even the strong if they are trapped there by storms. Even more challenging technical routes have been done on Peak Pobeda's north face.

Mountaineering base camps hosting foreign climbers operate seasonally on the South Engilchek Glacier. Halfway between the Engilchek Glacier's maw and the Engilchek River's confluence with the Sarydzhaz River, at elevation 8,333 feet (2540 m), sits Maida Adyr base camp, the main helicopter pad for flights into the South Engilchek. Just south of the tent camp at Maida Adyr, there's a special pocket of rare butterflies—one of several in Turkestan that make lepidopterists drool.

The International Mountaineering Center "Tien Shan" (IMC "Tien Shan," Bishkek, Kyrgyzstan) operates one of the main camps on the South Engilchek Glacier between Peaks Gorkovo and Diki, and also the helicopter service from Maida Adyr, below the South Engilcheck Glacier base camp. The International Mountaineering Camp "Khan Tengri" (IMC

A climbers' base camp on the Engilchek Glacier

"Khan Tengri," Almaty, Kazakhstan) also has a base camp on the South Engilchek Glacier, with transport arranged from the Kazakhstan side. Both of these base camps on the South Engilchek are full-service base camps, complete with climbing guides who provide consultation and do rescues. The stupendously beautiful setting is reason enough to check in for a stay at one of these camps even if you're not a climber. (See the discussion of altitude sickness in the Health and Medical Problems section of chapter 3, Staying Safe and Healthy.)

Hiking options for inexperienced climbers are limited because of the extreme conditions. Pik Diki, 15,853 feet (4832 m), at the mouth of the Zvyozdochka Glacier (2 or 3 hours across the South Engilchek Glacier from the base camps below Peak Gorkovo), can be done in 8 to 10 hours round-trip. This is considered a "trekking peak," but crevasses near the summit require roping up. If you're looking to do a 16,000-foot or 19,000-foot (5000-m or 6000-m) first ascent, there are a number of these in the environs.

Getting There

Most climbers get to the Muztag via Bishkek (formerly Frunze) and Karakol, Kyrgyzstan; you can also get there from Almaty (formerly Alma Ata), Kazakhstan.

There is an international flight to Almaty from Urumqi, China. Currently there are no international flights to Bishkek, so from outside Russia or Central Asia you must first fly to Moscow, St. Petersburg, or Almaty.

From Almaty, fly to Bishkek and follow the directions from Bishkek, below, or take a bus (3 or 4 hours) to an advanced base camp at Karkara, then helicopter (2 hours) to the South Engilchek Glacier base camps. There's no climbing out of Karkara, which is set in low, rolling foothills.

From inside Russia, you can fly to Bishkek from Moscow (4 hours); from Turkestan, you can fly to Bishkek from Tashkent (30 minutes) or Almaty. From Bishkek, fly or drive (6 to 7 hours) to Karakol (formerly Przhevalsk) at the east end of Lake Issyk Kul. From Karakol, you can take a helicopter flight

(45 minutes) or bus (4 to 5 hours) to Maida Adyr base camp, and from Maida Adyr helicopter to the South Engilchek Glacier base camps between Peaks Gorkovo and Diki (45 minutes).

For the **Dzhergalan-to-Chon Tash trek** below, from Karakol drive another hour or so to the town of Dzhergalan. On this trek, you basically walk in to the Muztag across the Sarydzhaz Mountains.

Where to Stay

Hotels in Almaty, just like everything else, are more expensive than in Bishkek. There are several tourist hotels in downtown Almaty, where rooms start at $80. There are also some small guesthouses with much simpler accommodations at a fraction of the price. One, called the Uyut, charges $5 a night.

In Bishkek, the Dostuk Hotel is the most expensive ($60 and up) and least desirable lodgings. The Intourist hotel Alatoo, near the train staion, is a better deal. About ten minutes from downtown, the Issyk Kul is a Western-class hotel with rooms for about $45.

Maida Adyr, the last outpost of green life before entering the Muztag, has a good *banya*, cook and kitchen, and beds available in *vagonchiki* (recycled train cars). Both base camps on the South Engilchek Glacier between Peaks Gorkovo and Diki are complete, with mess tents, cooks, comfortable canvas stand up room tents, and *banyas*. Karkara base camp is run by Almaty-headquartered International Mountaineering Camp "Khan Tengry," which also operates the heliservice from here. The camp features stand-up room tent accommodations and a mess hall.

When to Go

Summer is short in the mountains. July and August are the best times to go. The climbing season begins after the middle of July and shuts down by the first week in September. The average temperature in the Muztag is 7°C.

In the western plains of the Central Tian Shan, where the bicycle trek described later in this section takes you, July to mid-September is best. In late June, there may still be snow in the mountain passes.

Equipment and Supplies

Base-camp cooks serve up good, hearty borscht and stews, so you only need to bring your own mountain food and equipment for your trek. (See the Climbing section of chapter 1, Introduction; the Climbers' Equipment section of chapter 2, Preparing for Your Trek; and the discussion on helicopters in the By Air section of chapter 4, Traveling in Russia and Central Asia.)

On the Dzhergalan-to-Chon Tash trek, there are two places where stores provide minimal supplies for herders: at the confluence of the Ashuairik and Chon-Dzhanalach rivers, and at the bridge over the Sarydzhaz River. If you count on finding food at these places, however, you may go hungry.

DZHERGALAN TO CHON TASH

A much more remote and wild hike than the one from Ozerny (near Almaty) to Lake Issyk Kul, this trek from Issyk Kul to the Muztag across the

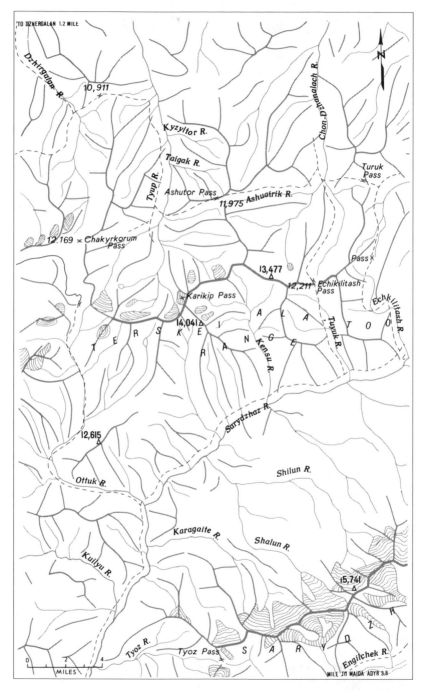

Sarydzhaz Mountains takes you in the footsteps of early exploring parties to the Engilchek Glacier. Allow **4 to 6 days of easy hiking** to Chon Tash. If you're fond of moraine slogs and crevasse hopping, you can waltz up the glacier itself, right into the heart of the big mountains. Add additional days for travel to the South Engilchek Glacier base camps between Peaks Gorkovo and Diki (and to hike all the way up the Engilchek Glacier).

Beyond the town of **Dzhergalan**, the trail follows the Dzhirgalan River, climbing slowly through mixed juniper and fir, to the **pass**, 10,915 feet (3327 m), **3 to 4 hours**. Drop into the scenic **Tyup River** basin and follow it south, past tributaries Kyzyltor and Taigak, with snowy peaks looming ahead. In some places, the trail is passable by all-terrain vehicle, which may carry supplies to herder settlements a few times in a season.

Ford the Tyup River and head up toward Ashutor Pass. There are drawings on the rocks. You'll come upon a small lake in the flat meadow area, and another just below the pass. The trail to **Ashutor Pass**, 11,972 feet (3649 m), winds through a cliffy gate (**3 to 4 hours**).

Across Ashutor, descend the Ashuairik River to the Chon-Dzhanalach valley. Where the rivers meet, there's usually a small settlement. This might be your chance to stock up on fresh milk and *kumys* (fermented mare's milk). Head up the east slope and into a dry riverbed to a **small pass** on the right (**1**

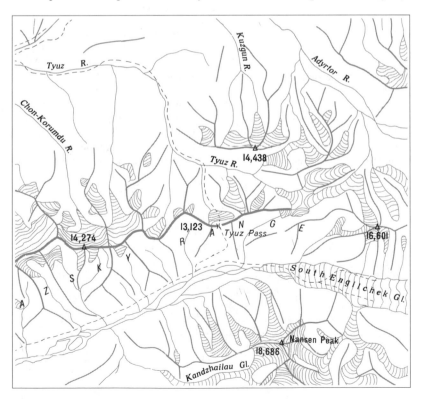

hour). From here you get breathtaking views of Khan Tengri and Pobeda. Traverse the slope south to flat-topped, swampy **Turuk Pass** which you can see in the distance (**2 to 3 hours**). In good weather, all of the Sarydzhazsky, Engilchek, and Tengri Tag mountains are visible, an unbelievable panorama.

Descend along the Echkilitash River until it pours into the **Sarydzhaz River** (**2 to 3 hours**). Here, near the bridge across the Sarydzhaz, is a little summer store, with something for sale on rare occasion. Until recently, there was also a border guards' checkpoint, although China is still miles away on the unpaved road you cross here.

Beyond the bridge, over a little hill, you come to the **Tyuz River**—not to be confused with the Tyup River, where you started out! Hike along the Tyuz River through open, rolling landscape with the Sarydzhaz Mountains dominating the horizon. After **4 or 5 hours** you pass the **last herders' camp**. Broken-up cliffs stripe the hillsides in red and black bands. In another **2 hours** or so you reach the **headwaters of the Tyuz River**, which flows from a gorge on your right.

It's best to cross the Tyuz early in the day when the water is low. The trail to Tyuz Pass ascends through verdant meadows to the cirque below the pass. On the left hangs a steep glacier. Ascend on scree to the right of the glacier. The last section of the ascent is steep, with snow covering the scree. From the broad ridge of **Tyuz Pass**, 13,000 feet (4000 m), **3 to 4 hours**, the Engilchek Valley extends below, the glacier itself off to the left. Peak Nansen towers opposite.

There's an equally long descent on scree to the **Engilchek River** (**3 to 4 hours**), and **Chon Tash** ("Big Stone") is **40 minutes** upstream at the foot of Engilchek Glacier. Chon Tash, across the Engilchek River, is a boulder 30 feet across that marks a freshwater spring. There's **nice camping** here (without any of the permanent facilities of the base camps at Maida Adyr or South Engilchek Glacier). You've now crossed the Sarydzhaz mountains.

If you've arranged through the IMC "Tian Shan" in Bishkek to be picked up by helicopter and flown into the South Engilchek Glacier base camps, you're only a half hour from the base camps. The IMC "Tian Shan" also has rafts on the Engilchek River for floating downstream to its Maida Adyr base camp, from where you can helicopter out to Bishkek. Or you can spend another 4 days conquering the Engilchek Glacier, hiking from Chon Tash to the South Engilchek Glacier base camps (see the Maida Adyr-to-Engilchek Base Camp trek, below).

MAIDA ADYR BASE CAMP TO ENGILCHEK BASE CAMP

This **strenuous trek** from Maida Adyr base camp, to which you've helicoptered or taken the bus, takes **4 to 6 days**. (If you're continuing from the previous trek, which ends 2 days farther upriver at Chon Tash, allow 3 to 4 days.) **Experience in glacier walking** is required. **Rope up** when crossing ice bridges, ice rivers, or snow on the glacier's surface.

From **Maida Adyr** base camp, a rough track continues about **9 miles (15 km)** up the Engilcheck River. Where the **Kan-Kzhailoo River** flows into the Engilchek River is a **good camp**.

From this confluence, **Chon Tash** is **1 more day**'s walk. Chon Tash ("Big Stone") is a 30-foot (9-m) boulder on the left bank as you face the glacier;

Chon Tash marks a freshwater spring and a **good camping spot**. (If you are continuing from the preceding trek, Dzhergalan to Chon Tash, pick up this trek description at this point.) The IMC "Tien Shan" has rafts on the Engilchek River for floating back down to Maida Adyr base camp, should you desire a 4-day circuit from Maida Adyr that bypasses any glacier travel.

Cross the Engilchek Glacier diagonally (2 to 3 hours), gaining about 2,600 feet (800 m) in the process. Continue up between the right slope and the side moraine. The walking is rough, sometimes on and sometimes beside the glacier. You'll cross several side glaciers flowing into the moraine. It's best to cover the whole distance between **Chon Tash** and **Merzbacher Glade** in a long day (**8 to 10 hours**). The glade, an inviting haven in this barren ice and rock world, marks the spot on the south edge of the Engilchek Glacier's southern arm opposite where the North Engilchek issues into it.

From Merzbacher Glade, a side trip of several hours going directly north across the glacier brings you to the Merzbacher lakes.

For the main trek, past Merzbacher Glade continue on the main glacier's south bank to the **Shokalsky Glacier moraine** flowing into the Engilchek on the right (2 to 3 hours). Here you can find crystals, topaz, and other pretty rocks and minerals. When you're even with Shokalsky, skip to the second moraine over and continue on it as far as the **Komsomol Glacier** (3 to 4 hours). About 1,600 feet (500 m) before you reach the Komsomol Glacier, turn hard left and get on the **Red Moraine** (**5 to 7 hours from Merzbacher Glade**), which flows from the Zvyozdochka Glacier. You can **camp** here.

The Red Moraine is the turnpike of debris from Peak Pobeda's glacier, the ferocious Zvyozdochka. Stay on the Red Moraine until you're even with where Zvyozdochka carves around Peak Diki and cascades into the Engilchek. Then cross over to the glacier's north edge below the slopes of Peak Gorkovo to the IMC **South Engilchek Glacier base camps** (**5 to 7 hours**).

From the base camps, you can continue higher up the glacier and climb some peaks, you can helicopter out, or you can hike back down to Maida Adyr and helicopter or bus out.

PEAK KHAN TENGRI ASCENT

The Gorkovo–Chapayeva–Khan Tengri traverse is considered a test of climbing mettle by Russian mountaineers. The route up **Khan Tengri from the north**, from the North Engilchek Glacier, is a direct line to the top of the Chapayeva ridge.

The ascent is unrelentingly steep, broken only by one small shoulder suitable for an intermediate camp at 17,700 feet (5400 m). Climbing guides from the mountaineering base camp fix a series of lines up the ridge, but a misstep can be fatal. A Japanese climber who slipped near the top of the ridge in 1989 fell nearly 7,000 feet (2000 m); his body was recovered from just above the glacier.

From the Chapayeva ridge, drop to the east saddle, 19,360 feet (5900 m). This saddle is the upper edge of the narrow chute between Chapayeva and Khan Tengri, down which cascades the Semenovsky Glacier. From the saddle, continue to the summit, as described below.

The route up **Khan Tengri from the South Engilchek Glacier**, less haz-

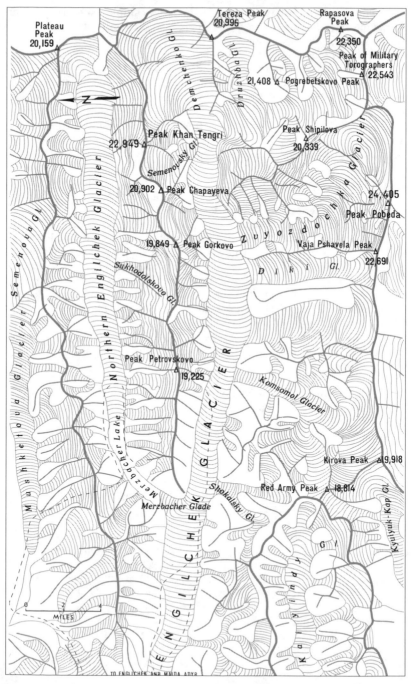

Plateau Peak 20,159

Tereza Peak 20,995

Rapasova Peak

22,350

Peak of Military Torographers 22,543

21,408 Pogrebetskovo Peak

Demchenko Gl.

Druzhba Gl.

Peak Shipilova 20,339

Peak Khan Tengri

22,849

Semenovsky Gl.

20,902 Peak Chapayeva

Zuyozdochka Glacier

24,405

Peak Pobeda

19,849 Peak Gorkovo

Vaja Pshavela Peak

22,691

D i k i Gl.

Semenova Gl.

Mushketova Glacier

Northern Engilchek Glacier

Sukhodolskovo Gl.

Peak Petrovskovo

19,225

Komsomol Glacier

Merzbacher Lake

Kirova Peak 19,918

Shokalsky Gl.

Red Army Peak 18,814

Kyuliuk-Kap Gl.

Merzbacher Glade

E N G I L C H E K   G L A C I E R

Kaltinda Gl.

0 2 4
MILES

TO ENGILCHEK AND MAIDA ADYR

ardous than the north ridge, ascends Semenovsky Glacier. From the **South Engilchek Glacier base camps**, proceed up the South Engilchek Glacier to the **Semenovsky Glacier** (**1 day**). Proceed up the Semenovsky to the **saddle** between peaks Chapayeva and Khan Tengri (**1 day**). There are a couple of snow caves at the saddle.

The **summit** can be climbed in a **long day** from the saddle, although some choose to bivy on intermediate ledges. Over a half mile (1 km) of mixed rock and snow scrambling, some of it technical, leads to Khan Tengri's summit.

BISHKEK TO KASHGAR, CHINA, OVERLAND

This is a trip of **strenuous mountain biking**, taking **9 to 12 days** from Bishkek, Kyrgyzstan, across Turgart Pass to Kashgar, China. (It can also be done by motor vehicle.) Rough mountain roads lead fom Bishkek through Naryn to Turgart Pass, passing several historical sites that date back to the Silk Road. Because of the rough terrain and distances involved, mountain bikes are an ideal mode of transportation. **Maps:** 1:200,000 quadrangles: K-43-IX, K-43-X, K-43-XVI, K-43-XV, K-43-XXI, K-43-XXII, K-43-XXVII, K-43-XXXIV.

If you intend to cross the border into China, your visa should state Turgart Pass (see the Visas section of chapter 2, Preparing for Your Trek). This pass is officially the only open border post between Kyrgyzstan and China, although it's rumored you may be able to cross the border farther south at Irkeshtam. (From Kazakhstan, you can cross into China at Khorgos.) The Chinese have been known to turn back travelers who do not have prearranged Chinese escorts waiting for them at the border. For this reason, the officials on the Kyrgyz side require proper papers; they radio to the Chinese to verify China's willingness to all passage. (Reportedly, Chinese border officials at Khorgos are less strict.)

There are numerous ways to make your way across central Kyrgyzstan. The route given here is one that's been popular with several mountain-bike groups. This relatively direct north–south course loops around several of Kyrgyzstan's beautiful mountain lakes; Song-Kol and Chatyr-Kol both have protected park status (*zakazniki*). Much of this route is above 10,000 feet (3000 m), with spectacular mountain scenery. Along the way, there are also reminders of the bold travelers who traced the Silk Road trail through treacherous terrain hundreds of years ago, like Tash Rabat, the fifteenth-century fortress and caravanserai south of Naryn.

From **Bishkek**, ride southeast to **Tokmak**; there's a recommended camp at Kegeti Priut.

From here, ride west on the Kegeti River road up and across the pass to the **East Karakol Valley**, another good campsite.

The next stops are Tunuk and Kyokyo Meren Gorge on the way south to **Aral village**, where there is a guesthouse.

From Aral, head back northeast to the Jumgal River, Chaek, and Kairma en route to the south side of **Song-Kol Lake** (a recommended campsite).

From Song-Kol Lake, proceed east over **Dolon Pass** to **Saryibel** (another recommended campsite).

Kyrgyz horsemen near Turgart Pass (Photo: Peter Bogardus)

Then ride south to **Naryn**, where there's a hotel.

From Naryn, **Tash Rabat** is slightly off the route and up a side valley, but it's well worth the **side trip**. Named for the ancient stone fort that served as a trading post in the days of the Silk Road, the Tash Rabat valley was a central location, with main roads going south to Kashgar, China, north to Lake Issyk Kul, and west to Osh, Kyrgyzstan.

Tash Rabat is a great place to set up a base camp for day treks into the mountains to the south. The climate in the lush green valley is often milder than the lower valleys toward At Bashi and Naryn. An old Kyrgyz couple, the caretakers of the fort, live next door to Tash Rabat. They are very friendly, can offer advice on day hikes, and may even be able to provide pack horses. The caretakers have the key to the fort, which has been restored so you can view the dungeon pits into which thieves were thrown.

Return to **Naryn** and proceed southwest to **Chatyr-Kol Lake**, **18 miles** (**29 km**), where you can camp before crossing Turgart Pass.

Nearing Turgart Pass, you can see the military bunkers from 1982 when the Chinese army crossed this border, but was turned back. Turgart Pass itself is at 12,306 feet (3752 m), a 18.5-mile (30-km) uphill climb of about 1,000 feet (300 m) of elevation gain. At the border on the Chinese side, there are some small kiosks that sell cookies and noodles. There are a few more noodle stalls along the roughly 62-mile (100-km) stretch to Kashgar.

The only flights out of Kashgar (which appears on some maps as Kashi) are to other cities in China, including Aksu and Urumqi. A popular overland route west from Kashgar is over the Karakorum Highway to Pakistan. Tour bureaus in Kashgar offer vehicles that can take you as far as the Pakistani border.

A shorter alternative is to bus from Bishkek to Naryn or At-Bashi, and then bike 2 days from Naryn to the border, about 36 miles (58 km), and over Turgart Pass (if desired).

Part 3

Siberia and the Russian Far East

Few places in the world can be called untouched. Wilderness everywhere is in demand, and even the well-meaning leave some trace of their passing. But to this day there are vast tracts of Siberia and the Russian Far East that have never seen a human foot.

The Altai Range in southern Siberia, equidistant from four oceans, is the geographic heart of Asia. It pumps the lifeblood of one of Siberia's major waterways, the Ob River. Many believe Asia's spiritual heart also beats here. Oriental philosophy and Indian legends place the metaphysical kingdom Shambala in the vicinity of the Altai's Mount Belukha.

Siberia, the vast territory east of the Urals, encompasses Russia's enormous central landmass from the Arctic Ocean in the north to the southern border with Mongolia, and from the Kazakhstan border in the west to the mountainous region around Lake Baikal in the east. The great rivers of Siberia—the Ob, Enesei, and Lena—flow north into the Arctic Ocean. The highest of Siberia's mountains, in the Altai and Sayan ranges, stretch in a band across southern Siberia.

Lake Baikal is the oldest, deepest, most voluminous lake on the planet. It is surrounded by several mountain ranges, including the Khamar Daban, Barguzin, Muisky, and Baikalsky. This is a remarkable part of Siberia, considered sacred by indigenous peoples.

To Russians, Siberia does not extend all the way to the Pacific. The easternmost reaches of Russia, comprising more than a quarter of the country—and the most sparsely populated areas—are known as the Far East, or the wild east. In the north it includes Yakutia, Magadanskaya Oblast, Chukotka, and Kamchatka; in the Sea of Okhotsk are Sakhalin Island and the Kuril Islands; and in the south, near China and Japan, are Chita, Amurskaya Oblast, Khabarovskii Krai, and Primorskii Krai.

Independent travel in Siberia and the Russian Far East is a taiga experience. There are no deserts or canyons here: dense forests cloak the mountains of Siberia, the river basins, the islands of Sakhalin and the Kurils. Only the summits of peaks are treeless alpine tundra. It's hard to conceptualize a band of coniferous woods 6,000 miles (10,000 km) long, but when you wander for days on end through larch and Siberian stone pine (the Russians call it *kedr*, so it's often mistranslated as cedar), you begin to comprehend the immensity of the taiga. Berries and mushrooms glut the forest floor in late summer. The taiga shelters wolves, foxes, bear, deer, elk, squirrel, sable, and a variety of birds (see the Logging section of chapter 5, Environmental Challenges).

Siberia, inhabited since the Stone Age, became part of the Mongol Empire when Ghengis Khan's armies pushed across the continent from the area south of Lake Baikal, conquering everything in their path to Central Asia and the Black Sea, and controlling it from the thirteenth to the fifteenth century.

The great Russian wave of exploration and settlement didn't happen until the sixteenth century. Up until that time, Russians had been trading furs as far east as the Ob River, on the eastern side of the Urals, for several centuries. The fur market drove the Russians across Siberia between the 1580s and 1650s. The vanguard was the Cossacks—a "cowboy" class that included deserters, trappers, traders, criminals, and fiercely independent vagabonds. Curiously, they were also the official representatives of the tsar: they established *ostrogs* (forts) and forced the natives to pay *yasak* (a tax to the crown). For several decades they plundered Siberia and the Far East. The Russian Orthodox priests followed closely on the heels of the fur traders.

The great rivers of Siberia—the Ob, Enesei, and Lena—and their tributaries and the portages connecting them provided the original route east from Moscow and St. Petersburg. After the Russians established a fort at Irkutsk near Lake Baikal in 1650, their focus moved to the Amur River, from which they forged east to Ussuriland and northeast to Chukotka and Kamchatka.

Under the tsars, Siberia became a place of exile for political prisoners and common criminals. In this century, Stalin developed the Siberian penal system to a vast network of forced labor camps (*gulags*), in which millions of innocent people were murdered or worked to death. Most Russians can tell you of relatives who disappeared during Stalin's purges.

Most of Siberia was closed to foreign travel until around 1990, thanks to a xenophobic, totalitarian government intent on protecting its military secrets. Much of the Russian Far East was closed even to Soviet *citizens*: in general, all cities in which there was military production or army or naval bases, or that were located anywhere near a foreign border, were closed to visitors. Unless you had relatives on Kamchatka or in Vladivostok, or you had professional access to a *propusk* (permit)—geologist, ornithologist, or high-ranking Party official on a bear hunt—you didn't go to these places. Even for those few who were allowed to roam the Far East, the controls were strict. Reknowned Russian nature photographer V. Gippenreiter recounts how the KGB agent accompanying him in the Kurils would repeat over and over "*Nelzya!*"—[You're] "not allowed" [to photograph that].

Aside from the travel restrictions, the sheer remoteness of the Siberian and Russian Far Eastern wilds limited the amount of travel there. Decent topographical maps were impossible to come by until very recently. There are few roads and the railroad only runs west to east. Helicopters or small planes are the only way to get into many areas unless you are prepared for an extended, extreme approach.

Russia's "wild east" resembles America's west in more than just an abundance of wide roadless expanses on the map. It was the land of opportunity for the Cossacks in the seventeenth century. Now, in the last years of the twentieth century, the gold rush is on for Western traders.

In the past several years, Siberia and the Russian Far East have wriggled out from beneath the heel of Moscow's foreign trade conglomerates, and foreign companies are pouring into the region to exploit the territory's wealth, from diamonds to salmon. The Far East cities of Petropavlovsk-Kamchatsky, Yuzhno-Sakhalinsk, Khabarovsk, and Vladivostok, teeming with oilmen and traders, resemble Klondike towns. Other large Siberian cities like Omsk, Ekaterinburg, Novosibirsk, and Irkutsk have also seen large influxes of foreign business people eager to develop resources.

Much closer geographically to Korea, China, Japan, and the North American Pacific Rim, the Russian Far East is rapidly developing closer economic ties to these countries. Only a short time ago, travelers to the Far East flew around the world via Moscow; now there are a variety of options for direct international travel to the Far East.

Aeroflot has an Anchorage–Magadan–Khabarovsk route. Alaska Airlines flies from Anchorage to Magadan, Khabarovsk, and Vladivostok in the summer. Bering Air hops across the strait from Nome, Alaska, to Providleniya. You can fly to Vladivostok from Niigata, Japan, and Seoul, South Korea. You can fly to Khabarovsk from Niigata, Japan; Harbin, China; and Pyongyang, North Korea. You can fly to Blagoveshchensk from Harbin. You can fly to Yuzhno-Sakhalinsk from Hakodate, Japan. All of these new international connections make a trip to the Far East a much less expensive, and less exhausting, proposition.

If you're going to Lake Baikal or western Siberia, depending on where you're coming from, it may be cheaper to fly through Moscow. Just about anywhere east of there, you're better off flying the Pacific route.

You can go by train to Siberia from China: to Irkutsk from Beijing via Ulaanbaatar, Mongolia; to Blagoveshchensk or Khabarovsk from Harbin; or to Vladivostok from Suifenhe.

There are also ships to Vladivostok from Japan (see the information on getting there in the Ussuriland section of chapter 12, The Russian Far East).

The very adventurous traveler may manage to make the passage across the Pacific by freighter. The main shipping line, the semi-private Far Eastern Shipping Co. (FESCO), is based out of Vladivostok, with offices in most major Pacific ports. FESCO boats, which make stops at all the major Russian Far Eastern ports, have been known to carry passengers, but their foreign offices don't handle booking passage. This option of stowing away on a freighter is mostly employed by Russians, and is particularly popular to places like Australia that are very expensive to reach by air. Basically, you have to find out when there's a ship in town and strike a deal with the captain. You also have to have a very flexible schedule.

In 1991, my mother, Judith Maier, spent Christmas on a freighter anchored off the godforsaken port of Vostochny when the boat from Vladivostok to Nagoya made a loading stop there and was stalled for 5 days. The 3-day crossing ended up taking 8 days. The return from Nagoya to Vladivostok was less eventful, except that the ship, which had set out under the hammer and sickle of the USSR was now flying the white, blue, and red flag of Russia. Judith's "holiday cruise" set her back 186 rubles (the equivalent of $3.50 at the time)—but you won't find such a bargain any longer. Current costs for freighter passage reputedly range as high as $75 per day.

Within the Far East, passenger boats cruise the Amur River.

Aeroflot flies within Siberia and the Far East between the major cities. Many smaller towns that used to have regular air service are stranded now: fuel distribution problems and the expense of flying jets mean that less economically viable runs are the first to go. Delays and cancelled flights have become particularly common in the Far East. To get into the most remote areas, you can hire a helicopter or charter a small plane.

The Trans-Siberian Railroad links European Russia with the Urals and then Western Siberia; at Lake Baikal it dips south and follows along the southern periphery to Khabarovsk, and finally down to Vladivostok. From Moscow, the journey takes six days. You can get to wild places at Lake Baikal's north end and farther east on the Baikal–Amur Mainline (BAM) Railroad. The BAM forks north from the Trans-Siberian at Tayshet (near Bratsk, northwest of Irkutsk), and reaches the Pacific at Sovetskaya Gavan (east of Khabarovsk). There are several sections of this railroad that are not open to travel.

Many cars in the Russian Far East are used cars brought over from Japan, with steering wheels on the right. In Vladivostok and other port towns, these right-side–driver cars far outnumber lefties, even though, as in the rest of Russia, the rule is to drive on the right. Driving or being a passenger in Russia is scary enough; this only makes it more exciting!

Many of the people who live in Siberia and the Russian Far East today trace their roots to those who survived the *gulag*s. Then there are those who came to make their fortune in the mines, and never went home to Russia or the Ukraine. In some of the most remote reaches of Siberia nestle villages of Old Believers, descendants of those who fled religious persecution in the last century.

In Siberia, you'll find a different breed of Russian than in the cities. Many people end up out east seeking alternative life-styles, or to escape the city. I had been to Moscow fifteen times before I was first in a Siberian village. Now I've seen a few of them and am always struck by the resilience and earthiness of these hospitable people. Siberia and the Far East, with their tough, tragic history, are populated by an independent breed of pioneers.

Traditional Siberian food is *pelmeni*—little meat-stuffed dumplings. In winter, people make up large quantities and store them on the porch, which serves as a freezer for almost half the year. Hunters carry frozen *pelmeni* in their rucksacks and boil them up over the campfire.

In the Far East, people eat a lot of fish. Come autumn, solid masses of spawning salmon crowd the coastal streams, shoulder to shoulder from one bank to the other. Locals catch them with their hands; they throw the fish away, reserving only the eggs. They clean the caviar by pouring scalding salted water over it in a stocking or cheesecloth sack. The fresh caviar is eaten by the spoonful, sometimes for breakfast, lunch, and dinner. For the uninitiated palate, this takes some getting used to. But the Russians know dozens of delicious ways of preparing salmon. My favorite are salmon cutlets: patties mashed with potatos and fried.

Siberia and the Russian Far East are at least as challenging for the traveler

A ribbon of river meanders through the Far Eastern taiga. (Photo: Sergei Smirensky)

as anywhere else in the country. The tourist infrastructure is very raw and information sources limited. What experience Siberians have had with foreign tourists tends to fall into two categories: the sightseers who stay in Intourist hotels, and the fishermen and hunters who pay fat trophy fees. The backpacking, dollar-stretching traveler is still a novelty to them.

Many Russians see all foreigners as moneybags and the tourist trade as a chance to make easy money. In the Far East in particular, there's a gold-digger attitude toward foreign travelers. Prices are generaly higher in the Far East than elsewhere in the country. Especially in Ussuriland (also known as Primorye), the cost of tourist services is largely determined by what Japanese will pay: usually a lot. Don't be surprised if you're quoted seemingly astronomical prices for some services. And remember, many things, even hotel room rates, may be negotiable. In hiring guides, vehicles, et cetera, if you're reasonable and clear about what you can pay, you'll probably strike a deal. For more tips on keeping expenses down, see the Money section of chapter 4, Traveling in Russia and Central Asia.

In the Far East, there is no organized system of hiking and backpacking trails. There are game trails and hunters' trails, but these don't look like any groomed path you ever saw. Overgrown and cluttered with deadfalls, they can be slow going. The "trails of choice" for most outdoor enthusiasts are the waterways. Part of the appeal of rafting trips, in addition to avoiding the bushwhacking, is that it's a good way to observe animals and birdlife. Many backroads are suitable for bicycle travel. Distances are vast, population centers far between.

Even the solo backcountry traveler in Siberia and the Far East is likely to have plenty of company. Mosquitoes, flies, no-see-ums, and a host of other insects are worse in certain areas and at certain times of the year. They're at their most ferocious in early and midsummer. In many places, they're gone by late summer. Russians like to say, "The best way to deal with them is to get used to them." But you should also have insect repellent and, in high-activity areas, head nets.

The bugs can do more than drive you crazy. In Ussuriland (Primorye), there is some mosquito-borne Japanese encephalitis. The risk of Japanese encephalitis is primarily in rice-growing and pig-farming areas; anyone who will be spending more than a month in these field conditions should get vaccinated (see the Immunizations and Health and Medical Problems sections of chapter 3, Staying Safe and Healthy).

A prime concern for backcountry travelers in southern Siberia and the south of the Russian Far East is tick-borne encephalitis. If you're going for a short trip, it is probably sufficient to be very careful. However, most travelers and scientists spending extended time in the woods of southern Siberia or the Far East during the risk season try to get vaccinated. (See the Immunizations and Health and Medical Problems sections of chapter 3, Staying Safe and Healthy.)

With these precautions said, the fact remains that Siberia and the Russian Far East are the last frontier for wilderness. In return for putting up with a little chaos and inconvenience, you can experience the expanse of the world's largest forest and get close to bears and rare birds. Given its proximity to Alaska, the Russian Far East has the potential to become a very accessible outdoor recreation destination.

11   Siberia

The parts of Siberia that this chapter explores include the Altai Mountains, the Kuznetsky Alatau Mountains, the Sayan Mountains, and the Lake Baikal area. Many of the descriptions included in these sections are merely outlines of routes, rather than detailed hike descriptions. There is simply so much of Siberia that this guidebook cannot hope to cover it all.

The Altai Mountains, south of Novosibirsk on the Kazakhstan border, contain many mountain ranges, as well as Mount Belukha, Siberia's highest mountain. On the outskirts of the Altai is Teletskoye Lake, large and relatively accessible for outdoor pursuits.

North of the Altai, and more accessible from the cities of southern Siberia, is the Kuznetsky Alatau. The Ob River finds its source in these mountains, winding its way northwest to the Kara Sea at the northern end of the Urals.

East of the Altai are the Sayan Mountains, which run parallel along the border with Mongolia. Most of the area of the Sayans covered in this chapter is the Eastern Sayans, in the vicinity of southern Lake Baikal.

The Lake Baikal area includes the Tunka Valley, the Khamar Daban Mountains, the Baikalsky Mountains, the Muisky Mountains, the Barguzin Mountains, as well as the lake itself. Many islands, bays, and beaches of Lake Baikal offer opportunities for exploration on foot and by water. Lake Baikal is accessible from Irkutsk and Ulan Ude, located on the west and east, respectively, at the lake's southern end, as well as from Severobaikalsk at the lake's northern end.

Altai Mountains

The Altai Mountains straddle the border where Siberia, Mongolia, and China meet. The abundance of wild rivers, mountain lakes, and meadows makes this one of Russia's most beautiful ranges. The white faces of the mountains shimmer like icing castles levitating above the green ridges. The taiga, Siberia's legendary forest, covers the land with a dense, dark cloak. Glaciers—more than a thousand of them, covering 344 square miles (890 square km)—drop right into the taiga. Teletskoye Lake, the largest lake in the Altai, is the source of of the Biya River, which together with the Katun River forms the Ob River, one of Siberia's major rivers.

The Altai Mountains are remote and vast, hundreds of miles removed from major cities. It is a place only truly committed adventurers go. Just reaching the town of Gorno-Altaisk, south of Novosibirsk, is a marathon journey from anywhere in the world. Yes, the countryside is beautiful, but even the most spectacular scenery loses its charm when viewed for too long from inside a dusty vehicle with minimal shock absorption. From Gorno-Altaisk, on the fringe of the musky Altai foothills, you travel another full day to get into the alpine country (unless you're helicoptering). When the Englishman Samuel Turner attempted the first ascent of the Altai's Mount Belukha at the turn of the century, it took him nearly a week traveling by sledge from Novo-Nicolaevsk (as Novosibirsk was then known) to reach the mountains. In 1905, he wrote, in *Siberia: A Record of Travel, Climbing and Exploration*:

> The climber must make preparations, both in summer and winter, for much colder mountain tops and much colder winds than on the Swiss Alps. It is of vital importance to have the thickest under-clothing, a short seal-skin or bear-skin coat down to the knees, and a very thick shuba *(all-fur coat)* to go over all.

Turner also wrote about the abundance of big game he sighted—and shot—on his turn-of-the-century expedition to Mount Belukha. Thanks to the many avid hunters like Turner, many big-game species (including ibex) no longer exist in the Altai and can be seen only in stuffed form in the natural history museum in Gorno-Altaisk. Among the animals still found in the mountains are bear, marals (Siberian red deer), goats, sable, and fox. Tracks in the deltas prove that snow leopards still stalk these mountains, but don't count on seeing one.

Nicholas Roerich, a remarkable artist-writer-explorer-archaeologist-philosopher born in St. Petersburg in 1874, followed the legends to the Altai, where he lived for a while in the village of Verkhny Uimon. One of the foremost painters of the Himalaya, Roerich produced thousands of mountain-scapes during his lifetime. His paintings capture the spirit of the mountains with uncanny depth. Standing before a Roerich watercolor in the Novosibirsk picture gallery, I felt transported by the light and power as if I actually stood on a ridge surrounded by high peaks.

The way south from Novosibirsk and Gorno-Altaisk takes you along the Katun River. A favorite for white-water rafting, this stormy river is fed by the peaks of the Belukha range. At Biysk, it joins the Biya River, which flows from Teletskoye Lake, to make the mighty Ob River.

The Chuisky Tract, the major highway transversing the Altai Mountains, is a very rough, unpaved artery. Cutting through the valley of the Chuya River, the Chuisky Tract provides access to numerous fabulous alpine areas, including the Saldzhar, Kuraisky, and North Chuisky Ranges. Before crossing into Mongolia at Tashanta, the Chuisky Tract bisects a band of steppe. Kosh Agach, the last outpost of civilization, sits in a mostly flat basin about 12 by 18 miles (20 by 30 km) encircled by mountains. The Chuisky Steppe is so barren and parched, the helicopter pilots call it the other side of the moon. At these lower elevations, the locals herd camels. The steppe is broken by low, sparsely vegetated ridges and mountains rise on its periphery. Even along the Chuisky Tract, villages are few and far between. On the capillary roads branching out from it, many miles separate population pockets.

The neat villages set in golden fields of wheat and sunflowers against the dark forested hills seem like little pieces of paradise. The farther you get from the cities, the more the villages glow with prosperity. The Altai is famous for its abundant crops. In fact, the fertile region derives its name from a Mongol word—*altan*—meaning "golden."

Driving the road to Tyungur lined with fields of hops, my Russian companions noted a classic Soviet paradox: "all these hops and no beer." The Altai has a reputation for excellent honey. We visited a beekeeper in Tyungur who poured the honey out of a tall metal milk can into one of our water bottles.

The hamlets the road passes through are inhabited mostly by Altaitsi, the native people of the region. Their faces—especially the children—very much resemble Eskimo faces, a reminder that the ancient transmigration of peoples crossed in the Altai.

Horse travel is still a common mode of transportation here. For hours at a time the only people you pass are on horseback. There's almost no traffic. The absence of development impresses as much as the scenery. There are no hamburger joints, no neon signs, no motels.

In Ust-Koksa, a large billboard in front of the town hall features Lenin expounding "We will achieve the victory of communist labor." This struck me as a sign of how slowly change moves in the Altai (in the cities, most of the communist slogans have been replaced by advertising), and also a cruel mockery of the hard-working local folk. These people were never poor before the revolution. In the 1930s, they were brutally collectivized; one sixty-something woman told me, "We worked barefoot for eleven years."

Chronic alcoholism plagues most of rural Russia and the Altai is no exception. When vodka is delivered to the villages, these peaceable people can get rough; it is advisable to take precautions with your gear and to avoid conflicts.

Every year, committed pilgrims trek to the Mount Belukha area in search of the legendary kingdom of Shambala. These believers gaze at the snowy heights and describe seeing white horses and other fantastic visions. A peak neighboring Belukha is named for the painter Roerich, and the Akkem climbing rangers refer whimsically to his mystical followers as *Roerichovtsi* ("Roerichites"). A new-age gathering, "Altai-Himalaya," convenes annually in Novosibirsk.

The Altai may be Russia's best-kept secret. I had made numerous trips to the Caucasus, Pamir, and Tian Shan before I ever saw the Altai, which I dismissed as a minor mountain range. Ironically, many Soviet outdoorspeople neglected it for the same reason: it lacked the high-altitude appeal of the mountains of Central Asia.

In the Altai, you can enjoy stunning alpine scenery while trekking at moderate elevations through valleys carpeted with wildflowers. This would be great mountain-biking country. There are some organized horsepacking trips and theoretically it should not be difficult to find horses for trekking here. (See the discussion of pack animals in the Hiring Local Assistance section of chapter 1, Introduction.) Kupol Mountain, 11,155 feet (3400 m), is an easy hike (10 hours up and down) about 50 miles (80 km) from Kosh Agach. It's possible to fly into Kosh Agach from Gorno-Altaisk. If one continues south from there, the road crosses into Mongolia at Tashanta.

Two treks in this section are reached by bus or car from Gorno-Altaisk and end up on the south end of Teletskoye Lake, the largest lake in the Altai. Teletskoye Lake, because it is accessible by vehicle, is not one of the pristine tarns sprinkled on ridges throughout this range. Tourist ferries run the length of the lake and parts of its shores have been developed for recreation. Both of

A Kazakh family's summer home in the southern Altai near the "Four Corners" of Central Asia (where the borders of Kazakhstan, China, Mongolia, and the Russian Altai Republic intersect)

these treks, however, are quite wild and good samplers of the Sumultinsky Mountains in the northeast Altai.

Opportunities for hiking and climbing in the Altai, the third largest mountain system in the former Soviet Union after the Caucasus and Central Asia, are limitless. The routes described later in this section are relatively easy to find because they are well traveled. But they barely scratch the surface of the vast possibilities for mountain adventure in the Altai. Only a handful of foreigners have been in the big alpine peaks concentrated in the Katunsky and North and South Chuisky Mountain systems near the border with Mongolia.

In the North Chuisky Range, 13,691-foot (4173-m) Aktru is a white mirage of loveliness. Between the Aktru massif and Mount Belukha, just across the border from Mongolia, the summits Shavlo, Skazka, 11,500 feet (3500 m), and Krasavitsa, 12,139 feet (3700 m), echo on the surface of dazzling Shavlo Lake. All of these, and nearby Iiktu, a beautiful 12,930-foot (3941-m) peak, have challenging technical routes, as well as easier ones.

The biggest challenge to rambling in the Altai may be the numerous wild rivers. Since this is largely pristine country, many of the high-spirited mountain streams are bridgeless. Be prepared to wade across or to use ropes for the major fords.

Getting There

Novosibirsk and Barnaul, the main access points to the Altai Mountains, are about midway between Moscow and Khabarovsk.

There are daily direct flights to Novosibirsk from Moscow (5 hours) and Khabarovsk (5 hours). Aeroflot also flies from Moscow and Khabarovsk to Barnaul, which is a more convenient jumping-off point in some cases, since it is farther south and closer to the mountains.

The Trans-Siberian Railroad runs to Novosibirsk from Moscow (about 45 hours) and Khabarovsk (also about 45 hours).

From Novosibirsk or Barnaul, you can fly to Gorno-Altaisk; the airport is at Maima, about 6 miles (10 km) away. You can also take a train to Biysk (overnight from Novosibirsk, less from Barnaul), and from there drive to Gorno-Altaisk (2½ hours). One advantage of driving from Biysk to Gorno-Altaisk: if you like the Russian novelist Shukshin, you can stop at the village of Srostki where he was born.

For the **Lake Kucherla-and-Akkem Lake Loop** and **Mount Belukha Ascent**, from Barnaul fly to Ust-Koksa (Aeroflot flies from Barnaul by puddle-jumper to Ust-Koksa). From Ust-Koksa, it's only a couple hours' drive to Tyungur. You can also fly from Barnaul to Gorno-Altaisk and then take the bus all the way to Tyungur, but this is grueling—10 hours on rough, mostly unpaved roads. The bus to Tyungur leaves Gorno-Altaisk around noon, stopping in Ust Kan overnight before continuing on the next day. If you want to fly into Mount Belukha, helicopters can be hired from Gorno-Altaisk and (with some trouble) from Ust-Koksa. (See the discussion on helicopters in the By Air section of chapter 4, Traveling in Russia and Central Asia.)

For the **Katun River-to-Teletskoye Lake trek**, fly to Gorno-Altaisk and then drive the Chuisky and Chemalsky highways south to Ust-Sema, following the Katun River. As you drive south, the Chemalsky tract diverges from the Chuisky at the town of Ust-Sema. Cliffs next to town are popular with rock climbers. Continue south to Edigan, about 68 miles (about 110 km) from Ust-Sema. Along the way, you'll pass Chemal and Eland, where the Katun dam (successfully blocked by environmentalists) was to have been built. The bus only goes as far as Chemal, so it's about 30 miles (48 km) farther to get to Edigan.

For the return trip from where you end up on the south end of Teletskoye Lake, the ferry travels the length of Teletskoye Lake in 8 to 10 hours. From the north end of Teletskoye Lake you can take the bus to Biysk (3 hours). Or you can do this trek in reverse, driving to Teletskoye Lake from Biysk (3 hours), and taking the ferry to the south end of the lake (8 to 10 hours) to the trailhead in the Chulishman River Valley.

For the **Balyktuyul-to-Teletskoye Lake trek**, fly to Gorno-Altaisk and then drive to Balyktuyul. This is a long day's journey. The bus goes as far as Ust Ulagan, about 9 miles (15 km) south of Balyktuyul. Or, do this route in reverse, driving to Teletskoye Lake from Biysk (3 hours), and taking the boat to the end of the lake (8 to 10 hours). The approach to this trek is much longer than for the preceding Katun River-to-Teletskoye Lake trek.

Where to Stay

There are a number of hotel options in Novosibirsk and Barnaul, including Intourist hotels. In Biysk, a Western-class vacation hotel is under construction, scheduled to open its doors in 1994.

If you drive the Chuisky Tract south to the snowy peaks of the Altai, you are likely to see locals on horseback. (Photo: Vadim Gippenreiter)

The bus from Gorno-Altaisk pulls up in the main square of Ust Kan outside the central hotel. Don't expect too much from this hotel, or the two in Gorno-Altaisk. In fact, Ust Kan, the regional center, is more run-down than the smaller villages. Outside of Ust Kan, you shouldn't count on finding accommodations. For long stretches, there are no towns at all, then villages of single-family houses.

On the **Katun River-to-Teletskoye Lake trek**, there are cabins at "Katun" camp south of Ust-Sema, Chulishman (the south end of Teletskoye Lake), and Zolotoye Ozero (the north end of Teletskoye Lake).

On the **Balyktuyul-to-Teletskoye Lake trek**, there are cabins at Pazyrykskiye Kurgany south of Balyktuyul, as well as those at Chulishman and Zolotoye Ozero on Teletskoye Lake. There are hotels in Aktash, Ongudai, and Shebalina, which you pass through en route to Ust Ulagan.

When to Go

July and August are a good time to go to the Altai; best is early September, when the larches are turning color. The average temperature in Novosibirsk in January is -19°C, in July 19°C. For winter trips, February and March are the best time.

Equipment and Supplies

Effective rain gear is a must for the Altai Range, where extended periods of wet weather are common even in summer. If you go in spring or early summer, take precautions against ticks (see the Immunizations and Health and Medical Problems sections of chapter 3, Staying Safe and Healthy).

Many of the Altai families are self-sufficient farmers, so don't plan on finding necessary provisions in stores or markets in the countryside. It's best to stock up in Gorno-Altaisk or before. You can probably buy meat and dairy products and some fresh garden stuff from people in the villages, but don't expect any luxuries.

LAKE KUCHERLA AND AKKEM LAKE LOOP

This is an **easy trek of 5 to 6 days**, covering **100 miles (162 km)**. **Add 2 more days each way** for travel time between the major city of **Novosibirsk or Barnaul** and the trailhead at Tyungur. This trek can, conceivably, be done in as little as a week, if you fly into Ust-Koksa, rather than Novosibirsk or Barnaul. But a week is not enough time to spend in this region. The distances are too great and the mountainscapes too impressive to do it justice in a few days.

This hike carries you into the Katunsky Range, to Akkem Lake at the hem of Mount Belukha, 14,784 feet (4506 m)—the highest summit in the Altai—and beautiful neighboring Lake Kucherla. A loop forest trail, it also offers fantastic alpine panoramas and opportunities to explore up to the edges of glaciers.

In Tyungur and Kucherla, two villages separated by a bridge and the Katun River, the homes still have *ails*, yurt-shaped wooden structures in which Altaitsi traditionally lived. Now, they live in houses, but keep the *ail* as a summer kitchen in the backyard within the fenced plot usually crowded with

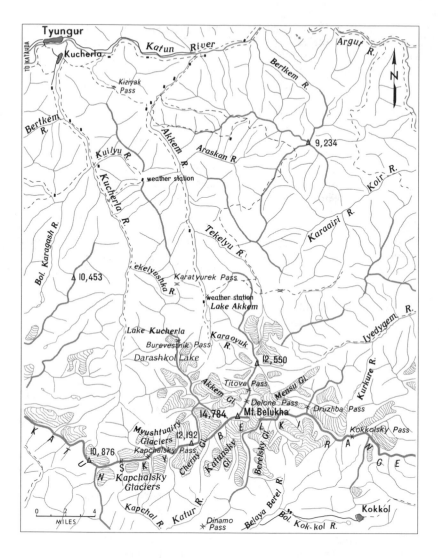

potatoes. It's possible to drive about 9 miles (15 km) up the road out of Kucherla, cutting off some monotonous road-walking.

The trail along the Kucherla River starts out from **Tyungur/Kucherla** through meadows and wheat fields gold against dark, forested hills. Especially in late summer, golden hues dominate the whole palette, birches mixing with larch. In August, it's berry heaven: we enjoyed a progressive feast of currants, bird cherries, buckthorn berries, and honeysuckle. As the trail rises gradually, the forest thickens. In the woods, the ground holds up well even after extended periods of rain, making this trail easy walking in spite of roots and mud. There are **good campsites** in the woods on streams flowing into the **Kucherla River**. Where the Tekelyushka River meets the Kucherla, the trail divides, the left fork going up the Tekelyushka River, the main trail continuing right to **Lake Kucherla** (**10 to 12 hours**).

Lake Kucherla, not as frequently visited as Akkem Lake, is lower in elevation and the prettier of the two lakes. The surrounding trees drop right into the lake, whose azure depths offer good fishing. There are some **cabins** on the lake, where you may be able to arrange a stay. To the south is another lovely mountain tarn, Darashkol Lake.

The trail to Akkem Lake branches off to the right a couple kilometers downriver from Lake Kucherla. Two passes stand between the lakes. Sepuchi Pass can be avoided by descending the Lake Kucherla trail back to the **Tekelyushka River** and following it up to where it meets the Sepuchi Pass–Karaturek Pass trail. From the top of **Karatyurek Pass**, you can see a few buildings on the top of the ridge—an outpost of the weather station headquartered on the lower reaches of **Akkem Lake** (**7 or 8 hours**). The trail drops rather abruptly to this main weather station, in Russian *gidro-meteo stantsiya* (*GMS*).

I don't know that I've ever seen anything more beautiful than Belukha's north face reflected at sundown in Akkem Lake. All movement on the lake's surface came to a standstill. The mountain glimmered there inverted, a perfect mirror image as through veiled fog. Mount Belukha, not a high-altitude giant, has the compelling presence of a very big peak. Its north face, a sheer headwall about a half mile (1 km) long, overpowers everything around it. We were lucky to see the mountain at all, it turned out. According to the meteorolo-

In small Altai towns, potatoes crowd the yards beside ails *like this one. These yurt-shaped wooden structures are the traditional homes of this region.*

gists, Akkem Lake gets 86 sunny days a year, Karaturek Pass 56, and only a few days a year are clear above 12,800 feet (3900 m) on the mountain.

Besides the weather station at the bottom of the Karatyurek Pass trail (where Akkem River flows out of Akkem Lake), there is a **small permanent camp** 0.5 mile (1 km) up on the right shore of the lake. Three dirigible-style huts, originally brought in for the International Mountaineering Camp that operated there for a couple of seasons, are home to three year-round rescue workers. In the summer, a small colony of tents swells this camp, set in a field of fireweed and yellow poppies at 6,700 feet (2042 m) in full view of Mount Belukha. You can stay at the camp for a fee, which is worth it if only for the use of the wonderful *banya*.

Even if you don't plan to climb Belukha, consider a **day hike** up to the **Akkem Glacier**. From Akkem Lake camp, the path leads through boggy grasslands along the lakeshore. A second lake higher up is now filled with mud, braided by streams. The rescue guys say they often see snow leopard tracks on the lakeshore, but have yet to see any tracks with a leopard in them. The trail picks its way through talus slopes to gain the Akkem Glacier, a flattish expanse of ice cut by a gorgeous ice river. Above looms Belukha's headwall, draped with hanging glaciers. It is surprising to find oneself in this extreme alpine setting only a few hours' hike from woods and meadows. The glacier is easy walking—basically flat until you come to an icefall and have to maneuver around its left side to reach the Tomsky camp, a hut at 9,700 feet (2957 m). From Akkem Lake to the Tomsky camp takes 6 to 8 hours.

Some other possible **day hikes** from Akkem Lake include Burevestnik Pass (rating of 2A), elevation 9,500 feet (2900 m), 7.5 miles (12 km); and Titova Pass (rating of 2A).

From Akkem camp back down to Tyungur, the Akkem River trail drops quickly to **Tekelyu River** (2 hours). Dense larch forest obscures the mountain and even the wild Akkem River is mostly hidden in the canyon below, making itself known by its constant roar. There's a **good campsite** here, in view of the Tekelyu waterfall. The trail is more strenuous than the Kucherla River trail. Although you descend 3,600 feet (1100 m) overall from Akkem Lake to Tyungur, there are numerous steep uphills.

Occasionally you get glimpses of the canyon walls, but there are no views of mountains. At about 3,500 feet (1065 m), the trail emerges into open meadows and the slopes on the opposite side of the Katun River appear in the distance. For a mile or so (a couple km) you hike through a wheat field dotted with sunflowers, turning left about 500 feet (150 m) above where the Kiziyak flows into the Akkem and they head northeast to the Katun. A very rough road comes this far. If you've been able to make prior arrangement, you can get picked up here and spare yourself 4 or 5 more hours of walking all the way to the town, over Kiziyak Pass (1 hour up, 2½ hours down) and through fields. If you're lucky, from Kiziyak Pass you'll get one last peek at Belukha, before arriving back in **Tyungur/Kucherla** (**12 to 15 hours**).

A 5- to 6-day extension of this loop explores the area to the south of Mount Belukha, traversing the Katunsky Range. This makes for a 10- to 12-day total, a trek that requires basic mountaineering skills, an ice axe, and crampons.

Trekking in to Mount Belukha

From Lake Kucherla, walk up the Koni-Airy River 7.5 miles (12 km) to Kapchalsky Pass (rating of 2A), elevation 9,186 feet (2800 m); drop over the pass to the Katur River, 9.25 miles (15 km). From Katur River walk up Dinamo Pass (rating of 1A), elevation 8,858 feet (2700 m), 8.5 miles (14 km), and cross the pass to Belaya Berel River, 6.25 miles (10 km). From Belaya Berel River, walk to Bol. Kok Kol River, 7.5 miles (12 km); from Bol. Kok Kol River, cross Kokkolsky Pass (rating of 1B), elevation 9,800 feet (3000 m) to Kurkul Glacier, 6.25 miles (10 km). From Kurkul Glacier cross Druzhba Pass (rating of 2A), elevation 10,500 feet (3200 m), to Mensu Glacier, 6.75 miles (11 km). From Mensu Glacier, cross Titova Pass (rating of 1B), elevation 10,000 feet (3050 m), to Akkem Glacier, 11 miles (18 km). From Akkem Glacier, follow the directions from the Akkem Glacier day-hike description back to Akkem Lake; from Akkem Lake, follow the rest of the hike description back to Tyungur/Lucherla (12 to 15 hours).

MOUNT BELUKHA ASCENT

Not only does Belukha make an impression much bigger than its 14,784 feet (4506 m), it is a more serious climbing objective than most mountains of this elevation. The "standard" Akkem Glacier route virtually circumnavigates this immense mountain, presenting a series of technical challenges. The unstable weather patterns in these parts mean that even in summer, you may often find yourself in dangerous winter storm conditions.

For the Akkem Glacier route, follow the Lake Kucherla-and-Akkem Lake Loop description (above) to Akkem Lake, and the Akkem Glacier day-hike description to the Tomsky camp. The hut is small and basic, but it's a good refuge in bad weather, and three to four people can sleep inside.

From Tomsky camp, another hour over low-angle glacier brings you to the steep—approximately 1,000 feet (300 m) vertical—slope leading to Delone Pass. In icy conditions, this slope could require roping up. It is also a potential avalanche hazard when loaded with large volumes of snow. Upon attaining Delone Pass, drop off the other side to a plateau, skirting extensive crevasses and bergschrunds, then climb the right shoulder to Berelsky Pass, 11,200 feet (3400 m). (Belukha is sometimes climbed from the south side via a route that joins the Akkem Glacier route at this point.) Climb 1½ hours up snow slopes over mostly closed crevasses to the saddle between Pik Berelsky and the Berelsky Ridge, which leads to the summit. This ridge, the classic route (Soviet Climbing Route rating of 3B) is ten pitches of low fifth-class rock, interspersed with knife-edged snow.

KATUN RIVER TO TELETSKOYE LAKE

This **easy 7- to 10-day trek** has lots of up-and-down over **124 miles (200 km)**: it crosses a dozen passes (all easy passes used by herders) and as many rivers as it traverses the Sumultinsky Mountains. Theoretically, there should be bridges because this is an "official" trail (*planovyi marshrut*).

Begin hiking from Edigan, which is a few miles up the Edigan River from the Katun River, heading east through the mixed forest. Higher up, the hillsides are mostly pine. There's **good camping** in wildflower meadows or groves.

The trail zigzags gradually up to Tashan-El Pass, 7,200 feet (2200 m), then down through birch undergrowth to the Chemal River. Hike to the Toguskol River and follow it to a group of mountain lakes. Before you rise the towers of Mount Temir-Kaya. Climb to Sarikonush Pass. You'll be rewarded with good views of the Maly Sumulta River valley and also Mount Albagan, 8,577 feet (2615 m), one of the highest peaks of the Sumultinsky Mountains. The descent from the pass is steep, through talus. Drop down to the Saigonosh River, where there's **good camping**. Hike through the valley to the confluence of the Tyurdem and Izhima rivers. From here, the trail heads up to Tyurdem Pass and the Konyi River valley on the other side. In the mountain meadows leading to Karasu River and Bezymyanny Pass, the grass grows tall as a person.

Hike up the Aksaazkan River valley to its headwaters. The valley widens and the trail winds up the rocky slope to Uimensky Pass. Another steep, rocky descent brings you to beautiful Uimen Lake. With a little luck, you'll get to soak out your trail aches in the *banya* here. Follow the Uimen River where it flows out of the lake, then turn off toward Karasaazkan Pass at the first branch on the right. The next pass—Shtativ, 8,500 feet (2600 m)—is the highest on this route. From the pass, you can see Mount Belukha on a clear day. Below Shtativ Pass, you hit the valley of the Uikaratash River and follow it until you come to the stream draining Samuralu Pass and head left. On the other side of

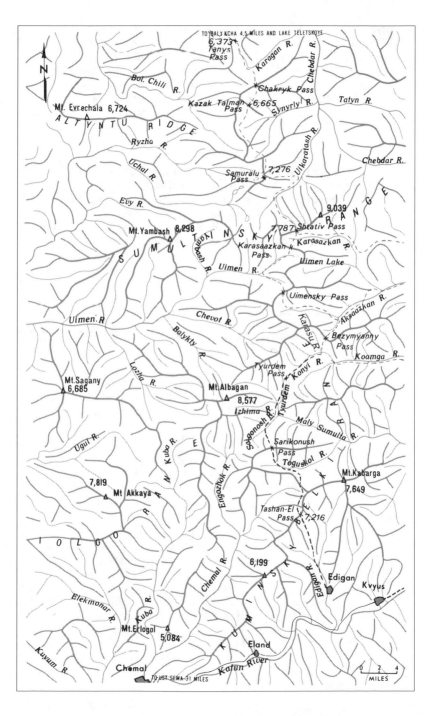

Samuralu Pass, in the Samuralu valley, is a herders camp.

The broad top of Kazak Talman Pass is really more of a plateau. You'll cross several spurs of the ridge dividing the Ryzha and Chebdar rivers before you reach Chakryk Pass. The trail disappears for awhile in boulder slopes before reentering the forest. Cross the Karagan River, and walk through the valley of the Yuch-Alanchik to reach the last pass, Tanys. From Tanys Pass, the trail descends to the Achelman River, twice crossing the river and leading into the Chulishman River valley at Teletskoye Lake's south end.

BALYKTUYUL TO TELETSKOYE LAKE

This **5- to 8-day trek** covers **83 miles** (**134 km**) traversing the Chulyishmanskoye Foothills, from the village of Balyktuyul to Teletskoye Lake.

From **Balyktuyul**, set out on the marked trail north. The trail ascends gradually through coniferous and pine forest to a saddle, then drops down to some lakes. It veers right through a valley choked with bushes; here you pick up the horse path that leads to **Kok-Kyol** ("Black Lake").

From Kok-Kyol the horse trail continues northwest and then north over an unnamed 6,858-foot (1975-m) pass to the Onysh River. Follow the **Onysh River** northeast to the herders' camp at the end of the valley. Off to the left you can see **Uzungol Pass**, 6,500 feet (2000 m); take the trail winding up to it. Beyond the pass, cross two spurs of the Chulyishman Ridge to reach the **Belkash-Tuyan shelter**. You'll find another **hut at Arachok**, before coming upon **Koo Pass**, the hardest pass on this route. From the top of the pass, there are great views of the Abakansky and Shapshalsky ridges, the natural border between Gorny Altai and Tuva. Drop down to the **Chulyishman River valley**, a 5- to 6-hour descent from the pass. **Two more days** of hiking through the Chulyishman valley bring you to the south end of **Teletskoye Lake.**

Kuznetsky Alatau

By Peter Christiansen

Just north of the Altai, the Kuznetsky Alatau is lower in elevation and lacks the remote mountain appeal of the mystical Altai, but it's much more easily accessible from major industrial cities of the Kuzbass Basin.

The Podnebesniye Zubya Mountains are located in the southern half of the Kemerovo Oblast, approximately 62 miles (100 km) south of the coal-mining center of Mezhdurechensk. The western edge of this area is roughly defined by the Tom River, and the eastern portions give way to the vast Siberian taiga.

The ridges and peaks of the Podnebesiye Zubya range from 4,600 to 6,500 feet (1400 to 2000 m). The highest peak is Verkhny Zub, 7,146 feet (2178 m). The mountains are granitic, with much evidence of extended periods of freeze and thaw. They are characterized by extensive boulder fields, which often extend far below tree line, which is at about 3,200 feet (1000 m). The ridges tend to be knife-edged, with cliffs encountered along cirques and near summits. Lakes nestle in the valley floors. Snow hangs on at the higher elevations until midsummer. The ridges are long and rolling, with large expanses above tree line.

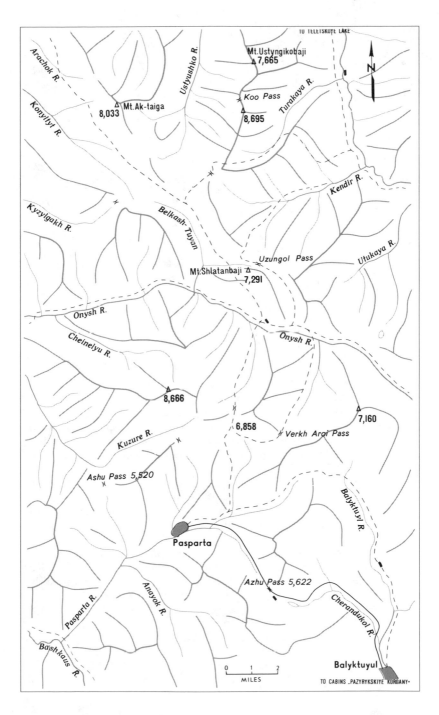

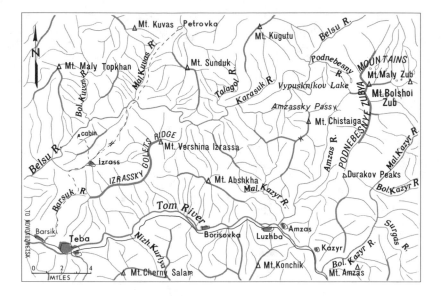

This is a good place to experience the stunning biotic diversity of the taiga, with birches, maples, and other hardwoods occurring in stands along the edges of meadows and bogs. The forest in this area has never been cut and is in full climax stage. Trees up to 100 feet (30 m) tall stalk the valleys. The forest is host to a variety of edible mushrooms, berries, and medicinal herbs and plants.

The taiga is crossed with streams and rivers and dotted with lakes and ponds of all sizes. The water is clean and pure, and supports a large population of *taimen*, a local relative of the trout, and many other sport fish. The forest here boasts large populations of bear, wolf, deer, moose, mink, and many other indigenous smaller mammals. The avian community includes eagles, hawks, owls, ducks, geese, ptarmigan, and many songbirds.

The indigenous people, the Shortsi, are oppressed and suffer a high incidence of alcoholism. This problem is not unique to the native peoples, however. The local Siberians are hospitable to a fault but tend to show their joy at meeting people by attemping to persuade them to drink to the point of unconciousness.

Kemerovo Oblast contains a huge industrial and mining region known as the Kuzbass. All of the cities in this area are industrial cities and are among the least attractive spots to be found in Russia and Central Asia. Mezhdurechensk is a monument to bad construction practices in concrete; Kemerovo is pleasant enough except for the pervasive sulpherous chemical smell that dominates the city; and Novokuznetsk is just plain dreary.

But outside of the cities, the Kuznetsky Alatau is a unique and lovely combination of taiga, mountains, and rivers offering a playground for all kinds of outdoor sports. Hiking is popular along developed trails. There are endless opportunities for cross-country trailless hiking and peak bagging in the higher elevations. Off-trail travel through the taiga is not difficult, as there are many open meadows and boulder fields to follow; however, it can be time consuming and strenuous in places. The rivers in the Podnebesniye Zubya are well known for their white-water rafting and kayaking opportunities during the spring runoff. In the winter, the Podnebesniye Zubya is renowned for cross-country skiing and ski mountaineering.

Getting There

The main access point, Novosibirsk, is about 150 miles (240 km) west of the Kuzbass Basin and about midway between Moscow and Khabarovsk.

There are daily direct flights to Novosibirsk (5 hours from either Moscow or Khabarovsk), or you can take the Trans-Siberian Railroad (about 45 hours from either Moscow or Khabarovsk).

From Novosibirsk, travel to Novokuznetsk; from Novokuznetsk, drive to Luzhba and then cross the Tom River by boat to Amzas (about 8 hours).

The trek ends at Barsik, about 20 miles (32 km) downstream on the same road, from where you can get a bus back to your starting point. Or you can river raft from Barsik to Mezhdurechensk, which is 68 miles (110 km) from Novokuznetsk.

Where to Stay

There are a number of hotel options in Novosibirsk and Novokuznetsk; Amzas has a *turbaza*.

When to Go

Primarily because of insects, this area is best suited for excursions beginning in mid-August at the earliest. In August, temperatures are mild during the day (10°C to 20°C) and cool at night (5°C to 10°C). The region is wet. It rains every three days or so, with rainy seasons in late fall and late spring/early summer. Locals say the weather is stable in August and September. Also, in late August, there are an amazing quantity of wild berries.

Equipment and Supplies

Stock up in Novokuznetsk before you head out.

AMZAS TO BARSIK

This **7- to 10-day trek**, approximately **75 miles (120 km)** long, begins at the Amzas Baza, near the village of Luzhba on the Tom River. The route, which is rated an **easy hike**, traverses two mountains, follows a large river, and ascends two passes. Although it's located just 75 miles (120 km) south of Mezhdurechensk, this trek is in the remote Podnebesniye Zubya Mountains, an area that sees few hikers.

Amzas Baza is at the junction of the Tom and Amzas rivers. It is a renovated Siberian village in a scenic setting, with electricity and a traditional Siberian *banya*. From here, you can do a day hike up to Shorskii Pass, about 12 miles (20 km) round-trip along an old tote road. The pass features fine views of the Durakov Peaks.

Ford the Amzas River and ascend **Chistaiga Mountain**, 4,200 feet (1280 m). The mountain is a gradual ascent through taiga, with occasional views of the Podnebesniye Zubya. Descend to **Belsu River, 9 to 12 miles (15 to 20 km)**. This is a wild and unspoiled river in a remote area. The Belsu has a reputation as one of the best fishing rivers in the Podnebesniye Zubya.

From here, a possible side trip is Vypusknikov Lake, elevation 3,800 feet (1162 m), 25 miles (40 km) round-trip.

Hike down the Belsu to junction with the **Kuass River, 18.5 miles (30 km)**, then along Kuass River on an old road to **Kuass Pass, 9 miles (15 km)**.

From here there's an optional day hike up Sunduk Mountain, 4,600 feet (1400 m). This is a large, open plateau with taiga in places and excellent views. The ascent is easy and even possible on horseback.

Descend from Kuass Pass back to the **Belsu River**. Ford the Belsu and continue along an old road to the abandoned village of **Izrass, 18.5 miles (30 km)**. Hike from Izrass to **Barsik station** on the Tom River, **9 miles (15 km)**. It's recommended that you descend the Tom River in a *taidonka*, the traditional Siberian river boat. The *taidonka* is a long, narrow, flat-bottomed canoe with a shallow draft that makes it ideally suited for navigating the rocky riffles of the upper Tom. The descent to Mezhdurechensk, 62 miles (100 km), takes about 3 or 4 hours. There are fine views of the taiga along the way, a few descents of easy rapids, and many Shorskii villages on the river.

Sayan Mountains

The Sayan Mountains have their western edge near the Kuznetsky Alatau, from where they sweep southeast toward Mongolia, the town of Irkutsk, and Lake Baikal. The eastern Sayan rise steeply against the Tunka Valley at the southeastern end of Lake Baikal. The Sayan are wild, with still many unnamed, unclimbed summits. Zum Bortoy and Altan Mudarga, both over 10,000 feet (3000 m), share space in the Sayan Mountains with Buryat gods (for a description of the Buryat people, see the Lake Baikal section later in this chapter).

The eastern foothills are mixed forest that transitions to *goltsy* ("naked," for bare hills) and alpine. Cascading, health-giving water creases these mountains. Arshan Resort is located on a northern flank of the Tunka Valley, where the Kynarga ("Drum") River cascades out of the Sayan. A mile or so (2 km) up the Kynarga River from Arshan Resort is the largest—50 feet (about 15 m) high—of numerous waterfalls. As you go higher in the watershed, you come to one more, then another series of waterfalls.

Bubbling with various sources of mineral waters, the hot-springs town of Arshan was turned into a popular resort in the Brezhnev era. Trails lead out from Arshan into the mountains, to Peak Lyubov, 6,955 feet (2120 m), and other nearby summits. Several volcanoes are within striking distance from Arshan.

On the border with Mongolia near Tunka Valley, the Tunka Pinnacles offer challenging routes for alpine rock climbers. The Tunka Pinnacles are an all-day bus ride from Irkutsk to Mondy, near the Mongolian border. The highest of them, Munku-Sardyk, 12,930 feet (3491 m), is a 2-day climb from the Muguvek Gorge, with some fifth-class sections.

Reindeer herders in the Sayan Mountains (Photo: Vadim Gippenreiter)

Getting There

The jumping-off point for the eastern Sayan is Irkutsk.

International connections with Irkutsk are growing: there are now regular flights to Irkutsk from Ulaanbaatar and Beijing, as well as charter flights from other cities in China. Irkutsk has regular flights from Moscow (about 7 hours) and Khabarovsk (about 5 hours). Other cities connected by air to Irkutsk incude St. Petersburg, Novosibirsk, Bratsk, Ulan Ude, Vladivostok, and Magadan.

From outside Russia and Central Asia, you can take the train to Irkutsk from Ulaanbaatar, Mongolia, via Ulan Ude (24 hours) or from Beijing, China (50 hours).

From within Russia, you can take the train to Irkutsk from Moscow (72 to 88 hours, depending on the train) or from Khabarovsk (49 hours).

For the **Shumak Hot Springs hike**, from Irkutsk drive or take the bus via Slyudyanka to Turan (3 to 4 hours), then turn north to Nilova Pustyn, and go beyond there another 9 miles (15 km) up the road to Khoitogol.

Where to Stay

There are a number of tourist hotels in Irkutsk, and a low-star establishment in Slyudyanka.

When to Go

July and August are the best times for good weather in the eastern Sayan. If you go in spring or early summer, take precautions against tick-borne encephalitis. (See the Immunizations and Health and Medical Problems sections of chapter 3, Staying Safe and Healthy.)

Equipment and Supplies

Stock up in Irkutsk or Ulan Ude. The availability of a variety of foodstuffs (i.e., anything but bread) is unpredictable. You can buy milk from farmers in rural areas.

SHUMAK HOT SPRINGS

This is a **short hike—31 miles (50 km) one way**—that can be done in **2 days** if you're in a hurry. But why rush to leave an area so rich in mineral springs and beautiful scenery? There are more than thirty springs of varying mineral content and temperature, with wooden baths.

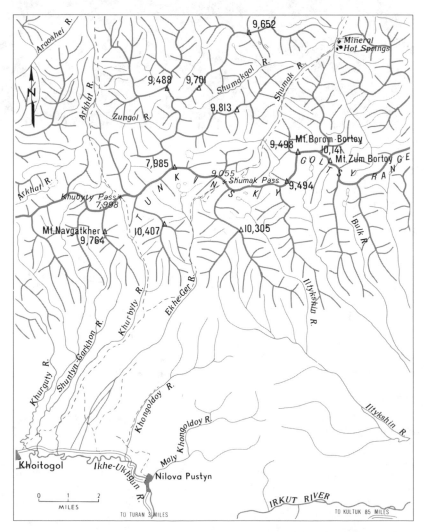

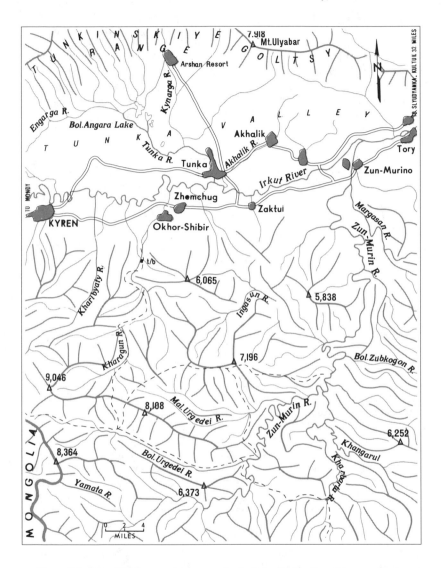

From **Khoitogol**, hike up the watershed of the **Ekhe-Ger River** and across **Shumak Pass** (Soviet Mountain Pass rating of 1A), 9,053 feet (2760 m). From the pass, descend along the **Shumak River** to **Shumak Hot Springs**. Lots of people **camp** in the forest on the streambanks or stay in **cottages** the nearby *kolkhoz* (collective farm) has built at this popular springs.

It's possible to continue the trek, hiking from Shumak Hot Springs to Arshan Resort, a longer trip. Ben Hanson, a graduate student in Russian studies, has spent a lot of time around Lake Baikal. Notes from Ben's journal of a hike in the eastern Sayan area:

Past Turan, our bus drops us at the desolate spa village Khoitogol with the bluish giants of the Sayan in the distance. We hike for 17 kilometers on the dirt road to the trailhead that takes off steeply through the forest, before leveling off to a more gradual slope. We camp on a lake surrounded by small cranberry bushes that, brewed with tea, make a wonderful before-bedtime drink. We awake to a misty morning. Autumn has already come to the Sayan in late August. The firs are a lighter shade of green, the few birch yellow, the bushes red; all these colors are reflected in the lake. And in the distance are tall, brown-carpeted mountains. It rained during the night, so the trail is muddy in places. After several kilometers of thick forest, we break onto a trail side-hilling the mountain. The trees become sparser until, eventually, we come to the tree line. We see squirrels, chipmunks, and marmots, but the most common animal here is cows. The Buryats use the mountains as summer pastureland.

Lake Baikal

Whatever you believe about evolution, Lake Baikal amazes. Statistics make this gigantic crescent, cracked open to depths more than a mile below the surface of the Siberian land, one of the seven wonders of the world. Lake Baikal's southern foot nearly reaches Mongolia, from whence the lake arcs northeast in a long crescent, surrounded by mountain ranges that parallel it.

The Tunka Valley, sandwiched between the eastern Sayan and the western reaches of the Khamar Daban at the south end of Lake Baikal, runs into Mongolia about 200 miles (300 km) west from Irkutsk. The valley around Tunka is marshy, draining into the Irkut River, a twisty, oxbow bending stream that cuts through the valley's bud-green fields on its way to the Angara downriver from Irkutsk.

The gentle slope of the Khamar Daban Mountains fringe Lake Baikal's southern extremity, abutting Mongolia in the Tunka Valley region. Most of the summits are rounded bumps on barren ridges, linked by easy trekking passes. While the Khamar Daban are small fry next to the Sayan, there is a lot of nice, relatively accessible hiking here. Cattle graze in the forest and out on *goltsy* (bald mountains) and alpine openings. The locals collect medicinal herbs and grasses and the multitude of mushrooms that glisten in the damp, foggy forest.

To the east lie the Ulan Burgasy, Ikatsky, Barguzin, and North Muisky mountain ranges. To the west lie the Primorsky and Baikalsky ranges. From the western flanks of the Baikalsky Range flows the Lena, one of Siberia's three great rivers. And the Lake Baikal area contains a number of *zapovedniki* and national parks.

Barguzin *Zapovednik*, the first of Russia's nature reserves, was created in the southwest Barguzin Mountains in 1916, specifically to protect the sable population. By this time, commerce in furs had already decimated the sables (Russian traders had been in the Barguzin since the 1600s). Tsarist authorities forbade sable hunting for several years and, in establishing this reserve that stretches from the crest of the Barguzin Ridge to Baikal's shore, laid the cornerstone in what would become the *zapovednik* system. The *zapovednik*'s headquarters are in the sole village, Davsha, which can be reached only by water. Most of the east Baikal coast is as wild and unpopulated as the Barguzin Mountains.

Olkhon is the biggest island in the lake. Olkhon is a dry place, an island where steep, rocky cliffs guard the shore. The indigenous Buryats believe the mountains are inhabited by gods, and the deity Burkhan dwells here. It's important, when partaking of a meal with the Buryat people, to flick a bit of vodka with the middle finger of the right hand in deference to Burkhan.

North of Olkhon Island, from Cape Ryty, the western coastline of Lake Baikal becomes increasingly rugged and mountainous, the snow-covered peaks of the Baikal Range plunging straight into the lake. These peaks separate Baikal from the watershed of the Lena River. Only a few turbulent streams flow eastward off this ridge and into the lake.

North of Cape Malaya Kosa, the northern edge of the Baikalo-Lensky *Zapovednik*, the Baikalsky Mountains pull away from the west shore, with broad valleys framed by mountain spurs. On this section of the lake, there are no towns for many miles; before the arrival of the Baikal–Amur Mainline (BAM) railroad, and more recently the road south from Severobaikalsk, this was very remote country.

The Barguzin Mountains, hugging the eastern shore of the lake from the Svyatoi Nos Peninsula all the way north to the end of the lake, surpass all

Traditional Siberian-style carved shutters still grace the windows of villages around Baikal.

other Baikal mountains in scale and remoteness. Most Barguzin summits are over 8,000 feet (2400 m); the highest is Peak Baikal, 9,315 feet (2840 m). Accessible from the Barguzin Valley, there's an easy route up it from the Iakhana River side. The other side plunges in a half-mile-long (1-km-long) cliff. In this beautiful high-alpine country, brightly colored wildflowers, including anemone, columbine, and Siberian globeflower, grow in hillocks between the lakes.

A particularly appealing feature of the Barguzin Mountains is that the volcanic forces express themselves here in clusters of hot springs tucked into the river valleys. There's one about 6 miles (10 km) upstream from the mouth of Bol. Chevyrkui River. What more perfect finishing touch on a lovely high-tundra hike than a mineral bath?

Rivers from the Barguzin Mountains' gentler western slopes run directly into Lake Baikal, while those on the eastern side of the watershed, the Talinga and Iakhana, feed the Barguzin River. The Barguzin Mountains catch precipitation coming off the lake, dumping large volumes of snow on the western slopes.

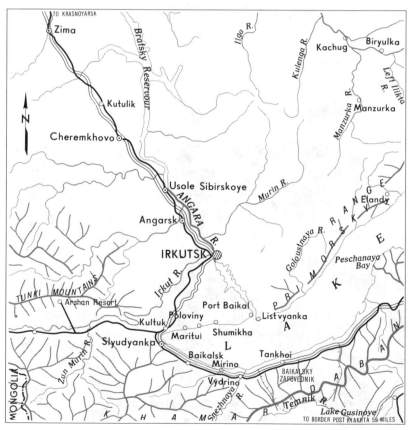

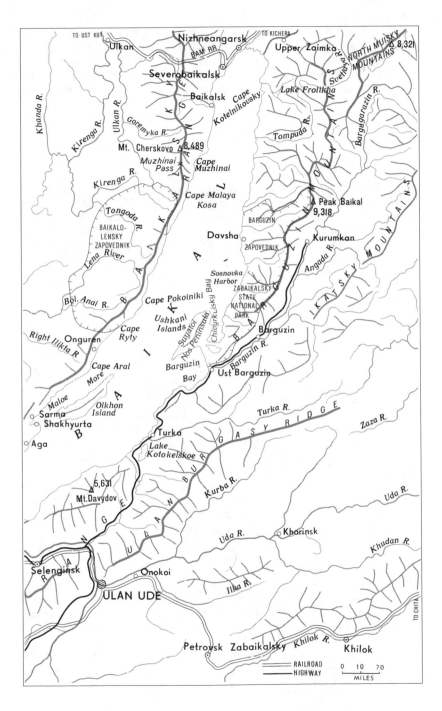

Most of eastern Lake Baikal is uninhabited. It is amazing to look at topos of the northeastern corner of the lake, ribbed by ridges of the Barguzin, Ikatsky, and Muisky Mountains, and realize that no road cuts through most of this vast territory. On this range's eastern edge, the last towns peter out in the Barguzin Valley. On the north, the only settlements are along the BAM railroad line.

The road north, not long after leaving Ulan Ude, climbs into the mountains and becomes a dirt road through the taiga. It descends to the lakeshore, with many places to stop at the lake along the way, including the village of Ust Barguzin. You can take a ferry barge across the Barguzin River to the area north of Ust Barguzin.

The farther north one ventures, the wilder the terrain and the topography, and the steeper and closer the mountains are in relation to the lake. From the fishing village of Kurbulik, a short boat ride north brings you to Snake Bay (named for the harmless grass snakes that inhabit the area), the site of a hot spring. Along the eastern coast of Baikal there are long stretches of good beach walking, for example, from north of the Selenga delta to the Barguzin Range, and even farther north.

But even the facts—the oldest, deepest, most voluminous body of water on the planet—don't account for the charisma of Lake Baikal. Baikal is not so much a lake as a legend. The indigenous Buryats call it the "Sacred Sea." Baikal gives life to an astonishing numbers of species of plants and animals found nowhere else in the world.

Baikal shimmers to the horizon and beyond. Slopes of Scotch pine and larch, cliffy in places, drop into the lake. Hillsides and uplands swim in delphinium, astors, edelweiss, pinks, butter-and-eggs, wild rose, fireweed, cinquefoil, and forget-me-not.

Chivyrkui Bay and Maloe More, as well as the Selenga and Upper Angara deltas, are major stopover sites on the Siberian Flyway, providing excellent birdwatching in early spring and fall. The Siberian capercaillie, a member of the grouse family, shares these forests with chickadees, nuthatches, warblers, sandpiper, grosbeak, and pine bunting, among many other species of birds.

Late spring and early summer is a good time to see bears, wolves, and foxes. Most big game were shot out long ago, and it's not common to see caribou, moose, or red deer around the immediate Baikal watershed.

The *nerpa*, cute little ringed seals, are year-round residents in Baikal; in winter they maintain breathing holes in the ice. They favor the Ushkani Islands, an archipelago off the Svyatoi Nos peninsula about halfway up the lake's east shore. Hunting has decreased *nerpa* numbers to about 60,000, and 6,000 of them are still taken every year for their furs and meat. The *nerpa* skin, so valued by hunters, is sleek and rich from a diet of *golomyanka*, an oily fish also endemic to Lake Baikal. Besides hunting, another major threat to this freshwater seal is pollution in the lake, which drastically affects the fish *nerpa* feed upon.

The climate around Baikal is extreme continental, moderated somewhat by the lake. In Irkutsk, the temperature in January averages -20°C, though it can get down to -50°C (high is 2°C!). April can be as cold as -32°C or as warm as

29°C. July is hot in the city, up to 36°C. In October the maximum is 26°C, the minimum -30°C. Ulan Ude is similar, but even more extreme. Most of the precipitation comes in midsummer, 4 inches (102 mm), in July, with a little less than a half inch in January (12 mm), a little more than a half inch in April (15 mm), and a little more than three-fourths inch in October (20 mm).

The water temperature in the lake, frozen January through May, rarely rises above 10°C to 12°C—making for a brisk swim even on the hottest day. Temperatures are milder along the shore year-round than inland, with the mean winter temperature at the lakeshore around -20°C, and the summer temperature 10°C.

One group of people that lived around Lake Baikal since ancient times, the Evenks are nearly gone. The Evenk life-style was similar to the American Plains Indians, but revolved around reindeer herding. The earth religion beliefs of the Evenk culture linger among the Buryats in the form of shamanism. North of Irkutsk, it is still possible to meet shamans, most of them very old.

The Buryat, people of Mongolian extraction who've lived at Lake Baikal for centuries, are gentle folk, with laughing eyes and warm hearts. Many remain Lamaist Buddhists, in spite of Soviet attempts to annihilate this belief system. The communists brutally suppressed the practice of their religion, destroying the *datsans* (monasteries) and liquidating the monks. Only now are the *datsans* being rebuilt. One can be visited just a few miles outside of Ulan Ude, the Buryats' administrative center. A monk there is said to predict the future, which may explain how his *datsan* has managed to persist.

The Barguzin Valley, sprinkled with Buryat settlements, also used to be an enclave of many of the *datsans*. You can still visit several *datsans* that survived the Soviet genocide. And, all around Lake Baikal, you'll see trees beribboned with tatters of cloth and paper, the local version of a custom apparently drawing from the Buddhist prayer flag.

The Buryats have settled throughout the vast lands east and south of the lake, and in the Ust-Urdinskii Buryat Autonomous Region on the west side, interspersed with the descendants of transplanted Russians. The Baikal fishing culture is a Russian phenomenon; the Buryats were never much for fishing. With horse culture in their blood, they subsisted mainly on horses and cattle.

The descendants of seventeenth-century Cossack settlers live in the Tunka Valley and east to the lakeshore at Kultuk. Tunka Valley industry is mostly collective farming, with villages spread out around the valley. The bottomland is used for haying and grazing, pushing the forests ever farther up into the foothills.

Michael Jones, a Russian interpreter who has spent many months at Baikal working on a team that made recommendations for sound environmental management, describes a horse trip in the area in his journal:

> *We start our horse trip at Zhemchug, along a trail that extends south into the Khamar Daban along the Kharagun River valley. As we near the Mongolian border, the trail moves away from the river, bending south and up over a 6,500 foot pass that leads into the headwaters of the Bolshoi Urgedei. Rafters like to put in here to float the Bolshoi*

Urgedei, working their way into the Zun Murin River basin. We wanted to trail down to the confluence of the Zun Murin, but high waters change our plans. Fords are out of the question. Instead we climb back over the ridge by a different trail. My Buryat friends give me an army-type raincoat to keep the saddle dry. We bunk down on the Malyi Urgedei. East along the ridge, up past hard rock extrusions worn up from the earth, there is a brief, storm-emptied moment with bits of dark blue Sayan Range across the valley. At the headwaters of the Ingasun River, we leave behind the alpine and goltsy highlands to drop into the forest again. At the water's edge of the Ingasun, we travel north in a floodplain deep in tall, wispy grass, crowned in an airy canopy. A granite wall, a low-entrance zimovka (cabin), and a rushing left-entering tributary mark the trail that runs along the left bank of the drainage. The trail zigzags through a recent fire zone before cracking the cat-tracked ridge, then drops back down into the valley along a flank of high pasture and mixed forest. On an evening thick with fog and mosquitoes, and with a close, rich aroma, we reach the village of Ozhor-Shirib.

The Krugobaikalka, a 53-mile (86-km) stretch of railroad hugging the scenic shoreline at the southwest end of the lake between Port Baikal and Kultuk, is a special part of the Lake Baikal experience, chronicling events at the turn of the century. Until that point, Lake Baikal had interrupted the railroad tracks stretching from St. Petersburg to Vladivostok, and cargoes were ferried across the lake in summer; in winter, temporary tracks skated loads over the ice. The Krugobaikalka, built when the Russians were preparing for war with Japan, linked the west and east branches of the Trans-Siberian Railroad for the first time. The line was built hurriedly, in just two years (1902–1904), but with a great deal of care and attention to design of the railroad and the whistle-stop towns.

This stretch of track became a virtual ghost line when the dam across the Angara River flooded the section connecting the Krugobaikalka with Irkutsk. Now, the Trans-Siberian Railroad circumvents it and only two trains a day still rumble along the Krugobaikalka, toting berry pickers, mushroom gatherers, and supplies for the villages and homesteads in the valleys along the route.

While the lake's south end is the most developed, villages and towns mark the anchorable bays up and down the coastline, most of them fishing communities. Baikal is oceanlike in scale, and the people who live there are seafarers. Fishermen brave the summer storms kicked up by the Barguzin, the wicked wind of the east, and the Sarma that howls from the west, to harvest the fish that thrive on Baikal's rich ecosystem. Foremost among these is *omul*, Baikal's native whitefish delicacy. In winter, the locals gillnet *omul* with nets slung between two holes chopped through the ice. The fishing towns tend to be on the rough-and-tumble side.

Inland, where farmers cultivate the valleys, lingers a delightful picture of traditional rural Russian life. Villages of neat larch cottages suggest a proud, self-sufficient life-style. Pots of flowers peep from windows edged with elaborately carved or painted shutters. If you're invited in for fresh milk or *pirozhki*, you'll see traditional Siberian stoves, giant affairs 6 feet (nearly 2 m)

This church is one of many beautiful old Siberian buildings collected in the open-air museum at Taltsy.

across that the whole family can sleep on top of when it's -40°C. Many of these hamlets are now "grandfathers' villages"; the young people have all slipped away to the cities and only the elderly remain.

There are three relatively good-sized cities near Lake Baikal: Irkutsk to the southwest, Ulan Ude to the southeast, and Severobaikalsk to the north.

Irkutsk is on the Angara River, about 50 miles (80 km) downriver from the Angara's source at Lake Baikal. The Angara is the only outflow from Baikal; all the other more than 400 streams flow into the lake. A cultural capital from the rough Siberian frontier days, Irkutsk still boasts numerous onion-domed churches and neighborhoods of classic wooden Siberian houses with beautifully painted and carved shutters, many of them lopsided from decades of sinking into the permafrost. A good highway connects Irkutsk with Listvyanka, the town on the lake where most tourists go, staying in the Intourist hotel there. Halfway to Listvyanka, there's a beautiful open-air museum of old wooden architecture at Taltsy.

Ulan Ude is a pit of a town that nestles in the bends of the Selenga River. The facade, like so many other Soviet cities, is "concrete realism": Khrushchev flats and Brezhnev skyscrapers. For a superb example of how the Evenki, Buryat, and other indigenous people lived, visit the outdoor ethnographic museum near Ulan Ude.

On the lake's northern end, the town of Severobaikalsk, offspring of the BAM railroad, lacks any old Siberian charm. Hastily constructed barracks house the residents of this new railroad town.

Baikal, not long ago considered the world's cleanest great lake, is threatened by the Baikalsk Pulp and Paper plant on its southeast shore and by the BAM Railroad at its north end. The lake's fisheries and the seal population are in danger. Local environmentalists failed in their efforts to block the construction of the pulpmill in the late 1950s, but still hope to shut it down. Scientists and environmentalists worldwide are concerned about saving Lake Baikal.

Because of the immensity of Baikal as a body of water, the first thought of many who go there is water travel. But there's plenty to do on foot, too. Mountains grasp Baikal in a close embrace. There's even a special Baikal term—*goltsy*—(from the word "naked") for the bald mountains found on the perimeter of the lake.

It's hard to fathom, let alone describe, all the opportunities for mountain adventure around this lake. I give an overview of the main ranges and popular recreation spots along the shore. Several, like the hike along the Krugobaikalka tracks, are trips easily planned and executed. Exploration of the remote northern ranges is for those experienced at orienteering, who don't mind getting their feet wet. Some possible hikes I mention only briefly here in the next few paragraphs.

The Tunka Valley can be reached by bus or car from Irkutsk via the town of Slyudyanka, on the lakeshore south of Irkutsk. Slyudyanka, the jumping-off point for the Khamar Daban Mountains, is just south of the Krugobaikalka Railroad's southernmost whistle-stop, Kultuk. From Sludyanka, it's a 3- or 4-day hike into Pik Cherskovo (not to be confused with Mount Cherskovo in the Baikalsky Mountains on the other side of the lake).

Russian hikers like to cross the Khamar Daban from Lake Baikal, ending up in the Selenga valley (or vice versa). In the valley of the Selenga River, from

Taezhny, a trail follows the Temnik River west, with trails fanning out right (to the Khamar Daban ridge crest) and left (to the Selenga Basin). Taezhny can be reached by road from Irkutsk via Sludyanka and Babushkin, or from Ulan Ude.

The protected near-bay between Olkhon Island and the western shore of Lake Baikal is called the Maloe More ("Little Sea"). The south end of the Maloe More is one of the most popular recreation spots at Baikal. You can get information about the area at Malomorskaya, the tourist center at Sakhyurta village. There's also a resort at Peschanaya Bay. To reach Olkhon Island, bus from Irkutsk to Sakhyurta, on the middle western shore of Lake Baikal; from there, ferry to the island. There's good kayaking in the warm bays of the Maloe More, but you can't put in everywhere along the shore. A possible hiking route leaves from Sarma, on the mainland on the south end of the Maloe More, going north up the Left Ilikta River and crossing the southern end of the Baikalsky Mountains, to end at the town of Biryulka, on the highway about 185 miles (300 km) north of Irkutsk.

Another possible hiking route from Lake Baikal to Biryulka takes you through the Baikalo-Lensky *Zapovednik*, which is north of the Maloe More. From near Cape Pokoiniki, at the Solnechnaya weather station, the route takes off up the Bolshoi Anai River to eventually come out at Biryulka. To reach Baikalo-Lensky *Zapovednik*, from Irkutsk fly to the airport at Onguren, 12.5 miles (20 km) north of Cape Aral, or drive; Onguren is where the west coast road ends. Farther north along the west shore, there are several cabins in Muzhinai Bay and a trail from here over Muzhinai Pass leads into the Ulkan River valley. More from Michael Jones's journal:

> For a foggy couple of days we pick mushrooms back up under Cape Ryty in the (Baikalko-Lensky Zapovednik) foothills just up from the shoreline. A trail leads up the Ryty River toward the headwaters of the Lena. There's snow in the beginning of September; we're on our way back from Ushkanii Island. Crossing the lake, we rode the trough to the inside before the coming northwest blow, great yaws to starboard and port, barefooted Nikolai and Sasha the helmsman talking omul [whitefish] under an eleven o'clock moon that lit the bridge.

Twenty years ago, the mountains at Baikal's northern tip were virtually untouched, until the BAM tracks opened up access to the region. On both sides of the tracks, in the Baikalsky Mountains to the west or the North and South Muisky Mountains to the east, there's infinite wilderness hiking country where you likely won't see another person. If you're adventurous and competent at backcountry navigation, this is the place to go for a week or two of exploring. To reach the North Muisky Mountains, take the BAM train from Severobaikalsk east to Kichera (3 hours), and then drive south 9 miles (15 km) to Verkhnaya ("Upper") Zaimka. Or travel north over-lake to Upper Zaimka.

Most of the passes in these parts are easy: you won't find glaciers or cliffs obstructing the way. You *will* find, in places, thickets of stone pine that make manzanita bushwhacking seem like a picnic. It is particularly frustrating to wedge yourself into a tangle of limbs, when you can't see where you're stepping until *after* you sink into a trap of branches, when carrying a large pack.

Where there *are* trails, they are often cluttered with deadfalls. External-frame packs are best avoided, because they tend to hang up in the taiga. This undergrowth, wild rivers, and *kurumnik*—rock fields of varying size, from pebbles to large boulders—present the main obstacles to cross-country travel in this area.

The Barguzin Mountains can be reached by driving north from Ulan Ude (possibly a good bike trip); there's a road up the Barguzin Valley to Kurumkan. There are also flights from Ulan Ude to Kurumkan. There are ferries from Turka (south of Ust Barguzin) and Onguren (on the west side of the lake) to Davsha, on the lakeshore in the Barguzin. Coming from the north, you can take the BAM train from Severobaikalsk to Kichera (3 hours); from Kichera, drive south about 9 miles (15 km) through the village of Upper Zaimka on the Verkhny Angara River to the end of the road a couple of miles (a few km) past the town of Verkhny Akuli.

In the South Barguzin is Zabaikalsky National Park, where there are traces of trails from the Barguzin valley across the mountains to Lake Baikal. These are a combination of paths to food-gathering (berry, wild onion, and pine nuts) sites on the lower slopes, from which one picks up trappers' and Buryat trails. Often these connect with winter huts. Above tree line, the paths are not distinct. It is tempting to camp up here where the vistas go on forever, but the weather is extremely changeable and it is advisable to move downslope for the night.

Most visitors to Zabaikalsky National Park come in winter, when thousands of fishermen flock to the shallow, *omul*-rich waters of Chivyrkuisky Bay from throughout the lake region, traveling over the ice. (Another big ice-fishing camp convenes in the Maloe More on the opposite side of the lake.) To reach Zabaikalsky National Park, drive or fly to Ust-Barguzin; from here, you can ferry across the Barguzin River to the park.

A slender isthmus anchors the Svyatoi Nos Peninsula off of Ust Barguzin. The highest point on the peninsula, 6,158 feet (1877 m), is a popular hike. About 6 miles (10 km) off of Svyatoi Nos are the Ushkani Islands, where the *nerpa* hang out.

Activities other than hiking include bicycling, kayaking, spelunking, and cross-country skiing. The backroads offer good—though often very muddy—mountain biking. Once you're outside the major cities, the only traffic is local. And most of the locals don't have cars. You can go all day without being passed by a single motorcycle. In the uplands north of Irkutsk, ride through fields rolling in sunflowers and rye, wide-open expanses that tilt with light. The road north from Ulan Ude to the Barguzin Valley could be a good bike trip.

Kayaking has also become popular on Lake Baikal. There's great kayaking in Chivyrkuisky Bay, between the Svyatoi Nos Peninsula and the east coast. This bay is sheltered from the forces of Baikal by the narrow sand isthmus connecting it to the mainland and by the mountains of Svyatoi Nos. It's interesting to explore the narrow inlets, putting in on the forested shores. Several other places you're protected from the storms that rock Baikal's open shores are along the Upper Angara River in the vast delta at the north end of the lake, and in the Maloe More on the west coast near Olkhon Lake.

White-water enthusiasts can find plenty to do on Baikal's many tributaries, ranging from class VI carnival rides in the Barguzin Mountains to the Irkut

River, a class II that meanders east toward Lake Baikal for 124 miles (200 km), then turns away from the lake to flow north into the Angara River at its namesake town, Irkutsk.

Numerous caves carve out Baikal's coastline. Especially accessible for spelunkers are Mechta and Buryatskaya at Mukhor Bay (across from Olkhon Island), and Aya, Oktyabrskaya, and Ryadovaya just south of there on Aya Bay. Innokentevskaya Cave is next to the village Razdole 50 miles (80 km) from Irkutsk.

Cross-country skiing is fantastic, and it's especially nice to end up at a hot springs in the Barguzin Valley at the end of the day.

Getting There

The main towns in the Lake Baikal region are Irkutsk and Ulan Ude on the south and Severobaikalsk on the north.

There are regularly scheduled flights to Ulan Ude from Moscow, Irkutsk, and Khabaraovsk. Severobaikalsk is serviced by air from Bratsk, Irkutsk, and Ulan Ude.

You can take an international train to Irkutsk or Ulan Ude from Ulaanbaatar, Mongolia (24 hours), or from Beijing, China (50 hours).

Within Russia, you can take the Trans-Siberian Railroad to Irkutsk or Ulan Ude from Moscow (72 to 88 hours, depending on the train) or from Khabarovsk (49 hours). You can take the Baikal–Amur Mainline (BAM) Railroad from Tayshet or Bratsk (where the Trans-Siberian meets the BAM), which are west of Irkutsk, to Severobaikalsk (24 hours).

Hydrofoils run the length of the lake and a variety of ferries cruise the shores. If there's not a scheduled ferry to where you want to go, you can probably hire some small craft. In winter, Baikal locals use the lake as a highway, driving everything from motorcycles to semis over the ice.

For the **Port Baikal-to-Kultuk hike**, from Irkutsk drive or bus to Listvyanka (about 1 hour). The ferry across the Angara River to Port Baikal goes several times a day. At the Kultuk end, drive or catch the electric train back to Irkutsk.

To reach the Baikalsky Mountains for the **Mount Cherskovo or Cape Kotelnikovsky-to-Baikalsk hikes**, take the BAM train to Severobaikalsk or take a ferry up the coast over-lake to Severobaikalsk from Irkutsk. From Irkutsk you can also either fly to the airport at Onguren, 12.5 miles (20 km) north of Cape Aral where the coast road ends, or you can drive as far as Onguren. From Onguren, you then need to hire a boat up the coast to Cape Kotelnikovsky to get into the Baikalsky Mountains.

To reach the **Lake Frolikha and Aya Bay-to-Verkhny Akuli hikes,** trailhead at Aya Bay, you can take a boat across the lake from Severobaikalsk to Aya Bay (2 hours). A ferry also runs between Severobaikalsk and Khakusy, just south of Aya Bay. From the end of the Aya Bay-to-Verkhny Akuli hike, you can drive from the end of the road at the town of Verkhny Akuli for a couple of miles (a few km) past the village of Upper Zaimka on the Verkhny Angara River and continue north about 9 miles (15 km) to Kichera; from Kichera take the BAM train to Severobaikalsk (3 hours).

Where to Stay

There's a very nice Intourist hotel overlooking Lake Baikal at Listvyanka, an hour's drive from Irkutsk. Otherwise, outside of Irkutsk's and Ulan Ude's tourist hotels, you have to be somewhat creative about lodgings.

This can lead to interesting encounters: residents of many of the Baikal villages have some experience with foreigners renting a room overnight. Some locals have actually converted their homes to bed-and-breakfast–style lodgings, and actively seek paying guests. In Slyudyanka, there's one of these small, independent "hotels," and another just past Cape Tolstoy as you head south along the Krugobaikalka tracks from Port Baikal to Kultuk. These little establishments are mushrooming, and you're sure to find more scattered in out-of-the-way places. They're not necessarily a bargain, though; the Cape Tolstoy chalet charges $40 a night.

When to Go

The first snow falls in the mountains as early as the end of August. In the north, Baikal gets more snow and is generally chillier than the south. Also, it is significantly colder in the northeast, averaging -35°C in January. For outdoor trips, go in July and August, or in winter if you really like it cold. By August the mosquitoes aren't bad. If you go in spring or early summer, take precautions against ticks (see the Immunizations and Health and Medical Problems sections of chapter 3, Staying Safe and Healthy).

Supplies

Stock up in Irkutsk or Ulan Ude. You should be able to resupply on fuel in towns and villages along the coast, but the availability of a variety of foodstuffs (i.e., anything but bread) is unpredictable. You can buy milk from farmers in rural areas.

On the **Port Baikal-to-Kultuk hike**, you should plan to be self-sufficient. While there are stores in several of the villages you go through, you can't predict what you might find there in the way of foodstuffs. If the store's locked, knock at the house next door for the storekeeper.

For the **Lake Frolikha and Aya Bay-to-Verkhny Akuli hikes**, rubber boots are ideal footgear for tramping through the swampy territory of the North Barguzin Mountains. Crampons (at least one pair per party) are advisable for travel in these mountains early in the season, when snow slopes may still be verglas.

PORT BAIKAL TO KULTUK

The track of the Krugobaikalka ("Circumbaikal") Railroad runs along **53 miles (86 km)** of Lake Baikal's southwest shoreline. This is an **easy 5- to 7-day hike**, part of the time on railroad tracks, otherwise on trails following the tracks. You can also do just a couple of days by hiking in and out again, or catching the train that goes by once a day. (Inquire in Port Baikal or Kultuk about what time the train goes by and whether it will stop for hitchhikers.)

On the Krugobaikalka route, fifty-two tunnels thread the rails through the rock promontories of Lake Baikal's coastline. No route finding is necessary here: The trail worn alongside the track is flat, easy walking for a couple of miles (several km) outside the towns, although the path fades the farther you get from either Kultuk at the south end, or Port Baikal at the track's north end. For about 19 miles (30 km), you have to walk the ties or gravel railroad bed.

There's easy access to the lake almost everywhere, with pebbly beaches and a few broad, sandy ones. There are places to **camp on the lakeshore and in the woods**. You never have to worry about finding water with Lake Baikal always right there. Along the tracks, on the shoulder, a band of bushes and wildflowers hems the alders.

The Krugobaikalka is popular with campers and fishermen, and there are often tents pitched along the tracks, especially a day's walk in at either end of the line. Few people walk the whole distance; in the middle section you see fewer campfire rings and trash. The lack of environmental ethics among Soviet campers is actually a hazard on the Krugobaikalka, where *turisti* tear up the wooden railroad ties for firewood. Notes from my Baikal journal:

> *Headquartered in Maritui's town hall, Nikolai Shishelov chairs the one-man Historical Society and Greens Party. The retired military careerist plays gentle host in the immaculate turn-of-the-century cottage he restored next door. Pouring the* zavarka *(strongly brewed black tea) and topping it off with boiling water from the samovar, Shishelov describes winter life on the lakeshore and pleads the cause of the relic of railroad he calls home. "The engineering feats of ninety years ago, the tunnels and larch bridges that endure to this day, must be preserved as a historical monument to the proud Russian tradition, just as Baikal must be saved as a unique phenomenon."*

It's easy to keep track of where you are, because each kilometer is marked. Starting at **Port Baikal**, you pass the 72-kilometer marker (measured from Irkutsk). The path is good to 80 kilometers. Go through your first tunnel at 76.9 kilometers. The tunnels are a bit eerie, especially when the train comes through. A headlamp helps. Off on the right at 79.9 kilometers are three beautiful wooden **cottages** that the railroad's Commercial Department rents out.

From 84 kilometers, there's no trail. At 101.2 kilometers, you come to the village of **Shumikha**. At 105 kilometers is a building housing the Atomic Research Institute. At 106.5 kilometers is the village **Ponamarevka**. Past 106 kilometers, the path's mostly there, with the exception of particularly bad sections between 141 and 144 kilometers and 149 and 150 kilometers. At 108 kilometers you'll find a nice sandy beach just before a kilometer-long tunnel. This tunnel (Tunnel 19) spits you out in the village of **Poloviny**.

In **Maritui**, 118.5 kilometers, beautiful wooden dormitories, a boarding school, and a hospital still stand, abandoned and boarded up now. Home to 300 families in its heyday, only 120 people remain, most of them very old. A landslide wiped out the main street and the taiga creeps ever closer into what's left of what was once the main town between Kultuk and Port Baikal.

At 137.4 kilometers, a youth camp, Sharyzhalgai, headquarters summer campers in old train cars. You'll pass a few more homesteads and small settlements before coming into **Kultuk** at the 158-kilometer post.

MOUNT CHERSKOVO

This **4-day hike** covers **50 miles (80 km)** in the Baikalsky Mountains, taking you to Mount Cherskovo and the only glacier on the west side of Lake Baikal. The trail's rough, with its share of bushwhacking. The trailhead is at Cape Kotelnikovsky, with thermal springs that make it a popular spot.

From **Cape Kotelnikovsky**, the trail heads up the **Kurkula River** with its beautiful waterfalls. About **19 miles (30 km)** in, you come to **Gitara Lake**, a high-alpine lake stuffed with grayling.

Another **6 miles (10 km)** farther is **Mount Cherskovo**, 8,491 feet (2588 m), not to be confused with Pik Cherskovo in the Khamar Daban range to the southeast of Lake Baikal. If you're interested in climbing, the route (Soviet Climbing Route rating 2A) up the peak requires rock-climbing gear.

LAKE FROLIKHA

This is an **easy 3- to 4-day hike** in the North Barguzin Mountains. The trailhead is at Aya Bay on the northeast shore of Lake Baikal. There are organized campsites on Aya Bay and may be some charge for camping here.

Lake Frolikha is part of a protected area, so you need to get a permit for the area. Permits may be obtained in Severobaikalsk from the City Zakaznik Office (Gorispolkom, Otdel Zakaznikov, tel. 6619) or in Nizhneangarsk. You may also be able to get permits from the rangers at Lake Frolikha.

A **4.25-mile (7-km)** hike in from **Aya Bay** brings you to beautiful **Lake Frolikha**. There are places for tents at either end of the lake. Along the southern edge, it's a 1-day hike from the west end of the lake to the southeast end, the second half of the hike being along the rocky shore. You can also cross the lake by boat. At the southeast corner of the lake you can camp in birch and pine, within spitting distance of great fishing.

A trail from the southeast end of the lake cuts back to Lake Baikal, following the **Bireya River**. The trail ends just **north of Khakusy Bay**, which is on the south side of the Khakusy Peninsula. At Khakusy Bay, the hot springs resort of Khakusy until recently catered to vacationing Party functionaries, so the facilities are good.

AYA BAY TO VERKHNY AKULI

This is a **wilderness hike** in the North Barguzin Mountains taking **2 weeks**, based on 6 to 7 hours of hiking a day.

From **Aya Bay**, hike **4 miles (7 km)** to **Lake Frolikha**. From Lake Frolikha, head southeast on the trail along the **Frolikha River**. It's a **2-day hike** through forest to a **cabin** (one of several along the way), with the trail muddy underfoot, possibly even submerged in places.

Climb gradually to **Ukoinda Pass**, overlooking Ukoinda Lake. The pass itself may be swampy, as is much of the land here where permafrost starts thawing in July. A steep boulder descent from the pass puts you on the **Tykma River**. There's **good camping** at this stream's confluence with the **Tompuda River**.

Turn north and hike up the Tompuda for **2 days**. The better path, where hikers have pieced together animal trails, is on the east side of the river. This

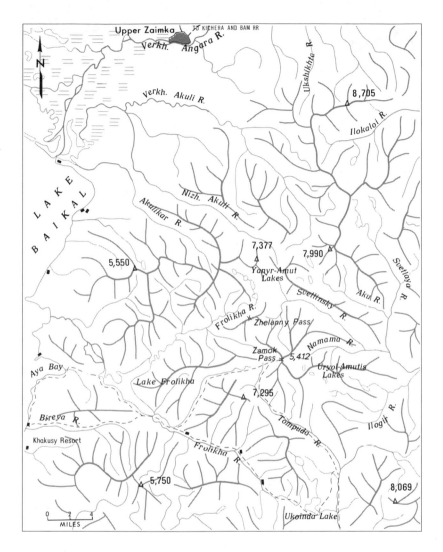

trail travels through forest and meadows by turns, the meadows very wet as a rule. Past the Ilbikaitsi River, you'll come to a hunter's cabin. The trapper's the only resident for miles around, and he only winters here. Wander on up the Tompuda. (In the December 1992 issue of *Russian Far East*, Don Croner describes rafting this river—which has a class VI rating—with a bunch of Russian rafting enthusiasts.)

There's not really a trail, but the walking is easy and level. To reach **Zamok** ("Fortress") **Pass**, 5,413 feet (1650 m), you climb only about 1,600 feet (500 m). There are nice views from here of mountain cirques on either side of the pass, the Tompuda Valley and the rest of the Barguzin Mountains.

Now you're deep into the mountains. To the north crowd rocky pyramids. Many of these summits are accessible only by technical routes, although all of the passes on this route are rated 1A or easier.

Dropping north across Zamok Pass, you cross the headwaters of the Frolikha River's left fork, and across the next pass, **Zhelanny** ("Desired"), the right fork.

Continue north, winding through the **Yanyr-Amut Lakes**. The trail veers east into a knot of unnamed mountains, several over 7,500 feet (2300 m). Between **Medovy Pass** and **Pass Simferopoltsov**, you go through another series of tarns. Beyond this cluster of peaks, walk **3 more days** to **Verkhny Akuli**, down the river of the same name. From here you can drive to Kichera and take the BAM train to your starting point.

12   The Russian Far East

The Russian Far East circles the Sea of Okhotsk, from the cluster of mountain ranges between Yakutsk and Magadan, northeast to Chukotka and its southern appendage, the Kamchatka Peninsula, across the sea to the chain of the Kuril Islands and Sakhalin Island that nearly link Kamchatka to the south mainland of Ussuriland (also known as Primorye). Northwest from Ussuriland are the Stanovoy Mountains and, farther west, Lake Baikal. The Lena River, whose source is the western mountains of Lake Baikal, completes this vast circle in its northeasterly route to Yakutsk and the western foothills of the Verhkoyansk Range.

This enormous region extends from the Arctic Ocean on the north to the Sea of Japan on the south, where Ussuriland shares borders with China and North Korea, and Sakhalin and the Kurils nearly touch Japan. The Russian Far East encompasses climates from arctic to subtropical, and its geography is defined by the volcanic activity in the Pacific "ring of fire."

Yakutia

Far to the northeast of Lake Baikal, the northern Far East begins in Yakutia, the Republic of Sakha. It contains the Verkhoyansk Range, to the west of which winds the great Lena River, coursing from its source in the mountains west of Lake Baikal of the Laptev Sea at the foot of the Verkhoyansk Range. Southwest of the Verkhoyansk, on the Lena River, is Yakutsk, the nearest major town to these mountains. East of the Verkhoyansk is the Chersky Range, in which Peak Pobeda (not to be confused with Peak Pobeda in the Tian Shan) rises to the highest point in the Siberian subcontinent. Yet farther east, connecting Yakutia to the Chukotka peninsula, are the Kolyma Mountains, which extend to Magadan and the Sea of Okhotsk on their southern end.

The Chersky Range and the Verkhoyansk Range rise from the tundra. These are truly untamed mountains. The Buordakh Massif, where steepled summits over 9,800 feet (3000 m) jostle, has been described as a miniature Himalaya. No inviting alpine meadows here: this corner of the Ulakhan-Chistai Mountains is a land of rocks, water, snow, and ice. Even alpine lakes are few. Siberia's highest peak, Peak Pobeda, 10,325 feet (3147 m), crowns this massif.

The Chersky Mountains defend themselves well against visitors. In winter, this is one of the coldest places on earth. In summer (which lasts about five weeks), the surrounding land is swampy, making access on foot difficult. The mosquitoes devour you as you contend with numerous fords, bushwhacking, and steep rocky passes. There are no trails in the mountains and few in the lowlands.

The coldest temperatures in the northern hemisphere have been recorded in Yakutia. In this extreme continental climate, the average January temperature is -40°C, but the mercury's been known to drop to -70°C. The warmest month

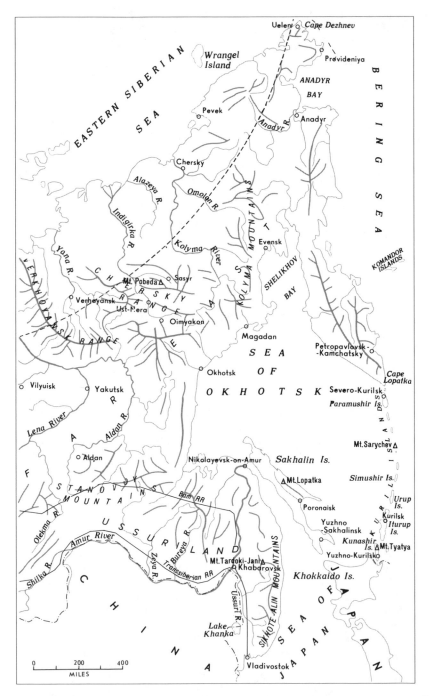

is July, with average temperatures of 13°C to 15°C, although it can get up to 35°C.

Why do I even bother telling you about this place? To remind you that there are mountains in the world that are not on anyone's peak-bagging list, with no summit registers and, often, no names. Russians didn't start climbing here until the 1960s. According to local sources, no Westerners have climbed Peak Pobeda or other giants of the Chersky Range. If you do choose to go into this area, be sure you have good guides or good maps. You're unlikely to see other people, though you may well see bears and wolves.

Getting There

You can fly to Yakutsk within Russia from Moscow (six hours), Khabarovsk, Magadan, and Irkutsk. You can also get there by road from Magadan or Khabarovsk, or by train from Khabarovsk.

There are local flights from Yakutsk to Ust-Nera, or even Sasyr for Peak Pobeda and to Predporozhny. You'll enjoy the mountains a lot more if you can swing a helicopter direct to the high country and avoid driving or hiking through the swamps. Some of the first Russian adventurers in these parts chose to tackle the swamps in spring on skis.

Where to Stay

Yakutsk offers a number of hotels.

When to Go

July and August are the warmest time to go to this land of abbreviated summer, but not necessarily the driest. The Verkhoyansk and Chersky region gets one half its annual precipitation between June and August, this falling as snow at elevations over 4,900 feet (1500 m). By mid-May the rivers open and snow disappears in the lowlands, but the snow hangs on in the mountains for another month after that. There's relatively little snow, with the snowline generally between 7,200 and 7,500 feet (2200 and 2300 m) in July. The rivers freeze and snow arrives in October.

Equipment and Supplies

Outside of Yakutsk, don't count on finding much of any supplies.

PEAK POBEDA ASCENT

The ascent of Pobeda, 10,322 feet (3147 m), is a technical climb, complete with glacier travel and icefalls. A snow cap sits on the summit year-round. The cliffy ridge considered the "standard route" starts at about 7,900 feet (2400 m). There is nothing harder than minor technical moves, but most parties do the route roped. Because of the mountain's remoteness and the generally extreme geographic conditions, this is a climb for experienced mountaineers only. Allow yourself a week for this adventure if you helicopter in to Pebeda; two if you hike from Sasyr.

The village of Sasyr is the gateway to the Buordakh Massif in the Chersky Range. From here, you can see the summits Pobeda and Oiunsky, and the gla-

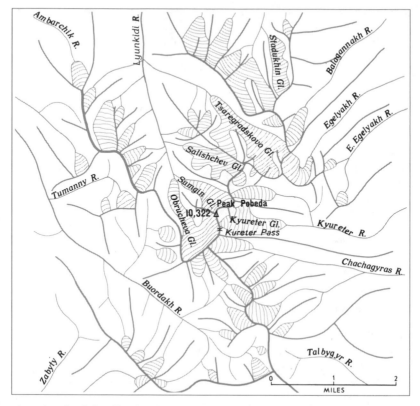

ciers that feed the Chachagyras and Kyureter rivers. Close as the mountains are, the 25-mile (40-km) approach is a real test. Much of it is across swampy lowlands, with challenging fords. If at all possible, arrange for an all-terrain truck to take you at least part of the way.

From **Sasyr**, follow the path northwest along the left bank of the **Moma River** through sparse taiga, coming to the **Onkuchak-Yuryak River** after **5 miles (8 km)**. The trail turns southwest and in another **1.75 or 2.5 miles (3 or 4 km)** you cross the **Onkuchak-Yuryak River**. To call this area swampy is a gross understatement: your ankles may be submerged for several miles. Beyond the bog, you emerge into forest. The mountains loom near now, including the great white cap of Tirekhtyakhsky.

Follow the edge of the forest west, crossing a branch of the Tirektyakh River to come out at **Ulakhan-Kyol Lake**. Head northwest, tracing the rough track to the **Arga-Tarynnakh River** where there's a single grave on the bank. Cross the river and go up the tributary Chachagyras River. Finally, continue northwest toward the grassy ridge extending from the mountain massif. Cross a plateau with a little wooden tower to the banks of the **Kyureter River**. Now you're below **Peak Pobeda**, whose rocky bastions tower above its skirt of glaciers.

The standard route is the cliffy ridge that starts at about 7,900 feet (2400 m).

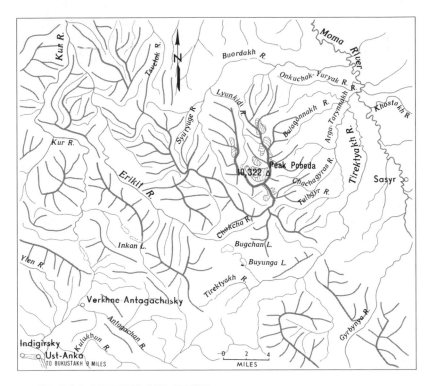

PREDPOROZHNY CIRCUIT

This loop starting and ending at the village of Predporozhny is **112 miles (180 km)**—about a **2-week** hike. This hike does not require climbing gear, but you better take your rubber boots.

From the village of **Predporozhny**, about 56 miles (90 km) west of Peak Pobeda on the Indigirka River, walk along the Maly Kuobakh-Bag River to the Kenner-Sal River. Go up this river to Yubileiny Pass (rated 1A), and descend to the Lyunkidi River. Continue to the Echenk River and Sukhoi River. Ascend to Ekho Pass (rated 1A), and descend to the Tumanny River. Continue to the Mitrei-Ongokhtakh River. From here cross a 5,741-foot (1750-m) pass and descend to the Sredny Kuobakh River. Continue to the Bolshoi Kuobakh River, which you follow back to Predporozhny.

Chukotka

Chukotka is Russia's easternmost point of land, a large wedge with the Eastern Siberian and Chukchi seas to the north, the Bering Sea to the southeast, and Alaska at its eastern tip. Southwest of Chukotka is the Magadan region; until recently, Chukotka was administratively part of the Magadan Oblast.

Much of Chukotka consists of alpine or low-bush tundra. Trees, including larch, pine, birch, poplar, and willow occur only in scattered locations in the valleys of major rivers. The shores of the Bering Sea and the Arctic Ocean are bare tundra and around the town of Provideniya on Chukotka's tip, there are no trees. But you can see Chukotka's gentle mountains from anywhere on the peninsula.

The Anadyrsky Mountains, running east–west with elevations of over 6,500 feet (2000 m), separate the watersheds of the Bering and Chukchi seas. The Chukotsky Mountains run parallel to the east, extending to the peninsula's eastern-most area. The highest point in Chukotka, Mount Matachingai, is just north of the village Egvekinot in the Chukotsky Mountains. The eastern-most part of Chukotka, in the Provideniya–Cape Chukotsky area, is especially mountainous and rugged. Much of the mountainous terrain of Chukotka shows the effects of glaciation during the last ice age; for example, a huge ice field extending south from Mount Matachingai carved out present-day Holy Cross Bay.

Mountains, many over 6,000 feet (1800 m), cover much of the peninsula, and blue rivers cut through the medial valleys. On this wild northern land neck, light plays in the green expanse of tundra in summertime, and highlights the bonfire of colors in early fall. The eastern part of Chukotka, along the tributaries of the Kolyma River, is forested intermittently.

To the west of Chukotka, the Magadansky *Zapovednik*, established in 1982, protects the unique flora and fauna in several different parts of the Magadan region. Sparse larch forests predominate in the reserve. The mountainsides covered in stone pine and birch provide habitat for brown bear, moose, Siberian bighorn sheep, sable, and other taiga animals. You can also see a wide variety of birds, including Steller's sea eagles, capercaillies (grouse), and numerous ducks and owls.

Wrangel Island, 87 miles (140 km) off Chukotka to the north, with moun-tains up to 3,596 feet (1096 m), is one of the more unusual tundra reserves. Aside from a small native village, this Arctic island is wild, inhabited by about 250 polar bears and large populations of walruses and musk oxen. It's an important nesting ground for snow geese, sandpipers, and other birds.

Off Chukotka, whales fluke in the bays and walrus pile on top of each other in coastal haul-outs. Among the cliffs edging this side of the Bering Sea breed colonies of numerous seabirds: puffins, auklets, kittiwakes, and many other rare species. Bushes and grasses grow in the permafrost that blankets Chukotka, feeding the herds of domesticated reindeer. There are about a half million domesticated reindeer on Chukotka. With the reindeer of Koryakia, this is the largest herd in the world.

At Cape Dezhnev on the far east end of Chukotka, only 55 miles (89 km) separate Siberia from Alaska. Because of the direction of prevailing winds, the climate on the Russian side is more severe than on the North American coast, and the vegetation sparser.

Chukotka's a cold place. Average winter temperatures range between -15°C and -30°C, and in summer from 5°C to 13°C. The first snow falls in Septem-ber, hanging on most places until June. Winds blowing from the Pacific and Arctic oceans make the weather on the coast. Cold fogs are common in sum-mertime—and snow flurries are a possibility. In Central Chukotka, with its continental climate, the extremes are felt even more sharply—here it gets

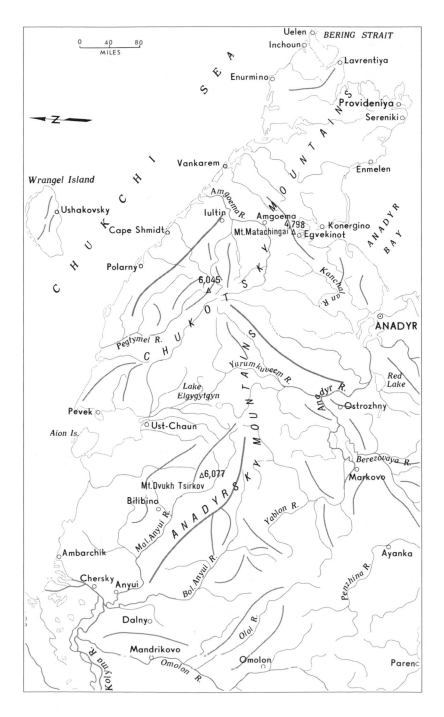

Uelen

BERING STRAIT

Inchoun

Lavrentiya

Enurmino

Provid?niya

Sereniki

Enmelen

C H U K C H I S E A

MOUNTAINS

Vankarem

Wrangel Island

Ushakovsky

Cape Shmidt

Iultin

Amgoema R.

Amgoema
4,798
Mt.Matachingai Δ
Egvekinot

Konergino

ANADYR BAY

Polarny

6,045
Δ

Kanchalon R.

CHUKOTSKY

Pegtymel R.

Yurumkuveem R.

Anadyr R.

ANADYR

Lake
Elgygytgyn

Red
Lake

Pevek

Ust-Chaun

Ostrozhny

Aion Is.

ANADYRSKY MOUNTAINS

Berezovaya R.

Δ6,077
Mt.Dvukh Tsirkov

Markovo

Bilibino

Mal.Anyui R.

Yablon R.

Ambarchik

Ayanka

Chersky
Anyui

Bol. Anyui R.

Penzhina R.

Dalny

Oloi R.

Mandrikovo

Omolon

Parenc

Omolon R.

Kolyma R.

0   40   80
MILES

N

down to -50°C in winter, and as hot as 40°C in summer.

More than 12 millenia ago, some folks living in northern Siberia crossed over into Alaska and scattered across North America. Talk about exploration and adventure! None of our late-twentieth-century ideas of intrepidity, of first ascents and first descents, even come close to the act of walking off into a new continent. Yet these people were doing a very ordinary thing, following the animals they hunted for a livelihood. And, chances are, they weren't concerned with making history.

Then the glaciers of the last Ice Age melted, turning the Bering Land Bridge into the Bering Strait. But the people of Chukotka and the Seward Peninsula, which mirrors Chukotka across the strait, were still closely tied, sharing the same language and subsistence marine hunting way of life.

Three hundred fifty years ago, the Cossak Semyon Dezhnev sailed down through (what we now call) the Bering Strait to Anadyr, demonstrating in the process that the Eurasian continent ended there. For many years, it remained too remote and difficult of access for the Russians to settle there. Yankee whalers started coming to the coast in 1848 and continued into the early 1900s. It is said that during this time more people in Chukotka spoke pidgeon English than Russian. You can still find American shotgun shells from the last century here.

The port of Magadan, on the north shore of the Sea of Okhotsk southwest of Chukotka, has been the gatekeeper to the Arctic since the late 1600s when the first Russian explorers passed through in search of fur riches. Settled in the early 1930s as a support base to exploit the region's mineral resources, Magadan became the center of one of the largest "islands" of the Gulag Archipelago described by writers like Solzhenitsyn, Shalamov, and Ginzburg. Human cargo by the thousands was freighted east on the Trans-Siberian Railroad in airless, windowless cars, then transferred to ships and barged north to Magadan. Prisoners built the infamous Kolyma Highway, the "road of bones," reaching north to the gold fields and west to Yakutsk. Other labor camps in the Magadan system worked prisoners to death in the gold and uranium mines and on construction projects. While no one knows exactly how many, more than a million people who were declared "enemies of the people" during the Stalin repressions died in Magadan camps. Few people *chose* to live in Magadan. Most of the camp administrators were sent to Magadan as punishment or exile.

In this century, Chukotka (labeled Chukchi Peninsula on some English maps) was estranged from Alaska by politics, splitting many Eskimo families down the middle. Opened to travel in the late 1980s as the Cold War thawed, Chukotka welcomed some of the first Americans to Russia's Pacific Coast. Separated for decades by the "Ice Curtain," the Eskimos of Chukotka found they still spoke a common tongue with visiting Alaskan and Canadian Eskimos, and could teach dances that had been forgotten on the other side of the Bering Strait.

In large part, the Chukchi people maintain their traditional life-style, following the herds, living in reindeer-hide tents called *yarangas*. There are about 11,000 Chukchis on Chukotka, and another 1,500 Yupik Eskimos. In

Chukchi drawings on a walrus tusk (Photo: Vadim Gippenreiter)

Tent Life in Siberia, George Kennan describes the significance of the reindeer to the native people of the Siberian North:

> *Besides carrying them from place to place, he furnishes them with clothes, food, and covering for their tents; his antlers are made into rude implements of all sorts; his sinews are dried and pounded into thread, his bones are soaked in seal oil and burned for fuel, his entrails are cleaned, filled with tallow, and eaten; his blood, mixed with the contents of his stomach, is made into* manyalla; *his marrow and tongue are considered the greatest of delicacies; the stiff, bristly skin of his legs is used to cover snow-shoes; and finally his whole body, sacrificed to the Koryak gods, brings down upon his owners all the spiritual ... blessings which they need.*

Many people in the villages still lead a subsistence life-style—the satellite dishes ubiquitous in Alaskan Eskimo villages have yet to arrive. In Sereniki, they still make *umiaks*, the walrus-skin boats in which Eskimos have traditionally hunted the Bering Sea. In Uelen (see the Cape Dezhnev Circuit description later in this section), there's an ivory-carving workshop and museum. There are many ivory carvers in Chukotka and you're likely to be offered ivory souvenirs. It's illegal to bring marine mammal parts back into many countries, including the United States.

Soviets like to make Chukchis the butt of jokes, in the way that Americans make fun of Polacks. They caricature Chukchis as stupid and simple-minded people from the sticks. In reality, most Soviets know little or nothing about life in Chukotka: Moscow is nine time zones and more than 5,000 miles (8000 km) away. Far enough, as Egvekinot journalist Yuri Skorobogatov remarks, "that it takes an outbreak of flu a month to reach us from Moscow. And you can escape the flu altogether if you're out fishing or herding reindeer. Other events pass us by, too, like the military conflicts and crime problems plaguing some parts of the country now."

Administratively part of Magadan Oblast until it declared independence in 1991, Chukotka is about half the size of Alaska in territory and population. In these most remote reaches of Eurasia, you'll find one of the last traditional Arctic cultures. Most of the remaining 150,000 people are Russians and Ukrainians; 19,000 of them live in Anadyr, the capital city.

Most of Chukotka's towns are coastal, with the exception of a few inland tin and gold-mining centers, like Bilibino. Aside from the chance to meet local people, you probably won't want to spend too much time in Chukotka cities, which are a sobering reminder of the peninsula's harsh history: Egvekinot was a supply post for the Gulag. Not far outside town, you can see the remains of one of these camps. At Provideniya, military hardware rusts—a monument to the Cold War in this border outpost. The Gulag and the Soviet military machine have left their mark: rusting oil barrels litter the beaches and the tundra's torn up by personnel carriers. Still, those expecting a frozen wasteland cordoned with barbed wire will be surprised by Chukotka's charms.

Magadan was opened to travel in 1990, becoming an international city when Alaska Airlines started flying there in 1991. It's the major transportation hub for the region. High wages paid in this northern outpost for jobs in mining and fishing once attracted laborers to the city, but now its economy is in a slump.

Downtown Magadan straddles the isthmus of an anvil-shaped piece of land, hugging Nagaeva Bay. The airport's about 40 miles (65 km) north of town along the Kolyma Highway. Here, settlements are identified by their kilometer post: The airport's the 56th kilometer, the turnoff to Snow Valley is the 23rd kilometer, the insane asylum's the 19th kilometer. There are regular buses between the airport and downtown, and taxis are generally available.

Magadan takes pride in its mining and minerals industry. There are two geological museums. One of them, off Lenin Square, boasts a model of baby mammoth "Dima," recovered some years ago from a glacier in the Magadan region. In the regional museum, the "Memorial" exhibit, opened in 1992, portrays life in the camps. There are also several halls dedicated to the history, culture, and arts of native peoples of this vast region.

The name Kolyma strikes terror in the heart of anyone who's read Russian history, but the river-laced Kolyma Mountains, in the now-liberated 1990s, offer countless outdoor recreation possibilities. And you can mix adventure with history study. As far as we know, no foreigner has ever traveled the length of the Kolyma Highway from Magadan to Yakutsk. This could be done on motorcycle, mountain bike, or even hitchhiking. The "Road of Bones" is only recommended for the most hardened and experienced traveler.

Antiquity emanates from Chukotka. It's common to find artifacts that have washed up on the earth's surface after being buried for centuries: dishes, articles, human bones, polar bear skulls. Ken Leghorn of Alaska Discovery has spent several summers exploring Chukotka; he describes walking the beach

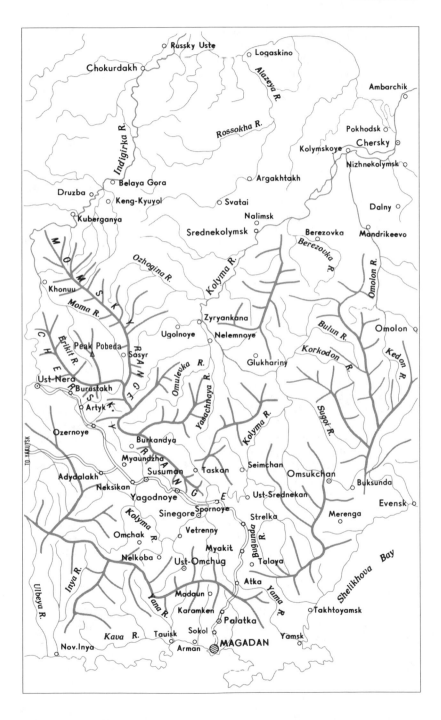

and finding "mind-boggling archaeological sites ... long jawbones from bow-head whales rising in graceful arcs from the tundra where they had been placed hundreds of years earlier by Siberian Yupik hunters." When you find interesting objects literally lying on the ground, it's tempting to collect them as souvenirs. But these bones, shards, or domestic articles are part of an ancient heritage. The fact that many artifacts can be found unprotected on Chukotka is all the more reason to leave them; you have the privilege here of walking through an open-air museum.

Most of Chukotka is accessible to the traveler only by air. And once you're there, small planes and helicopters are the only way to get very far inland. Thus, even though it is the closest point to America, it's not the cheapest place to travel. Travel by water is a good way to experience the peninsula, but most of the coastline is very committing open-water kayaking. Alaska Discovery offers umiak trips along the coast, and the Siberian Alaska Trading Co. does charter boat cruises (see Appendix A, General Resources).

Sport fishing is taking off on Chukotka, where arctic grayling, northern pike, sheefish, whitefish, arctic char, and salmon run in the rivers. Arcsovtour operates trips on the Amgoema, Berezovaya, and Anadyr rivers and to Lake Elgygytgyn in the Anadyrsky Mountains. Other rivers that offer good rafting are the Omolon, Bolshoi Anyui, Maly Anui, and Pegtymel, although these are farther from the coast and harder to reach. On Chukotka, as elsewhere in Siberia, river rafting is a more popular form of wilderness travel than hiking.

Judy Brakel, who leads trips to Chukotka, reports that the mountains in Chukotka are not so much fun to climb because their surfaces are usually frost-sharded rocks. Even ascending a 3,000-foot (900-m) peak can be a chore, given the loose footing. Wandering in the lower elevations, the terrain is fairly gentle, with large valleys and little vegetation.

On boat trips along the coast, in addition to birds and marine life you'll see defense batteries built to protect Magadan during World War II. Helicopters hired for fishing or river trips can also stop to see out-of-the-way labor camps.

The Ola River, which enters the sea at the settlement of Ola east of Magadan, is a popular and accessible place for fishing throughout the summer. Cars crowd the road for several miles and clog the one-lane bridge over the Ola, bonfires line the banks, and family members take turns with the fishing rod.

In the Magadan region, cross-country skiing lasts all winter and into the spring. According to Alaska Airlines Far East Station Manager Mark Dudley, Snow Valley is a good ski bowl; watch for the most popular Russian spring ski fashion: the swimsuit!

Getting There

The best direct international route to Chukotka is to fly across the border from Alaska (unless you want to swim, which is what extreme swimmer Lynne Cox did—from Little Diomede to Big Diomede Island). Bering Air's Cessna does the trip from Nome, Alaska, to Provideniya (50 minutes). There is an international flight to Magadan from Anchorage, Alaska.

From within Russia, you can fly to Anadyr, Chukotka, from Moscow (8 hours) and from Khabarovsk (5 hours). There is regular jet service to Magadan from Moscow, St. Petersburg, Khabarovsk, Vladivostok, and Yakutsk.

By road, Chukotka is a *long* way from anywhere. There's talk of a tunnel that would connect Alaska and Chukotka, but the digging hasn't started yet.

From Magadan, small planes and helicopters provide access to the native towns and mining centers. Ports on the Sea of Okhotsk are serviced by freighters and irregular ferries.

For the **Cape Dezhnev Circuit**, fly from Provideniya or Anadyr to Lavrentia, and from there, helicopter to Uelen.

For the Lake Elgygytgyn-to-Anadyr River raft trip, helicopter to the lake from Anadyr or Egvekinot. You can fly to Anadyr from Provedeniya; to Egvekinot from Anadyr.

Where to Stay

In Magadan, there's the Hotel Magadan on Lenin Prospect and the Business Center Hotel in former Communist party digs. The new hotel Okean is comfy, with a good restaurant and steep prices.

Hotel accommodations in Chukotka towns range from very limited to non-existent, but homestays are a common practice in Anadyr, Provedeniya, and Egvekinot, whose residents are accustomed now to visitors coming across the sea from Alaska.

When to Go

In Chukotka, for hiking and most other outdoor activities, mid-June to mid-September is the time to go.

In the Magadan region, the maritime climate moderates temperatures in both summer and winter, producing lots of fog and rain. Slightly inland, there arc many more clear, dry days. Temperatures may drop to -40°C in winter, and reach 30°C to 35°C in summer.

On the **Cape Dezhnev Circuit**, where the Arctic Ocean meets the Pacific Ocean at the Arctic Circle, the weather can change without warning several times a day. In general, east winds mean good weather.

For the **Lake Elgygytgyn-to-Anadyr River raft trip**, the best rafting season is the first half of August.

Supplies

Stock up in Anadyr or Providerniya before you go. You can't count on finding much in the way of familiar foodstuffs or other camping items in Chukotka stores.

Stores in Magadan sell more and more foreign goods, but don't expect to be able to find camping-type food.

CAPE DEZHNEV CIRCUIT

On the easternmost spit of the Chukotka peninsula, at Cape Dezhnev, an oval of mountains about 9 miles by 6 miles (15 km by 10 km) pushes up from the tundra, the highest being Mount Lev, 2,430 feet (741 m). The east slopes of this massif are cliffy, the western side much more gradual and swampy in

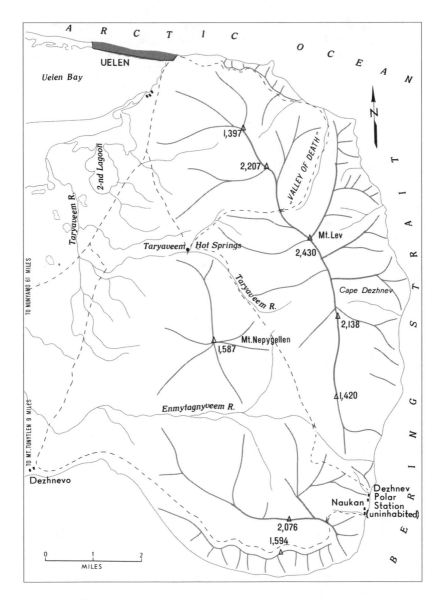

places. On this **5- to 7-day hike** from Uelen to Dezhnev Village, you'll circle these mountains' northeast flanks, cross over them north of Mount Lev, and walk along their west side to the Bering Strait. From here, where you'll likely see bird colonies and the remains of ancient civilizations, you walk the coast to Dezhnev Village and then return inland to Uelen.

From **Uelen**, hike west up to the **Cape Dezhnev plateau**, passing the border guards' station. On a clear day, you can see the striking coastal cliffs, and whales fluking in the bay. Off to the west is the triangular Cape Inchoun. Drop down to the **"Valley of Death," 4.25 miles (7 km)**; the steep slope is overgrown with berry bushes.

Hike south along the "Valley of Death," climbing gradually to the pass over the mountains, with several rocky rises. At the end of the valley is a last steep 300-foot (100-m) slope before the trail levels out. Off to the left from the pass is flat-topped Mount Lev, 2,430 feet (741 m), and to the southwest is Mount Nepygellen, 1,588 feet (484 m). Below Mount Nepygellen you can bathe in a pool at the **Taryaveem Hot Springs, 6.75 miles (11 km)**; there's also **camping** nearby.

From the hot springs to Dezhnev Peninsula Polar Station is hilly hiking. Climb through the brushy **Taryaveem River Valley** to the **pass** between Mount Lev and Mount Nepygellen. Stone pillars at the "pass" (actually a flat, boggy saddle) hark back to the days when there was a polar station and border post on the Dezhnev Peninsula. Among the local residents here are owls, marmots, and bears. For the descent from the pass, traverse up and right on a rough track; the direct route down is a steep one over a permanent snowfield. This track disappears in rocks just before the Dezhnev lighthouse. There are great views of the coastline and the lighthouse perched on the cliff, and of the old Chukotkan village Naukan. Descend to the lighthouse through steep scree and boulders. You may be able to stay in the buildings of the **polar station, 8.75 miles (14 km)**.

From the Dezhnev Peninsula, ascend a steep slope to the plateau, the south edge of which drops down to the sea in 1,000-foot (300-m) cliffs. Beyond the plateau, hike through rock fields trimmed with moss. On a clear day, you can see the Diomede Islands and the outline of the North American continent, as well as the mountains of southeast Chukotka. After 1.25 or 1.75 miles (2 or 3 km), you can make a side trip down to the old village of **Naukan**. Ahead is an ancient ritual site marked by stone monuments, and cliff gates leading the way down to the coast.

At the village of **Dezhnevo, 10.5 miles (17 km)**, there are just a couple of buildings housing the border guards and the whale hunters who put in here.

From Dezhnevo village back to Uelen, it's flat hiking north on a rough track, with many rivers to ford. (You can also do a side trip from Dezhnevo village, 9 miles (15 km) round-trip, west along the shore to Mount Tunytlen, where there's another ancient settlement.) A couple of miles (several km) before reaching **Uelen, 11 miles (18 km)**, you come to the cemetery—a field of bones of whales that were fed to foxes.

LAKE ELGYGYTGYN TO ANADYR RIVER BY RIVER RAFT

By Don Croner

In central Chukotka, Lake Elgygytgyn is surrounded by the Anadyrsky Mountains, ice-covered October to July. Not long ago, icthyologists discovered a new genus of char in the mysterious lake, which scientists have recently determined to be the crater of a fallen meteorite.

The Enmyvaam River flows out of Lake Elgygytkyn, combining with the

Yurumkuveem River to form the Beláya River, which in turn flows into the Anadyr River, Chukotka's major stream. The float from Lake Elgygytgyn to the mouth of the Belaya River at the Anadyr River is **218 miles (352 km)** long—about **50 hours** of river rafting when the water is at average flow.

From **Lake Elgygytkyn**, the valley of the **Enmyvaam** narrows at the mouth of **Kuivyneretveten Creek** and the river enters a canyon. This part of the Enmyvaam is the most picturesque: the river has only one channel 200 feet (60 m) wide surrounded by high rocks. Wild sheep paths are clearly visible and the animals themselves are often seen here. The water is quite slow in this section. After passing the mouth of **Tabunnaya Creek** you encounter the **Leonovskie Rapids**, which are easily passable even in low water.

After flowing out of the canyon, the river splits into many channels and the valley becomes wider and wilder with every passing mile. High willow branches growing in the flood plain and rocky outcrops on the banks create an unusual landscape. The remains of Mukhomornoye village, the first settlement of Native collective farmers in Chukotka, is located at the foot of a mountain 10 miles (16 km) upstream from the confluence of the Enmyvaam and **Yurumkuveyem rivers**.

Where the Enmyvaam joins the Belaya, it is already a major river—more than 800 feet (240 m) wide and 7 feet (2 m) deep. This part of the Belaya valley is forested, quite a change from the barren tundra of the Enmyvaam valley.

Kamchatka

The Kamchatka Peninsula is so narrowly attached to Chukotka it seems like a big earthquake would break it off. Separated from Moscow by nine time zones and at least as many "cultural zones," Kamchatkans refer to Russia as "the mainland." This dog-tail peninsula doesn't fit in geologically, either. The northern arm of the Pacific "ring of fire," Kamchatka percolates with geothermal activity. Several dozen of the more than 200 volcanoes chaining the peninsula have erupted in this century. Hot springs dot the landscape.

Kamchatka's Kronotsky *Zapovednik* on the peninsula's east-central coast is a mountainous wilderness of nearly 2.5 million acres (1 million hectares) containing, among many other natural wonders, Kronotskoye Lake, Kamchatka's largest. The park also includes a marine ecosystem, because its boundary extends 3 miles (4.8 km) into the Pacific Ocean.

A small ravine tucked into the mountains of southeastern Kamchatka has particularly piqued the interest of the "outside world." The "Valley of Geysers," Dolina Geizerov in Russian, crowns the Kronotsky *Zapovednik*. This several-mile-long canyon on the Geyser River bubbles with 200 geysers, making it the second-largest geyser field on the planet, runner-up only to Yellowstone. At most places on the planet, you are only peripherally aware of perpetual motion. In this place, the earth's inner forces churn with an insistence that demands nothing less than awe.

Multiple tiers of geysers dress the steep slopes to about 600 feet (183 m) above the river. Multicolored algae that flourish in the high water temperatures of the geyser outflow paint an abstract mural. The valley bottom is punctuated by boiling mud cauldrons, azure blue pools, and steam vents. No fish

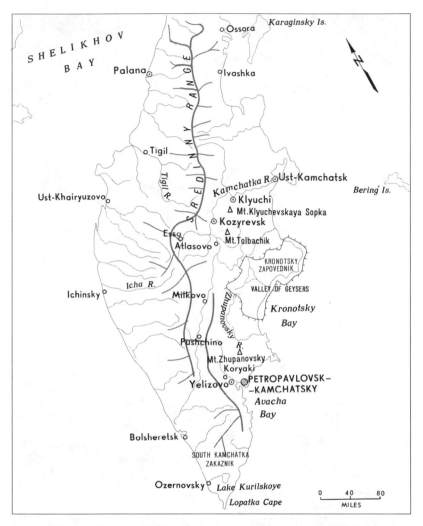

swim in Geyser River, which has been recorded as warm as 27°C in winter.

It has been estimated that hot-spring activity has been taking place within the Valley of Geysers for at least 100,000 years, but it was discovered only in 1941 by geologist Tatyana Ustinova. It was not open for general visitation for most of the past 50 years. For a brief period in the 1970s, hikers were allowed into the valley. Then, in the 1980s, the park management decided human visitors were impacting the fragile terrain too much and the valley was banned to all but a handful of scientists. This treasure went unseen again by Western eyes until 1990. In fact, geyser specialists outside the USSR were skeptical about Kamchatka having a geyser field of world significance.

The Valley of Geysers may be the most dramatic geothermal show within

The Kamchatka Peninsula's geothermal activity reaches the surface in its most spectacular concentration at the Valley of Geysers. These bubbling mud pots were geysers in a past life. (Photo: Vadim Gippenreiter)

Mount Klyuchevskaya (far right), *which erupted in 1993, is the most recent of Kamchatka's frequent volcanic explosions. Clustered around it are Kamen* (center) *and Bezymyanny.* (Photo: Vadim Gippenreiter)

the confines of Kronotsky *Zapovednik*, but there are other exciting features. In addition to 200 geysers, the park has twenty-two volcanoes, some of which have erupted within recorded history.

Just a few miles north of the Valley of Geysers at the headwaters of Geyser River, Kikhpinytch Volcano was active during the 1890s. Karimsky is the most active volcano on the peninsula, regularly spewing smoke. At the southern edge of the *zapovednik*, the summit of Karimsky holds a distinctive crater pool as blue as Crest toothpaste. The *sopka* Semlyachik also erupts frequently. The elegant cone of Kronotskaya, on the shores of Kronotskoye Lake, beckons on a flight into the valley. South of the Valley of Geysers bubbles the basin of Uzon. Luscious colored pools surrounded by supernatural green grass are what remain of the dead crater.

Outside of Kronotsky *Zapovednik*, there are scores of other volcanoes as well. Klyuchevskaya *Sopka*, North Asia's highest summit at 15,584 feet (4750 m), is the ringleader of a concentration of volcanoes at the center of the peninsula known as the Klyuchi group. With its twin, Kamchatka's second-highest, Mount Kamen, 15,148 feet (4617 m), it's a picture of wild beauty.

Besides Klyuchevskaya and Kamen, the Klyuchi group includes Plosky (Blizhny and Dalny), Bezymyanny, Zimin (Bolshoy and Maly), Udin (Bolshoy and Maly), and Tolbachik, ranging from 6,476 to 13,222 feet (1974 to 4030 m). Four of these are more Fuji-like than Fuji. Perhaps the most famous of Kamchatka's volcanoes, nearby Tolbachik blew in September 1962, pouring liquid lava for miles in a spectacular eruption.

The volcanoes of Kamchatka have always been shrouded in mystery. The native peoples, the Koryaks, regarded them with cautious awe. Stephan Krasheninnikov, the earliest chronicler of life on the Kamchatka Peninsula, recorded in *Explorations of Kamchatka 1735–1741* that the natives believed the volcanoes hopped from place to place. The Kamchatka volcanoes are in a class of their own. They are conical and elegant, rising from the flat coastal lands and the labyrinth of ridges inland. The Russians don't call them mountains; they refer to them by a special term—*sopka* ("cone")—unique to these volcanoes.

The botanical diversity of Kronotsky *Zapovednik* is unparalleled, according to T. Scott Bryan writing in the July 1992 issue of *Earth* magazine. In "Kronotsky Nature Preserve," he describes the flora and fauna of Kamchatka:

> *Stone birch trees dominate the forests, growing to huge size over hundreds of years. Members of the beech, ash, willow, and elm families mingle with conifers. While some small plants, such as roses and strawberries, seem familiar to outsiders, a great many flowering species are endemic to Kronotsky and considered endangered; one variety of grass has been found only in one small portion of Dolina Geizerov....*
>
> *Kronotsky Nature Preserve was established as a wildlife refuge in 1882, primarily for its concentration of sable, a rich dark fur reserved for the nobility. The refuge became a full nature preserve in 1934. In recognition of its great biodiversity, the United Nations designated it a World Heritage Site....*
>
> *Kronotsky contains a tremendous concentration of wildlife, with more than 600 grizzly bears (nearly three times as many as in the entire Yellowstone ecosystem), along with wolves, foxes, and lynx. The park houses the greatest known populations of the Pacific and white-tailed eagles, and rumor persists of a Kamchatkan variety of the Siberian tiger....*

The Kamchatka Peninsula overall has one of the largest concentrations of grizzlies (*Ursus arctos*) anywhere in the world. Estimates of the total Kamchatka brownie population range from 10,000 to as many as 25,000. Foreign hunters present an irresistible temptation to Kamchatkans desperate for cash. The more significant peril to the bears than foreign hunters are poachers, who sell the bears' furs, gall bladders, and other parts on the lucrative Asian market (see the Poaching section of chapter 5, Environmental Challenges). Local experts estimate that well over 1,000 brownies were shot in 1991—and possibly several times that number.

Warm currents from Japan moderate the climate of the Kamchatka Peninsula. Summer is surprisingly long, the land snow-free and reasonable for hiking and exploring for four months in the summer.

Flying over Kamchatka's mountainous backbone, you see wisps of steam rising from the earth and patches of hillside painted in surreal bright colors. Anywhere else these would be remarkable phenomena; on the Alice's Wonderland of Kamchatka, one takes them for granted. My first visit to Kamchatka took my breath away. I wrote in my journal:

*We float the Zhupanovsky River, its meanders twirling us so the
Zhupanovsky volcano is now ahead, now behind us on the horizon.
From the river's edge, stone birch march their lonely way up the hills,
white skeletons against a veil of rain. Only a golden fringe remains of
their canopy now in late September. Splotches of mountain ash brighten
the evergreens here and there. Bear trails come right down to the water. Big tracks in the mud. My companions and I cluster around the
table in Vadim and Nina's cozy cabin, a table crowded with six kinds of
salmon: light-smoked, strong-smoked, salmon soup, fried salmon, red
caviar, and salmon cutlets. These are true frontier-people. Their genu-
ineness, hospitality, and calm acceptance of the rugged land they live in
take me back to my Alaskan childhood. Many of these people are refu-
gees from the cities of Russia and Ukraine, all trace their roots to European Russia, and yet they are a different breed.*

The earliest inhabitants of Kamchatka were the Itelmen and Koryak
peoples. In some references the Itelmen, who lived primarily on the southern
part of the peninsula, are called Kamchadal. The Koryaks occupied the
northlands, their life-style based on reindeer herding. It may have been these
peoples, or tribes related to them, who first crossed the passage we know today as the Bering Strait.

Cossack Semyon Dezhnev was the first Russian to attain the strait between
Alaska and Chukotka (1648), but his report never reached the capital. The
"discovery" was claimed by Vitus Bering (1728). The Cossack Atlasov explored Kamchatka in 1697, establishing a brutal system of subjugation of the
Itelmen and Koryaks. For several decades, the Russian interlopers plundered
Kamchatka, collecting taxes by force and ultimately inciting the natives to re-
volt. Atlasov himself was a pirate who served time more than once for amass-
ing personal wealth unscrupulously. He and many of the other Cossacks who
ruled the *ostrogs* (settlements) scattered around South Kamchatka were eventually killed by the natives.

The pillage of the Kamchatka Peninsula for furs changed indigenous
Kamchatkan culture irreversibly, decimating the Itelmen and Koryak populations. Descriptions of these peoples' way of life and their battles with the Cossacks are to be found in the observations of Stephan Krasheninnikov. Invited
along on Bering's second expedition as a young scholar, Krasheninnikov
wandered Kamchatka for three years. He lived among the natives and documented in great detail their dwellings, food, feasts, ceremonies, child-raising
practices, war strategies, language, shaman rituals, and many other customs.
Krasheninnikov's *Explorations of Kamchatka 1735–1741* is a must-read for
anyone seriously interested in the region. His book, which includes the notes of
the botanist George Steller, also describes the natural history of Kamchatka.

Another fascinating Kamchatka travel story is George Kennan's *Tent Life
in Siberia*. In 1865, Kennan explored Kamchatka and Chukotka with the mis-
sion of surveying a telegraph line to connect Europe with the United States.
The telegraph never happened, but Kennan wrote an entertaining account of
his adventures.

Russian settlement virtually wiped out the Itelmen people; only about 1,500 who consider themselves Itelmen are left. The remaining Koryak population is larger, with reindeer herding still the mainstay of many of their villages.

Out of Kamchatka's population of about 500,000, about 300,000 live in Petropavlovsk-Kamchatsky. Petropavlovsk-Kamchatsky (usually called simply Petropavlovsk, although you should be specific when placing a call through the international operator, or you'll end up talking to Petropavlovsk, *Kazakhstan*) is the biggest fishing town on the Pacific. A dreary place, Petropavlovsk-Kamchatsky resembles all Soviet cities with its dilapidated high-rise apartment buildings, but lacks the redeeming charm of many old Russian towns. In conspicuous contrast to the ugly, run-down facade, Petropavlovsk-Kamchatsky's natural setting is stupendous: beautiful Avacha Bay and the trio of snowy, alluring volcanoes. One of the significant battles of the Crimean War was fought here when the British and French navies attacked Petropavlovsk-Kamchatsky.

There are a few fishing outposts and scattered towns and villages. The peninsula is largely undeveloped. Apart from a few roads on the outskirts of Petropavlovsk-Kamchatsky, there is only one major road, which runs north–south down the middle of the peninsula through a break in the knot of mountains. Helicopters are the pickup trucks of the Kamchatka Peninsula. The MI-8s deliver hunters and trappers to their cabins. They haul furs, fish, and, now, seekers of adventure.

In addition to the Pacific Ocean and Sea of Okhotsk fisheries, thousands of tons of salmon are harvested annually from Kamchatka's rivers. Furs are still big business on the peninsula. For many city dwellers, trapping is a way of life; they spend several months of the winter in the woods setting their traplines for sable. These trappers are allocated sections of land by the governmental hunting agency, in return for which they must return a certain part of their catch to the government.

Petropavlovsk-Kamchatsky Harbor is also home to the Soviets' largest submarine base on their eastern seaboard. It was this base that kept Petropavlovsk-Kamchatsky off limits longer than almost any other city. Now that the peninsula has opened its doors, Western companies are competing to develop Kamchatka's oil and gold. There have even been proposals to tap Kamchatka's geothermal power and drilling is going on in South Kamchatka *Zakaznik*, part of a feasibility study for a plant that would channel power to Japan.

Resource development is unavoidable for the peninsula, which is faced with conversion from its mostly military economic base. The challenge is whether Kamchatka can develop these resources without destroying the pristine wilderness that was preserved through xenophobic totalitarian restrictions on travel there. The voices of local environmentalists are faint and stand little chance against the forces pushing to open the peninsula to mining and logging. One of the immediate, direct threats is to the grizzly bear.

Kamchatkans as a rule are very warm, hospitable people, but Kamchatka's official policies toward tourists have been anything but welcoming. As the peninsula's tight seal began to crack, Party bureaucrats grasped control of "tourist reception," demanding exorbitant fees for everything from a permit to climb Klyuchevskaya to filming wilderness documentaries. Notwithstanding arguments about a country or region's right to charge visitors for the enjoyment of its wilderness resources, in Russia funds collected for this purpose usually benefit the individuals extorting them rather than bolstering the regional economy or supporting natural resource management (see chapter 5, Environmental Challenges).

The biggest obstacle to growth of a stable tourist industry on Kamchatka that would facilitate travel there *and* provide tourism income to the region is infighting among the various local players. The struggle over ownership of land and resources is being waged all over Russia, but in Kamchatka it is particularly barbarous. Turf battles between individuals and agencies here obstruct a cohesive approach to wilderness tourism development.

Regulations requiring permission from the Kamchatka KGB and military authorities for a tourist visa facilitated the government insiders' monopoly. Only after the Party was banned (following the August 1991 attempted coup) did the way open for independent tourist agencies to compete in providing services at reasonable prices. It will probably be some time before Kamchatka is "tourist-friendly."

Cross-country hiking is easier over much of Kamchatka than other parts of the Far East, because there is relatively little undergrowth. The high tundra is free from bushwhacking, lending itself to easy exploration. And even the birch woods are relatively open, with tall grasses covering the forest floor. The beachs of the Pacific Coast make for easy travel. They are sandy and barren, not much tide nor driftwood.

Still, the peninsula is not an easy place to travel independently, especially if you don't speak Russian. Even the hike of Avachinskaya *Sopka* (see the Petropavlovsk-Kamchatsky's Backyard Volcanoes hike later in this section), right out of Petropavlovsk-Kamchatsky, is challenging to arrange on your own unless you have friends with an all-terrain vehicle. For anyplace farther away, hiring a helicopter or truck is a virtual necessity; as elsewhere, you'll probably find it prohibitively difficult and expensive to do this without going through an organized tour agency (see the discussion on helicopters in the By Air section of chapter 4, Traveling in Russia and Central Asia).

To Kamchatkans, who live off the land, travel in the outdoors has traditionally been for subsistence: fishing, hunting, trapping. Because there is not the long tradition of outdoor recreation found in other ranges of Russia, the tourist infrastructure is still rough. No trains traverse the peninsula. Regular bus service is basically limited to one route up the peninsula's spine. There are no *turbaza* or climbing camps. Most cabins are in private hands. There is no network of hiking trails, although the forests are laced with animal trails and some ancient human trails. George Kennan wrote in *Tent Life in Siberia* in 1865:

> *"Oh Bahrin!" "How does the come-pass know anything about these* proclatye *mountains? The come-pass never has been over this road before. I've traveled here all my life, and, God forgive me, I don't know where the sea is!" Hungry, anxious, and half-frozen as I was, I could not help smiling at our guide's idea of an inexperienced compass that had never traveled in Kamtchatka, and could not therefore know anything about the road.*

Along with the lack of amenities or transportation network outside of the city, Kamchatka travel is complicated by a certain comprehension gap. Kamchatka was completely isolated from the West for so long that locals have very little concept of low-budget, low-impact wilderness adventure. Their impressions of what foreign visitors want, and can pay, has been formed by the first foreign tourists to hit Kamchatka: sport hunters who pay $10,000 to $20,000 each, demand to be pampered, and leave behind expensive equipment and gifts.

If you have a lot of time, and are very flexible, go on your own. Helicopters don't figure in the "classic" Cossack travel style. Krasheninnikov, in *Explorations of Kamchatka 1735–1741*, described the eighteenth-century trip down the southeast coast from Bolsheretsk *ostrog* to Lopatka Cape, a journey of nine days in winter:

> *The first night is spent on the seashore near the mouth of the Bolshaia; the second, in the wilderness; the third, on the banks of the Opala. The fourth night is passed in a yurt on the shores of the Koshegochik. On the fifth night one stops on the Yavinaia; the sixth night, a short distance from Kozhokchi, seven* versts *before one reaches the Ozernaia River. On the seventh night one is on the shores of Lake Kurile; the eight night is spent at Kambalina, and on the ninth day one reaches Cape Lopatka. From Bolsheretsk* ostrog *to this latter place, the distance is 210* versts *300* sazhens, *a trip which is easily made in four days. The Cossacks in this part of the country never pass an* ostrog *without stopping, both to carry out their orders and to rest their dogs. I went from Kozhokchi to Bolsheretsk* ostrog, *and arrived early in the morning of the third day without strain. It is about 150* versts *from one place to the other, as will be seen below:*

> Route from Bolsheretsk *ostrog* to Cape Lopatka—in versts
> Bolsheretsk *ostrog* to the mouth of the Bolshaia R.—33 *versts*
> The Bolshaia to the Opala River—85 *versts*
> Opala River to Koshegochik or Kilgta River—18 *versts*
> Koshegochik River to Yavina River—15 *versts*
> Yavina River to Ozernaia River—15 *versts*
> Ozernaia River to Kambalina River—36 *versts* (plus 300 *sazhens*)
> Kambalina River to Cape Lopatka—27 *versts*
> > —*Excerpt from Explorations of Kamchatka 1735–1741. Translated by E. A. P. Crownhart-Vaughan. Oregon Historical Society Press, Portland, 1972.*

If you just strike out hitchhiking, you're sure to have interesting adventures, though you may not end up where you thought you were going. People you meet along the way will probably welcome you with open arms, stuff you full of salmon cutlets, and give up their bed for you.

If you *do* go on your own: be careful. Kamchatka is bear country, so you should know how to behave around them. Hang your food away from your camp, carry bear flares and bear spray, avoid getting between a sow and cubs,

A research vessel tugs anchor in Vilyuchinsky Bay, against the backdrop of Vilyuchinskaya Sopka. (Photo: Vadim Gippenreiter)

and, if attacked, play dead and try to protect your head and face. Hot pots, superheated earth, and sulphuric pools are also nothing to mess around with. Serious burns can result from a step too close to a steam vent, and enticing pools may have dangerous concentrations of minerals. Most of us have no experience with things like this in the mountains, so it pays to be extra cautious.

Any of the local outfitters listed in Appendix A, General Resources, can probably help you arrange trips described later in this section. At present, travel to the Valley of Geysers is by permit only. The park management granted a temporary concession to the agency Sogjoy, and some of the revenues generated through sale of permits go toward maintenance in Kronotsky *Zapovednik*. Helicopters transporting passengers who failed to obtain the proper permits through Sogjoy have been forced to turn around as soon as they landed at the valley, and have also been subjected to stiff fines. It is to be hoped that the keepers of this fragile gem will be able to resist pressures to develop the Valley of Geysers in order to attract tourist dollars. We should take a lesson from the degradation of Yellowstone, and create an international Valley of Geysers Preservation Foundation.

Getting There

The airport on Kamchatka Peninsula is at Yelizovo, a town of about 50,000 located 12.5 miles (20 km) outside of Petropavlovsk-Kamchatsky on the banks of the Avacha River.

Currently, there are no direct, scheduled international flights from the United States to Petropavlovsk-Kamchatsky, although these are slated for late 1994. Alaska Airlines' flight from Anchorage to Magadan (4 hours) is the closest connection (1 more hour from Magadan to Petropavlovsk). Aeroflot's Magadan–Petropavlovsk-Kamchatsky service is unreliable. Due to fuel distribution problems, they've been known to cancel these flights, requiring passengers to fly all the way to Khabarovsk to pick up a flight to Petropavlovsk-Kamchatsky.

Within the peninsula, there are Aeroflot flights from Petropavlovsk-Kamchatsky to Kozyrevsk, Ozernovsky, Ust-Kamchatsk, Milkovo, Klyuchi (a closed city), Ust-Khairyuzovo, and Ossora, dependent on fuel availability. Foreigners must pay dollars for these flights; for a small group it is often cost-effective to charter a small plane (see the discussion on helicopters and charter flights in the By Air section of chapter 4, Traveling in Russia and Central Asia).

There's bus service from Petropavlovsk-Kamchatsky to Esso, Klyuchi, and on to Ust-Kamchatsk.

Due to serious fuel shortages, there is no longer dependable ferry service to Kamchatka's distant seaside settlements.

To reach the **Petropavlovsk-Kamchatsky's "Backyard Volcanoes" ascents**, drive from Petropavlovsk-Kamchatsky over an all-terrain road to the saddle between Avachinskaya and Koryakskaya *sopkas* (4 hours).

Access to the **Valley of Geysers** is by helicopter. The nearest road ends more than 60 miles (100 km) away to the west, and it's a 4-day hike from the Pacific Coast. Flying into the valley over the Shumnaya River, a series of pristine waterfalls tumbles out of ravines. The Valley of Geysers, a hidden pocket in the landscape thick with plumes of steam, pops into view as a complete surprise.

To reach the **Klyuchi Volcanoes ascents**, you can fly to Kozyrevsk from Petropavlovsk-Kamchatsky, or drive there via Milkovo (about a 12-hour drive). From Kozyrevsk, helicopter to a base camp in an extinct crater between Kluchevskaya and Ushkovskii (½ hour). The closest town to the mountain is actually Klyuchi. It is possible to drive an all-terrain vehicle south some distance from Klyuchi, although a Swiss group that did this in 1993 got stopped by a mudslide.

Where to Stay

In Petropavlovsk-Kamchatsky, the softest beds are at the old Party hotel, the Oktyabrskaya. The Avacha Hotel and Petropavlovsk Hotel are the best of a grim lot of fishermen's hostels. Outside of Petropavlovsk-Kamchatsky, anything called a hotel is probably best avoided in favor of a tent. Outside of the city, especially at Paratunka (the hot springs south of Yelizovo), there are some lodges that can be arranged through some of the organizations listed in Appendix B, Contacts. In smaller towns, it's best to try to rent a room or an apartment.

When to Go

June through September is the most pleasant time for hiking, photography, and other outdoor activities, although in the old days most travel was done by dogsled in winter over the frozen waterways. Weather can be chilly even in summer on Kamchatka, due to wind and latitude. Average temperatures range from -11°C in February to 14°C in July. Throughout the summer months until the first frost, mosquitoes and flies are a problem (see the Immunizations and Health and Medical Problems sections of chapter 3, Staying Safe and Healthy). By late August and September, the mosquitoes are gone.

The locals recommend climbing *sopkas* early in the season in order to do as much elevation gain as possible on snow, because many of the *sopkas* are piles of volcanic slag, making for difficult, two-steps-forward-one-step-back climbing. Avachinskaya can be done year-round, although a winter climb is a serious mountaineering undertaking.

Equipment and Supplies

Clothes should be light enough to keep you cool during the day, but thick enough to discourage insects. In addition to mosquito-net hats and insect repellent, you may want to treat clothes with permethrin (see the Special Considerations section of chapter 2, Preparing for Your Trek). Also be prepared for extended rainy periods.

Lay in your food supply in Petropavlovsk-Kamchatsky. Locals don't eat many fruits or vegetables in this part of Russia, although in summer you can find some fresh stuff in the market at astronomical prices.

PETROPAVLOVSK-KAMCHATSKY'S "BACKYARD VOLCANOES" ASCENTS

Avachinskaya and Koryakskaya are the twin volcanoes that command Petropavlovsk-Kamchatsky's horizon on a clear day. "Avachi" is a mountain evolving constantly. It erupted most recently in January 1991, dumping lava thousands of feet and blanketing the city in ash. One whole slope of the mountain now glows a reddish hue from the lava; smoke billows from the crater.

Avachinskaya's crater rim, a **4- to 6-hour hike** from the **saddle** between it and Koryakskaya, provides a close-up look at the steam vents, sulphur pots, and other activity in the crater. The lower part of the climb is a slag pile. Although there's not actually a trail through the slag lumps, route finding is simple. Higher up, on snow, there's almost always a track through the snow. On a mild day, this is an easy hike. In inclement weather, however, this can be a wintry mountaineering challenge even in August, as we discovered. The top 1,000 feet (300 m) are steep, and in icy, windy conditions with poor visibility, ice axe and crampons are a must and a fall could be serious.

Koryakskaya, Avachi's sister volcano, has kept its summit pyramid. This is a long climb: 9,000 vertical feet (2700 m) of scrambling to the top. The last few hundred feet of climbing are steeper and may require roping up if it is icy.

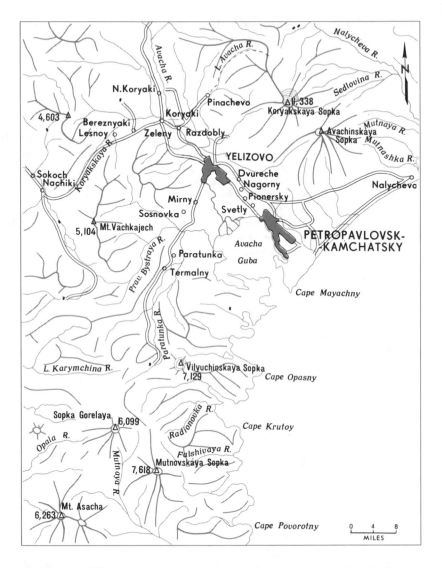

The ascent of Koryakskaya is a **long, exhausting day** for even the fit climber. From the summit, there are terrific views of Petropavlovsk-Kamchatsky harbor, and the pyramids of east-central Kamchatka's volcanoes circle around: Mutnovskaya, Vilyuchinskaya, and, off to the southwest, Opala. To the north, you can see Zhupanovsky, Korimsky, and all the way to Kronotskaya's delicate cone in the distance.

(For a several-day excursion, from the pass between Koryakskaya and Avachi, you can drop down to the north and hike along the Nalycheva River valley.)

More notes from my Kamchatka travel journal:

Often, travel in Russia reminds me that it's not achieving the goal that's the adventure, it's the process of getting there. The drive to **Mutnovskaya Sopka** *is one of these. For the first third or so of the approximately* **6-hour drive** *from Petropavlovsk-Kamchatsky, we actually drive a road, striking off beyond Paratunka in the direction of Vilyuchinsky [Vilyuchinskaya], on the south side of the bay.*

In Russia, even mountains can be military secrets. Vilyuchinskaya is one of those. From the summit of this graceful peak, all of Petropavlovsk-Kamchatsky harbor fans below, including the hidden inlet and submarine berths about which no one is supposed to know (although, of course, everyone does). This puts "Vilyuchi" off limits, beyond the pale of legality, a fact that helped fuel our clandestine ascent.

Russians seem to take a certain pleasure in demonstrating to Americans the exceptionally bad state of Russian roads and the superiority of Russian all-terrain vehicles. A popular joke about how Russian drivers can outdrive any other drivers—no hands, they just stick the wheels in the ruts and go—isn't completely tongue in cheek.

When our truck driver turns off on the "road" to Radionovka, he basically heads into the tundra and straight down a 30-degree hill. We all exchange silent glances like passengers in an airplane experiencing turbulence ... is he really doing this? We'll never get the "Ural," a six-wheel-drive monster, out of this ravine. Radionovka, one of many mineral baths that spout from the Kamchatka earth, is such an unassuming place we have trouble finding the hot springs. After a stream crossing and some stumbling around in the bushes, we locate the series of five pools of varying temperatures and mineral concentrations and have the natural hot tub in the tangled Kamchatka undergrowth all to ourselves. And the truck does get out!

This is only the beginning of the drive to Mutnovskaya. The rest of the "road" is just a track across the tundra, much of it still under snow in late August. The truck churns right through the snow patches. A half dozen times the monster tires spin out in the snow. Once we mire so deeply our fate seems uncertain, but even that one we dig out of.

We are not driving into the unknown. We're following a supply route for the geothermal power research station where a grandiose experiment has been underway for the past decade. Across a broad basin, hydrologists have punched dozens of holes deep into the earth, exploring ways to harness Kamchatka's underground forces. Hot water spouts constantly from these punctures, sending up plumes of steam and making the basin look like a field of constant geysers.

We **hike about 3 hours** *to* **Mutnovskaya Sopka** *from the hill above the research station across a spongy moss carpet. The lowbush cranberry and blueberry bushes sag with berries and wildflowers still decorate the alpine tundra. The vegetation is typical tundra: dwarf bushes, alder. Rhododendron grows up to about 3,200 feet (1000 m); I imagine these hills are a riot of color in early summer. We enter the bowels of* *the earth through a striking canyon, a gash in the hillside rent unceremoniously by volcanic outburst. Steep rock walls give way to crevassed glaciated slopes, plumes of steam rising from them, and we find ourselves in an amphitheater about 500 feet (150 m) deep. The crater floor sizzles with pulsating geysers and fumaroles spouting sulfurous fumes and acidic steam at high pressure. Extraterrestrial-looking sulphur chimneys spit out bright yellow rocks in their sulphurous moats. According to our escort, molten magma boils only a couple hundred feet below ground, periodically leaking to the surface and changing the configuration of the crater floor.*

To journey into Mutnovskaya Sopka is to walk into a fantasy world—or house of horrors. As we leave, Chuck compares it to the Gates of Mordor.

SKI -TOURS AROUND PETROPAVLOVSK-KAMCHATSKY

Peter Christiansen, a Pacific fisheries researcher who is wintering his second season on Kamchatka, raves that the peninsula is a ski-touring paradise, especially in the spring when the days are long and the snow settled.

Crab Peak and Kamchatka Rock is a series of small summits in the south end of Petropavlovsk-Kamchatsky that offers fine backcountry skiing for an afternoon. Go to the **ski area near the *CPB*** ("ship-repairs wharf") and ski into the obvious valley—usually there's a track to follow. Pick any line up the open slopes and skin up to **Kamchatka Rock and Crab Peak (1 to 2 hours)**, then zoom down open meadows. The view from the top includes five volcanoes, the city, and the Pacific.

The following ski tours are outside of Yelizovo, beyond Paratunka. The large plain along the **Paratunka River** is fun skiing in spring under a full moon. All of these routes outside Paratunka have the additional attraction of an apres-ski hot springs soak.

Myshinsky Mys ("Bear Peak") is the lumpy, obvious mountain above the village of **Termalny** near Paratunka. Ski up the ravine from town and then on to the summit. There are many possibilities for ridge skiing and "shots" into the valley. Expect about **1 hour** of **strenuous climbing**.

Koldun is the obvious peak in front of the Okean resort. Go to **Nikolayevskaya Vorota** and head up through the *dachas* (country houses) to the woods. Climb about **30 minutes**.

Distinguish **Pik Ostry** ("Sharp Peak"), in the range above the Paratunka Valley, by its long, knife-edged ridge. Go to Nikolaevka and find the locals' tracks toward the mountain, then skin up and ski the bowl north of the peak to the col, then up to the summit (**4 to 6 hours**). You'll have magnificent views and a nice run down.

There's a nice hot springs about 40 minutes south of Paratunka on Goryachaya *Sopka*. The hot springs are located across the road from a volcanologists' research base. The path up to the hot springs is across the stream—look for a plank bridge and head up the hill. There are three sets of springs on the hill. The best is the highest one, with an excellent pool and views of the distant hills.

(There's also good hiking on the Karim-Sha River, south of Paratunka. This is a large river just north of Goryachaya *Sopka*. The hiking trail begins on the north side of the river and goes into a lovely forest for many kilometers, paralleling the river. The upper reaches of the valley, in a bowl filled with rhododendrons and flowers, is truly outstanding, and offers access to the hills beyond.)

VALLEY OF GEYSERS

While access to the Valley of Geysers is still controlled by the agency Sogjoy, other tour agencies can arrange visits there through Sogjoy. The Valley of Geysers has been preserved completely in its natural state. The only facility there is the rustic, rickety wooden structure that is home to the caretaker and the seasonal researchers. A limited **boardwalk** stair system connects the **helicopter landing pad** and the most accessible geysers. There's a trail from the **Valley of Geysers to Uzon**; it's **3 or 4 hours** up a muddy 800-foot (240-m)

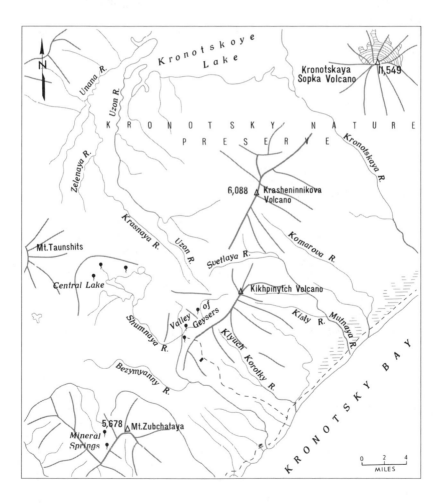

slope to the pass, then a gradual drop 1,000 feet (300 m) across tundra embroidered with bear trails and marmot holes.

KLYUCHI VOLCANOES ASCENTS

A concentration of volcanoes at the center of the Kamchatka Peninsula is known as the Klyuchi group. **Klyuchevskaya Sopka**, North Asia's highest summit at 15,377 feet (4750 m), is the ringleader. With its twin, Kamchatka's second-highest, **Mount Kamen**, 15,019 feet (4617 m), it's a picture of wild beauty. The Klyuchi group of volcanoes is very active. Klyuchevskaya itself erupted in August 1993.

Besides Klyuchevskaya and Kamen, the Klyuchi group includes **Plosky Blizhny** and **Plosky Dalny**, **Bezymyanny**, **Zimin (Bolshoy and Maly)**, **Bolshoy Udina** and **Maly-Udina**, and **Tolbachik**, ranging from 6,476 to 13,222 feet (1974 to 4030 m). Perhaps the most famous of Kamchatka's volcanoes, nearby Tolbachik blew in September 1962, pouring liquid lava for miles in a spectacular eruption. The area around Tolbachik offers interesting hiking with terrific views.

There are few mountaineers on Kamchatka and, because the region has been closed so long to outsiders, many of the alluring summits of the volcanoes have been climbed by only a handful of people. Because of its nearly perfectly conical shape, to climb Klyuchevskaya is to be constantly bombarded by falling rock and ice. David Koester, who did the first American ascent (1992) of the peak together with Tim Byrnes and Fred Menger, describes the climb:

> *It was sometimes like climbing under gunfire. Some of the rocks were large enough to kill. As soon as they gained much speed, they would break up as they crashed into other rocks. One particularly impressive one flew by 40 feet above the slope at what looked like 100 mph, spinning and whirring like a firework. The climb to the intermediate tent was fairly straightforward snow climbing on very old snow, which was sometimes mixed with ash and sometimes covered ice. From (the intermediate tent) up, loose lava chips characterized the rest of the climb. One had to look carefully to distinguish the fixed from the flaked.*

Koester, a Columbia University ethnographer who studies native Kamchatka cultures, also did the first American ascent of Kamen via a technical, 50-degree ice route. In June, the team he was with climbed through snow from about 6,000 feet (1830 m) on Kamen. At this writing, none of the other Klyuchi volcanoes have been climbed by Americans.

Ussuriland

On a political "peninsula" bounded by Manchuria, China, on the west and south, the Sea of Okhotsk on the north, and the Japan Sea and Hokkaido, Japan, on the southeast, the tropical jungles meet the taiga, creating a fascinating ecosystem in an area known historically as Ussuriland. To the northeast are Sakhalin Island and the Kuril Islands, arcing north from Ussuriland across the Sea of Okhotsk in a "chain" stretching to the Kamchatka Peninsula.

The Sikhote Alin Mountains wall Ussuriland off from the Sea of Japan.

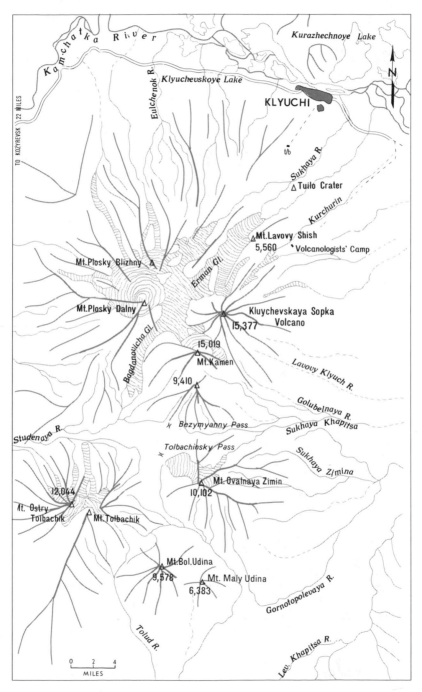

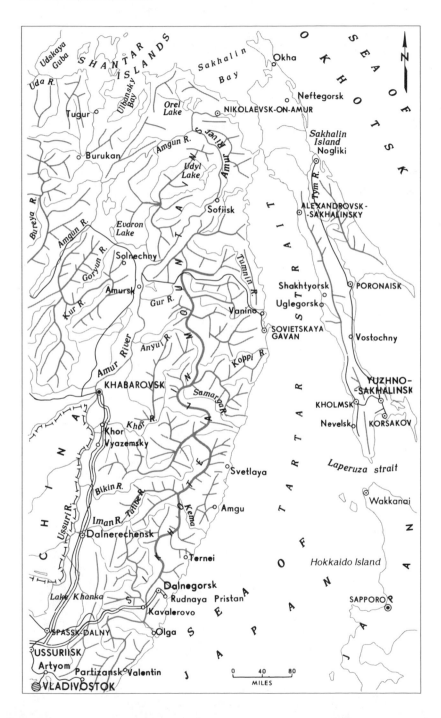

Most of the peaks are around 3,000 feet (1000 m). The lower slopes of these mountains are forested, with alpine tundra higher up. Two passes cut across the central range, one along the Sista-Sankhobe River, the second along the Belimbe River. Rivers flow west off the Sikhote Alin watershed, making their indirect way to the Pacific Ocean via the Amur River.

The Ussuri River begins a ways north of Vladivostok, at the southern tip of Ussuriland. The Ussuri flows north, forming Ussuriland's western border with China and joining the Amur River at Khabarovsk. The Bikin River, which flows westward from the Sikhote Alin Mountains, is one of the main tributaries to the Ussuri River. The Bikin River's watershed, where northern boreal, temperate, and subtropical forests converge, contains the most biologically diverse forests in Russia. The forests of the Bikin and Samarga river basins are the only ones in Ussuriland that remain unlogged, but they are presently threatened by foreign logging operations. (For more on the clearcutting crisis there, see the Logging section of chapter 5, Environmental Challenges.)

Twelve percent of Ussuriland falls under the *zapovednik* designation—a territory the size of Switzerland and Czechoslovakia together. There are six individual *zapovedniki* located in the southern part of Ussuriland.

The **Sikhote Alin *Zapovednik***, spreading across the main watershed of the range, in the Kolumbe and Serebryanka river basins, is not only the largest of the *zapovedniki*, but, by dint of its isolated location, also remains the least affected by development and human activity. The summits Pamyatka and Ostraya, both just shy of 5,000 feet (1500 m), stand guard over the *zapovednik*. The *zapovednik*'s headquarters are in Ternei, at road's end in the reserve's northern end; the logging town of Plastun is just south of the *zapovednik*. The road from Plastun to Ternei bisects the reserve. A steady stream of logging trucks clogs this corrugated dirt road shooting straight through the forest, with rarely a bend to break the monotony.

The forest here is a cornucopia of biodiversity, with more than 1,100 species. On the surface, though, it feels familiar to a native of the New England woods or the Pacific rain forest alike. Stands of virgin Siberian pine, some 200 to 300 years old, mix with yew trees, Mongolian oak, and rhododendrons. It is hard to believe that 800-pound felines roam these woods. Sikhote Alin *Zapovednik* harbors many of Ussuriland's Siberian (Amur) tigers. There's a good chance here of seeing the mountain goats or deer the tigers feed on.

In the spring and fall, the *zapovednik*'s Blagodatnoye Lake is a stopping place for thousands of migrating birds. This place is a peaceful sanctuary among the rosehips. Blagodatnoye Lake is about 10 miles (16 km) from either Plastun or Ternei; it's just a 10-minute walk to where the Pacific rolls in, sweeping the beaches clean, where the teal hills of the Sikhote Alin slide into the sea.

Farther south, where the Sikhote Alin Mountains drop into the Sea of Japan, is **Lazovsky *Zapovednik***. Lazovsky has traditionally been home to a large number of Ussuriland's Siberian tigers, but their territory is increasingly threatened because of its proximity to Vladivostok.

The **Khanka *Zapovednik***, an "island" among the vast rice fields—wetlands set aside for the many species of cranes, herons, and other waterfowl that nest in the marshes south of Lake Khanka—straddles the border with China west of Lazovsky *Zapovednik* and north of Ussurisk. One of the earliest chroniclers of bird activity at Lake Khanka was Przhevalsky. He spent several springs and summers at the lake, in which exquisite lotus flowers grow. Przhevalsky documented 120 species and boasted of shooting cranes and ibis. The birds were rare even then; now, four of the seven species of cranes found in Russia are on the endangered species list. The best season to visit Khanka is early spring or later autumn, during birds migration, or May through June, during nesting.

The Ussurisk–Primorsk highway cuts through the Khanka region. Trails lead up rivers from virtually every town along this highway: from Nezhino, Tikhov, and Terekhovka. Anyone doing wilderness hiking in this rice-growing region should be aware of the risk of mosquito-borne Japanese encephalitis (see the Immunizations and Health and Medical Problems sections of chapter 3, Staying Safe and Healthy).

Ussuri *Zapovednik* is only 62 miles (100 km) from Vladivostok, and just 12.5 miles (20 km) from Ussurisk (population 200,000), so it's much less wild than the other *zapovedniki*.

Kedrovaya Pad *Zapovednik* is in the southernmost Khasanskii Raion (Khasan is the North Korean border town), running along the edge of China on the west side of Amursky Bay west of Vladivostok. The Kedrovaya Pad forest has an exotic feel. In this oldest of Russian Far East *zapovedniki* (it was founded in 1916), the vines of aktinidea (a kiwilike fruit) wrap around the trunks of the Korean pines and wind between the trees like spider webs. Light filters through the canopy of the forest, which is knee-deep in ferns, and lilacs line the trails. Within tiny Kedrovaya Pad Zapovednik's 45,000 acres (18,000 hectares) 900 botanical species are concentrated—half of the plant species of Ussuriland, including some endemic to this southern realm that escaped the last ice age. All eight types of Ussuriland maples are found here.

With its neighboring Barsovyi *Zakaznik*, Kedrovaya Pad *Zapovednik* is prime Amur leopard habitat. Here, as in Sikhote Alin *Zapovednik*, you may be able to "listen" to the movements of several leopards and tigers that have been radio-collared by a joint Russian–American team under the auspices of the Hornocker Wildlife Research Institute.

The **Primorsky *Zapovednik*** is the only such reserve created to protect marine life. It includes the magically beautiful Rimsky-Korsakov Islands in Peter the Great Bay south of Vladivostok. The islands are named for members of the first sailing expeditions to these shores: De Livron, Durnov, Gildebrandt, Matveev, and Furugelm. It takes at least 3 hours by boat from Vladivostok to reach these islands. Also part of the *zapovednik* is the coastline from Cape Lev to Cape Telyakovsky—a series of sandy beaches linked by cliffy points. This rocky coast, silhouetted by Korean pines, resembles an Oriental painting.

The clash of climatic zones in Ussuriland produces a fantastic diversity of species and remarkably lush flora. The animal kingdom of the tropics mingles with that of Siberia in Ussuriland, the last haven for many species no longer found anywhere else on the planet. It's a birdwatcher's paradise, with a wide array of exotic birds and butterflies. Manchurian deer (*izyubr*), roe deer (*kosulya*), *goral* (a rare mountain goat), and bear share the woods with amazing reptiles and amphibians—and with leopards and tigers. The last twenty or

The last few dozen Amur leopards (above) *and Amur tigers in existence live in Ussuriland. (Photo: Yuri Shibnev)*

thirty Amur leopards on the planet live in the southern part of Ussuriland, and the only surviving wild Siberian (Amur) tigers roam throughout the region.

The political and economic chaos in Russia has brought the Amur leopard and Siberian (Amur) tiger to the verge of extinction. Researchers estimate that in 1992 alone fifty Siberian tigers were poached—this represents perhaps a quarter of the remaining population in the wild. But the greatest wild cat in the world doesn't recognize boundaries of reserves, and the *zapovedniki* don't have the means to combat poachers, especially where roads pass too close. (See the Poaching section of chapter 5, Environmental Challenges.)

North of Ussuriland, across from the northern tip of Sakhalin Island, are the Shantar Islands. Offshore of Nikolaevsk-on-Amur, a port city of 40,000, the Shantar Archipelago offers fantastic marine wildlife and birdwatching. They're inhabited by Shantar brown bear, sable, ermine, and red fox. The Shantar Islands have a microclimate much colder than other parts of the Far East. Ice grips these fifteen mountainous islands eight to nine months of the year.

Summer starts in May in Ussuriland and it is *hot*—sometimes 25°C in the shade. Ussuriland is typhoon country. The summer storms blow up from the south, bringing with them high winds and torrential rains sometimes as late as August. Once they hit Vladivostok and Peter the Great Bay, they generally veer off toward Japan, although they sometimes sweep through all Ussuriland and the lower Amur basin. On the coast, temperatures are always more moderate and it doesn't really get hot here until July. Summertime rain flurries are usually brief downpours. The waters of the Ussuriland bays get quite warm in summer—up to 22°C in August.

In September, berries are ripe, the taiga is changing color, temperatures drop to 15°C to 20°C during the day and the weather is more stable. Ussuriland has cold winters. The average January temperature in Vladivostok is -15°C, and Khabarovsk is even colder: -22°C!

Between the seventh and thirteenth centuries, between the Amur River basin and the Japan Sea, fairly advanced industry, agriculture, and arts developed under the Bohie Empire and the Chzurchzen Empire that succeeded it. The descendants of this culture are the indigenous Udege people.

The Amur River was the path east to the Pacific for the Cossacks. When they reached the Sea of Okhotsk in 1639, the Chinese were already there; the Manchu tribes claimed the Amur and Ussuri regions as their birthright. Through the second half of the seventeenth century, the Russians and Chinese fought over these lands. The Russians' incursions were checked and China continued to rule the Amur until the 1850s, when Count Muravyov, the governor-general of eastern Siberia, once again challenged Chinese dominance in the region. By 1860, Muravyov had finally captured the lands between the Ussuri and the Pacific down to the Korean border, leaving Manchuria without access to the sea. The boundary stuck. Today Ussuriland is known as Primorskii Krai—the "Maritime Region"—or simply Primorye.

Late in the fall of 1867, the explorer Nikolai Przhevalsky trekked the Ussuri coast north from Korea, then crossed the Sikhote Alin Mountains, a walk of some 600 miles (970 km). At that time there were few Russians in these parts (Vladivostok was a town of 500) and the Russians had only just secured their empire's claim to Ussuriland.

The Udege, the indigenous people who live today in the basins of the Bikin and Samarga rivers, trace their roots to the early Tungus inhabitants of this region. The Udege, who number about 1,000, still maintain a fairly traditional life-style. They live mainly in the Bikin River basin, subsisting off the river and the forest. They harvest the abundant medicinal plants and trees, including wild ginseng.

In the notes of his explorations in Ussuriland in the last century, surveyor Vladimir Arsenev described meeting Dersu Uszala. A century later, Akira Kurosawa immortalized the Udege woodsman in a movie (of the same name: *Dersu Uszala*), bringing to most Westerners for the first time images of this wonderfully strange corner of eastern Russia.

Krasny Yar Village, the Udege "capital," is a 6-hour drive from Khabarovsk. From Vladivostok, the nearest city is Luchegorsk (overnight train). Another Udege village nearby is Olon. Bill Pfeiffer, who has been instrumental in supplying Russian grass-roots environmentalists with electronic communications, was one of the first Westerners to visit Krasny Yar. From Bill's Krasny Yar journal:

> Our four-wheel-drive vehicle stops on the other side of the Bikin River ... all people and goods must travel across the river to the village proper. When I first set foot in Udege territory, the Bikin River basin, I have the feeling time has stopped. Not in the sense of seeing so-called "primitive" people because the Udege wear Western clothes, watch TV, use machinery, et cetera. What's profoundly different is the apparent sense of harmony between them and the wilderness they inhabit.

Udege people dance at a festival in Krasny Yar. (Photo: Yuri Shibnev)

> *When it comes time to depart, we're escorted 50 kilometers downriver on that classic piece of appropriate technology: the Udege outboard canoe. To my amazement, there's not one human settlement along the whole stretch.*

When Przhevalsky came through in 1867, Vladivostok was a town of 500 people. Today, the population of Vladivostok is 633,000, and it's Russia's largest and most important Pacific port. Vladivostok spreads over several hills on the peninsula jutting into Peter the Great Bay, bounded on Amursky Bay to the west and Ussurisky Bay to the east. Before the revolution, Vladivostok was a cosmopolitan city. Some traces remaining from those days are Chinatown and the Catholic and Lutheran churches. Vladivostok's striking natural setting is marred by the run-down high-rise apartment buildings typical of all Soviet cities and the massive heaps of waste dumped on the shores by the city's industries and the Pacific Fleet, which is based in Vladivostok.

Today, Vladivostok is on the verge of becoming a Pacific Rim hub once again. During the years it was a closed port, all foreign tourists went through Nakhodka, to the north, and business and foreign governments' Far East representations were in Nakhodka or Khabarovsk. Now that Vladivostok has re-opened, it has regained its status, with Khabarovsk, as the center of foreign activity in the Russian Far East.

The archipelago of islands south of Vladivostok is green and inviting. Many residents of the city have garden plots and *dachas* (country houses) on Popov Island. The ferry goes out there from town, or you can hire a boat. Russky Island is the citadel of the Pacific Fleet. Shmakovka is a popular hot springs resort not far from Vladivostok. There are good hotels there.

Aside from Vladivostok, there's not much in the way of city sightseeing in Primorye. The region's cities are "working towns": fishing slums, the cement capital of Spassk-Dalny, the aircraft center of Arsenyev, the pulp-mill burgs of Lesozavodsk and Dalnerechensk, and the nuclear submarine repair town Bolshoi Kamen.

The highway running south–north between Vladivostok and Khabarovsk, along with the road running northeast from Vladivostok to Dalnegorsk near the Sea of Japan, form two sides of a triangle in southern Primorye. The third side of the triangle is formed by a dusty road from Spassk-Dalny (north of Ussurisk) that cuts east through Primorye's midriff. This west–east road bisecting the province spans fields of corn, wheat, and potatoes in the valleys of the Ussuri tributaries. The hills that pop up on the horizon recall Japan. The road, periodically blacktopped, turns into a winding gravel washboard as it begins the climb up the west side of the Sikhote Alin. This is the main artery through the interior. Aside from the few tentacles of roads branching east from the Vladivostok–Khabarovsk highway, this is the only road access to the hinterlands. There is essentially no infrastructure here for travelers; towns and cafeterias are few in these parts, hotels fewer.

The names of many Primorye cities incorporate *dal*, a prefix meaning "far away." Dalnegorsk, for example, is really out there. Before you see the gouged hills of Dalnegorsk ("Far Hills"), you'll smell it. The polluted city is ringed by scars from mining boron, ore, and other minerals since before the revolution, when the local mine belonged to the father of Yul Brynner. Dalnegorsk's other claim to fame is that lots of UFOs are reported to land here. The town has an excellent mineralogical museum, but little else of appeal.

About 22 miles (35 km) farther east from Dalnegorsk, you come to the Sea of Japan at Rudnaya Pristan ("Mineral Harbor"). Outside of Rudnaya Pristan about 2.5 miles (4 km) is a place called Smychka, where there's a very nice, simple resort set on the shores of a lovely lake. From Smychka, you can hike along the coast 4.25 miles (7 km) out to seacliffs to the south. From Rudnaya Pristan, the road leads north to Plastun and Ternei, in the Sikhote Alin *Zapovednik*. The road effectively ends at Ternei. The few coastal villages and towns, including a *maral* (elk) farm north of Ternei, are accessible by sea.

Khabarovsk sits at the northern edge of Ussuriland, where the border turns the corner west. Administratively, Khabarovsk is the center of gargantuan Khabarovskii Krai, which covers the coast all the way up to Magadanskii Oblast. Khabarovsk is the terminus of the highway from Vladivostok, as well as the Baikal–Amur Mainline railroad; the Trans-Siberian railroad parallels the highway from Vladivostok to Khabarovsk, then follows the border west. Less than an hour south of Khabarovsk is the Bolshe-Khektsirsky *Zapovednik*. You can hike to the Ussuri River from south of Khabarovsk.

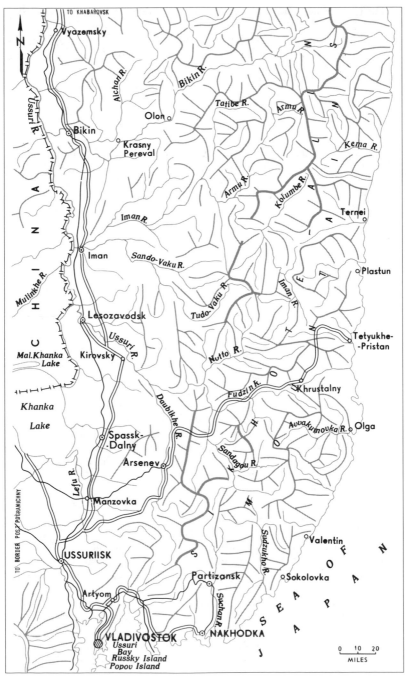

TO KHABAROVSK

N

Vyazemsky

CHINA

Alchan R.

Bikin R.

Bikin

Olon

Krasny
Pereval

Tatibe R.

Armu R.

SIKHOTE ALIN

Kema R.

Armu R.

Kolumbe R.

Iman R.

Iman

Sando-Vaku R.

Ternei

Plastun

Tudo-Vaku R.

Iman R.

Mulinkhe R.

Lesozavodsk

Ussuri R.

Mal. Khanka
Lake

Kirovsky

Nutto R.

Tetyukhe-
-Pristan

Khrustalny

Fudzin R.

Khanka
Lake

Daubikhe R.

Spassk-
-Dalny

Avvakumovka R.

Olga

Arsenev

Sandagou R.

Lefu R.

Manzovka

SEA

Sudzukhe R.

Valentin

TO BORDER POST POGRANICHNY

USSURIISK

Partizansk

Sokolovka

OF

Artyom

Suchan R.

NAKHODKA

JAPAN

VLADIVOSTOK
Ussuri
Bay
Russky Island
Popov Island

0   10   20
MILES

The undergrowth of the Ussuriland forests, a dense thicket of *limmonik* (a variety of wild grape from which the locals make a delicious wine), yew, and creeping stone pine doesn't lend itself to hiking. What trails there are, the animals maintain. While an encounter with a tiger is probably wishful thinking, running into a boar in these parts is a distinct possibility. It's best not to tangle with these mean critters. The taiga is abuzz with insects, and hiking with a head net is often the only way to enjoy the scenery.

In Kedrovaya Pad *Zapovednik*, reserve director Viktor Korkishko can guide you on hikes through this magical forest with leopard tracks fresh in the mud, up to hilltops with views to China. Kedrovaya Pad *Zapovednik* is reached via Perevoznaya (1½ hours south of Vladivostok by ferry): from Perevoznaya, drive 2.5 miles (4 km) to the military town of Sukhaya Rechka, and then another 7.5 miles (12 km) along a very rough road to the *zapovednik* headquarters.

Some hikes can be reached via the road north from Vladivostok. Go through Partizansk, Sergeevka, and, finally, Arkhipovka to reach an area just north of Lazovsky *Zapovednik* where you can climb Oblachnaya, 6,086 feet (1855 m), the highest summit in the Sikhote Alin Mountains. Nakhodka, due east of Vladivostok, is reached by a road that winds along the twisting coastline. Outside Nakhodka, Mount Pidan, 4,377 feet (1334 m), in the Livadiskii Mountains is a good hike, with views of Amerika Bay and the environs of Nakhodka. You can take a bus from Nakhodka across Benevskoye Pass and past Alekseevka to the outskirts of Lazovsky *Zapovednik*, where you can explore some of the Sikhote Alin caves.

A great bike tour would be along the dirt road circling Lazovsky *Zapovednik*, following the Cherny and Kievka rivers. Another would be to ride north up the coast from the fishing village of Preobrazheniye to Valentinin.

There are also recreational possibilities in Sikhote Alin *Zapovednik*. The *zapovednik* staff can guide you on a variety of hikes into the classic, tangled Ussuriland undergrowth; some of these hikes are accessed by vehicle over extremely bad roads. From Maisa to Shandui, 6 miles (9.5 km), is a nice hike to primary forest. Blagodatnoye Lake, where the *zapovednik* has a guesthouse, is the starting point for a couple of hikes east to the sea. (It's just a 10-minute walk to the shore from the lake, but there are trails that explore en route.)

Blagodatnoye Lake to Mys Severny ("North Cape"), 2.5 miles (4 km), takes you to a large fur seal colony, home to 400 seals during the fall–winter migration; in Blagodatnoye Harbor a rare form of edelweiss grows.

Blagodatnoye Lake to Kantami, 2.5 to 3 miles (4 to 5 km), takes you to the next drainage, where there's a cabin. The trail heads through broad deer meadows, where it's possible to observe thirty or forty deer. At Kantami, the river drops into the sea in a beautiful, cliff-walled bay. (Kantami is also called Golubichnaya, but the locals tend to use the original Chinese names for places, although on maps the Russian names are used.)

Another recreational possibility around Ternei in Sikhote Alin *Zapovednik* is the Kema River, popular for rafting. From Ternei, you drive 62 miles (100 km) north, then hike 12.5 miles (20 km) farther to get to the river's headwaters.

In fact, the main arterials through Ussuriland are the rivers. In places the only reasonable way to travel through the taiga is via the river systems. The

In the exotic Ussuri forest, aktinidea vines entwine a Korean pine in a tangled embrace. (Photo: Viktor Korkishko)

rivers that flow west to the Ussuri are longer and quieter. The Khor, Army, Iman, and Ussuri rivers are all popular with river-rafters. The rivers of the eastern Sikhote Alin are more accessible and also wilder white-water descents: the Kema, Amgu, Svetlaya, Edinka, and Samarga rivers. You can raft from the settlement of Ulunga (1½ hours by helicopter from Khabarovsk), where the Svetlovodnaya River flows into the Bikin, and raft all the way to Krasny Yar, a beautiful 130-mile (210-km), 7- to 9-day float trip.

You can take local trains north from Khabarovsk through this vast and beautiful country, to connect with the BAM, and get dropped off on a remote river like the Tuyun, in the Vernebureinsky District. The Tuyun River has class III rapids that take you swiftly through the Turana Mountains, bounded by rugged rock walls. In other places, it cuts through forests reminiscent of the Pacific Northwest, but for the silver birch scattered among the fir and pine trees. With a good guide, this river's fine for people with limited white water experience.

Paseta Bay, south of Vladivostok, could be very interesting for sea kayaking. While sea kayaking has yet to catch on in Primorye, scuba diving has long been popular around Vladivostok, especially in the coral reefs near the Korean border. Mollusks are an important part of the local diet, so the scuba diving tradition has practical roots. For pure sport diving, the region is incomparable. Sailing's also popular around Vladivostok, especially in the beautiful islands of the Primorsky *Zapovednik*.

Getting There

The two main access cities for Ussuriland are landlocked Khabarovsk in the north and the port of Vladivostok in the south.

There are direct international flights to Khabarovsk from Anchorage, Alaska; Seoul, South Korea; Niigata, Japan; Harbin, China; and Pyongyang, North Korea. There are now regular direct international flights to Vladivostok from Niigata and charter flights from Seoul; Alaska Airlines also flies to Vladivostok in the summer from Anchorage, Alaska. (The Vladivostok airport is 50 km from the city.) There are also international flights between Blagoveshchensk (east of Khabarovsk) and Harbin.

The Badzhal Mountains, north of Khabarovsk, under the cloak of this clime's brittle winter (Photo: Sergei Chebotov)

There is international train service to Khabarovsk from Pyongyang (41 hours), North Korea, and Harbin, China. There is also a train to Vladivostok from Suifenhe, China.

The ship *Antonina Nezhdanova* carries passengers between Vladivostok and Niigata and Toyama, Japan. Another route from Vladivostok services Yokohama, Japan.

It's about a 1-day drive from the Russian border town of Pogranichnii to Suifenhe, China.

There are flights to Khabarovsk from Moscow, Novosibirsk, Yakutsk, Magadan, Petropavlovsk-Kamchatsky, Yuzhno-Sakhalinsk, Vladivostok, and the towns of Amur Oblast and Primorye. Aeroflot flies to Vladivostok from Moscow, Magadan, Petropavlovsk-Kamchatsky, Khabarovsk, and other major Russian cities.

The Trans-Siberian Express runs to Khabarovsk from Moscow (5½ days) and Irkutsk (about 60 hours), and to Vladivostok, the terminus of the Trans-Siberian Railroad (6 days from Moscow). There's an overnight train between Khabarovsk and Vladivostok.

Boats run from Khabarovsk's River Station up and down the Amur River, stopping at other cities on the river. Ferries from downtown Vladivostok go to Perevoznaya through Golden Horn Harbor toward the entrance of Amursky Bay, past the fishing port with its refrigerator and factory ships. On the right is the commercial port, with container ships flying flags of many countries. The ferry passes Russky Island on its way across the bay to Perevoznaya, a typical Russian village (1½ hours). Skyrocketing fuel prices in 1993 disrupted service on this and other Primorye ferries. Boats that formerly operated on a fixed schedule became irregular and unpredictable. Information about this ferry's sailings can be obtained at Dock 36 in downtown Vladivostok next to the train station.

There's bus service from Vladivostok to nearby Primorye cities: Nakhodka, Partizansk, Ussurisk, and Bolshoi Kamen.

To reach the **Khasan Coast hike** from Vladivostok, take the ferry to Perevoznaya and drive or walk to Sukhaya Rechka, 2.5 miles (4 km), and then to Kedrovaya Pad Zapovednik "lodge," 7.5 miles (12 km). To shorten the hike by 33 miles (53 km), you can take the *elektrichka* from Vladivostok to Ryazanovka. It leaves Vladivostok's Central Station around 2:00 P.M. Change trains at Baranovsk (2 hours) to the Novochuguevko-Khasan train and ride to Ryazanovka (another 5 hours).

From Gamov Cape at the end of the hike, you can hitch a ride to Andreevka and then catch the bus to Sukhanovka and train from there back to Vladivostok (8 hours); the train leaves about 2:00 A.M. If you can arrange it, travel by boat is easier. It's possible to drive back to Vladivostok from Gamov Cape, if you have arranged in advance to be picked up.

Where to Stay

In Khabarovsk, there's an Intourist hotel (2 Amursky Blvd., tel. 339313, 399351; double rooms are currently about $100, although summer and winter rates vary), Tsentralnaya (ul. Pushkina 52, tel. 336731, cheaper than the

Intourist hotel), Tourist (52 Pushkin St., tel. 334759, also cheaper than the Intourist hotel), Amur Hotel (29 Lenin St., tel. 335043), and floating hotel Vasily Poyarkov (tel. 398201). At the train station there is a small hotel in a train car parked alongside the tracks.

Two joint-venture restaurants have the best food in town: the Sapporo (3 Muriaviev-Amursky St.) and the Harbin (118 Volochaevskaya St.). Don't go to the third-floor sushi bar at the Sapporo unless you have a lot of dollars to burn!

In Vladivostok, the top of the line is the Vlad Motor Inn (kilometer 19 outside Vladivostok, call 604-787-1030 in Canada for reservations). Nearby, the Equator Hotel has two nice floors for foreigners. There's also Hotel Vladivostok (ul. Naberezhnaya 10, tel. 222208) and Hotel Amurskii Zaliv, right next door (tel. 225520). There are several *turbazas* outside town, including Tikhii Okean and Lazurnii Bereg.

Past Dalnegorsk, northeast of Vladivostok en route to Sikhote Alin *Zapovednik*, is a place called Smychka, where there's a very nice, simple resort set on the shores of a lovely lake. Smychka Camp is about 2.5 miles (4 km) outside of Rudnaya Pristan, which is about 22 miles (35 km) farther east from Dalnegorsk. Smychka Camp, run by Aleksei and Lydia Kobtsev (Lydia is an excellent cook) has clean cabins that sleep two or three, and a great *banya*. Rates are around $5 a night; tel. (272) 98541.

The Sikhote Alin Zapovednik has a guesthouse at Blagodatnoye Lake, about 10 miles (16 km) from either Plastun or Ternei. This simple dormitory has cots, wooden furniture, and gas lamps. From the second story you can see where the Pacific rolls in.

When to Go

May through August is very hot, as well as typhoon season; September is more stable. On the coast, temperatures are more moderate, and it doesn't get really hot until July.

Equipment and Supplies

Long-sleeved pants and shirt and tick-protective headgear are a must in the summer; in the Lake Khanka area, precautions should also be taken against mosquito-borne Japanese encephalitis (see the Special Considerations section of chapter 2, Preparing for Your Trek). Be prepared for mud, and for very deep mud after one of the torrential rains.

A good variety of food is available in Khabarovsk and Vladivostok due to the Chinese influence, with fruits and rice relatively easy to come by. There are no special hard-currency grocery stores, but the central markets are well stocked with fruit, vegetables, meat, and cheese—also gypsies and pickpockets!

KHASAN COAST HIKE

The Khasan Coast takes in some of the wildest and most beautiful parts of Primorye. The woods are crowded with a dozen different kinds of mushrooms. Getting to them is not an easy proposition through the thick and prickly tangle of undergrowth. The beautiful sandy beaches are decorated at low tide by sea stars and anemones. On the cliffy promontories between the bays, twisted Korean pines overlook the sea, a reminder of the thick coastal forests that were cut over the centuries. In places, it is necessary to climb up and around these cliffs.

This **41- to 42-mile (66- to 68-km**) hike begins from the Kedrovaya Pad *Zapovednik* "lodge," hiking along the coast and crossing the big bays to Gamov Cape in the Primorsky *Zapovednik*. reach Ryazanovka. If you want to shorten the hike to 8 miles (13 km), you can travel directly to Ryazanovka, from where the more scenic part of this hike begins, and hike from there. This option has the advantage of avoiding the south side of Klerk Bay, which has been used as a heavy-metals dumping ground. In either case, the most beautiful part of the Khasan Coast is much farther south, beyond Cape Lev. The hike ends at Gamov Cape.

From the Kedrovaya Pad *Zapovednik* lodge, hike **12.5 miles (20 km)** down the coast to the village **Bezverkhovo**, where from the high point on the treeless Lomonosov Peninsula you can see the islands of Amursky Bay and the lagoons of Narva harbor.

There's a private lodge, called the Atoll, across **Slavyansky Bay**. The Atoll has its own yacht and can ferry you across. The lodge is used as a base for dives in the Sea of Japan, shimmering with phosphorescence.

From the **Atoll Lodge**, continue hiking the shore of **Baklan Harbor**, where the coast is marshy, around **Nerpa Cape** and the **Klerk Peninsula** with meadows and the salt lake Ryazanovskoye to the high right bank of the **Ryazanovka River**. There's a fish hatchery here. You're likely to see snipes, wingtails, herons, and many other birds. Cross to the other side of the Ryaznovka River, to **Krasny Utyos Cape**, **10 to 11 miles** (**16 to 18 km**) from Atoll Lodge. If you've opted for the shorter version of this hike and taken the train from Vladivostok to Ryazanovka, this is where you'll begin to hike.

From Krasny Utyos Cape to the **Gamov Peninsula** is a 12.5-mile (20-km) walk as the crow flies, but beach walking and crow-flying are different things, and by the time you get around all the coves and capes, it ends up being at least **19 miles** (**30 km**). About 4.25 miles (7 km) south of Cape Krasny Utyos, from Cape Lev (in Russian Mys Lva) on, you're in the **Primorsky *Zapovednik***. In the distance float the Rimsky-Korsakov Islands, also part of the Primorsky *Zapovednik*. Walking the shores of coves Srednaya (the *zapovednik* has a shelter here), Nerpichei, Astafyev, and Telyakovsky, you're treated to some of the most spectacular scenery of this hike. The hike ends at Gamov Cape.

Sakhalin Island

Sakhalin Island, 620 miles (1000 km) long, lies off the Ussuriland coast north of Hokkaido, Japan, with its northern end in the Sea of Okhotsk and its southern end in the Sea of Japan. Separated from the Ussuriland coast by the Tartar Strait, at one point the island is a mere 4 or 5 miles (6.5 or 8 km) away from the mainland.

Two ridges shore up south Sakhalin Island: the West Sakhalin Ridge rises to 4,347 feet (1325 m), while the highest point in the East Sakhalin Ridge is Mount Lopatka, 5,280 feet (1609 m). The train ride up the spine of the island between these ridges gives one a sense of how wild a place this still is. Aside from the widely spaced small villages where the train stops, the countryside is undeveloped. This train provides easy access to the coast and the wild north of the island, a great place to see bird colonies and sea lion rookeries. Sakhalin intrigues birdwatchers, with its unique species of marsh birds, like the rare spotted greenshank and the long-toed stint.

If your mental image of a bamboo grove is one of Japanese calendar photographs—kimonoed ladies tiptoeing through stands of tall, graceful trees shot through with soft light—you're in for a surprise on Sakhalin. The bamboo here is a slender-trunked bush that grows to 6.5 to 10 feet (2 to 3 m). Thickets of this inhospitable bamboo brush, mixed with alder and Indian rhubarb, cover much of Sakhalin. In the clearings, I saw dogwood, fireweed, Indian paintbrush, and geranium.

January temperatures average -13°C in the south, and -20°C in the north. In July, the average temperature is 15°C, though it can get as hot as 30°C.

The history of Sakhalin records the shifts in regional preeminence between Russia and Japan over the last two centuries. During the early nineteenth cen-

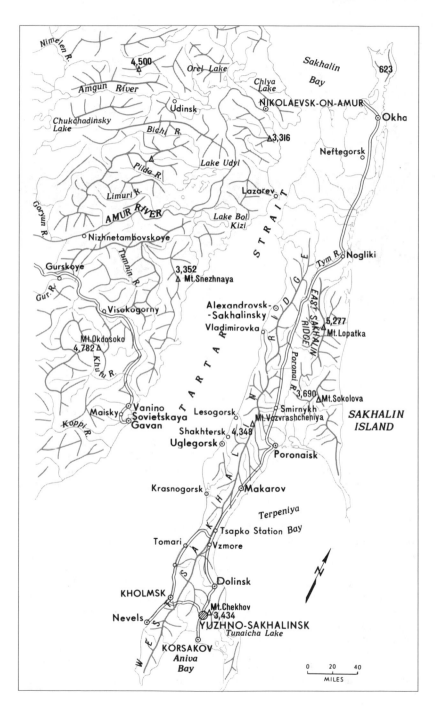

Hiking the eastern coast of Sakhalin Island

tury, Russia and Japan split Sakhalin north and south. In 1875, the Japanese gave up control of south Sakhalin in exchange for all of the Kuril Islands, but in 1905 they reclaimed it, keeping their foothold there until they were forced to surrender at the end of World War II.

Under the Soviet regime, Sakhalin Island was the world's biggest Alcatraz—a huge sea-locked penal colony. The island's main industries are fishing and timber. The fisheries of Sakhalin Oblast, which includes the Kuril Islands, are the third largest in the Far East, after Kamchatka and Primorye. Now foreign oil companies are eagerly pursuing off-shore drilling. Even though Sakhalin is visible on a clear day from Cape Soya at Hokkaido's northern tip, until 1990 the two islands were part of separate, alien worlds, with no communication or transportation between them.

Of Sakhalin Island's 700,000 people, 170,000 live in Yuzhno-Sakhalinsk, a rough Far Eastern dustball of a town. It was a Japanese city from 1905 to 1945. While little pre-war Japanese flavor remains in the city, called Yuzhny or Yuzhno ("South") by locals, new construction is largely financed by, and targeted at, Japanese money. The museum has good exhibits on the natural history and earliest inhabitants of the island. Just outside town is a ski area that was an Olympic training course. The ski hill has a T-bar and about a 1,200-vertical-foot (365-m) run. There are also groomed cross-country trails. At the north end of the island, there's excellent cross-country skiing in the winter.

The semi-tropical Sakhalin vegetation makes it difficult to explore off-trail. Sakhalin outdoor enthusiasts like to do coast hikes, hiking one trail out to the sea, walking the beach for miles north or south, and rejoining the railroad at the next station down the line. In late summer, the *elektrichka* is crowded with locals in rubber boots, carrying baskets for gathering berries and mushrooms. These coast hikes are not for those who prefer to stay dry. The high tide submerges most of the cliffy points dividing one cove from the next, so at times you're climbing around rocky capes knee deep in water.

A good 5- to 6-day ski trip at the north end of the island is to take the overnight train from Yuzhny to Timovsk and make your way on skis out to the western coast. You can overnight in hotels along the way at Smirnykh, Poronaisk (a coal and paper town), and Makarov. At Makarov, ski tour along the shore of the Tatar Strait before taking the train back to Yuzhny.

Getting There

There's ferry service to Yuzhno-Sakhalinsk from the port of Wakkanai, Japan, reportedly twice a week. For schedule information, try contacting Times Travel in Tokyo, which books passage to Sakhalin (fax [03] 3572-2279), or the Russian Government's Tourist Information Bureau in Tokyo (fax [03] 3584-6618). By 1994, there is supposed to be an international flight from Hakodate, Japan, to Yuzhno-Sakhalinsk.

Ferries from Vanino (the port of Sovietskatya Gavan) north of Vladivostok to Kholmsk (about an hour's drive from Yuzhny) connect Sakhalin with the mainland. Aeroflot currently flies to Yuzhny from Moscow, Petropavlovsk-Kamchatsky, Khabarovsk, Vladivostok, and other cities.

For the **Tsapko Station Circuit**, hop the train north from Yuzhno-Sakhalinsk to Tsapko Station (2½ hours).

Where to Stay

In Yuzhno-Sakhalinsk, there's Hotel Sapporo (tel. [7] 504- 415-1001, fax [7] 504-415-2001) and Hotel Lada (fax [7] 504-415-2002). Among a number of second-string hotels, the *vedomstennaya gostinitsa* Geolog and Sakhryba's *gostinitsa* Yakor are pretty good.

When to Go

If you choose to go skiing on Sakhalin, dress warmly. January temperatures average -13°C in the south, -20°C in the north. By March and April, the temperatures are less extreme and the days are longer. In July, the average temperature is 15°C, though it can get as hot as 30°C.

Equipment and Supplies

All the ports of the Russian Far East are flooded with goods, and Yuzhno-Sakhalinsk is no exception—but Chinese liquor and clothing are not necessarily useful to the traveler and food supplies may be hit or miss. It's worth stocking up for a backcountry trip before you even get to the island.

TSAPKO STATION CIRCUIT

This is an **easy overnight hike** to the Pacific coast from the rail line (**4 to 5 hours**), and back out the same way.

From **Tsapko Station**, hike east toward the Pacific coast on a muddy trail through dense bamboo brush, climbing about 1,000 feet (300 m) up across **Zhdanko Pass**. Reaching the pass, the Sea of Okhotsk spans blue below, dotted with fishing boats. The trail down to the water is steep and even muddier. Nearing the shore, the grass grows as tall as a woman's head. The Japanese homesteaded these shores, and you can still see the remains of buildings dating back before the war. From my Sakhalin journal:

> *The salmon are jumping like crazy just off the shore. Sasha throws out a handline and reels in a big* gorbushcha *(humpy). Down the beach, people drag nets in the low-tide shallows for shrimp. They pull in piles of bright green algae and sea grasses, then pick through it for the prawns.*

Kuril Islands

By Bob Moore ˙

The Kuril Islands "link" the Kamchatka Peninsula to Hokkaido, Japan, arcing across more than 620 miles (1000 km) of ocean in the Sea of Okhotsk. This is an arc of fire, the islands marking the fault line between the Pacific and Eurasian plates. The largest islands in the chain are Paramushir in the north and Kunashir, Iturup, and Urup at the southern tail. Many of the islands in between are the summits of giant volcanos poking out of the ocean. "If the ocean were to recede," writes Y. Markhinin in *Pluto's Chain*, "the mountains rising above the Kuril valley would be higher than Everest." Markhinin is one of the few people to have explored these islands.

In the Kurils, geology is never static. With more than 100 volcanoes, including 31 that have erupted in the islands' recorded history of several centuries, this is one of the most geothermally active places on earth. Mount Sarychev, on Matua Island, has erupted frequently and violently a number of times. There was a major eruption in 1957 on Simushir, the largest island in the Central Kurils, where there are three active volcanos: Goryachaya Sopka, Zavaritsy, and Prevo Peak. On Paramushir, the eruption of Ebeko in 1952 killed hundreds of people in the town of North Kurilsk. Now, people swim in the lake in the crater.

Along the coasts of these islands, impressive cliffs drop into blue lagoons and bays. The taiga extends to Sakhalin Island and the southern Kurils. Dark conifer forests of Yeddo spruce and fir give way at higher elevations to dwarf birch and pines.

Kunashir Island, just north of Hokkaido, is 75 miles (121 km) long and only about 8 miles (13 km) wide for most of this length. Throughout the island, the smell of sulphur and clouds of steam from fumaroles remind you this is the "ring of fire." Climate and vegetation types cover the spectrum from arctic barrenness to tropical rain forest of tree ferns and bamboo. Above 1,000 feet (300 m) there are hardwood and conifer forests. The north and south ends are quite different from each other. The north half of the island is beautiful but trackless wilderness. The south half, with its geothermal wonders and abundant birdlife, is more accessible.

In the Kurils, striking cliffs, such as this one at Cape Stolbchaty on Kunashir Island, drop into pristine bays. (Photo: Anatoly Suschenko)

Facing the Sea of Okhotsk, Kunashir's northwest shore is steep and cliffy down to the island's midpoint. Formed by lava flows and other igneous activity, this northwest quarter of the island, from the shoreline through the hinterland to the island's ridgetop spine, is rocky and formidable. The northern half of Kunashir teems with bears.

Mount Tyatya, 5,978 feet (1822 m), a cinder cone of the Fuji type, dominates the north end of Kunashir Island. The new cone rising from within the old cone gives this volcano a "hatted" look. Tyatya is young and active, with cinder and ash showers every few years. It last blew its top in 1972, but is still smoking. To its northwest is a string of four lesser volcanoes ranging from 3,000 to 5,000 feet (900 to 1500 m).

The northeast quarter of the island is flat along the shore, and an easy trekking area through which Mount Tyatya can be reached. Much of this area is swampy away from the immediate beach line. It's inhabited by only a dozen people on a small homestead and two game wardens 15 miles (24 km) into the wilderness.

The remaining island population of 25,000 live on the southern half of Kunashir Island. While still volcanically active in the same sense as Yellowstone, it supports some farming and cattle in nooks and crannies. The Golovnino Caldera on the island's south end is more than a mile across and contains two crater lakes.

Between the two volcanoes at each end of the island, there are scores of lesser cones, domes, and vents that run up and down the island as a spine. The most accessible of these for hikers is Mendeleev, 2,913 feet (888 m), only a few miles from the Golovnino Caldera.

Markhinin's book, *Pluto's Chain* (see Appendix C, Bibliography) is a fun and informative account of the volcanologist's adventures in the Kurils. He describes the fantastical island of Ushishir, with its crater bay behind steep walls, where he was followed by curious silver foxes:

> *At Hot Beach the villagers warm their meals on jets of subterranean steam and use it to heat their homes; there is always hot water in the bathhouse and laundry even though there are no stoves.*

Enormous colonies of seabirds nest on these islands and the Komandor (variously spelled Commander) Islands, reaching out to the Aleutians. Some species are found only in the Kurils. In fact, a *zapovednik* was established on the south end of Kunashir Island in 1985 to protect the rare and interesting plant and animal life.

Ironically, the islands are known not for their amazing natural history, but as a political hot potato. The Japanese built their first fort in the southern Kurils in 1800. Part of the same Far Eastern "Great Game" as Sakhalin Island, the Kurils changed hands between Russia and Japan several times in the last 150 years. Japan acquired all the Kurils under the 1875 treaty that gave Russia control of Sakhalin Island. After World War II, the Soviet Union seized the islands and have occupied them ever since, in spite of Japan's persistent demands for return of what to Japanese is *Hoporyodo* (the Northern Territories). This encompasses the south four islands: Shikotan, Kunashir, Iturup, and the Habomai rocks.

This territorial argument continues to be a sticking point in Japanese–Russian relations. Japan has held foreign aid hostage to the return of the islands, and the issue impedes large-scale trade between Russia and its economically powerful neighbor.

Residents of the Kurils are caught in the middle. Most of the Japanese living on the Kurils in 1945 were repatriated, but many of the citizens of Sakhalin and the Kurils are of Japanese or Korean ancestry. Otherwise, the population is Russian. Their standard of living would undoubtably improve were they to become citizens of Japan. On the other hand, Russians are proud people; politicians, in particular, don't want to set a precedent of trading away land for Japanese investment. Today, all the Kurils are still administratively part of Sakhalin Oblast.

The only towns in the Kurils are on the larger islands. These towns are called, confusingly, Severo-Kurilsk (North Kurilsk) on Paramushir Island, Kurilsk on Iturup Island, and Yuzhno-Kurilsk (South Kurilsk) on Kunashir Island. Some of the smaller islands are inhabited only by foxes.

Yuzhno-Kurilsk has a magnificent natural harbor, but is otherwise a miserable place. Ninety percent of Kunashir's residents live here in the half dozen concrete apartment blocks and 100 more tar-paper shacks. None of the streets are paved. Shipwrecks and debris litter the shore. The town's only industry is fishing and fish processing at a couple of dilapidated factories. For much of the post-war period, the Soviet military presence dominated this and the nearby islands. While most of the troops are gone now, around Yuzhno-Kurilsk, you see junkyards of abandoned military equipment, as well as World War II– and Korean War–era T-34 tanks that have been buried in the ground with only their turrets exposed. These fixed beach-front fortifications were to have defended against invasion.

Few outsiders have set foot on the Kurils. These islands were among the last of the formerly closed Soviet eastern realms to be pried open for tourism. In the past year, Japanese journalists have been allowed to visit the south Kurils, and Japanese whose relatives died on the islands come visiting graves.

There is no infrastructure for travelers; to the contrary, obstacles to getting there and getting around are numerous. The Japanese had developed an extensive road system on Kunashir Island in particular, when the island was exploited for sulphur and timber. The Soviets did not maintain most of these roads and many of them have faded back into the wild. Still, some of these overgrown roads provide a way through the bamboo that chokes the forests of the southern islands. This tenacious bush discourages cross-country travel; if you strike off from roads and trails into an impenetrable bamboo thicket, you may be sorry. Most transport is now by military truck along the beach at low tide.

Kunashir is the first shore touched by the Japanese current and the island's beaches are piled with nets, crates, and trash. The islanders burn this refuse for firewood, helping to preserve Kunashir's native trees. There is so much netting that you need only pick up a length and make a pass at the nearest creek for a superb salmon dinner.

Getting There

There is irregular ferry service from Hokkaido, Japan, to Kunashir Island. The Japanese National Tourist Bureau may have the most current information (tel. 212-757-5640).

There are regular flights and some charter planes between Petropavlovsk-Kamchatsky and Paramushir; in the past, there has also been ferry service. There used to be scheduled ferry service from Vladivostok and Korsakov (on Sakhalin Island) to Yuzhno-Kurilsk. There also were flights from Sakhalin, weather-dependent. Fuel distribution problems apparently have disrupted both services. If you're traveling independently, probably the only way to get information about flights and sailings is to check in Yuzhno-Sakhalinsk or Vladivostok.

For intra-island transportation, ferries carry passengers between Yuzhno-Kurilsk and Kurilsk. Large ships cannot dock at these towns. Passengers and goods are off-loaded into a landing barge and ferried ashore.

Where to Stay

On Kunashir Island, visiting government officials use rooms in the former Party offices in Yuzhno-Kurilsk, on top of the hill. Down the road from the dock where passengers land are barracks that serve as a hostel.

You can camp on the harbor beach: from the dock, go left down the beach, cross a creek and walk about a half mile (1 km) beyond. Off the beach from the campgrounds is a wrecked ship. There's a frame shelter on the beach with a totem pole in the yard. The campground caretakers should be paid something for your stay.

When to Go

Mild, humid winds of the Japanese current lull the southeast shore of Kunashir Island, while severe winds roar across the Sea of Okhotsk out of Siberia, rocking Kunashir's northwest shore. Mid-July to mid-September is the "dry" season, but even it's not immune to the frequent typhoons.

Equipment and Supplies

Take a copy of *A Field Guide to the Birds of Japan,* published by the Wild Bird Society of Japan. Even the non-birder will thrill at the majesty and brute power of the white-shouldered Steller's sea eagle, found along the southwestern shore across from Hokkaido. And don't even think of going without insect repellent. The mosquitoes are especially ferocious on the island's north end.

Bring your own food. There are no eateries on Kunashir. The campground caretakers will sell you milk and eggs, and you can buy bread in the stores.

MOUNT TYATYA ASCENT

This hike covers **62 miles (100 km)**, **6 days** into and back out of north Kunashir Island, along the beachfront to Mount Tyatya. Expect **flat, easy walking** and numerous fords, none more than waist deep. The climb of Mount Tyatya is a walk-up, worth it for the view into an active volcano.

From Yuzhno-Kurilsk, take the dirt road north out of town. For 0.5 mile (1 km), it runs past a gigantic trash heap that lies between the road and the sea. At its far north end, where sand dunes begin to appear, you can find Ainu pottery shards and arrow heads, remains of ancient civilizations that are now

mixed with AK-47 shell casings from Soviet soldiers' target practice.

The road carries you inland around some cliffs jutting into the sea. However, return to the sea as soon as you can and continue north on the beach. About **4 miles (6 km)** from town, there are the remains of a thermal spring-heated **Japanese bath**. By adjusting the hot and cold piping, bring the temperature to your liking. The custom is to soak, then soap up out of the pools, rush into the cold sea to rinse, and return for more soaking. Russians consider vodka an integral part of this ritual.

Beyond the Japanese baths, the road literally goes off into the sea to get around a protruding cliff. Wait for low tide. About **2 miles (3 km)** beyond this point, and again on the road that has retreated from the sea, you come to a **homestead**, appearing on maps as Grigoryevo. The homesteaders do not speak English, but are friendly and may let you camp nearby.

The road ends at the homestead, although a rutted track continues, left by the armored personnel carriers of Border Guard troops. Avoid left turns, and bear to the right wherever you have the option. You want to get back to the beach. Beyond the homestead, the inland area is quite swampy. The road is a quagmire, especially the last **couple of miles (2 to 3 km)** before it **rejoins the beach**, but it beats the swamp.

Once back on the beach, you come to a river and, across it, the hut occupied by summer rangers. There's no point fording this deep river; it's better to take the road another **6 miles (10 km)** to another big stream where there is a flat sand and gravel bar on which to camp. Maps show a hatchery near this sandbar, but it appears to no longer exist. Beyond this **campsite** is wilderness bear country. You may need to take directly to the beach to make good progress.

Another **day's walk** along the beach brings you to the base of Mount Tyatya. The best **campsite** is probably at a point directly southeast of the summit of the volcano cone, but any of the flat spots near the beach with a stream for freshwater nearby will do as your base camp for the climb.

There is no trail up Mount Tyatya; you're on your own with a compass. Follow one of the streambeds from the sea up the mountain. Immediately back from the beach, the vegetation is primarily 6-foot-tall (about 2 m) bamboo grass and a variety of wild rhubarb 13 feet (4 m) high, but then it becomes a jungle. Very large rain-forest trees, ferns, and vines cover the lower 3,000 feet (900 m), with many fallen trees. The going is tough, over volcanic cinders and ash. Shortly up the slope the stream disappears, so it's essential to carry water. By sticking to the gully and not losing sight of your basic compass direction, you pass out of the jungle into a smothered forest where only the bleached white tops of dead trees poke through the black cinders. It is spectacular, and gets more so as you climb into the next zone of pure cinders and ash with large volcanic bombs thrown across the landscape by the most recent eruption.

At the rim of the crater, the new cone is visible. It's worth proceeding on to its rim, from where you can look down into the active volcano. Beware of gas clouds or smoke. Tyatya is remote; the locals don't climb it or go anywhere near it. Descend the route by which you climbed and retrace your steps to Yuzhno-Kurilsk.

MENDELEEV VOLCANO

This is a **13-mile (20-km) day trip** or an overnight camping trip where you sleep on the edge of Hades.

Catch a ride from **Yuzhno-Kurilsk** on the road south to the airfield. Mendeleev is the big volcano that you see from town. Steam rises from the fumaroles on its flank in the morning air. The Japanese used to mine sulphur at these fumaroles. The fumes kill off all vegetation, leaving an eroded moonscape of white rock gullies with bright yellow cones of sulphur crystals. You can reach these fumarole fields by hiking old, overgrown Japanese roads. If you come to the airfield, you've gone too far.

GOLOVNINO CALDERA

This hike of **2 to 5 days** allows one day in to the caldera and another day back, with additional time as desired for exploring the caldera from a base camp.

Unlike Mount Tyatya, Golovnino is frequently visited. The area is alpine. The caldera is 2 miles (3 km) across and has two very different lakes. The larger lake is cold and absolutely clear; no algae clouds the water. The smaller lake is an acidic mud bath, fed by boiling fumaroles. You can scald to death swimming in this lake if you break through a fumarole crust.

From Yuzhno-Kurilsk, follow the same route as to Mount Mendeleev, taking the road south to the airport, but continuing on this road for about 6 miles (10 km) past the airport. Ask directions to the rutted road cutting off to the caldera. Try to get a ride as far as this point. From the cutoff, it's about **5 miles (8 km)** in to the lip of the **caldera**, then a steep descent to the two lakes.

Once in the caldera, hike to the place on the large clear lake where the stream from the mud lake enters. Facing the clear lake, turn right and walk the shore until you are about 300 feet (100 m) into a wooded area. When you come to a small stream, turn right again and walk directly away from the lake about 100 feet (30 m). You then come to a dry clearing where there's a picnic table and **good campsite**. A good **alternative campsite** is near the rangers' hut on the shore of the clear lake.

From the caldera, day hike out of the caldera to Nemuro Strait, which separates Kunashir Island from Hokkaido. Hike along an old Japanese road, overgrown and washed out in places, but still an easy hike. After emerging from the forest and catching your first glimpse of the sea, find a knotted rope tied to a tree on the edge of a deep gorge formed by the discharge stream from the caldera. Use the rope to descend to the beach. One of the world's greatest concentrations of Steller's sea eagles nests on this coast.

You can rock-hop the beach in either direction, south to the town of Golovnino or north to Alekhino. From either, you can make your way back into the caldera by way of the cutoff road or on other local trails.

CAPE STOLBCHATY

This is a long **1-day hike** or an overnight to Cape Stolbchaty. On the Sea of Okhotsk, almost due west of Yuzhno-Kurilsk, at Cape Stolbchaty there are impressive lava formations and thermal springs.

Take the road toward the airfield to about the 21-kilometer mark, where an old Japanese road leads off to the right. Trek west to the sea on the opposite side of the island. The thermal springs about halfway there has a nice pool.

Upon reaching the shore, turn right and walk the beach, which gets rockier as you approach the cape. Don't attempt to climb to the top of the cliffs, where you can be stranded. North beyond the cape, less than 0.5 mile (1 km), you come upon a military road leading back to Yuzhno-Kurilsk.

APPENDICES

Kyrgyz elders playing a dice game with sheep bones (Photo: Vladimir Maximov)

A. General Resources

TRAVEL AGENCIES/AIRLINES

Aeroflot: New York, tel. (212) 332-1050; Washington, DC, tel. (202) 429-4922 or (800) 535-9877

Exodus Expeditions, 9 Weir Road, London SW12 0LT, tel. [081] 675 5550; British company most experienced at USSR treks

Inturtrans, ul. Petrovka 15, Moscow; air and rail tickets

REI Adventures, P.O. Box 1938, Sumner, WA 98390, tel. (206) 891-2631 or (800) 622-2236; American company most experienced at USSR treks

Yak & Yeti, BP 126, 74403 Chamonix Cedex, France, tel. [50] 535367, fax [50] 558440; heli-skiing

AMERICAN EMBASSIES

U.S. State Department: tel. (202) 647-5226; has separate "desks" for different areas of Russia and Central Asia (e.g., the Western Slavic desk, the Trans-Caucasus desk) to which the U.S. ambassadors in each area report

Kazakhstan: 551 ul. Seyfullina, Almaty, tel. [3272] 631375, fax [3272] 633883

Kyrgyzstan: 66 ul. Erkindick, Bishkek, tel. [3312] 222270, fax [3312] 223551

Russian Far East: U.S. Consulate, 12 Mordovtseva St., Vladivostok, tel. 26-84-58, 26-84-45, 26-67-34. To write to the consulate from the U.S.: United States Consulate General, Vladivostok, AmEmb Moscow, PSC-77, APO AE 09721; mail stamped with U.S. postage can be posted from a mailbox at the consulate

Tajikistan: Hotel Independence, 39 ul. Ainii, Dushanbe, tel. [3772] 248233

Uzbekistan: 82 ul. Chilanzarskaya, Tashkent, tel. [3712] 776986

EQUIPMENT AND SUPPLIES

Alpindustriya, near Izmailovo metro, tel. [095] 367-3183; the only climbing-gear store in Moscow—or all of Russia for that matter!—selection is far from complete

Russia/Central Asia Travel Resources, 117 N 40th St,, Seattle, WA 98103, fax (206) 633-0408; maps

National Oceanic and Atmospheric Administration, tel. (301) 436-6990; Defense Mapping Agency topographical maps

MEDICAL RESOURCES

American Medical Center, Moscow, tel. [095] 256-8212

Centers for Disease Control (CDC), Atlanta, Georgia, tel. (404) 332-4565; gives update on medical concerns for travelers in Russia and Central Asia

Flughafenklinik, Frankfurt Airport, tel. [069] 690 66 767; clinic that will administer the vaccine for tick- and mosquito-borne encephalitis

The Medicine Man, Tschernaiakhovskovo 4, tel. 155-7080; a Moscow pharmacy

Sana, Nizh. Pervomaiskaya 65, tel. 464-1254; a Moscow pharmacy

Unipharm, Skaterny Per. 13, tel. 202-5071; a Moscow pharmacy

COMMUNICATIONS

American Express, ul. Sadovaya-Kudrinskaya 21-A, Moscow, tel. [095] 254-4305; address at which you can receive mail from overseas, if you're a member

American Express, ul. Brodskovo 1/7, St. Petersburg, tel. [812] 315-7487; address at which you can receive mail from overseas, if you're a member

CompuServe, tel. (800) 848-8990; E-mail to Russia

Econet, 18 De Boom St., San Francisco, CA 94107, tel. (415) 442-0220; E-mail to Russia

Khabarovsk Sprint, 58 Muravev-Amurskii Blvd., tel. [4210] 218799

MCI Mail, tel. (800) 444-6245; E-mail to Russia

SovAm Teleport, tel. (800) 257-5107; the pioneers in E-mail communications with the USSR

Sprint, tel. (800) 736-1130; E-mail to Russia

Vladivostok Sprint, 69 Svetlanskaya St. #210, tel. [42322] 222114 or 224797

ENVIRONMENTAL ORGANIZATIONS

Numerous Russian and foreign organizations are involved in environmental projects in the former USSR. Most of these are listed in the next section, "Contacts," under the specific area where they are active. Here are a few whose reach extends more broadly.

International Snow Leopard Trust, 4649 Sunnyside Ave. N, Seattle, WA 98103

ISAR (formerly Institute for Soviet–American Relations), 1601 Connecticut Ave., NW, Ste. 301, Washington, DC 20009, tel. (202) 387-3034; environmental activism

Sacred Earth Network, 267 East St., Petersham, MA 01366, tel. (508) 724-3443, environmental activism

B. Contacts

The following organizations may be able to help you with information, visa support, permissions, vehicles, accommodations, guides, support staff, and other travel arrangements. Grouped by region, the list includes private companies, environmental organizations, national parks, and *zapovednik* offices. I can't vouch for all of the firms and organizations listed, although I have excluded those with poor reputations.

Telephone numbers change frequently; see Section I, chapter 4, Communications.

PART 1. WESTERN RUSSIA

Moscow and St. Petersburg

There are literally hundreds of travel agencies in Moscow and St. Petersburg. Because this book's focus is wilderness adventure, it does not detail these city services. You can find lists of travel agencies in *Where in Moscow, Where in St. Petersburg, Moscow Yellow Pages,* and *St. Petersburg Yellow Pages* (see Appendix C, Bibliography). One Moscow agency of good repute is Pilgrim Tours, 1st Kirpichny Per. 17A, Moscow 105118. Tel./fax [095] 365-4563 or 369-0389, E-mail: pilgrimtours@glas.apc.org.

6. Crimea

Alpclub Krim, ul. Zagorodnaya 5, Yalta 334200, tel. [0654] 328950, fax 321951

7. Urals

Bryilyakov, Konstantin and Yakov, 10a ul. Bessarabskaya Apt. 46, Ekaterinburg 620007, tel. [3432] 260804, fax [3432] 572571. These hard-working, resourceful brothers are good company and very dependable guides in the Urals. While they are city folk—Konstantin's a historian, Yakov a computer programmer—they're as at home in their Urals as *tayozhniki* (taiga woodsmen). Yakov is also a white-water enthusiast who has descended rivers all over Asia, Siberia, and the Far East.

8. Caucasus

Central Caucasus

Alpbaza Shkhelda KSP, Anatoly Makhinov, Pos. Elbrus, Kabardino-Balkaria, Russia 361603, tel. 78421

Kabardino-Balkarskii *Zapovednik*, Verkhnyaya Zhemtala, Sovetskii Raion, Kabardino-Balkaria

Kavkazkii *Zapovednik*, Sukhumskoye Shosse 7a, Sochi X-67, Krasnodarskii Krai

Pilgrim Tours, 1st Kirpichny Per. 17A, Moscow 105118, tel./fax [095] 365-4563 or 369-0389, E-mail: pilgrimtours@glas.apc.org; this outfit does a good job with Elbrus programs

Teberdinskii *Zapovednik,* Badukskii 1, Teberda 357192, Stavropolskii Krai, Russia

Eastern Caucasus

Dagestan *Zapovednik,* Makhachkala 367010, Dagestan (Eastern Caucasus)

Gadjiev, Bagaudin, ul. Oskara 4, 237112 Makhachkala, tel. [87200] 78310, fax [87200] 52288. Bagaudin, "Din" to his friends, is an energetic and reliable mountaineer. Descended from the revered Shamil (Din's ·grandfather, an Islamic holy man, lived to the ripe old age of 137), Din made my visit to Dagestan in the Eastern Caucasus much more meaningful by translating my questions for the mountain people from Russian into Avarsky.

Ramazanov, Akhmed, ul. Vaskieva 61, Apt. 12, 237007 Makhachkala, tel. [87200] 71222. Akhmed, who speaks excellent English, is of Avarsky descent. He has a delightful wife and family, five sons and daughters who play Big Band swing on the piano and cook delicious Dagestani dishes. Recommended for Eastern Caucasus treks.

PART 2. CENTRAL ASIA (TURKESTAN)

9. The Pamir Mountains
High Pamir

Dushanbe KSP, tel. [3772] 245914 or [3772] 245373

The Kuhiston Foundation, 1515 Tenth St., Boulder, CO 80302; contact for information about an international effort to create new parks and protect existing nature reserves in Tajikistan

Navruz Company, Vladimir Mashkov, Director, Box 364 Gorno-Spasatelnaya Sluzhba, 734003 Dushanbe 3, tel. [3772] 245068, 245373, or 245914 (one may be a fax); primary organizer of expeditions on Peak Communism

Sindbad Trekking Agency, Dushanbe, tel. [3772] 277367, fax 276543

10. The Tian Shan
Western Tian Shan

Alpclub "Chatkal," Artur Zakirov, ul. Kombriga Sinitsina 28/31, Namangan, Uzbekistan, tel. 32859 or 34817; contact for Western Tian Shan

SEU local branch, union for the protection of the Aral and the Amu Darya, E-mail: nukus@glas.apc.org

Tashkent Tourist-Sport Club, Radiy Shakirovich Bakaev, ul. Shevchenko 44, 700060 Tashkent, Uzbekistan, tel. [3712] 323440, fax [3712] 337258

Northern Tian Shan
Asia Tours, 8 ul. Korolenko, Apt. 25, 480032 Almaty, Kazakhstan, tel. [3272] 478164; Zailiisky Alatau in the Northern Tian Shan

Environmental activists, E-mail: eco@glas.apc.org, or isarata@glas.apc.org

International Mountaineering Camp "Khan Tengri," ul. Abaya 48, 480072 Almaty, Kazakhstan, tel. [3272] 677024, fax [3272] 675352, telex 251232 PTB SU; Zailiisky Alatau in the Northern Tian Shan

Pilgrim, 68/74 Abai Prospekt, Almaty 480008, Kazakhstan, tel. [3272] 426209, fax [3272] 426209

Central Tian Shan
International Mountaineering Centre "Tian Shan," Vladimir Biryukov, Director, 17 ul. Togoloka Molko, 720033 Bishkek, tel. [3312] 272890 or 272885, fax [3312] 270576, telex 245149 DOS SU. This organization has more experience running treks and expeditions than any other group in Central Asia. They are competent, professional, and pleasant to deal with.

PART 3. SIBERIA AND THE RUSSIAN FAR EAST

11. Siberia
Altai Mountains
Altaiskii *Zapovednik*, Pos. Yailyu, Turochokcskii Raion 659564

Ecofund, Nikolai Fotiev, 66 ul. Lenina, 656099 Barnaul, tel. [3852] 23 03 08, E-mail: katun@glas.apc.org; Ecofund has been active in resisting the Katun dam project and is working to create a national park in the Belukha region.

Kuznetskii Alatau *Zapovednik*, ul. Stroitelei 13, Pos. Belogorsk, Tisulskii Raion, Kemerovo Obl. 632238

Sayano-Shushenskii *Zapovednik*, ul. Zapovednaya 7, Pos. Shushenskoye, Krasnoyarsk Krai 662720, tel. 32300 or 31449

Sibalptur, Sergei Kurgin, 155/1 ul. Nemirovicha-Danchenko Apt. 47, 630087 Novosibirsk, fax [3832] 46 51 60, E-mail: sibalp@niee.nsk.su; Sergei is a native of Gorno-Altaisk. He and his staff are experienced mountaineers.

Lake Baikal
Baikal Ecological Museum, 281 ul. Lermontova, Room 220, Irkutsk 664033, tel. [3952] 46 06 09, E-mail: bem@glas.apc.org; Dr. Molozhnikov has organized an international environmental youth camp near the village of Goloustnoe about 130 kilometers north of Irkutsk.

Baikal Institute for the Rational Use of Nature: E-mail: buryat@glas.apc.org

Baikalo-Lenskii *Zapovednik*, ul. Dekabrskikh Sobytii 47, 664026 Irkutsk-26, tel. [3952] 332007

Baikalskii *Zapovednik*, pos. Tankhoi, Kabanskii Raion, Buryatiya 671120

Baikal Watch, Earth Island Institute, 300 Broadway, Ste. 28, San Francisco, CA 94133, tel. (415) 788-3666; Baikal Watch, a Russian–North American environmental group, has been active in promoting protection for Baikal as a World Heritage Site and Biospheric Reserve.

Bamtour, Rashit Yahin, 16 ul. Oktyabrya, Apt. 16, Severobaikalsk 671717, telex 288126 DWC SU

Barguzin *Zapovednik*, pos. Davsha, Severo-Baikalskii Raion, Buryatiya 671715

DIMIS, Dimitry Mashkin, 231 Baikalskay St., Apt. 42, Irkutsk 664075, tel. [3952] 245434, telex 231716 TURNE SU

Friends of the Russian National Parks Society, Michael Tripp, Director, 2816 Seaview Road, Victoria, BC V8N 1K8 Canada, tel. (604) 477-4407

Russian Geographic Society, Baikal Section, Vladimir Molozhnikov (Doctor of Biology), Chairman, Baikal Ecological Museum, 281 ul. Lermontova, Room 220, Irkutsk 664033, tel. [3952] 46 06 09; Dr. Molozhnikov has organized an international environmental youth camp near the village of Goloustnoe about 130 kilometers north of Irkutsk.

Shapkaev, Sergei, E-mail: root@techn.buriatia.su; Baikal and forestry issues

Shishelov, Sergei Nikolaevich, Slyudyansky Raion, Irkutsk Oblast, Maritui 665920

Stalker, P.O. Box 3673, 664074 Irkutsk, tel. [3952] 433466 or 433448, fax [3952] 432322, telex 133153 INST SU; local climbers who provide guides and other tour services

Vitim *Zapovednik*, ul. Stoyanovicha 99, Bodaibo, Irkutsk Obl. 666910, tel. [3952] 92117

Zabaikalsky National Park, per. Bol. 9, Ust Barguzin, 671623 Buryatskskaya SSR

12. The Russian Far East
Yakutia
Olekminskii *Zapovednik*, ul. Logovaya 31, Olekminsk, Sakha 678100, tel. 21032 or 21482

Yakutsk Obl. KSS, ul. Lomonosova 25, 677000 Yakutsk, tel. 28242

Chukotka
Alaska Discovery, Juneau, Alaska, tel. (907) 586-1911

Arcsovtour, Egvekinot, Chukotka, tel. 3773 (via international operator), fax (907) 274-9614 in Anchorage

Bering Air, Nome, Alaska, tel. (907) 443-5620

Beringia Conservation Program, Audubon Alaska-Hawaii Regional Office, 308 G St., Ste. 217, Anchorage, AK 99501, tel. (907) 276-7034. In concert with other environmental nongovernmental and governmental agencies, Audubon is working for creation of an international park that would protect marine wildlife on both sides of the Bering Sea. It also has a publication on flora, fauna, and ecology of Beringia and a pamphlet on responsible tourism in Beringia.

Ectur, Magadan tel. [41322] 2-90-54

Magadansky *Zapovednik*, ul. Shirokaya 14, 685014 Magadan, tel./fax [41322] 20071

Siberian Alaska Trading Co., Anchorage, Alaska, tel. (907) 277-3042

Wrangel Island *Zapovednik*, Shmidtovskovskii Raion, Ushakovskoye Selo 686870, tel. 78 (!)

Kamchatka

Alpha Tours, 59 Kosmonavtov St., Petropavlovsk-Kamchatsky 683905, tel. [41500] 56728 or 55850

Kamchatka Adventures, 2A ul. Sovetskaya, Petropavlovsk-Kamchatsky 683000, tel. [41500] 24615, fax [41500] 62436, telex 244131 OKEAN SU

Kamchatka Greens, E-mail: sol@green.kamchatka.su

Kronotsky *Zapovednik*, Sergei Alekseev, Superintendent, ul. Ryabikova 48, Elizovo, Kamchatka 684010, tel. 62847

Snow Leopard, 19-29 Pogranichnaya St., Yelizovo, Kamchatka 684010, tel. 64254, fax [41500] 24364, E-mail: service@post.kamchatka.su

Sogjoy, ul. Sopochnaya 13, Elizovo, Kamchatskaya Obl. 684010, tel. 61493, 62984, or 61083, telex 144124

Terra Ros, tel. [41500] 92209, fax [41500] 21917, E-mail: svetlana@net.kamchatka.su

Ussuriland

Fortuna, Sergei Chebotov, 5 ul. Frunzenskaya, Khabarovsk 680000, tel. [4212] 216401, telex 141134; Fortuna specializes in outdoor programs

Geosouvenir, Okeansky Pr. 29/31, Vladivostok 690000, tel. [4232] 260285

Hornocker Wildlife Research Institute, P.O. Box 3246, University Station, Moscow, ID 83843, E-mail for tiger protection: dalm@glas.apc.org. The Hornocker Institute has been conducting joint research with the Russians on the Siberian tiger. Their work in the Ternei area has focused attention on the plight of the tiger. The institute can direct donations to anti-poaching controls and ranger salaries in the Sikhote Alin *Zapovednik*—areas where even a little money goes a long way toward saving the tiger.

Institute of Water and Ecological Problems, E-mail: kras@glas.apc.org

International Crane Foundation, E 11376 Shady Lane Rd., Baraboo, WI 53913

Pacific Energy and Resources Center, Fort Cronkhite, Bldg. 1055, Sausalito, CA 94965. PERC's Siberian Forests Protection Project works with Russian and Siberian environmentalists to defend their fragile, boreal forests. The project facilitates the exchange of information about destructive logging practices currently taking place, policies that promote forest protection, and sustainable forestry practices.

Primorsky Regional Association Indigenous Peoples (PRAIP), 1st Ul. Morskaya 2/414, 690007 Vladivostok, tel. [4232] 229997, fax [4232] 228949, telex 213122 MRH SU, E-mail: amba@stv.sovam.com or amba@amba.marine.su; this group of native guides offers boating and fishing trips, in particular in the Bikin River area

Prout Institue for tiger protection, E-mail: proutfe@nk.igc.org

SEU Khabarovsk branch, E-mail: 4000@as.khabarovsk.su

SEU Vladivostok branch (Anatoly Lebedev), E-mail: swan@glas.apc.org

Sikhote Alin *Zapovednik*, E-mail: sixote@glas.apc.org

Vladivostok Mountaineering Club, Igor Zheleznyak, tel. [42322] 71521

Zov Taigi environmental journal, E-mail: solkin@stv.marine.su

Kuril Islands
Gert, Evgenii, 9 Sovetskaya St., Apt. 3, 694500 Yuzhno-Kurilsk, tel. 21343 or 21852

Kurilsky *Zapovednik*, Mikhail Dykhan, Superintendent, Yuzhno-Kurilsk, 694500 Sakhalin Obl., tel. 21586 or 21968

Zapovednik Moscow Representation: Priroda Rossii, P.O. Box 55, Moscow 125047, tel. [095] 264-9948, fax [095] 264-9927 or 292-6511 for Box 16049, telex 411720 for Box 16049

C. Bibliography

ENVIRONMENT

Feshbach, Murray and Alfred Friendly, Jr. *Ecocide in the U.S.S.R.* New York: Basic Books, 1992. Depressing litany of ecological ills. Feshbach is as thorough and unsparing in his cataloging of incidents and examples as Solzhenitsyn's *Gulag Archipelago*. Focuses on the disastrous health effects in the Soviet population of air and water pollution.

Pryde, Philip. *Environmental Management in the Soviet Union.* Cambridge: Cambridge University Press, 1991. Academic (but very readable) overview of state of Soviet air and water pollution, energy resources, toxic waste, conservation, national parks, and landscape preservation before the disolution of the USSR.

NATURAL HISTORY

Bannikov, A. G. *Nature Reserves of the USSR.* Moscow: Mysl, 1966. Translated from the Russian by the Israel Program for Scientific Translations.

Belt, Don. "The World's Great Lake." *National Geographic.* June 1992.

Bryan, T. Scott. *Geysers of "The Valley of Geysers."* Apple Valley, CA: GOSA (15107 Burns Dr., Apple Valley, CA 92307), 1991. A report that provides detailed scientific notes on the area.

Durrell, Gerald. *Durell in Russia.* New York: Simon & Schuster, 1986. Anecdotal accounts of travel to several of the nature reserves. Photographs.

Knystautas, Algirdas. *The Natural History of the USSR.* New York: McGraw-Hill, 1987. This encyclopedia by a Lithuanian naturalist of the physical geography, climate, soil, plant and animal distribution, nature reserves, and national parks of the former Soviet Union is *the* best, most comprehensive natural history guide. It's Soviet-era politically correct—there's no acknowledgment of Soviet eco-blunders here. Beautiful photos.

Krasheninnikov, Stepan Petrovich. *Explorations of Kamchatka 1735–1741.* Translated by E. A. P. Crownhart-Vaughan. Portland, OR: Oregon Historical Society Press, 1972.

Markhinin, Y. *Pluto's Chain.* Moscow: Progress Publisher's, 1971. This is the only book I've ever read by a Russian scientist that displays any humor. Volcanologist Markhinin's stories of Kamchatka and the Kurils are interesting and entertaining. Good translation.

Matthiessen, Peter, photographs by Boyd Norton. *Baikal: Sacred Sea of Siberia.* San Francisco: Sierra Club, 1992.

Sparks, John. *Realms of the Russian Bear.* London: Little Brown, 1992. Companion volume to the documentary aired on PBS. Focuses on birdlife and wildlife in selected wilderness areas. Good photos.

St. George, George. *Soviet Deserts and Mountains.* Amsterdam: Time-Life Books, 1974.

EARLY TRAVEL AND EXPLORATION

The few titles mentioned here represent a small fraction of the wonderful travel and exploration accounts from the nineteenth and early twentieth centuries. Any good university library has scads of these great reads.

Curtis, William Eleroy. *Turkestan: The Heart of Asia.* London: Hodder and Stoughton, 1911.

Freshfield, Douglas. *Travels in the Central Caucasus and Bashan.* London: Longmans, Green, 1869.

Gordon, T. E. Edmonston and Douglas. *The Roof of the World: Being a Narrative of a Journey over the High Plateau of Tibet to the Russian Frontier and Oxus Sources on Pamir.* Edinburgh: 1876.

Kennan, George. *Tent Life in Siberia.* Salem, NH: Ayer Publishing, 1989.

Krasheninnikov, Stephan. Petrovich. *Explorations of Kamchatka 1735-1741.* Translated by E.A.P. Crownhart-Vaughan. Oregon Historical Society Press, Portland 1972.

Mundt, Theodore. *Krim Girai: Khan of the Crimea.* London: J. Murray, 1856. A nineteenth-century account.

Newby, Eric. *The Big Red Train Ride.* New York: St. Martin's Press, 1978. Account of Trans-Siberian journey.

Olufsen, O. and Wm. Heinemann. *The Emir of Bokhara and His Country.* 1911.

Schuyler, Eugene. *Turkistan: Notes of a Journey in Russian Turkistan, Khokand, Bukhara and Kuldja.* New York: Scriber, 1876. This comprehensive (two volumes) travel diary devotes much more attention to local people and customs than most explorers' books.

Seymour, H. D. *Russia on the Black Sea and Sea of Azof: Being a Narrative of Travels in the Crimea and Bordering Provinces.* London: John Murray, 1855.

Turner, Samuel. *Siberia: A Record of Travel, Climbing and Exploration.* London: Unwin, 1905. With the quintessential pomp of the early British explorer, the first man to explore up to Mt. Belukha describes traveling by sledge into the heart of the Altai. Although the author spends more time talking about the local butter industry than climbing, this book is a classic.

Wood, Capt. John. *A Journey to the Source of the River Oxus.* London: Oxford University Press, 1976. This is a reprint of the 1872 classic describing the south Pamir.

BIOGRAPHY, HISTORY, AND REGIONAL FICTION

Oriental Research Partners. *Petr Petrovoch Semenov-Tian-Shanskii: The Life of a Russian Geographer.* Newtonville, MA: 1980. This biography of the great Russian explorer includes little information about his travels in the mountains whose name he took.

Rasputin, Valery. *Live and Remember.* Author is a well-known contemporary Russian writer who lives and writes on Lake Baikal. Among his books are this long novel and many short stories.

Rayfield, Donald. *The Dream of Lhasa: The Life of Nikolay Przhevalsky (1839–88).* London: Elek Books, 1976.

Stephan, John J. *Russian Far East: A History.* Stanford, CA: Stanford University Press, 1993.

——. *Sakhalin—A History.* Oxford: Clarendon Press, 1971.

TRAVEL AND GENERAL INFORMATION GUIDES

Bender, Friedrich. *Classic Climbs in the Caucasus.* London: Diadem Books, 1992. (Distributed in U.S. by Menasha Ridge Press, 3169 Cahaba Heights Road, Birmingham, AL 35243; tel. (800) 247-9437; ISBN 0-89732-116-2; $24.95.) This new guidebook gives detailed technical descriptions to eighty climbs in the Elbrus and Bezengi regions. This book is a must for mountaineers.

InfoServices International, Inc. *Yellow Pages and Handbook for St. Petersburg.* Cold Spring Harbor, NY: 1992. (InfoServices International, 1 St. Marks Pl., Cold Spring Harbor, NY 11724, tel. 516-549-0064.)

——. *Yellow Pages Moscow.* Cold Spring Harbor, NY: 1992. (InfoServices International, 1 St. Marks Pl., Cold Spring Harbor, NY 11724, tel. 516-549-0064.)

Kelly, Lawrence. *St. Petersburg: A Traveller's Companion.* New York: Atheneum, 1981.

Magowan, R., photographs by V. Gippenreiter. *Fabled Cities of Central Asia.* New York: Abbeville Press, 1989.

Matlock, David and Valeria. *Russia Walks.* New York: Holt, 1991.

Noble, John and John King. *USSR—a travel survival kit.* Berkeley: Lonely Planet Publications, 1991. For traveling in European Russia and Central Asia, in particular. Accompanied by street maps of major cities, this is the best standard travel guide available for historical glimpses and sightseeing opportunities in cities you pass through. It also covers internal transportation by bus and rail very comprehensively. However, it came out just as the USSR was disintegrating, and tends to rely on old tourism structures (Intourist) that have gone by the wayside.

Richardson, Paul E. *Russia Survival Guide.* Montpelier, VT: Russian Information Services (Box 2, Montpelier, VT 05602, tel. (802) 223-4955),

1993 (updated annually). Well-informed, up-to-date information about prices and essential travel information, especially in Moscow and St. Petersburg.

Rosen, Roger. *The Georgian Republic.* Chicago: Passport Books, 1992. This is a beautiful, entertaining, and useful guidebook.

Russian Information Services. *Where in Moscow.* Montpelier, VT: Russian Information Services (Box 2, Montpelier, VT 05602, tel. 802- 223-4955), 1993 (updated annually).

————. *Where in St. Petersburg.* Montpelier, VT: Russian Information Services (Box 2, Montpelier, VT 05602, tel. 802-223-4955), 1993 (updated annually).

West Col Productions. *Mt. Elbruz Region.* (Can be ordered through Chessler Books, P.O. Box 399, Kittredge, CO 80457; tel. 800-654-8502.) A thin guide that has useful general information about travel in the Caucasus. They also have done trekking guides and maps for Teberda; Bezengi, Sugan, and Laboda region; Ada Khokh, Gimarai, and Kazbek.

Whittell, Giles. *Central Asia: The Practical Handbook.* London: Cadogan Books, 1993. Very current and thorough guide to the cities of Central Asia.

RUSSIAN LANGUAGE TEXTS AND PHRASEBOOKS

Berlitz Russian for Travelers. New York: Berlitz Guides, 1992. Tapes also available.

Jenkins, James. *Russian Phrasebook.* Hawthorne, Victoria: Lonely Planet Publications, 1991.

TRAVEL MEDICINE GUIDES

Bezruchka, Stephen. *Pocket Doctor.* Seattle: The Mountaineers, 1988.

————. *Trekking in Nepal.* Seattle: The Mountaineers, 1991. The chapter on Health and Medical Problems is the best treatment on medical concerns for trekkers.

Forgey, William, M. D. *Travelers' Medical Resource.* Merrillville, IN: ICS Books, 1990.

Houston, Charles, M. D. *Going Higher: The Story of Man and Altitude.* Boston: Little Brown, 1987.

Jong, Elaine, M. D. and Russell McMullen, M. D. *The Travel and Tropical Medicine Manual.* 2d ed. Philadelphia: W. B. Saunders, 1993.

Rose, Stuart, M. D. *International Travel Health Guide.* Northampton, MA: Travel Medicine, 1991 (tel. 800-872-8633).

Wilkerson, James, M. D., ed. *Medicine for Mountaineering.* Seattle, WA: The Mountaineers, 1992.

PERIODICALS

There are good city guides available for Moscow and St. Petersburg. Several other publications available in the book kiosks of hotels list Moscow and St. Petersburg services and phone numbers—this is valuable information in a country where there are no phone books.

CIS Environmental Watch. Monterey, CA: Monterey Institute of International Studies (tel. 408-647-4154), biannual.

Commersant. Chicago: Refco Publishing (111 West Jackson Boulevard, Chicago, IL 60604), weekly. *Commersant* is usually available in its English-language edition at good newsstands in major U.S. cities; the address given is for those who want to subscribe in the United States. This is the most popular business weekly throughout Russia. You can find the English edition at newsstands in major Russian cities (sometimes).

Communicating to and from the Russian Far East. Russian Market Information Services (P.O. Box 22126, Seattle, WA 98122), periodically updated. A special publication that is very helpful.

Moscow Magazine. Moscow, monthly. Usually available in an English -language edition at good newsstands in major cities.

Moscow News. Moscow, weekly. Usually available in an English-language edition at good newsstands in major cities.

Moscow Times. Moscow, daily. This paper periodically publishes phone listings for businesses serving the foreign community, including travel agencies, banks, airlines, medical services, and Western-style supermarkets. You can pick up the English-language daily in major Moscow hotels.

Russian Far East Update. Russian Far East Update (P.O. Box 22126, Seattle, WA 98122, tel. 206-447-2668, fax 206-628-0979), monthly ($275/year). This provides business briefing on trade and economic developments in the Russian Far East, plus information on hotels, transportation services, et cetera. It's carefully researched and condensed and easily readable.

Russian Travel Monthly. Russian Information Services, Inc. (89 Main St. #2, Montpelier, VT 05602, tel. 802-223-4955, fax 802-223-6105), monthly ($36/year).

Surviving Together. ISAR (1601 Connecticut Ave. NW, Washington, DC 20009, tel. 202-387-3034), triannual ($25/year). This journal reports primarily on environmental issues and action projects; it's packed with information.

D. Trekkers' Phrasebook

There are a number of travel-size Russian-English dictionaries and phrasebooks. Some of them are mentioned in the Bibliography. I list here terms that are useful specifically to the wilderness traveler, many of which you are unlikely to find in a standard pocket dictionary. This is intended to supplement a basic Russian phrasebook or text.

Gear	снаряжение (sna-rya-JE-ni-ye)
alarm clock	будильник (boo-DEEL-neek)
backpack	рюкзак (ryuk-ZAK)
boots	ботинки (bah-TEEN-kee)
bowl	миска (MEES-ka)
candles	свечи (SVEEYE-chee)
cup	кружка (KROOJ-ka)
gas	бензин (ben-ZEEN)
down parka	пуховка (poo-KHOV-ka)
electric heating coil	кипятильник (kip-ya-TEEL-neek)
first aid kit	аптечка (ap-TECH-ka)
flight plan	контрольное время (kon-TROL-no-ye VREM-ya)
gaiters	гетры (GET-ree)
headlamp, flashlight	фонарик (fah-NA-reek)
jacket	куртка (KOORT-ka)
jacket--windbreaker	анорак (ah-no-RAK)
knife	нож (noj)
pan	кастрюля (kah-STROOL-ya)
poles (for tent)	стойки (STO-ee-kee)
pot (for cooking)	котел (kah-TYOL)
raingear	непромокаемая одежда (nee-prah-ma-KA-ye-ma-ya ah-dee-EJ-da)
rain fly	тент (tent)
rain coat	непромокаемая куртка (nee-prah-ma-KA-ye-ma-ya KOORT-ka)
rain pants	непромокаемые штаны (nee-prah-ma-KA-ye-mwee-ye shtah-NEE)
skis	лыжи (LEE-jee)
ski poles	палки лыжные (PAHL-kee LEEJ-nee-ye)
skins (for skis)	камусы (KAH-moo-see)

sleeping bag	спальник (спальный мешок) (SPAHL-neek/SPAHL-nee me-SHOK)
sleeping pad	каремат (ka-RE-mat)
spoon	ложка (LOJ-ka)
stakes	колышки (ko-LEE-shkee)
stove	примус (PREE-moos)
sunglasses	очки солнцезащитные (och-KEE soln-tse-zah-SHEET-nee-ye)
tent	палатка (pah-LAHT-ka)
toilet paper	туалетная бумага (too-ah-LEEYET-na-ya boo-MAH-ga)
water bottle	фляжка (FLYAJ-ka)
Climbing terms	альпинистские термины (al-pee-NEEST-skee-ye TARE-mee-nee)
approach	подход (pahd-KHOD)
ascent, climb	восхожедние (vos-khoj-DE-nee-ye)
basecamp	базовый лагерь (BAZ-o-vwee LAH-gare)
belay	страховка (stra-KHOV-ka)
bivouac	бивак (bee-VAK)
carabiner	карабин (kah-rah-BEEN)
climber	альпинист (al-peen-EEST)
climbing equipment	альпинистское снаряжение (al-peen-EEST-sko-ye sna-rya-JE-nee-ye)
crampons	кошки (KOSH-kee)
descender	восьмерка тормозная (vos-MYOR-ka tor-moz-NA-ya)
hammer	молоток (mah-lah-TOK)
hardware	крючья (KRYUCH-ya)
harness	обвязка/беседка (ob-VYAZ-ka)
Friend	френд (frend)
ice axe	ледоруб (le-do-ROOB)
ice screw	ледобур (крюк ледовый) (le-do-BOOR)
intermediate camp	промежуточный лагерь (prah-me-JOO-toch-nee LAH-gare)
jumar	зажим (za-JEEM)
knot	узел (OO-zel)
plastic double boots	пластиковые ботинки (PLAS-tee-ko-vwee-ye bah-TEEN-kee)

pulley	блок (blok)
rappel	спускаться по веревке (spoos-KAT-sya PO ver-YOV-kee-ye)
rock climbing	скалолазание (ska-la-LAZ-ah-nee-ye)
rope	веревка (ver-YOV-ka)
rope up	связываться (SVYA-ze-vat-sya)
shovel	лопата (la-PA-ta)
sling	петля веревочная (pet-LYA ver-YOV-och-na-ya)
Geographic terms	географические названия (geo-gra-FEE-ches-kee-ye naz-VA-nee-ye)
big	большой (бол.) (bol-SHO-ee)
bridge	мост (most)
cave	пещера (pe-SHARE-a)
chimney	камин (ka-MEEN)
cirque	цирк (tseerk)
cliff	скала (ska-LA)
cornice	карниз (kar-NEEZ)
couloir	кулуар (kool-WAR)
crevasse	трещина (TRE-shee-na)
crusted snow	наст (снежный) (NAST SNEJ-nee)
east	восток (vos-TOK)
downhill	спуск (spoosk)
glacier (hanging)	ледник (висящий) (led-NEEK vee-SYA-shchee)
(open)	(открытый) (ot-KREE-tee)
(closed)	(закрытый) (za-KREE-tee)
gorge, canyon	ущелье (oo-SHELL-ye)
ice	лед (lyode)
icefall	ледопад (le-do-PAHD)
ford	брод (brode)
lake	озеро (O-ze-rah)
landslide	обвал (ob-VAL)
lower	нижний (ниж.) (NEEJ-nee)
moraine	морена (mo-REEYE-na)
mountain	гора (go-RAH)
north	север (SEEYE-vare)
pasture	пастбище (PAST-bee-shche)

pass	перевал (PER-e-val)
plateau	плато (PLAH-to)
ravine	овраг (ov-RAG)
rib	ребро (re-BRO)
ridge	гребень (GREEYE-ben)
river	река (re-KA)
rock	камень (ka-MEEYEN)
roof	крыша (KREE-sha)
route	маршрут (marsh-ROOT)
saddle	седловина (sed-lo-VEE-na)
scree	осыпь (O-seep)
slope	склон (sklone)
small	малый (мал.) (MAL-yee)
south	юг (yook)
spring	источник (ee-STOCH-neek)
stream	ручей (roo-CHEY)
summit	вершина (vare-SHEE-na)
swamp	болото (bo-LO-ta)
trail	тропа (tra-PAH)
uphill	подъем (pod-YOM)
upper	верхний (верх.) (vee-YARE-khnee)
valley	долина (do-LEE-na)
wall, face	стена (ste-NA)
waterfall	водопад (vo-do-PAD)
watershed	водораздел (vo-do-RAZ-del)
west	запад (ZA-pad)

Health	здоровье (zdo-RO-vee-ye)
bandage (elastic)	бинт эластичный (BEENT e-las-TEECH-nee)
Bandaid	лейкопластырь (lay-ko-PLAS-teer)
bleeding	кровотечение (kra-va-tech-ee-EN-ee-ye)
break	перелом (per-re-LOM)
burn	ожог (o-JOGUE)
coughing	кашель (KA-shel)
diarrhea	понос (pah-NOS)
dizziness	головокружение (go-lo-vo-kroo-JE-nee-ye)
fall	падение (pa-DE-nee-ye)
frostbite	обморожение (ob-mo-ro-JE-nee-ye)
mountain sickness	горная болезнь (GOR-na-ya bol-EZN)

oxygen deficit	кислородное голодание (kee-sla-ROD-na-ya go-lo-DA-nee-ye)
painkillers	болеутолящие средство (bo-le-oo-tol-YA-shchee-ye SREEYE-dstvo)
shot	укол (oo-KOL)
snow blindness	снежная слепота (SNEEYE-jna-ya sle-po-TAH)
wound, cut	рана (RAH-nah)

Weather — погода (pah-GO-dah)

blizzard	метель (me-TEEYEL)
freezing	мороз (mo-ROSE)
fog	туман (too-MAHN)
lightning	молния (MOL-nee-ya)
overcast	пасмурный (PAS-moor-nee)
rain	дождь (dojt)
rockfall	камнепад (kam-ne-PAHT)
snow	снег (snee-YEK)
snowfall	снегопад (sneeye-go-PAHT)
thunder	гроза (gro-ZA)

Other useful terms:

accident	несчастный случай (nee-SHAST-nee SLOO-chay)
alcohol	спирт (speert)
altitude	высота (vwee-so-TA)
avalanche (wind-slab)	лавина (грунтовая) (la-VEE-na)
axe	топор (to-POR)
cairn	тур (toor)
climb	лазать (LA-zat)
danger	опасность (ah-PAS-nost)
deep	глубокий (gloo-BO-kee)
descent	спуск (spoosk)
dry	сухой (soo-KHO-ee)
fresh	свежий (SVEEYE-jee)
glissade	глиссировать (glee-SEE-ro-vat)
guide	проводник (pro-vod-NEEK)
(without guide)	без проводника (BEEYES pro-vod-neek-AH)
helicopter	вертолет (ver-to-LYOT)
help!	помогите! (pah-mah-GEE-tee-ye)

hut	хижина/приют/домик (KHEE-jee-na/pree-YOOT/DO-meek)
length	длина (dlee-NA)
level	пологий (po-lo-GEE)
load carries	заброски (za-BROS-kee)
pack animal	въючное животное (VYOOCH-no-ye ji-VOT-no-ye)
porter	носильщик (no-SEEL-shcheek)
radio	радиостанция (ra-dee-a-STANT-see-ya)
radio contact	радиосвязь (ra-dee-a-SVYAZ)
rescue party	спасательная команда (spa-SA-teeyel-na-ya ka-MAN-da)
route, itinerary	маршрут (marsh-ROOT)
scale	масштаб (mas-SHTAP)
slippery	скользкий (SKOL-nee)
smooth	гладкий (GLAD-kee)
steep	крутой (kroo-TO-ee)
stretcher	носилки (no-SEEL-kee)
tracks	следы (sle-DEE)
trail	тропа (tra-PAH)
vodka	водка (VOD-ka)
way, path, road	дорога (do-RO-ga)
wet	мокрый (MO-kree)
Food	пища/еда (PEE-shcha/ye-DA)
apricots, dried	курага (koo-rah-GA)
apple	яблоко (YA-blo-ka)
bread	хлеб (лепешка in Central Asia) (khlee-YEP)
butter	масло (mas-LO)
cabbage	капуста (ka-POO-sta)
candy	конфеты (kon-FEEYE-tee)
carrot	морковь (mar-KOF)
cereal	каша (KA-sha)
semolina	манная каша (манка) (MAN-na-ya KA-sha)
oatmeal	овсянка, геркулесовая (off-SYAN-ka)
wheat	пшеничная (pshe-NEECH-na-ya)
cheese	сыр (seer)
chocolate	шоколад (sho-ko-LAD)
cookies	печение (pe-CHEEYE-nee-ye)

cottage cheese	творог (tvo-ROK)
cucumbers (pickles)	огурцы (ah-goor-TSEE)
eggs	яйца (YA-ee-tsa)
flour	мука (moo-KA)
fruit	фрукты (FROOK-tee)
jam	варенье (va-REEYE-nee-ye)
kefir	кефир (in Asia, айран. Ряженка is another type of sour milk)
mayonnaise	майонез (my-OWN-ez)
meat	мясо (MYA-sah)
meat (canned)	тушенка (too-SHON-ka)
milk	молоко (mo-lo-KO)
milk (sweetened, condensed)	сгущенка (sgoo-SHON-ka)
mushrooms	грибы (gree-BWEE)
onion	лук (LUKE)
potato	картошка (kar-TOSH-ka)
rice	рис (REES)
sausage	колбаса (kol-bas-AH)
sour cream	сметана (sme-TAHN-ah)
sugar	сахар (SA-khar)
tea	чай (chai)
tomato	помидор (po-mee-DOOR)
vegetables	овощи (O-vo-shcee)

Animals and birds	животные и птицы (jee-VOT-nee-ye ee PTEE-tsee)
eagle	орел (or-YOL)
bear	медведь (med-VEEYET)
boar	кабан (ka-BAN)
burro	ищак (ee-SHAK)
cow	корова (ko-RO-vah)
deer	олень (ah-LEEYEN)
elk	марал (ma-RAL)
Manchurian deer	изюбр (ee-ZYOOBR)
roe deer	косуля (ka-SOOL-ya)
goat	козел (ka-ZYOL)
horse	лощадь (LO-shchat)
marmot	сурок/суслик (soo-ROK)

moose	лось (los)
mountain goat	горный козел (GOR-nee ka-ZYOL)
musk deer	кабарга (ka-bar-GA)
rabbit	кролик (KRO-leek)
sheep	баран (ba-RAN)
snow leopard	снежный барс (SNEEYEJ-nee BARS)

Trees and berries	**Деревья и ягоды** (dare-ee-EV-ya ee YA-go-dee)
apricot (wild)	урюк (oo-RYOOK)
birch	береза (bare-YO-za)
blueberry	голубика (go-loo-BEE-ka)
buckthorn	облепиха (ob-le-PEE-kha)
cranberry	клюква (KLYOOK-va)
fir	пихта (PEEKH-ta)
honeysuckle	жималость (JEE-ma-lost)
huckleberry	черника (CHER-nee-ka)
pine (Siberian stone)	кедра (KEDR)
pine	сосна (sa-SNA)

Administrative Divisions of Russia and Turkestan

Although political reform continues to redraw boundaries, the administrative divisions remain roughly as they were in the USSR. This list is in descending order of size, starting with the largest division. In parentheses are abbreviations you may encounter on maps.

Within the Russian Federation are several geopolitical divisions: Autonomous Republics may have significant autonomy from the central government. These are primarily areas where there is a majority non-Russian ethnic group.

Autonomous Republics and Okrugs are also usually homelands to smaller minority groups. These enjoy a limited degree of local autonomy.

край	krai	state or province in Russia
область (обл.)	oblast	city and its surroundings (county)
город (гор.)	gorod	city
районный центр	raionnii tsentr	largest town in oblast
поселок (пос.)	posyolok	small town
кишлак (к.)	kishlak	village (in Turkestan)

деревня (дер.)	derevnya	village
село (сел.)	selo	village

Other terms and abbrieviations you may encounter on maps:

а/л	альпинистский лагерь	
Б. or Бол.	большой	big
бас.	бассейн	lowland, basin
бр.	брод	ford
В.	восточный	east
в.	вершина	summit
Верхн.	верхный	upper
ГМС	Гидро-Метео Служба	weather station
г.	гора	mountain
изба		cabin
З.	западный	west
Л.	левый	left
лед.	ледник	glacier
лет.	летовка	shack, shelter
М.	малый	small
МТФ		dairy farm
Нижн.	нижный	lower
н/к	некатегорийный	easy pass
оз.	озеро	lake
ос.	осыпь	scree
ОТФ		farm
1А, 2Б, etc.		category of pass
П.	правый	right
п.	пик	peak
пас.	пастбище	pasture
пер.	перевал	pass
р.	река	river
пещ.	пещера	cave
пионерлаг	пионерский лагерь	pioneers' camp
руч.	ручей	stream
С.	северный	north
ск.	скалы	cliffs
сн.	снег	snow
Средн.	Средний	central
т/б	туристская база	hostel or lodge

xp.	хребет	ridge (this can also be a mountain range)
Центр.	центральный	central
ур.	урочище	grove
ущ.	ущелье	valley, gorge
Ю.	южный	south
зим.	зимовка	winterized shelter

GLOSSARY

ail (аил)--yurt-shaped wooden structure in which Altaitsi traditionally lived

airan (айран)--kefir: a yogurtlike dairy product (Turk.)

ak (ак)--white (Turk)

aksu (аксу)--white water (Turk)

alatau (алатау)-- literally, "colorful rocks" (Kazakh)

alatoo (алатоо) -- literally, "colorful rocks" (Kyrgyz)

alpbaza (альпбаза) --climbing camp/hostel

alpinisti (альпинисты)--climbers

alpinistky (альпинистский)--climbing (adj)

alplager (альплагерь)--climbing camp

arashan (арашан)--healing springs

aul (аул)--word for village in Dagestan

banya (баня)--steam bath; bathhouse

bazaar (базар)--farmers market in Turkestan

chabani (чабаны) --herders, in Turkestan

chai (чай)--tea

chaikhana (чайхана)--Turkestan teahouse

chon (чон)--big (Turk.)

dacha (дача)--country home

datsan (дацан)--monastery of Buryat people

diki turist (дикий турист)--"wild tourist"; independent hiker

do vostrebovaniya (до востребования)--general delivery; a place to receive mail

elektrichka (электричка)--local electric train from major cities to nearby countryside.

golomyanka (голомянка)--an oily fish endemic to Lake Baikal

golets (голец- sing.)--goltsy (гольцы-pl.) Siberian term for bare hills

gorbushcha (горбуша)--humpback salmon

gorny turism (горный туризм)--hiking, backpacking

gorny turist (горный турист)--"mountain tourist"; hiker, backpacker

grabinnik (грабинник)--scrub birch

gulag (гулаг)--forced-labor camp

halva (халва)--a mixture of honey and sesame butter; loved in Turkestan

izyubr (изюбр)--Manchurian deer

kak dogovorishsya (как договоришься)--"however you cut the deal"

kamen (камень)--rock

kara (кара)--black (Turk)

karasu (карасу)--black water (Turk)

kedr (кедр)--Siberian stone pine (often mistranslated as "cedar")

khan (хан)--prerevolutionary Turkestan ruler

kharius (хариус)--trout

kishlak (кишлак)--village in Turkestan

kishmish (кишмиш)--raisins (Turk)

kizyak (кизяк)--cowpies (in Dagestan); used for fuel

koksu (коксу)--blue-green water (Turk)

kolkhoz (колхоз)--collective farm

kompot (компот)--berry/fruit stew

kontrolno-spasatelnaya sluzhba (КСС) (контрольно-спасательная служба)--rescue service

kontrolno-spasatelny-punkt (КСП) (контрольно-спасательный пункт)--rescue post

kosh (кош)--summer mountain camps for herders, usually consisting of a large extended family

kosulya (косуля)--roe deer

kotleti (котлеты)--meatballs

kumys (кумыс)--fermented mare's milk

kurumnik (курумник)--rock fields of varying size, from pebbles to large boulders

lagman (лагман)--spicy soup with mutton and noodles

lepyoshka (лепешка)--wheel of chewy bread

letovki (летовка)--Dagestani summer camps

limmonik (лиммоник)--variety of wild grape from which locals of Primorye make a delicious wine

madrassas (мадрасса)--Islamic school

manti (манты)--steamed meat-stuffed dough (like pot-stickers) *mezhdugorodny punkt* (междугородный пункт)--inter-city phone post

mineralnaya voda (минеральная вода)--mineral water

mumeo (мумие)--folk remedy of sterilized turds of alpine mice

narodnaya meditsina (народная медицина)--folk medicine/remedies

nelzya (нельзя)--not allowed

nerpa (нерпа)--little ringed seals endemic to Lake Baikal

nomenklatura (номенклатура)--Soviet upper class

oblepikha (облепиха)--buckthorn

omul (омуль)--Lake Baikal's native whitefish delicacy

ostrog (острог)--fort

otchyot (отчет)--expedition report; includes hand-drawn maps

pelmeni (пельмени)--little meat-stuffed dumplings; Siberian food

piala (пиала)--special little ceramic bowl out which tea is drunk

pirozhki (пирожки)--baked or fried bread stuffed with meat or cabbage

planovyi marshrut (плановый маршрут)--"official" trail

plov (плов)--rice cooked with mutton, grated carrots, and onions; standard
    Turkestan fare

propusk (пропускк)--permit

puree (пюре)--mashed potatoes

putyovka (путевка)--all-expense-paid vacation voucher

razryad (разряд)--ranks, as in hierarchical levels in sports

Roerichovtsi (рериховцы) -- Roerichites, mystical followers of the painter Nicolai
    Roerich

ruble (рубль)--unit of money

rynok (рынок)--farmers market

sala (сало)--pork fat, much loved by Ukrainians in particular

samovar (самовар)--traditional Russian pot for boiling tea

samsa (самса)--baked meat-stuffed dough like pot-stickers (Uzbek)

shuba (шуба)--winter coat

shurpa (шурпа)--spicy soup with noodles and mutton; Turkestan dish

sopka (сопка)--volcano (Kamchatka)

spirt (спирт)--strong alcohol like Everclear

srochny peregovor (срочный переговор)--urgent call

stolovaya (столовая)--cafeterias

su (суу)--water (Turk)

taiga (тайга)--mixed boreal forest

taimen (таймен)--Siberian relative of the trout

tash (таш)--stone (Turk)

tayozhnik (таежник)--*taiga* woodsman

turbaza (турбаза)-- a hostel, usually found in small towns or rural areas

turagenstvo (турагенство)--travel agency

turist (турист)--tourists, travelers

turistsky (туристский)--hiking (adj)

tyubeteika (тюбетейка)--the square black cap embroidered with white stitching worn throughout Turkestan

urbech (урбеч)--spread made from ground apricot pits, hemp seeds, and honey (Dagestan)

vagonchik (вагончик)--abandoned train car turned into a cabin

vedomstvenniye gostinitsy (ведомственные гостиницы)--small hotels owned/operated by government ministries and institutes

venniki (венники)--cut and bound pine or birch boughs softened by soaking in hot water; used in *banyas*

vokzal (вокзал)--train station

yaila (яйла)--Crimean mountain meadow

yurt (юрта)--Mongolian-style round tent

zakaznik (заказник)--nature reserve where some recreation and hunting are allowed

zapovednik (заповедник)--nature reserve

zapovedno-okhotnıchye khozyaistvo (заповедно-охотничее хозяйство)--hunting preserve; for commercial hunting

zavarka (заварка)--strongly brewed black tea

zimovka (зимовка)--winterized shelter

Index

ABOUT THE AUTHOR

Friends have suggested to Frith Maier that in another life she must have been a Tajik: her soul seems most at home in Pamir mountain hamlets. As a student at Leningrad State University in 1984, she traveled solo to what was then Soviet Uzbekistan, where she managed to get arrested for abandoning her Intourist-arranged tour to sneak off to villages. Frith's fascination with the people of the former USSR, and with Central Asia in particular, inspired her to embark on a decade of exploratory mountain travel to remote corners of the USSR. As the Soviet Union's doors creaked open in the late eighties, Frith challenged the "closed to foreign travel" designation of many wilderness areas. In 1988, she created a Soviet adventure travel program for Recreational Equipment, Inc., pioneering climbing, trekking, and biking trips to places that had not seen Westerners in this century.

Frith grew up in Juneau, Alaska, where she cut her teeth on mountain bushwhacking. Her early passion for mountain adventures has led her to many less-brushy peaks in the Pamirs and Tian Shan. She was the first American woman to summit on Khan Tengri (22,996 feet) on the Kyrgyzstan-China border, and has climbed Peak Communism (24,595 feet), the highest peak in the former Soviet Union.

Fluent in Russian and conversant in Japanese, Frith lives in Seattle, where she continues to manage Russia and Central Asia operations for REI Adventures. Her current focus is on developing travel programs that provide revenues for preserving wildlife habitat in national parks and nature reserves.

I welcome readers' comments and suggestions about this book. Please write and share additional information or updates.

Задача этой книги--предоставлять любителям путеществии на природе информацию по общим возможностям туризма в разных регионах России и Средней Азии, и также описании конкретных маршрутов и координаты фирм, коротые могут осуществить прием туристов. Если Вы имеете информацию, которую нам стоит включить в следующее издание книги, пришлите, пожалуйста, по адресу:

Frith Maier
c/o The Mountaineers Books
1011 SW Klickitat Way
Seattle, WA 98134
U.S.A.